W9-BVE-593

JAMES BROWN

THE GODFATHER OF SOUL

BY JAMES BROWN
WITH BRUCE TUCKER

FOREWORD BY REVEREND AL SHARPTON
WITH KAREN HUNTER

EPILOGUE BY DAVE MARSH

THUNDER'S
MOUTH
PRESS

NEW YORK

Copyright © 1986, 1997 by James Brown and Bruce Tucker
Introduction © 1990, 1997 by Bruce Tucker
Foreword © 2002 by Reverend Al Sharpton and Karen Hunter
Epilogue copyright © 1990, 1997 by Dave Marsh

Reprinted by arrangement with Macmillan Publishing Company,
a division of Macmillan, Inc.

Published by
Thunder's Mouth Press
An Imprint of Avalon Publishing Group Incorporated
161 William St., 16th Floor
New York, NY 10038

Library of Congress In Publication Data
Brown, James, 1928–
    James Brown, the godfather of soul / James Brown with Bruce Tucker
    Discography : p.
    Epilogue by Dave Marsh.—1st Thunder's Mouth ed.
      p.   cm.
    Reprint. Originally published: New York: Macmillan, c1986
    ISBN 1-56025-115-8
—Biography.   I. Tucker, Bruce.   II. Title.
ML420.B818A3   1990
782,421644'092—dc20
[B]   90-31961
                                                         CIP
                                                         MN
ISBN this edition: 1-56025-388-6

9 8 7 6 5 4 3 2 1

Text design by Jack Meserole

Printed in the United States of America

Distributed by Publishers Group West

CONTENTS

PREFACE

I was marked from the getup. You might say that I've got a mark on my back that I never knew was there. That's because they fixed it where I couldn't see it myself. But now that I can look back on my life, I realize that what I've done was no accident.

I was marked a lot of different ways. With names, for example. I was marked with a lot of different names. And each one has a story behind it.

As a kid growing up in a whorehouse, I was known as Little Junior. After I broke my leg a couple of times playing football, I was nicknamed Crip. In prison I was called Music Box.

The name of my first group, the Famous Flames, caused Little Richard to say, "Y'all are the onliest people who ever made yourselves famous before you *were* famous."

As a performer, I've had names like Mr. Dynamite, The "Please Please Please" Man, The Hardest Working Man in Show Business, Soul Brother Number One, The Sex Machine, His Bad Self, The Godfather of Soul, and The Minister of the New New Super Heavy Funk.

My full legal name is James Joe Brown, Jr. Ben Bart, my manager for many years and a man who was like a father to me, always called me Jimmy. Today, I prefer to be called *Mr.* Brown.

But of all the names I've been marked with, James Brown is probably the most mysterious. In school the kids and the teachers always called me by it like it was one word. Jamesbrown. Just like that. But originally my name wasn't supposed to be James Brown at all. It should have been something else.

When I look back on my life and follow the different bloodlines, it's almost like I was a planted child, like I was sent here for a reason. I guess we all feel that way. But a lot of strange things have happened in my life, and by looking back I've been finding out who I am.

It's just beginning to come to me.

JAMES BROWN
1986

For the child deprived of being able to grow up
and say "Momma" and "Daddy" and have both of them
come put their arms around him.

J. B.

For Vereen Bell, Jr., and Sam Floyd, Jr.
—two juniors who are my
seniors, mentors, and friends.

B. T.

ACKNOWLEDGMENTS

I want to thank God first. And I want to thank my wife, who gave me a new look and a new outlook. I want to thank Macmillan Publishing Company for going through with the project all the way and realizing how important it is.

I want to thank Bruce Tucker for traveling around with me, seeing me in all different kinds of situations, and really getting to know James Brown so he could bring out the real story. I want to thank Gerri Hirshey for bringing me to the attention of other writers interested in my story.

I want to thank all the members of my band, who gave me the drive and the support that I need to demand an audience— not *command* but *demand*.

I want to thank my mother and father. I hope their son's story will thank them more by doing a lot of good things.

And I want to thank this country for allowing me to tell my story and for making it possible for me to have a story to tell. I'm also grateful to all the countries that allow me to come onto their soil and do a show that's Americanized to a point that it could hurt some of their culture—but they always take the good from it to help their culture along.

I'd like to thank in advance the libraries and the schools for a place on their bookshelves. And I want to thank in advance any young kids who can use this story as a role model. If this book helps somebody, then it will have accomplished what I want to accomplish.

JAMES BROWN
1986

Not many kids get to grow up and work with their boyhood idol. For giving me that rare opportunity, I have many people to thank. Jim Fitzgerald initiated the project, and Roy Blount drew me into it. My agent, Carol Mann, kept it going and, for the past year and a half, kept me going as well. At Macmillan the support of Hillel Black and the enthusiasm and incisive editing of Dominick Anfuso made the idea a reality.

For me, nothing would be possible without the unflagging support of my wife, Harriet Davidson, who, while I was out there with the Godfather, endured my frequent absences from home before and after the birth of our daughter.

I, too, wish to thank Gerri Hirshey, author of the incomparable *Nowhere to Run: The Story of Soul Music*. Her generosity with files and notes, her unfailingly sound advice, and her strategically timed encouragement helped immeasurably.

In Georgia, A. H. Dallas smoothed the way throughout. Mrs. James Brown offered hospitality and candor in equal measure. And if they gave Grammys to secretaries for handling with sympathy and tact the unceasing demands made on performers like James Brown, Becky Blanchard Miller would win hands-down.

My sister Mary Howell provided logistical support during a crucial stage of the project. The indefatigable Cliff White, on woefully short notice, produced the exhaustive discography that appears at the end of the book. Vicki Gold Levi gave me a crash course in photo research. John H. Johnson of Johnson Publishing Company generously made available photographs from *Ebony*.

Thanks also to the many people who provided information and interviews as aids to His Bad Self's own astonishing powers of recall: "Hoss" Allen, Thomas I. Atkins, Leon Austin, Sydney L. Avery, Dan Aykroyd, Johnnie May Wheeler Banks, Jack Bart, Steve Bloom, Robert J. Brown, Velma Warren Brown, Dr. William Calloway, William "Bootsy" Collins, Mal Cook, Richard Dostal, Tim Drummond, Roy Emory, Buddy Fox, Al Garner, Laura Garvin, Willie M. Glenn, Delois (Keith) Haley, Sylvester Keels, Gwen Kessler, Mike Lawlor, Ron Lenhoff, George Livingston, Jr., Lester Maddox, Warren A. Martin, Sparkie Martin, Mrs. Walter J. Matthews, Johnnie Miller, Silas Moore, Hal Neely, Bob Patton, Dora (Davis) Payne, Chuck Seitz, Reverend Al Sharpton, Charles Sherrell, Hamp Swain,

Donald E. Walters, Sr., Colonel Jim Wilson, Guy Wilson, Teddy Washington, and Perry Williams.

Just as he made a major contribution to James Brown and the Famous Flames, Bobby Byrd played a crucial role in the realization of this book. With Bobby and his wife, Vicki Anderson, two of the most generous and gracious people I know, I passed many pleasurable hours in my old hometown of Nashville.

It was there, back in 1962, after a rained-out James Brown show at Sulphur Dell, that I jumped from the grandstand and sneaked backstage. A fourteen-year-old already suffocating in surburbia, I wanted to shake the hand of the man whose music coming over WLAC late at night had blown away the teen crooning, cha-cha-cha and Mouseketeer rock found a little farther up the radio dial. Even then I perceived, however dimly, that I was thanking James Brown for far more than some enjoyable records. Twenty-three years later, after an arduous day of working together on this book, I tried to tell him all that. "You're kidding," he said.

No, James, I'm not.

BRUCE TUCKER
1986

INTRODUCTION:
Another James Brown and An Other James Brown

On a cool late-summer evening in 1985, we are driving down a tree-lined street in Augusta, Georgia, feeling good, nearly at the end of our work on *The Godfather of Soul*. Immaculately coiffed and vividly made up, James looks, as always, ready to step on stage. He is driving a new Lincoln supplied by his record company after "Living in America" has become an enormous hit and identified him, bizarrely, as he has been so many times before, with the country that has greatly rewarded him and greatly punished him throughout his life. After almost two years of working with him, I have finally managed to broach the subject of his outsize ego. Without a trace of resentment, he replies with the words that eventually become, verbatim, the book's concluding paragraphs, in which he makes the distinction between James Brown the man and JAMES BROWN the myth. As acutely as any star ever has, he understands that the commodity he is selling is *difference*—the projection of a personal extraordinariness.

"To get this well dressed, just to drive around and talk, you are living the life," he says. "I'm not letting my fans down or myself. They will pay to come see me. I look like somebody you would pay to see."

Difference may be most visible in the suit and the shades, but it begins on stage, for difference is not merely image. It is created out of all the resources a performer can command. For James Brown that has meant an impressive arsenal: the distinctive style of music, the signature vocals, the drop-dead dancing, the showmanship of his collapse-and-resurrection finale, the appearance of superhuman effort on stage. Haters of popular culture dismiss difference as an excrescence on talent or a cover-up for lack of talent—rhinestones on an empty suit—but the creation of the most enduring bearers of difference, such as JAMES BROWN, requires immense artistic abilities across categories of art, performance, and persona.

The people own JAMES BROWN, says James Brown, acknowledging that the reception of his painstaking creation is largely beyond his control. It's a problem for all performers, but a particularly pressing one for a black artist whose work is uncompromisingly rooted in black idioms and who nevertheless deeply yearns for universal acceptance. For black audiences, having lived inside those idioms all their lives, the difference James Brown projects is one of degree, not of kind. But for white audiences, even sympathetic ones, his difference always threatens to become otherness. Said to be singularly "raw," "uninhibited," "possessed," he becomes the mysterious, exotic, black Other of colonialist fantasy. (Diane Arbus, the late photographer celebrated for her prurient, condescending pictures of marginalized people, is said to have remarked, upon shooting James on assignment for the old *Herald Tribune*, "I love freaks.") The kicker, of course, is that otherness, no less than difference, sells tickets. But otherness, unlike difference, renders its bearer unreal.

The condition of unreality enveloping JAMES BROWN perversely complicates the question we bring to his autobiography: What is he *really* like? But it also suggests the direction in which we should look for the answer: not away from or beneath the public persona, but at the terms in which he has both chosen and been forced to realize that identity. No doubt there will one day appear a debunking biography dwelling on James' high-handedness with musicians, the reported domestic violence, and the problems that have recently landed him in jail. Before that baneful day comes, I want to offer a picture of another James Brown, of a man whose apparent contradictions, seemingly erratic behavior, and deep ambivalence about living in America grow out of a lifelong struggle to come to terms with the other James Brown, the hyperbolic figure not entirely of his own making that wins him wide acceptance and condemns him to misunderstanding.

The question as to what James is really like is also, as I soon came to find out, asked almost daily of his co-author. After a few tongue-tied attempts to answer, I quickly developed a stock response, the most truthful I could think of: He is the most complicated human being I have ever known. The incredulous looks this explanation often provokes speak volumes about the difficulty of being James Brown—or of portraying him as anything other than the cartoonish figure of recent newspaper accounts.

On the other hand, it is comparatively easy to assess his stature as an artist. It hasn't always been so, not even as recently as 1984, the year the barroom argument occurred out of which the idea for this book grew. Like most such arguments, it entailed large generalizations and sweeping claims. The contested category was something like "greatest living American musician." Another writer started it by nominating Ray Charles, whom he was preparing to interview for an article. I countered with James Brown. The discussion dragged on inconclusively until it was eventually resolved— in James' favor—when we refined the category to most *influential* living American musician.

Now, I'm not so sure I should have conceded anything. As a measure of the magnitude of James' accomplishment, you need only ask how many artists have created one musical revolution in their lives, not to mention *two*. Many celebrated musicians—Miles Davis comes to mind—have been among the first to synthesize and extend musical revolutions not originally of their making, but James Brown helped create one—soul—and single-handedly made another—funk.

Like many of the great southern soul singers, he brought to R & B a voice trained in gospel, but his rhythmic grunts and expressive shrieks harked farther back still—to ring shouts, work songs, and field cries. From a whisper to a scream, the timbre of that voice remains one of the unique sounds in the history of American singing, fully as distinctive as that of Louis Armstrong. As a bandleader and composer, James also reimported the rhythmic complexity from which, under the dual pressure of rock 'n' roll and pop, R & B had progressively fallen away since its birth from jazz and blues. The versions of "Think" and "I'll Go Crazy" captured in 1962 for *Live at the Apollo* show a performer in no danger of settling comfortably into a backbeat.

Though his rhythmic invention would carry him well beyond the confines of soul, its origins aren't readily explained. He played little blues and probably less jazz during his early years. And the amount of time he devoted to gospel is easily exaggerated—many other soul singers were far more steeped in it. In many ways, his music is simply *sui generis*. For unlike many of the other great soul artists, he was never associated with any of the three preeminent soul record labels—Atlantic, Motown, and Stax—and their formidable house bands or powerful producer-writers that tended to stamp the artist, rather than the other way around.

As a showman, he developed a full-scale musical revue, with the tightest orchestra—"band" doesn't do it justice—in the country. Some of America's finest musicians have come to grief when they tried to run a big band, but James has kept one going for more than thirty years, despite the well-publicized blowups, the ruthless discipline, the firings and resignations.

The consummate showmanship—the death-defying energy, the on-the-knees pleading, the cape routine—has sometimes obscured his importance purely as a dancer. Showmanship aside, he was quite simply the greatest vernacular dancer of his time, bringing an unequaled combination of precision and athleticism to popular dance. (In the eighties, Michael Jackson had the precision; Prince, the athleticism; but no one had both to the degree James did.) Always staying on top of the latest dance crazes—and integrating them into what came to be known as the James Brown, that inimitable combination of the camel walk, the mashed potatoes, the shimmy, and assorted other black dance idioms—he performed a nightly seminar in dance history.

Unfortunately, the filmed record of the peak dancing years has been lost or is largely nonexistent. There is a clip from the *Ed Sullivan Show*; there is the celebrated sequence from *The T.A.M.I. Show*; and there are a few other odds and ends. Metromedia filmed a live show at the Apollo in 1968, but destroyed the footage in a routine pruning of its archives (which an angry, impromptu lecture from me about destroying cultural history could of course do nothing to rectify). The WGBH show in Boston in 1968, a bootleg of which Dave Marsh describes in his epilogue, was lost or destroyed, possibly in a fire at the station. The *T.A.M.I.* sequence is indeed electrifying, but all too brief.

By the time James' passionate vocal style and raucous stage shows had opened the door for a whole host of soul shouters, including Wilson Pickett, Otis Redding, and Sam and Dave, he was already opening another door through which they did not go (an observation in no way meant to diminish their towering achievements, but to correct a mistake of emphasis in casual assessments of James' career). As James says in these pages, "Papa's Got a Brand New Bag" announced the change in 1965. By the time of "Cold Sweat" in 1967, when soul—both the shouting and churchy varieties—was peaking, James had already left it far behind for funk. Of that second musical revolution, he was the undisputed innovator and leader.

If "Brand New Bag" was the great departure, "There Was a Time," released two years later, was the destination. With that often overlooked record, James completed the journey that had begun with "Brand New Bag" and continued with "Cold Sweat," not only incorporating the polyrhythmic complexity of those undeniably revolutionary records, but also taking the music into new realms of sheer propulsiveness. As in "Cold Sweat," he dispenses with chord changes, stripping the music to its rhythmic essence. Horns, guitars, and voice—including a rich assortment of his trademark grunts, groans, shrieks, and shouts—are all employed percussively. Meanwhile, the bass digs into a relentless funk groove, sounding like a great resonant slingshot snapping the music forward. That bass virtually defines funk, for the goal in funk, as the title of another JB song puts it, is to be "Hot on the One." "It's not one AND two," James explained to me, beating it out with his fingers on the coffee table in his living room, "it's ONE and two." As the great bass player Bootsy Collins, who cut his teeth in James' band, told me simply and with obvious gratitude, "James Brown showed me where the one is." And he showed a whole host of others as well, from Sly Stone to George Clinton to Herbie Hancock to Prince.

Given today's international musical landscape of rock- and jazz-funk hybrids, dance-pop, rap, and African world beat—all rooted in the fertile funk of JB—what was a barroom generalization in 1984 is now readily apparent. But back then it was still highly debatable. The 1983 edition of the *Rolling Stone Record Guide* had accorded James only a short, dismissive entry (which, astonishingly, avers that "aesthetically it's hard to acknowledge 'Super Bad' . . . as quintessential JB"). The series of retrospective albums reprising his revolutionary funk of the late sixties and early seventies had only just begun to appear. In the relatively self-contained dance-club world, a few pioneering deejays were barely beginning to rediscover the dance potential of that funk, so long obscured by disco. And James himself had only just embarked on the series of appearances in New York, where opinion lives, that would utterly reverse Robert Palmer's ruefully accurate observation, made in 1980, that "Brown has never been a critics' favorite."

The rappers, of course, were way ahead of the critics, and they have paid James homage in every coin but money. Using advanced recording technology in a technique called sampling that digitally isolates from previous recordings virtually any sound—a bass line, a rimshot, or a Jamesian *aoowwwww*—innumerable rappers have created aural collages that freely and heavily sample his voice, his band, his beats, and even his backup singers. Many rap records simply name him explicitly as their source of inspiration, as poets do their muse. Afrika Bambaataa, a central figure in rap, claims that break dancing began at South Bronx house parties to James' "Get on the Good Foot." James' 1972 monologue "King Heroin," a nightmare vision of addiction, is sometimes said to be the first rap record. More broadly, the spirit of pride and uplift that comes under the umbrella of hip hop—the culture of graffiti, break dancing, and rap—owes as much to his indomitable sensibility as to his exemplary rhythms. Raps bursting with social criticism, cautionary tales, boasts, self-determination, and Afro-centricity all find forerunners in the JB canon. "Say It Loud, I'm Black and I'm Proud" is only one among many of his exhortations to pride and self-sufficiency, the short list of which would have to include "Don't Be a Drop-Out," "Get Up, Get Into It, Get Involved," and

"I Don't Want Nobody to Give Me Nothing." And, as with rap, you can dance to it.

Woe to the commentator today who tries to operate in ignorance of these immense contributions. Nevertheless, outside the mostly journalistic world of popular music criticism, large claims for black musicians still meet stiff resistance. Until relatively recently, to assert that Duke Ellington was America's greatest composer was to invite skeptical, if not hostile, responses from some quarters. Critical comparisons to Debussy and the orchestral palette and tone color and so forth made the way smoother for the acceptance of Ellington (though they miss the point about him). No such vocabulary is available to cover artists like James Brown. "Serious" music criticism elevates Western harmony and melody over African rhythm, though many of the great black music innovations, from ragtime to swing to bebop to funk, have been initially rhythmic. In performance, the great masters of these forms achieve an almost unimaginable subtlety that nevertheless eludes academics, who have been trained not to hear it, believing it to be "primitive" and therefore simple.

They equally ignore the meaning of black performance practices, disdain popular dance, and fall altogether silent on the crucial significance of such cultural icons as James Brown who have worked their way into the collective consciousness of America. I recently witnessed all of these wires crossed at once when members of the music department of a major university (located in a city overwhelmingly black and poor) took turns reviling Michael Jackson after one of their number had observed with outraged bewilderment that young children prefer to dance to Michael than to—*gasp*—Mozart. Jackson, as immensely talented a performer as we are ever likely to see, is finding, like James, that the carefully cultivated difference on which stardom depends can be transformed almost overnight into an out-of-control otherness. This melancholy fact is demonstrated by the hostility to Jackson, even in the music press, out of all proportion to his alleged sins: cosmetic surgery, androgyny, and general idiosyncrasy.

As an icon, James Brown is for many black Americans one of those definitive personalities of the culture, as resonant as

Muhammad Ali or John Coltrane—different but certainly not other. Despite his dabbling in Republican politics, James' records have always sold steadily and well in the inner cities, where excruciating political correctness counts for far less than attitude, which James has always had in abundance. For many white Americans, he is also representative of black culture, but as a figure who is both different *and* other. Like Elvis, with whom he almost obsessively compares himself, James Brown stands at that crossroads where the fascinating and fascinated interchange between black and white cultures takes place.

Elvis, too, was for a brief time both different and other. Being white, he was able to transform his borrowed black otherness into pure difference—to go from cat to king (and lose his edge in the process). For James there was no possibility that he could shed his otherness in a society that chose to regard him and his art as exotic. All he could do to overcome this perception was to continue to produce difference, inevitably translated by white America back into otherness, which only made him work harder. If all this gave him an edge as a performer, it also made for a tangled identity.

To untangle all these complications before beginning work in earnest on this book, James wanted to take me on a tour of his old haunts in Augusta. We are at his home, which sits on forty rolling acres cleared from a South Carolina pine forest. We're eager to get going, but the complications of being James Brown immediately reassert themselves; he must first look like a man you would pay to see. This requires some doing. He spends most of the morning in the pool house under a salon-style hair dryer. Occasionally, he pops out to take a phone call, to demonstrate a dance step, and once to show me his old pickoff move to first base. After lunch we go in the house and he disappears with his wife Adrianne through a door off the living room. There is much yet to do: the hair still to be tortured into place, the makeup to be applied, the clothes to be selected. Another hair dryer is heard to start up somewhere and the drone soon has me dozing on the couch. Suddenly, at the moment when the whole construct must have come together, I am jolted awake by his unmistakable shout coming from somewhere deep within the house: "AOWWW! JA-AAAMES BROWWWWWN!"

At last, we're almost ready. Willie Glenn, the cousin with whom James grew up in a brothel on Twiggs Street in Augusta, puts a .32 rifle in the trunk of James' red Lincoln Town car. "You got to be prepared," James explains, "because you always got a fool in the crowd." It is every celebrity's nightmare: the deranged fan who uses a bullet to close the gap between his felt intimacy with the performer and the performer's manifest difference from him.

The Augusta ghetto proves to be a 130-block pocket of poverty as grim as any I've seen in any American city. (The governments that have prosecuted James Brown have a lot more to answer for than he does.) We visit the DeSoto Lounge, a dim tavern where armchairs and sofas are circled comfortably around the pool table. The few patrons seem glad, but not surprised, to see the Godfather stroll in. The place is run by Leon Austin, who as a child had taught the young James how to improve his piano playing and as a man had talked him out of retirement, often coming over in the middle of the night to do the famous hair and propel him onto the road once again. "This is the only man," James announces, "who ever really did my hair right." James takes a brief turn at the table. Shooting left-handed, he deftly, delicately runs a few balls. He is among friends, appearing less like a star than like the member of a family who has done exceptionally well.

The different James Brown appears later, when we stop at one of the houses he had lived in as a child after the police closed down the Twiggs Street establishment. Four little girls, ranging in age from about four to nine, play in the tiny, dusty yard. Their father, a slender, friendly man of perhaps thirty, turns out to be a genuine fan. He says he has won amateur contests singing James Brown songs.

"You don't mean it," James says. "Let's hear it."

Unselfconsciously, the man stands in the middle of the yard, where a small crowd has begun to gather, and belts out "Please Please Please" note for note as James had originally recorded it. James beams. "There's so much talent just right here," he says to me, vaguely indicating the neighborhood. A shadow seems to flicker across his face. "Ain't that something?"

A chair is produced from somewhere and James sits on the porch, cordially receiving the neighbors and studiously avoiding going inside. Meanwhile, the man steers me in to see his extensive collection of James Brown records. The house is dark and sparsely furnished, with claustrophobically lowered ceilings of ragged acoustic tiles painted black and hung there presumably to replace long gone plaster. There is no sign of a woman's presence. The man is delighted to learn that James had lived there some forty years before, the only distinction the house is ever likely to have. While we stand in the kitchen talking, the youngest daughter wanders in, opens the refrigerator, and stares inside. The single shelf holds two pieces of uncooked chicken, nothing else. Say it loud: *There is no food*.

"Close it, baby," he says gently. He takes her by the hand and leads her back outside to admire James.

James still sits in the chair, smiling and talking easily with all comers. Though he often rants like a madman to journalists (largely because it's good for business—theirs and his), he speaks to fans with the utmost simplicity and sincerity. He inquires about their families, their jobs, their hopes, and their hometowns; he has played virtually every American city of any size many times and can talk about them in great detail. And he is always ready with advice and encouragement. In a restaurant once, a young black man who said he'd been in high school with Teddy, James' son who died in an auto accident, introduced himself. The young man had gone on to Georgia Tech and had taken a job with a big engineering firm. "Don't be a token," James admonished him, seeing in the young man what he had once hoped for Teddy. "Don't let them pay you for doing nothing."

But that day on the porch of his childhood home, there soon came an oddly discordant moment. Over the next two years I would come to recognize such moments as part of a pattern in James' encounters with the poorest of his fans, whether on Gwinnett Street in Augusta, Auburn Avenue in Atlanta, or 125th Street in Harlem. He would grow suddenly remote, withdrawing into himself, leaving the famous smile—a little fixed now—the immaculate coiffure, the shades, the sharp threads, and vivid makeup to do the work of celebrity until he returned from his brief meditative inner voyage. Whether on these occasions he was overwhelmed by memory or saddened by the misery confronting him is impossible to say. It was as if for those brief moments he wrestled with the conundrum of his fame, built on a sedulously cultivated difference, and found that as compensation—for him or for these admirers basking in its aura—that fame was not enough.

When the moment passes, he politely begins his departure, dragging the crowd with him to the car, a diversion that allows him quietly to dispatch Glenn back to the house. Out of curiosity I follow and see Glenn slip three $50 bills to the father of four.

In the car, later, I try to draw James out, without mentioning that I have seen the money change hands: "You know, there was nothing in the icebox."

As is his habit when he's deep in thought, he sucks his teeth, producing a faint sound like air slowly escaping a balloon. "That man was going to steal," he says at last. "To*night*. When a man's children are hungry, he'll do anything."

This observation is the closest James will come to admitting that he gave the man help. On other occasions I was to see him ostentatiously respond to appeals from some worthy cause or other, but his beneficences to ordinary people were always performed discreetly and with no illusions about their long-term good. Driving in silence, slouched down in his seat, he seems chastened somehow. "You know," he says many miles later, as we're crossing the Savannah River back into South Carolina, "after today I'll just go back to the stage and work that much harder." He doesn't elaborate, but it's pretty clear he doesn't mean he'll work harder in order to avoid falling back into the poverty from which he escaped, but in order to produce more of the fame that is not enough, in hopes that one day it could be.

He knows the fame didn't come solely through his own efforts. He readily credits Ben Bart and Syd Nathan, though he sometimes paints the latter as a foil. That both of these men were white, northern Jews is, in James' view, no accident. "Who else was going to give this poor black country boy a chance?" he asks. So great is his gratitude that to this day he will insist that any white person he likes has "got some Jewish in them," even if they deny it. The attraction remains strong because he sees himself in them, simultaneously identifying with Jews as cultural outsiders and wishing to make the historic journey into the mainstream that many of the great Jewish entertainers made a generation or more ago. It is the same thing he sees in the white-trash country boy from Memphis who turned himself into an American institution. But the difference that would take James there—his uncompromisingly black art—is readily confused with otherness, for James, unlike his models, bears the mark of otherness in his skin color. So, too, do many other black entertainers, but the problem is especially acute for someone famous for being "raw" and "uninhibited." It is a version of the problem faced by many ordinary black people daily, but James, possessed of a vast ambition and a talent to match, must play it out in public and on a grand scale. As a result, he often appears doubtful about the worthiness of the goal even as he pursues it more ardently than ever.

Over the years he has lived out this impossible dilemma through a kind of civic ambivalence: the jingoism of "America Is My Home" and the black nationalism of "Say It Loud, I'm Black and I'm Proud"; his admiration for Martin Luther King, Jr. and his invention of Al Sharpton; his identification with poor people and his endorsements of heartless politicians; his determination to be a role model and his unceasing legal problems. You can understand how a man might make a career of civic ambivalence when as late as 1968 *Billboard* magazine could call him in an editorial a "credit to his race." Or when as a sixteen-year-old in a city rife with corruption, he is sentenced to eight to sixteen years because he is a black nobody, and then some forty years later is sentenced to six years on a traffic charge because he is a black somebody.

Were I his psychobiographer instead of midwife for his story, I might trace the roots of his ambivalence to the separation from his mother described in the first chapter of this book. Hardly a day went by that he didn't mention it. In any case, whatever alternations of need and rejection that experience might have set up in him were soon complicated by his experiences of the society: growing up poor and black in a whorehouse in the Old South, going to prison and finding such kindly authority figures as the warden (so different from the men who had sent him up), going from prison to headlining at the Apollo seven years later, and from there—with the help of Jews for whom the entertainment industry was also one of the few paths of opportunity—to becoming a spokesman for black America courted by presidents.

"Is this the most important black man in America?" asked *Look* magazine in a 1969 cover story. It was a time when performers were often forced to choose sides, not about causes no one with any sense could oppose—fighting famine abroad, cleaning up the environment, saving family farms—but about race and class in America and whether violence was the answer. Much hinged on what Soul Brother Number One might do. He was . . . ambivalent. He preached nonviolence but told an Apollo audience, "Die on your feet, don't live on your knees." He bought a lifetime membership in the NAACP and gave money to the H. Rap Brown Defense Fund. Ultimately, of course, he came down firmly on the side of nonviolence, but the tax case the government soon began against him (and which still drags on) seemed an awfully clumsy attempt to insure he didn't change his mind.

The latest turn in this ambivalence has led him, once again, to prison.

"It's suffocating in here," he tells me over the phone, early in his stay there. Only once before have I heard him so low, and that was shortly after the hardcover edition of this book was published in 1986. "Now I know how Elvis felt," he had rasped on that previous occasion, nearly inaudibly in a late night phone call during a publicity tour for the book and his first major-label album in five years. He had flown into New York from an appearance in Las Vegas and without sleep found himself shuttled from one interview to the next. With the startling revival of his career had come all the old contradictions once again, and he sounded as if he dreaded the consequences that he knew must come, though in what form they would arrive he could not say.

In prison, he invokes Elvis once again: "You know I told you what I said when I saw Elvis in his coffin and put my hand on him," he observes. "Well, now I'm catching his flak *and* mine."

His latching onto Elvis, transfigured in death, suggests a resolution to the complicated logic of his own life that I don't want to pursue. I ask him more concretely how he's doing.

"Well, I'm all right, I guess, but, you know, you don't want to be *pleased* in a place like this."

As the talk turns to plans for a movie of his life, he grows more animated. The good humor and a healthier version of the old ambivalence return. He says he wants to get out the true story of how he wound up in prison, but he doesn't want it to "tear up the country." I remark on the harshness of the sentence.

"Yeah," he says, "they went way back—before civil rights, before Martin Luther King—on this one."

"Like to your childhood?"

"I think so, I think so," he says, and he's *laughing*. "But I'll tell you what," he adds just before we hang up, "if America can stand to have James Brown in prison, James Brown can stand it."

Suffocation is for him no metaphor. Even in New York hotels he invariably opens the windows, preferring the ozone of midtown to the climate-controlled atmosphere of presidential suites. "It's too funky in here," he sings in a song of the same name, "open the door, gimme some air."

One spring evening I got a glimpse of what breathing freely means to him. We are standing in his driveway talking after another day of exploring Augusta. James holds the .32 loosely at parade rest. Glenn, ordinarily a wary and melancholy man, is laughingly recalling his days as a policy runner in Harlem before the state of New York sent him to Rikers Island and legalized the numbers racket for itself. James teases him about what the North can do to a man. "You can't breathe up there," he says. "You ought to be in Toccoa this time of year, the mountains. The air's so fresh, the honeysuckle." He inhales deeply. "That's another *place* up there."

Adrianne, a dim outline in the late dusk, appears on the porch. James waves and smiles at her distractedly, but remains where he is. She calls him; still he lingers. He talks admiringly of some unlikely paragons of indomitability: southern farmers who would burn their farms before they'd let carpetbaggers get them, racist politicians whose straightforward stubbornness he respects. After much patience, Adrianne bellows, jokingly but insistently, "*I want my husbaaaaand!*" James laughs and takes his leave. On the porch he leans the rifle against the door and takes his wife in his arms and begins to waltz her around. It is almost dark now. The crickets are chirring, the bullfrogs down in the pond have started up, and James Brown—dancing with his wife under a Carolina moon out in the middle of what some people would call nowhere—begins to sing softly. He has plenty of air, and in a less crudely ironic world than this the song would not have been "Prisoner of Love," but it was.

To the devastating indictment, in Dave Marsh's epilogue, of both the criminal justice system and the hypocrisy and smugness of the national press, including some of the rock press, there is little I can add. In line with my argument about the burdens of otherness, however, I would point out that beneath the smugness in the reporting on James' plight, there was often a note of comedy, a nudge in the ribs about the wild man who *drove six miles on his wheel rims* before the police could catch him. Or, later, the sly dog who was caught with, *haw haw,* $40,000 in his cell. For me, the nudges in the ribs have been more than metaphorical. Perfectly well-meaning people, a risible gleam in the eye, talk to me about his troubles in tones usually reserved for the appreciation of Road Runner cartoons; though having twenty-three bullets pumped into your vehicle by enraged southern cops is no joke.

It is clear that part of the price of the difference James Brown sought—and the otherness he didn't—is to be treated like a cartoon figure, capable of popping back into shape no matter how many anvils land on him. Or, in an only slightly more affectionate form, of the same thing, he is regarded as a child. In a cover story, a writer for the *Village Voice*, explaining James' recent flight from the police in terms of his gamelike evasion of them nearly forty years before, quotes approvingly the old saying "once a man, twice a child." But as Gerald Early has written in a magnificent essay on Charles Mingus, Thelonious Monk, and Sonny Stitt—three black performers, he says, forced to live out their "deterioration . . . as the spectacle of a bitter public witness":

> To speak of the black male personality as being childlike—any black male's personality—is merely to describe euphemistically what white society perceives as the black male's psychopathology. . . . Surely, any half-thinking black male realizes it is only as an adult that the act of refusing to make concessions has any meaning beyond merely asserting the ego, in that such an act acquires a political aspect.

Regardless of the role chemical substances may have played in James' recent troubles—whether efficient cause or official canard—his struggle is no game. It is another public turning in the ambivalent identity of a man for whom—to borrow a phrase—the personal *is* the political. To love James Brown, you don't have to set his contradictory public actions to one side and focus exclusively on his music. Those actions are central to his identity as a performer and a man. They are not the actions of a hypocrite or a fool, but the essence of who James Brown is, markers along the impossible path he has chosen. No one has expressed this complicated dynamic of need and rejection better than he has: *if America can stand it, James Brown can stand it.* In there, wrestling with the logic imposed on him by the other James Brown, is where we will find another James Brown—not the reductionist construct of a debunking biography, but a man struggling with something much more complicated than private demons, a man who as recently as 1988 had this to say about himself: *I'm Real.* He said it as the title of an album with a picture of him on the cover looking—of course—like a man you would pay to see.

BRUCE TUCKER

In early 1990, when the first paperback edition of this book was being prepared, James Brown had been in prison for little more than a year. Among the people who love him there was still outrage mixed with hope—outrage at the manifest injustice of his six-year sentence, hope that the outrage would produce a quick remedy. Despite a spontaneous, nationwide Free James Brown movement, the public intervention of Jesse Jackson, and the behind-the-scenes exertions of other political and show business luminaries, no remedy materialized. The painful prospect of James serving the entire sentence was fast becoming a reality. Now, of course, we know how that particular story ends: after nearly two and a half years in prison and a halfway house, James Brown was granted early release on February 27, 1991.

Instead of a long twilight decline in the oubliettes of Southern justice, there was a triumphant return on pay-per-view television, the resumption of his recording career, and a return to the live performances that are the essence of James Brown. Awards and honors were heaped upon him. The immensity of his musical accomplishment was thoroughly documented on the indispensable four-CD retrospective *Star Time*. The double-CD sets *Messin' With the Blues* and *Soul Power* instructively gathered James's work in the blues and instrumentals. Documentary films about his life appeared; he was chronicled on A&E's *Biography*. He had a bridge, a street, and even a chocolate chip cookie named after him.

Yet, as befits a man of enormous contradictions, it is not a simple, cinema-ready story of irrepressibility and last laughs, of the life force outlasting and overcoming state-sponsored Thanatos. There remains the irreducible fact of two-and-half years stolen from a man's life. In addition, the sinister and unexplained events leading up to his arrest and conviction have gone largely unacknowledged and unreported, except for some enterprising, and necessarily circumspect, investigation by Stanley Booth. Meanwhile, the post-prison career, too, has been mixed: universally admired concerts and poorly received recordings. On January 6, 1996, however, there fell a blow of unequivocal tragedy: Adrienne, James's wife of 12 years, died while recuperating from cosmetic surgery. She was 47.

Her death brought to an end a marriage that most people know only through lurid accounts in the media. Reversing Tolstoy's maxim, we might say that all unhappy families are alike, at least if they are the families of celebrities. Their disputes and dysfunctions, spilling onto police blotters and back pages of newspapers, occupy an important place in our national morality play, feeding our prurience and smugness at the same time. They confirm our belief that our demigods have feet of clay, success brings unhappiness, and money can't buy love. Like everything else in life, and in James Brown's life in particular, the reality is far more complicated.

Adrienne's death is not only the most significant occurrence in James' life since he first told his story but also may well be the key to what is to come. But to understand what it might mean, it is necessary to have a corrective to the media's inevitably one-dimensional view of their marriage. Its excessive difficulty was far outweighed by an even more excessive—and enviable—devotion. Each of them, separately and unbidden, told the story, recounted in this autobiography, of their first meeting on the set of *Solid Gold* in early 1982, when James, ignoring a throng of admiring women, spied Adrienne from afar. As he puts it, "It wasn't love at first sight, it was recognition at first sight. Our souls had met a long time before." For James Brown, a man deeply conversant with portents and providence, this is not mere rhetoric. Even the most casual observer could not fail to see the profound affection between James and Adrienne, despite the widely reported domestic violence.

If the cost of living and loving at such a pitch is high, its aftermath is all the more devastating. When James's beloved son Teddy died in an auto accident, James dealt with it in much the same way he had always dealt with grief. He threw himself back into his work immediately, doing three one-nighters in a row the day after Teddy was killed. As he says here, he did it to hold onto his sanity. Not this time. For months after Adrienne's death, his despondency prevented him from working. Members of the band began wondering whether they should explore other options. Friends worriedly recalled the only other time James Brown had voluntarily stopped working—the period in the early seventies when a string of personal and professional reverses had pushed him into semi-retirement.

Another blow fell when Bobby Byrd, at almost exactly the same time that Adrienne died, was diagnosed with a serious, life-threatening illness. As both men readily affirm, James and Bobby have been like brothers since their first meeting as teenagers, when James was still an inmate at Georgia Juvenile Training Institute. From singing around the piano in Bobby's childhood home they had climbed to the pinnacle of success with the James Brown Revue, performing, co-writing, and producing until Bobby left the show for good in the 1970s. Though James and Bobby remained in close contact, the ensuing years have been a long period of estrangement and baffled misunderstanding that was painful to both.

It is easy to see how estrangement from Bobby Byrd might be painful—he is quite simply one of the most likable men imaginable. In a business notable for its backbiting and envy, no one has anything but words of genuine affection for Bobby. I still recall, some dozen years after the fact, a joyous birthday party for him in the basement of the church where he was then serving as music director. From the youngest members of the congregation to the oldest, there came an outpouring of love for Bobby of such depth and magnitude as to justify a life.

Since leaving James Brown, Bobby and his wife Vicki Anderson, whom James calls in these pages the best singer he's ever heard, have combined a quiet domestic life with performing here and abroad. Their stage show is a glorious family affair that includes Bobby's two sons, daughter, goddaughter, and daughter-in-law. They had most recently toured Europe and Japan and performed to a packed house in S.O.B.'s in New York, when Bobby's illness struck.

As soon as James learned of the diagnosis he roused himself from his grief to make the trip to Bobby's home near Atlanta. During a long, emotional day, he commiserated with Bobby and Vicki and poured out his sorrow—and his regrets—about Adrienne. Seemingly shaken by the prospect of mortality taking more misunderstanding to the grave, he said many of the things to Bobby that had gone unsaid for years. Soon the two men found themselves at the piano. For an hour or more, Bobby played while he and James sang. Reaching back across the years to the days before the complications of fame and money and temperament had come between them, they sang once again the duets they had worked up in Bobby's childhood home some 45 years before. They moved easily through their old repertoire of songs by the Clovers, the Dominoes, the Orioles, and the Five Royales. By the end of the day, the two childhood friends and veterans of a vanished era of show business represented by those songs, had reconnected on a plane beyond simple reconciliation. On the spot, they began laying plans for an album together.

Thus are private griefs likely to become public art. This is not to romanticize suffering (James's, Bobby's, and especially not Adrienne's) but to ask what it might mean that James Brown is returning to his psychic and musical roots. As this edition of the autobiography was going to press, plans for a major-label album with Bobby, who is now fully recovered, were well under way. Its working title is *The Beginning*. There is also talk of recording an album featuring the great lead female singers from the days of the Revue— Vicki, Lynn Collins, Marva Whitney, and Martha High.

What this return to James' beginnings is unlikely to mean, however, is exercise in nostalgia. Like most major artists, James is incapable of it. And he has stepped out of contemporary idiom before, with results that were far from nostalgic. In 1968, when he was at the height of his innovative funk, he recorded *Thinking About Little Willie John And A Few Nice Things*. It was not only a fitting tribute to the prodigiously talented singer who had died in prison in Washington state, despite James' two-year effort to get him released, but also a remarkable documentation of early R&B, without a trace of nostalgia.

It is worth recalling also that James is not hostage to a single, mannered style, unlike, for example, the seventies dinosaurs still lumbering through their endless reunion tours. Rather, he is the embodiment of vast musical traditions (blues, R&B, gospel, soul, funk, rap, and numerous hybrids) and the bearer of an expressive tradition (black performance) that has set the terms for much democratic art in the twentieth century.

Having spectacularly fulfilled most of his aspirations, he has nevertheless reached that time of life more familiar to ordinary people, when it becomes necessary, for whatever reason, to face down regret. As a result, he may very well give us not merely another hit or another improbable comeback, as with "Living In America," but something more enduring and difficult—late work by one of our great artists.

It is the kind of work of which only a few are capable—deceptively simple, rough, and direct, yet easily encompassing all of the resources and history of the form. The phenomenon is most familiar from fine arts and classical music—the late quartets, the last self-portraits—but there are examples in American popular music as well. Armstrong accomplished something like that in his singing, long after he had made his greatest instrumental contributions. Ellington did it in his sacred concerts. Now, James' restless genius, his undiminished drive, and his hard-earned humanism make him the most likely candidate to achieve it in our time. The only question, as with so much of James Brown's output over the years, is whether we will recognize it when we hear it.

BRUCE TUCKER,
OCTOBER 1996

FOREWORD

By Reverend Al Sharpton with Karen Hunter

The first time I ever laid eyes on James Brown was in the late 1960s. My father, who was one of his biggest fans, took me to the Apollo to see him in concert. I was the boy preacher at the time, and I remember sitting in my seat, not too far from the stage, and being absolutely mesmerized by this strange combination of gospel, rhythm and blues, and an accelerated kind of funk music that no one was calling funk back then.

But what caught me more than anything was the showmanship of this man. It was the highest energy I had ever seen in a human being. For more than two hours James Brown was in constant motion, with rapid-fire delivery, constant costume changes, cape draping, dancing, and doing splits. He was, to me, a one-person amusement park with all the rides in one body. It was fascinating. I was as awed by how much he could do and not seem to get tired as I was that he did it all while maintaining the music and the beat he was on. He completely mesmerized everybody. There were a lot of stars in his time, but he became bigger than all of them. He became a performer whom people wanted to see because he created a new category. And for me he wasn't just a star at the Apollo Theater that night; James Brown was a category unto himself.

Some years later I had the pleasure of knowing the man. Following the death of his son, Teddy, who was part of my National Youth Movement, James Brown took me under his wing. He did a benefit concert for me in New York in honor of his son, and after the concert he remarked on how well I did as a promoter. He told me, "If you listen to what I tell you, you can do this all over the world."

I listened. And James Brown took me all over the world. He would do a few benefit concerts for my National Youth Movement throughout the country and I did the promotions. He would even take me with him when he had radio appearances and I got to say a few words about my organization. That relationship grew one evening while we were in a studio in Greenville, South Carolina. We were there working on his first and only gospel recording, *God Is Smiling*. I was to do some preaching on the album in between his songs. While we were there cutting the album, James Brown got a call from Augusta, telling him that his manager, Al Garner, had a heart attack.

James Brown rushed back to Augusta but left me in charge in Greenville to tie up the loose ends. After Garner passed, James Brown put me in charge of collecting the money from the promoter at the different venues where he performed. He knew that I knew that end of the business and "I know you won't steal from me," he would tell me. I was still a teenager, but that kind of trust meant a lot to me. I wasn't his road manager, I was someone he trusted. I never held an official job in the James Brown camp, I was family.

A lot of people know that I wear my hair the way I do in honor of James Brown. But very few people really know why. My hair, like James Brown's whole persona, represents me. I wear it with honor because it is a reminder to always be myself.

James Brown taught me about self. He was a man who came from a tough beginning, growing up poor and black in the Jim Crow South, raised by a grandmother who ran a house of ill repute. He had been in trouble with the law. But somewhere he figured out for himself who he was. James Brown has an unusual sense of self that is never shaken. And within that knowing, he separates James Brown the man from James Brown the entertainer, the one whom fans never see with a hair out of place.

He would often tell me: "I've got to sell James Brown. That's all I have to sell."

After performances, where he spent two hours giving the crowd everything he had, he would come backstage drained and sweating. While most performers might simply change into dry clothes and head back to the hotel to rest, James Brown would spend forty-five minutes under the dryer, fix his hair, and change into his finest clothes before stepping outside. "Why are you going to all this trouble? We're just going back to the hotel," I once asked him. He told me that even if only one fan saw him on the way to his limo or on his way into the hotel, that one fan deserved to see him at his best. I always thought that attitude was the source of his achieving greatness.

You could not be around someone like that without wanting to learn who you were. And I learned that lesson.

During my travels with James Brown throughout the 1970s, I met just about every entertainer in the world, from Mick Jagger to Michael Jackson. And I don't care how successful, how popular, or hot any of these entertainers are, when they were in the presence of James Brown there was a reverence paid to him. To a person, I never saw any of them *not* be awed by him. James Brown's sense of self was so overpowering that even artists who may have been more commercially successful than he was at the time bowed to him. And I understand why. None of them has been successful in terms of setting a trend. When you think of soul, you think of James Brown. He was the creator and the King of Soul. There were many performers with hit records, but none who changed the entire course of music.

And I believe he was able to do this because he always believed he could. He was one of the first black artists who openly advocated a boot-strap philosophy—that black people should define their own success and shoot for their own standards. He felt we shouldn't complain about the concert hall that banned us, but go out and buy our own. Don't complain about the radio station that won't play your music, go out and buy your own.

We used to talk about this often in the wee hours of the morning while driving around Augusta. He used to park his car on Broad Street, in front of WAAW-FM, a radio station he owned. He loved it there because that spot represented so much pain in his early years and then so much redemption later in life. On that very street, young James Brown used to shine shoes for many of the soldiers at the nearby army base, Fort Gordon. He told me about how some of the soldiers would demean him by flipping a nickel or a dime at him as if he were nothing after he was done. He would pick the coins up and say to himself, "That's okay, one day I'm going to own something."

He told me about how he also used to dance for the soldiers, and when they flipped more coins at him, he would pick up those too, vow-ing internally to perfect his talent.

James Brown would drill into me during those predawn car conver-sations one simple mantra that I have never forgotten. He would look me dead in the eye and say, "Reverend, don't ever let anyone tell you what you can't be."

While those soldiers were tossing coins at him and seeing him as little more than an amusing nothing, he saw himself as an owner of something. He saw himself as somebody. Instead of getting angry, he used that energy to create something for himself.

"Reverend, real success wasn't that I got so good and that those nickels and dimes turned into millions and that I got paid to dance. No, Reverend, the real success was that those same soldiers who threw those coins at me started emulating me. When the world's way of marginalizing you becomes your way of making the world become like you, then you know you've made a difference."

Those who mocked James Brown ended up becoming his imitators. It was a message that helped shape who I am today. Because the same people who once ridiculed and mocked me are the same people who march with me and are arrested in protests with me today.

If you define yourself for yourself and you stay the course, eventually the rest of the world will catch up to you.

JAMES BROWN

1 | JAMES BROWN

I WASN'T supposed to be James. I wasn't supposed to be Brown. And I wasn't supposed to be alive.

You see, I was a stillborn kid. My mother and father lived in a one-room shack in the pine woods outside Barnwell, South Carolina, and when my mother's time came, they sent for my Aunt Estelle and Aunt Minnie to help. They'd helped at births before, and when I appeared, they did all the usual things, gave me the usual spanking, all that, but I didn't respond. They kept trying, but nothing happened. After a while, they just laid me aside.

All during the delivery my father paced outside the cabin, listening to the noise coming from inside. He could tell when it was over that nobody sounded too happy. When he came in to look at his child, my mother was sobbing. Aunt Estelle said, "He never drew a breath, Joe."

While Aunt Estelle tried to comfort my father, Aunt Minnie picked me up and started blowing breath in me. She just wouldn't give up. She patted me and breathed into my mouth and rubbed my back. Just about the time my father busted out crying, I did, too. He waited until he was sure I was all right, and then he walked nine miles into Barnwell to record my birth: May 3, 1933.

They were going to name me Joe Brown, Jr. Then, for no particular reason, they added James. Because they didn't understand the flow, they had it James Joe Junior Brown. Eventually it got straightened out to James Joe Brown, Jr., but the Brown should have been Gardner because that's what my daddy's last name was originally.

For a lot of reasons it's very hard for the Afro-American to trace ancestors. When I look at my family tree, the hardest thing to figure out is where the African came in. It must be from my

1

2 / JAMES BROWN

grandmother, on my father's side. But my grandfather on that side was pure Indian, a Cherokee, I think. My grandmother was working in someone's home and had a relationship with him. So on March 29, 1911, about three miles from Barnwell, my father was born Joe Gardner. When his mother, my grandmother, left South Carolina, he stayed behind with a woman named Mattie Brown, who used to take in children when their parents died or couldn't support them. She raised him, and he took her last name.

There's some mystery behind my daddy's mother. After she left South Carolina she married a white fella and went to New York and then to Philadelphia. Some of the first numbers banked in the numbers racket in Philadelphia were banked by them, and the white fella became very wealthy there.

On my mother's side there is a strong Asian element and some American Indian. My mother is Asian-Afro, but she's more Asian because her father, Mony Behlings, was highly Asian. I never thought that was possible until I visited Surinam, right next to Guyana north of Brazil, and saw dark-skinned Asians there.

Rebecca Behlings, my grandmother on my mother's side, was brown-skinned and had hair that hung way down her back. My great-grandmother on my mother's side, Susan Bryant, was almost a full-blooded American Indian—I'm not sure what tribe—and her hair was so long she could sit on it. She was married to Perry Bryant, who was Afro-American. I don't know how they got together, but it must have been unusual for a black and an Indian to be together back then. They were both around ninety-eight when they died, which was before my mother and father got together in 1929, so my great-grandfather, and maybe my great-grandmother, too, must have been slaves at one time.

Because of all these different bloodlines, I feel a connection to everybody, not to any special race, but to the human race. I'm very sensitive to the Oriental people, as well as to the African people, and I can tell that the African and the Oriental people have a very strong bond with me.

I know about my grandparents, but I can't say I really knew them. I saw Rebecca Behlings (she was called Becca) about twice, and I've never seen a grandfather in my life. Becca and

Mony Behlings lived in Bamberg, South Carolina, and had a son and two daughters besides my mother, Susie. Mony had an organ and used to play blues and gospel on it. That was unusual because most people who liked gospel wouldn't have anything to do with the blues, which were considered dirty and low-down. Mony later left for Florida with another woman, and the family never saw him again.

Everybody picked on Susie—Becca, the other two girls, everybody. They expected her to do all the work around the house, and they beat on her all the time, until Becca's sister, Eva Williams, took her away to live with her near Barnwell. That's where my daddy stole her from—from Eva's. He stole her because he had to.

Eva didn't want Susie to marry my father because she didn't know anything about him and was afraid that Becca would never forgive her if she let it happen. So my father worked out a plan to steal her away. On a certain day at a certain time he got a friend who owned a Model A Ford to drive him by the house. Over her real dress Susie put on an old dress, like she was going to do cleaning. When the car pulled up, she took off. Eva saw right away what was happening. She ran out of the house and hollered for her son Perry to catch my mother. But Perry was in on the plan with my father. He ran her down, but just before he grabbed her, he faked a fall. By the time he got up, she was in the car and gone. They drove off somewhere and got married and were living down in the woods near Barnwell when I was born.

I guess we lived about as poor as you could be. At that time my father did a lot of turpentine work. There were trees all around the cabin, and he worked them. He'd score the tree on each side and place a little trough there to catch the tar that ran down. He'd come back later with a scoop and a bucket and dip the tar into the bucket. When the bucket was full, he poured it into a barrel. When he had enough full barrels for it to pay, he'd take them in to the turpentine company. They paid by the barrel. There wasn't anybody out there with him, because the trees or the barrels, either one, would show him up if he was slacking. They were his boss.

When I was four years old, my parents split up. I didn't know why because I was too young to understand, but I understood it was happening. That's one of my earliest memories:

my mother standing in the door of the cabin getting ready to leave, my father facing her.

"Take your child," he said.

"You keep him, Joe," she said, "because I can't *work* for him."

I didn't see her again for twenty years.

2 LOST JOHN

LIFE out in the woods with my father was rough. We lived in a series of shacks all around the Barnwell and Elko areas. We lived in one as long as the people gave my father work. When he lost a job or tried to find better work, we moved on. The shacks were unpainted, didn't have windows except for shutters that you could pull together; and there was no electricity or indoor plumbing. But we did have plenty of firewood for the stove. My father chopped it, and we threw in some kerosene or fatty pine to start the fire.

We ate black-eyed peas and lima beans, fatback and syrup, polk salad that we picked in the woods, and corn bread. Although the diet never varied, there was almost always enough. But I was unhappy because I was alone all the time. Daddy was gone a lot, working in the turpentine camps, and the various common-law wives he had to take care of me didn't stay around very long, so I was left by myself a lot in the house or out in the yard. Every now and then I had a playmate, but we were so far out in the country I more or less had to be a loner. So I played with sticks and sang, I guess. Dug holes. Got up under the house. Played with the doodle bugs—"Bag, bag doodle"—that kind of thing. Years later I wrote and recorded an instrumental tune called "Doodle Bug."

I don't think you can spend that much time by yourself as a child and not have it affect you in a big way. Being alone in the woods like that, spending nights in a cabin with nobody else there, not having anybody to talk to, worked a change in me that stayed with me from then on: It gave me my own mind. No matter what came my way after that—prison, personal problems, government harassment—I had the ability to fall back on myself.

The best thing I remember from that time is the ten-cent

harmonica—we called 'em harps—my father gave me. I started playing it real early, when I was about five years old. I played "Lost John," "Oh, Susannah," "John Henry," and I sang. My father sang, too, but he sang blues songs he heard in the turpentine camps, things by Sonny Boy Fuller and Blind Boy Fuller, "Rattlesnakin' Daddy," things like that. I don't remember whether I sang them, but I know I never liked them. This is going to surprise a lot of people: I still don't like the blues. Never have.

My father also made home brew, and he was real good at it. Everybody wanted some. All the white people asked him to make it for them because he could beat anybody else making it. He made it out of apples. He'd let 'em sour and then peel 'em. Then he'd put 'em in a barrel and stir 'em and stir 'em and put sugar in. After that he let it sit a long time until it got real thick. You knew when it was ready because you could smell it. I guess it was really apple cider, but it was good stuff.

He had a capper, too. He washed out the bottles and scalded 'em and got the big old Co'-Cola caps and beat 'em flat. Then he'd put the bottles in the capper, put the caps on, and mash it down.

There was another thing my father had: a temper. He could be very mean, and a lot of times he gave me whippings I didn't deserve. He'd be away from home, and when he'd come back somebody would tell him I needed a whipping, and he'd give it to me, no questions asked.

He had a temper about white people, too, but he never showed it to *them*. Where white people were concerned, I would say my father threw a rock and hit his hand. He'd call white people "crackers," curse 'em and everything when they weren't around, but when he was in front of them, he'd say, "Yessir, nawsir." That's when I lost respect for my father.

I will not accept what my daddy accepted. I will not accept being a boy. If you push me, you got a problem. I was a boy *as* a boy, but as a grown man I will be respected. That's the reason I call everybody by his last name with a *Mr.* in front of it and insist on the same thing in return.

One of the things that probably makes me feel worse than anything in the world is to see a Caucasian walk up to my father and say, "How are you, Joe," and then walk to me and say,

"How are you, Mr. Brown." I think the man who does that is more ignorant than my father.

I love my daddy to death, but he has never looked a man in the eye and told him he didn't like him. That's the difference between us: I'd tell a man to his face I didn't like him. But I wouldn't be mad with his brother. My daddy would be mad at *all* of 'em but tell 'em, "Yessir, nawsir," and then be ready to kill 'em later.

People like that are dangerous. And that's what we're facing today: people who laugh with you and say you're all right and then kill you later. It's the same thing the Ku Klux Klan used to do. The same people you work with in the daytime come at night to lynch you.

My father gambled a lot, too. Never won. He'd gamble any place he could find. He played a lot of Georgia Skin. That's where you shuffle the cards and deal one to each player. Say, I have a seven and you have a five. You flip over cards from the top of the deck, and if a seven comes up before a five, I caught you and win your money. You bet any amount you want on it.

I don't know what Daddy had going for him. He's been a strange man for a long time. The mystery could have been in me, though, I don't know.

One thing about my daddy, he was always hardworking. I think I got a lot of my drive from him. He was never without a job for more than five days in his life. He did whatever work he could get. He did farm work. He did a lot of filling station attendant work, washing and greasing cars, and maintenance around the station. After all the turpentine work, he did a lot of highway work. He's a heavy-equipment operator, but he never had formal teaching so he couldn't get his certification papers. He stopped in the second grade in school. He is a jack of all trades and master of none because of the sheepskin he wasn't able to get.

My father had a very hard time trying to bring me through. He worked hard just to take care of his child, but the system really went against him because he didn't have very much knowledge. They deprived him of knowledge, and that's probably the greatest sin in the world.

The social system back then was like it is right today: economic slavery. One thing you have to understand about slavery:

A man never enslaved a man because he didn't like him; he enslaved him because he wanted him to work for him. It's about free labor. That's all it's ever been about. It works that way everywhere in the world.

My father did his best, but finally he had to get Aunt Minnie, who was really my great-aunt, to come take care of me—Minnie Walker, who first blew breath into me. The three of us were living around Robbins, South Carolina, in another one of those shacks, when my father decided that he could find better work across the Savannah River in Augusta. So the three of us moved into town, but he split from Minnie and me. He was still around, but from then on my father and I never lived in the same house again.

In Augusta, Aunt Minnie and I lived with another aunt of mine in a house at 944 Twiggs Street. That's one place I will never forget. Outside, Highway 1 ran right by the door. You could go all the way to New York on that highway. Inside, there was gambling, moonshine liquor, and prostitution. I wasn't quite six years old.

3 AUGUSTA, G-A

AUGUSTA was sin city: plenty of gambling, illegal liquor, and a lot of houses like the one I grew up in. The local government then was corrupt, the police could be bribed, and the law was whatever they said it was. It was like Phenix City, Alabama, on the other side of the state, just over the state line.

A lot of the corruption went back to Prohibition. Even after repeal, Georgia stayed dry for a long time, and a whole system of payoffs developed out of that. Augusta was also in the Bible Belt, and the ministers were all the time getting the city to crack down on the illegal activity. It just made it harder for the police to keep everybody happy. Half the time they were arresting you, and half the time they were looking the other way.

I got to Augusta at the end of 1938. The house was located in a section of the city called "the Terry," short for the Negro Territory. The Terry stretched west from Fifteenth Street to East Boundary and south from the Savannah River to Gwinnett Street. The streets were mostly unpaved red clay and sand. Rows of cabins in alleys and on the short streets stood side by side with regular middle-class homes.

The Terry was mostly black, but in 1938 there were still some whites and lots of Chinese. Most of the Chinese kept to themselves; they owned stores and lived above them. During a riot in 1970 all the Chinese people were burned out, but back then there was no trouble. There was a Moslem group there, too. Today you'd call them Black Muslims, but we called them Mohammeds. They wore beards, plaited their hair in back, and had a temple that was closed to white people. All I remember about them is that as kids we didn't care too much for their hairstyle.

Sometimes the Ku Klux Klan held parades right through the Terry. The funny thing was all the black folks turned out to watch. I never paid much attention. Kids just didn't think about things like that.

All up and down Ninth Street there were gambling joints run by a man named John S. He operated wide open—every year he bought the police a brand-new paddy wagon. When he died they carried trunks full of money out of his place.

My aunt who had the house on Twiggs Street was named Handsome Washington, but everybody called her Honey. She was very intelligent, and she supported a lot of people. We had about twelve to fifteen men staying there, in and out, and the woman ran the house because she was the most intelligent. A lot of the men were ex–farm workers who couldn't get jobs, and Honey just fed 'em all. She fed a lot of the people who lived in Helmuth Alley behind the house, too—young mothers who needed things. She brought them meat and sugar, and she gave them money for groceries. And she loved the children.

Honey just didn't want to see anybody hungry. I started eating better there myself. I kept her cleaned out of hog jowls, which I really liked, and I ate tripe (cow belly) for the first time. Honey knew I liked potato pone, too, and she'd fix me one any time I wanted it and I'd eat the whole thing. She also tried to give me chitlins, but I never did like 'em. When I finally got where I could eat chitlins, I had to have a lot of vinegar on 'em.

Honey had a grandson living there who was a year older than me. His name was Willie Glenn, but everybody called him Junior. Since I was called Junior, too, he became Big Junior and I became Little Junior. We were as close as brothers—wore each other's clothes, shined shoes together, and sometimes slept in the same bed.

The house itself was two stories, with a lot of rooms on each side. It must have been a funeral home at one time, because the rooms were so long. It was heated with stoves that burned wood and coal. In the winter Big Junior and I scoured the railroad tracks that ran nearby to pick up coal for fuel.

Honey paid off the police right along, but they still busted her about every three months. There was a detective who watched the house from Edwards' Texaco station across the street. He'd see men come and go with the girls or he'd see one of my cousins pull up with a car full of moonshine they'd made out in the country. Usually the car was driven by Jack Scott,

Honey's brother, the honcho in the family and a really vicious man. Big Junior and I sometimes helped stash the liquor because we were small enough to get under the house where they kept it hid. There was a loose floorboard in the front room, and Honey sold it out of there for 25 cents a half pint. I guess the floorboard was supposed to fool the police, but they'd walk in and reach right down and pull up the whiskey.

Sometimes, when they'd bust her, she woudn't even get all the way to the station before they'd let her go. Or sometimes they'd take her in and she'd pay her fine and be right back, and other times she'd spend a night in jail. It never seemed to make any difference; she was back in business right away.

When the police raided the place, they were always polite, at least for those days, because my people were extremely dangerous. The police usually called black people "niggers" and all that, but not at our house. That's when I learned that police are not brave: they just have a job to do. There's a whole lot of people badder than the police, and a lot of 'em were people in my family.

Everybody was afraid of Jack Scott and my daddy, who didn't think anything about taking a gun right out of a man's hand. They'd get in a scrape and a fella would pull a gun on 'em and be afraid to shoot because he knew if he missed he was a dead man. Jack or my daddy would dare 'em to shoot and then snatch the gun right out of their hands. Come home with a pocketful of pistols.

Jack wouldn't give up his own gun, though. One time when the police came, Jack had a gun in his hand and refused to surrender it to them. He let them arrest him, but he wouldn't hand over that gun. He just backed into the patrol car, still holding the pistol. "Now, shut the car door," he said. "Lock it up and I'll go to jail and come out with my gun in my hand." And they took him away like that.

Jack mistreated me a lot. He didn't live at the house, but he was around all the time and he beat me for nothing. Once, after a raid, Big Junior told Jack that I had told the police they were selling whiskey. I don't know why Junior said that because I hadn't told anybody anything. Anyway, Jack stripped me buck naked, hung me from the ceiling in a burlap sack, and beat me with a belt until I almost passed out. I stayed mad at him for a lot of years, but later on I wound up burying that man.

If any of the customers got too rowdy, they were taken care of by another cousin named Willie Washington. We called him Buck, and he didn't take no mess. He was a big fellow, double-jointed, a sort of Joe Palooka. I once saw him pick up a fifty-five-gallon drum full of water. People stayed out of his way.

Believe me, there were some bad cats around there. Out in the street you might see two men lock hands and cut it out with knives. Each one had a knife in his free hand, and they'd cut each other until one of 'em fell out. Not shoot it out, *cut* it out.

If Buck wasn't around, my daddy would take care of any problems. He was in and out of the house a lot, but he never lived there. During this time he worked a lot of different jobs; construction work, delivering vegetables for a truck farm by the levee, whatever he could find. He sure didn't get rich at it. I remember he got paid $4 a week for delivering vegetables, and I was spending some of that four dollars.

I said he's been a strange man for a long time. He had a strange sense of humor, too. Once, when I was about seven, he and a man he was working for had a bottle of gin they were having trouble opening. They handed it to me and asked me to open it. Back then I used to open everything with my teeth, thinking I was getting away with something. After I opened it and spit the cap out, they told me to drink some of it. I drank a little bit and handed it to my father.

"Naw, drink some more," he said and pushed the bottle back to me.

It was mint gin, and that's what fooled me—it tasted good. Before they could say anything, I chugalugged half of it. It made me drunk pretty quick and then I passed out. They got worried and carried me into a church nearby and dunked my head in the baptismal font. When that didn't do any good, they carried me to a river branch, took off all my clothes, and put me in the water to try to bring me back to life. Finally I came to, but I staggered around for the rest of the day. Boy, when I got sober the next day, I didn't want any more of that ever again. And I still don't know why they wanted me to drink that stuff.

It was around this time that I got my hands on an organ for the first time. My father was working at Eubanks Furniture Store, and they let him have an old pump organ with one of the legs off it. He brought it to the house on Twiggs Street and propped it up on a cheese crate on the porch. He set it up in the morning, and when he came back that evening he saw all the men and women from the house and some of the neighbors gathered on the porch. Thinking there was some kind of trouble, he pushed his way through and found me sitting there playing "Coon Shine Baby" on that old organ. I had taught myself to play it in one day. I don't know where I picked up that particular song, but I always figured it referred to Afro-American kids because they called us "coons" and they called us "shine" because we shined shoes. But I wasn't thinking about that, though; I was just happy making music.

After that, Honey really started taking an interest in me. She would bathe me and talk to me and listen to everything I had to say. One time she was having trouble getting into her chifforobe. It was locked, and she'd lost the key. I said, "Don't worry, Honey, I'll get it open for you." She looked at me real funny, like she was seeing me good for the first time. I went on out in the yard and walked straight to a spot where I found a piece of wire all bent up. I took it back inside and used it to unlock the chifforobe.

Honey, who was highly superstitious and knew things, thought she saw a definite sign with me. When she'd bathe me, she'd wash the hair on my arm, go crossways with it, and just stare at it.

"You're going to be a wealthy man someday," she'd say.

I'd laugh and say, "What you talking about, Honey?"

"You're going to be very wealthy," she'd say, pointing to the wet hair on my arm. "See the sign."

I told Big Junior what she said. We laughed at her and told her she must be crazy. She'd just smile. Next time she'd bathe me, she'd say it again.

Honey was a good woman and I loved her to death, but she was a madam with other things on her mind. It was Aunt Minnie who acted more like a mother to me. I shared a room upstairs with Aunt Minnie, away from what was going on downstairs. She read to me, talked to me, held me close. I'd lie there and daydream and try to envision something better. I felt terrible about what went on in that house. I knew people could live a lot cleaner, because I saw some who did, and I wanted to be like them. But then the war came and the soldiers with it, and things got a whole lot rougher.

4 PROSTITUTES AND PREACHERS

THE SERVICEMEN started pouring into Augusta in the fall of 1940, when I was seven. At first a lot of them were assigned to Daniel Field, an airstrip on the western edge of the city. Later, Jimmy Doolittle's men practiced there for their bomb attacks on Tokyo. The old Augusta Arsenal went into high gear making bombsights, and Camp Gordon was built out on Tobacco Road for the cavalry.

The soldiers brought a lot of money into the city and we tried to get our share of it on Twiggs Street. When the troop trains came through and stopped at a crossing, Junior and I and some of the other kids would run off and get sandwiches and Red Rock Creme Soda for them, and they'd tip us. When the cavalry came by in their truck convoys, I'd buckdance for them on the Third Level Canal Bridge. There was a canal that came off the Savannah River and ran through the Terry, and the Third Level Bridge was right beside our house. Big Junior would stand there and pat for me, and I'd do a little old country buckdance, same as you might see people doing in the South today. When I'd first come to Augusta, Big Junior showed me a few dance steps, and I guess I just took it from there. The soldiers loved it. They threw nickels and dimes, and I worked even harder, adding some steps of my own, trying to get them to throw quarters. Boy, I wanted those quarters. We picked up all the change, and then Big Junior and I would have an argument about it.

"We made the money together," he'd say, "so we ought to split it."

"Naw," I'd say, "I'm going to carry it to Honey."

And that's what we'd do. I've give it to her to pay the rent. Rent wasn't but $5 a month, but all of those men and women put together couldn't come up with it. I don't know where all the money from the bootlegging and prostitution went, but I know Honey was supporting an awful lot of people. Once we made the rent we might go back and make some money for ourselves so we could go to the picture show at the Lenox Theater, a "colored" movie house on Ninth Street, or to a little Chinese place to get wienie stew for 35 cents.

We steered money into the house another way, too. To get to Camp Gordon from town, the soldiers had to walk right by our house. Big Junior and I would stand out there and ask them did they want a woman. I wouldn't let 'em say no.

"Come on," I'd say, "there's some real pretty ones in that house yonder." I'd hook my arm in theirs and start tugging, pulling them toward the house. When they'd finally say yes I'd lead 'em right inside.

I guess I saw and heard just about everything in the world in that house when the soldiers were there with the women. It was a funny thing about the soldiers, though. They didn't want anything freaky. I'm not endorsing it or condemning it, but they didn't believe in oral sex; they thought it was unholy.

Even though we went out and got men for the women, we still had to stay in our place. We had to say "yessir" and "nosir" and "yes ma'am." We even said "yes ma'am" to those ladies, regardless of what they were doing.

By this time I had started school. Floyd School, one of the few in Augusta for black kids, had seven grades and about forty kids to a class. When I'd first gotten to Augusta the other kids initiated me by taking off my overalls and throwing them up in a tree. I was a real small kid so I had to get tough pretty quick.

I'd have to say that I was poorer than most of the other kids, and a different kind of poor, too. I was poor because nobody was really taking care of me. I came from a roadhouse, not an organized home. A couple of times the principal, Mr. Myers, called me into his office and sent me home for "insufficient clothes." It made me feel terrible, and I never forgot it.

Perry Williams, the man who had stolen my mother for my father, used to come by the house sometimes and bring me things, including my first store-bought underwear. Out in the country I'd worn stitched-together flour sacks. When I told him about getting put out for insufficient clothes, he carried me downtown in his truck and bought me some clothes I could go back to school in. That satisfied Mr. Myers, but when my new clothes wore out, it happened right again.

It was through the school that I began to get a sort of identity. At home I was Little Junior, but all the kids at school and all the teachers called me James Brown, like it was one word. I've always thought that was kind of strange. I was good at baseball and football, and I always got along with everybody. Sometimes I sang for the class. Once I sang "A Tisket, a Tasket" to the third grade.

Outside of school I was a hustler. Besides entertaining the troops, Junior and I worked at most any kind of job we could find. We shined a lot of shoes, delivered groceries, racked pool balls, picked cotton, picked peanuts, and cut sugarcane. The first time I picked peanuts I ate so many I got colic. Cane kept you bloody. Cotton was just *hard*.

Shining shoes was another story. There were a lot of shoeshine parlors in those days, and they all had licenses. They didn't like competition from freelancers, so they were all the time getting the police to run us off the streets. We had to do a lot of slipping around just to shine shoes. Sunday was the best day—we'd hit all the churches and at a nickel a shine make maybe as much as $20. I'd put some showmanship into it, too, popping the rag and beating the brushes behind my back. When we got tired of dodging the police we went to work for Shoeshine King, a parlor on Broad Street, but we only got to keep 30 cents for every dollar we made.

No matter how much money we hustled, it never seemed to be enough. I was carrying all my money home to help Honey, but we still needed everything and anything we could lay our hands on—including garbage. A grocery wholesaler down the street, C. D. Kennedy's, threw all its spoiled merchandise into oil drums in back of the place. We went through the oil drums and pulled out all the swollen cans and brought them home and ate the stuff. Everybody in the house ate it. Nobody thought about getting poisoned. We were just trying to survive.

That's what everything that went on in that house—gambling, bootlegging, prostitution—was about: survival. Some people call it crime, I call it survival. It's the same thing goes on right today in the ghetto. You can see kids standing on corners selling marijuana. You get it in a bag, and the funny thing is that the bag says "Church Offering." That's what hard times bring—makes pimps and prostitutes out of preachers. Prostitute don't have to be a person who lays down. A prostitute can be a prostitute for whatever.

One of the things that helped *me* to survive in those days was music. I didn't realize it at the time, but it was so. I wasn't thinking about music as a career or anything like that, it was just there in the community, and I fell into it, the way you will. At home I sang gospel with Junior and a fellow named Cornelius. We sang "Old Jonah," "Old Blind Barnabas," things like that, and tried to imitate the Five Trumpets and the Golden Gate Quartet. Really, gospel is what got me over, especially after I went to prison.

I was learning more instruments, too. A man named Mr. Dink taught me to play drums. At Jack Dempsey's, a liquor store where I worked as a delivery boy, I met Robert Graham, whose son, Robert, Jr., first taught me some piano. They lived at 707 Twiggs and had an old upright. Robert, Sr., had some good chords, and he could really play a lot of old songs. Robert, Jr., taught me some fingerings and let me fool around on the keyboard. Whenever I wanted I could go there and practice on that piano.

I also learned some guitar from a blues man named Tampa Red who was going with one of the girls at the house. His real name, I believe, was Hudson Whittaker, and in the thirties and forties he recorded a lot of party blues like "It's Tight Like That." When he passed through Augusta and stopped to see his girl he sometimes sat and played for us in the front room. He used an open tuning called Sebastopol and fretted with a broken off Coke bottleneck on his little finger. He bent those strings and got sounds out of 'em that I recognized later when I heard B. B. King play.

Tampa Red sang for us, too, and his songs reminded me of the blues my father used to sing when he worked the turpentine camps. I still didn't care for the blues that much. I'd *sing* 'em sometimes, but I didn't *like* 'em.

I liked country music even less. Whenever I worked for white people there was always a radio tuned in to country music. It was constantly forced on you. Much later on I got to where I listened to country music by choice—Lefty Frizzell, Jimmy Dickins, Tex Ritter—but back then I didn't pay any attention to it.

I liked gospel and pop songs best of all. I got all the Hit Parade books and learned all the pop tunes—Bing Crosby's "Buttermilk Sky," Frank Sinatra's "Saturday Night Is the Loneliest Night of the Week," "String of Pearls." I also admired Count Basie's "One O'Clock Jump," but I couldn't play piano good enough to do it.

I heard a lot of church music, too, because I went to all the different churches with a crippled man named Charlie Brown who lived in one of the shacks in Helmuth Alley. He had to walk with two sticks or with somebody on each side holding his arms. On Sundays when we weren't shining shoes, Junior and I walked Mr. Charlie to one or another of the churches because they'd take up collections for people like him.

At the churches there was a lot of singing and handclapping and usually an organ and tambourines, and then the preacher would really get down. I liked that even more than the music. I had been to a revival service and had seen a preacher who really had a lot of fire. He was just screaming and yelling and stomping his foot and then he dropped to his knees. The people got into it with him, answering him and shouting and clapping time. After that, when I went to church with Mr. Charlie, I watched the preachers real close. Then I'd go home and imitate them because *I* wanted to preach. I thought that was the answer to it.

Audience participation in church is something the darker race of people has going because of a lot of trials and tribulations, because of things that we understand about human nature. It's something I can't explain, but I can bring it out of people. I'm not the only person who has the ability, but I *work* at it, and I'm sure a lot of my stage show came out of the church.

One thing I never saw in the churches was drums until I went to Bishop Grace's House of Prayer. Those folks were sanctified—they *had* the beat. See, you got sanctified and you got holy. Sanctified people got more fire; holy people are more secluded—sort of like Democrats versus Republicans. I'm holy myself, but I have a lot of sanctified in me.

Bishop Grace was a big man, the richest and most powerful of that kind of preacher in the country, bigger than Father Divine or any of 'em. He had houses of prayer in more than thirty cities in the East and South, and he had these "Grace Societies" that just took in the money. Every year when he came back to Augusta there was a monstrous parade down Gwinnett Street for him, with decorated floats and cars and brass bands. Everybody in the Terry turned out for it, and other people came from as far away as Philadelphia to march in it. You could join in it with your car or, if you had a musical instrument, you could fall in with one of the bands.

He was called "Daddy" Grace, and he was like a god on earth. He wore a cape and sat on a throne on the biggest float, with people fanning him while he threw candy and things to the children. He had long curly hair, and real long fingernails, and suits made out of money.

His House of Prayer on Wrightsboro Road in Augusta resembled a warehouse. A sign over the door said: "Great joy! Come to the House of Prayer and forget your troubles." And everybody *did* come at one time or another, even people who didn't believe in him, because he put on such a show. Inside there were plank benches, a dirt floor covered with sawdust, and crepe paper streamers on the ceiling. At one end there was a stage where Daddy Grace sat on a red throne.

He'd get to preaching and the people would get in a ring and they'd go round and round and go right behind one another, just shouting. Sometimes they'd fall out right there in the sawdust, shaking and jerking and having convulsions. The posts in the place were padded so the people wouldn't hurt themselves. There was a big old tin tub sitting there, too, and every time they went by the tub, they threw something in it. See who could give the most. Later on he had various big vases out there, like urns, one for five-dollar bills, one for tens and twenties, and one for hundreds. It seemed like the poorest people sacrificed the most for him.

Daddy Grace had to be a prophet, but seeing him I knew I was an outsider because I couldn't believe in him. I believed in God, so that made me an outsider right away.

He had his house behind the church, and behind the house was a big pool where he baptized people. Instead of baptizing them just once, he baptized them over and over. Some people had so much faith in him that they took water out of that pool and carried it home by the gallon and drank it when they got sick. They paid for some kind of blessed papers that he put out, too, to put on themselves like a poultice.

That pool was the first place I ever swam in my life. We'd give him a dollar and he'd let us swim in there. They let him get away with that. But he brought a lot of trade to that city, and that's what it was about—trade. Like the Masters Golf Tournament. Elections. Or James Brown.

Meanwhile, the war was coming closer to home every day. First, there were all the soldiers, more every year it seemed like. Then the government started keeping hundreds of German prisoners of war at the Augusta Arsenal. I remember it because they were treated better than the American blacks around there. Pretty soon they started letting the German POWs do farm work around Augusta and in South Carolina, and the U.S. government paid them 80 cents a day for it. That was more than my father got a lot of times.

Eventually the government began to crack down on houses like ours. They put all the liquor joints and gambling places off-limits to the soldiers. Police raids came more often, and it took Honey a little longer to get released when she was arrested. Nobody said anything to me, but I could tell things weren't right. Finally, one day Honey fixed me a potato pone and set it down in front of me.

"What's this for?" I asked.

"It's for you to eat," she said.

She was acting funny, so I watched her the whole time I ate. When I was finished she said: "Baby, we got to move."

"How come?"

"We just do," she said.

"Junior and me can get some more money."

"That ain't the reason," she said. "Now go find Junior and bring him here."

She never would tell us straight out, but we knew it had something to do with the soldiers and the whiskey and the women. I guess the place really was a hellhole, but when you're a kid your home is home even if it's a roadhouse, and I was sorry to see it broken up. It wouldn't be the last time the government reached into my house.

5 CAL-DON-YA!

AFTER the Twiggs house was closed down, everybody kind of separated. Aunt Minnie and I moved into a two-room cottage by University Hospital near Fifteenth Street. There was a whole row of these unpainted two-room places up there. They called 'em cottages, but they weren't much different from the shacks I had lived in around Barnwell.

My father came and went like he always had, but it seemed like I saw less of him after the move. Pretty soon they took him right out of the service station he was working in and put him in the Navy. He was thirty-two-years-old with a second-grade education, and he eventually wound up a second-class seaman. In the service he operated bulldozers and set dynamite for construction projects. Every month he sent Aunt Minnie a check for $37.50, and we lived on that plus whatever I could hustle.

More and more I was getting to be a street kid, getting out and getting into everything. At school I was a little roughneck, a thug. You could tell the thugs because we wore baseball caps and jeans with a pocket on the side and a handkerchief tying down the pocket. We turned the sides of our sneakers down and then tied 'em back up real tight. We took Clorox and wrote on our clothes with it to impress the girls.

I had lots of girlfriends, and the teachers couldn't understand it. One day a teacher said to a bunch of 'em I was standing with, "I don't see what you all like about him; he hasn't got any money."

"Yes, I do," I said. I pulled out this little ratty wallet I had and kind of flashed a wad of bills stuffed in it.

"James Brown, let me see that," she said. She grabbed the wallet and pulled out the wad. It was $3 and a lot of paper cut the size of bills.

I was something, though. There was this new kid named

Henry Stallings who came from the country, and I used to take
his lunch every day. He had a lard bucket, and after I started
taking his biscuits and whatnot he started hiding the bucket
under the schoolhouse. I'd watch him from around the corner
and go get it right again. At lunchtime I'd watch him sneak back
around there, pull out the bucket, look inside, and then just
look all around, bewildered.

Henry was a lot more country than we were—he wore overalls instead of jeans, and his shoes were brogans—but he was a
lot cleaner than we were, too; his overalls were always spotless
and starched, and his shoes were always shined. That's what I
remembered about him when I ran into him years later coming
out of the Theresa Hotel in Harlem and hired him to work for
me. He became the first person ever able to really do my hair
right.

I met another kid around this time who would mean a lot to
me—Leon Austin. He was a few years older and played piano.
He showed me how to play with both hands and taught me how
to get rhythmic feel into it. I really wanted to practice playing,
but I couldn't always count on Robert Graham being at home,
so I started sweeping out Trinity Baptist Church in order to use
their piano when no one was around. At this time boogie-woo-
gie was the big thing, and like a lot of kids I wanted to play it,
but you'd better not be caught doing it in a church. I was always
careful to lock the doors before I started beating on that piano.
Never did get caught.

I was also hearing all kinds of new sounds around me—on
the radio, on records, around town. I listened to Louis Armstrong, Duke Ellington, Count Basie, Cleanhead Vinson, Louis
Jordan. Jazz, rhythm and blues, it didn't make any difference to
me. I tried to play whatever I could, and I imitated all the
singers no matter what their style. There was a local man
named Sammy Green who had a band of maybe ten pieces, and
I tried to hear them whenever I could. They were reading
charts, had a horn section, everything.

When the Lenox Theater started an amateur night, I decided to enter. I must have been about eleven, and it was the
first time I'd ever really sung in public. Without any accompaniment I sang "So Long" and won first prize. I think I won
because even then I had a real strong voice. The other people

on the program sang good, but real quiet. I sang loud and strong and soulful and the people felt it.

The Lenox was also where I first saw films of Louis Jordan performing. Louis Jordan and His Tympany Five. They played a kind of jumping R & B and jazz at the same time, and they were something else. They did a lot of comedy, but they could play a blues if they had to, or anything in between. The films were shorts of Louis doing whatever his latest song was, and they showed them before the regular picture. He played alto sax *real* good and sang *pretty* good. Louis Jordan was *the* man in those days, though a lot of people have forgotten it. His stuff was popular with blacks *and* whites, and he usually had several hits at one time, a lot of 'em that sold a million. "Choo Choo Ch'Boogie," "Early in the Morning," "Saturday Night Fish Fry," and "Ain't Nobody Here but Us Chickens" were all his. When I first saw him I think he had out "G. I. Jive" and "Is You Is, or Is You Ain't (Ma' Baby)?" but the one that knocked me out was "Caldonia, What Makes Your Big Head So Hard?" especially the way he'd go up real high: Cal-don-*ya!* I learned the words as quick as I could, picked it out on the piano, and started playing it and singing it whenever I got the chance.

"Caldonia" was a song you could really put on a show with, and I guess that Louis Jordan short is what first started me thinking along those lines. That and the preachers. The circus and the minstrel shows that came through town played a part, too.

Johnny J. Jones was my favorite circus. Junior and I used to crawl through a hole in the fence in the back of the fairgrounds to see him. Since he stayed for a whole week, they called it a fair, but it was really a circus. A circus is supposed to do all its stuff in one night and then move on to the next town, the way I did with my show years later.

We had to pay to get into the minstrel shows, but only because we couldn't figure out a way to sneak in. Silas Green from New Or-leans was the best. He presented a complete varied program with singers, dancers, musicians, and comics. That's what I tried to do fifteen years later when I put together the James Brown Revue.

It's strange: Even though I'd seen just about everything there was to see in the house on Twiggs Street, I thought the short dresses on Silas Green's girls were unbelievable. To me, those brown-skinned models were the prettiest things in the world. I saw some top talent in those shows, too, like Willie Mae Thornton, who first did "Hound Dog." I saw a lot of great comedians, too. In those days the comics still worked in black-face, but like everybody else I just thought it was funny.

What wasn't funny was some of the things that happened to me in the streets. Two incidents really stand out in my memory. The first involved a fella who tied kids to trees to try and break their spirit. His name was James, and he was a big, heavy, muscular fella. He'd been in the service, had gotten wounded in the war, and had a plate in his head. One day he grabbed ahold of me and said he was going to tie me to a tree.

"I'm not going to resist," I said, "but if you tie me up and then turn me loose, I'm going to kill you."

He laughed and started tying me to a chinaberry tree. First he tied my arms, then my legs, me not fighting it at all, while the other kids stood around watching and laughing. When he got me all tied up he stepped back and waited for me to try wriggling loose, but I never did. I just kept still. I was ready to stay tied to that tree for as long as he wanted. After a good while, he got bored and untied me. I never said a word. I just walked away, and he forgot about me and started bothering some other kid. In a lot next to a beer parlor nearby I found a big, heavy, broken-off tap. I picked it up, went back across the street, walked straight up to him, and hit him right on the head with it. It knocked him out, and he stayed knocked out for a long time. After that he didn't bother me again.

The second incident involved three white fellas who tried to electrocute me. Junior and I were working with them drain-ing a ditch and putting in some fence on farmland owned by a man who ran the filling station next to it. They had an electric air compressor or pump of some kind and somehow it slipped down into the water in the ditch. When they saw what had happened they started talking among themselves and laughing, and one of them turned to me.

"Cut on that air tank there," he said.

"Nosir," I said, "I don't want to."

"Goddammit, boy, I said cut it on!"

I stepped in the water and turned it on. When I did, it felt like a whole herd of horses was galloping over me. I couldn't let go of the tank—the electricity froze me to it. Junior was jumping around and yelling, "Turn it off, turn it off!" But the men stood there, grinning. Junior ran into the filling station and got the man we were working for. He came running, and when he saw what was happening he pulled the plug.

I collapsed, and Junior dragged me under a tree. When I came to, I just glared at the fella who'd told me to turn on the tank, but I didn't say anything. I didn't dare. The amazing thing is that when I recovered we all went back to work.

I don't know why I wasn't killed, but I decided from that day on I'd never take any mess like that again. There were still a lot of lynchings around Georgia and South Carolina in those days, but I was more aware of the everyday occurrences, black men getting kicked in the butt or beat up real bad, things like that. I wasn't angry, but I promised myself it wasn't ever going to happen to me again.

Later, I used to walk down the street with my first wife in Toccoa, Georgia, and smile a crocodile grin, and just *pray* that the white man didn't come up and mess with me like he messed with them other people. "Lord, don't let it happen," I'd say. Because if it did, I knew I was going to kill the man.

But when I was a kid, standing in that ditch water with all that electricity running through me, I was just beginning to put the race thing together. There was still a lot I didn't understand —like the end of the war. When the atomic bomb was dropped on Hiroshima, we were glad because we knew it meant my father would be coming home soon. We were glad, too, because from the first we were a lot madder at the Japanese because of Pearl Harbor than at the Germans. Now I think about it a lot differently because I realize that a bomb like that would never be dropped on white people.

Right after the war I formed my first band, the Cremona Trio. I don't know where I got the name and can't even remember the names of the others in it, but I know we thought we were hot stuff. We had to borrrow instruments from the school or from anybody who would lend us a beat-up old guitar or a snare drum or whatever. I played piano when the places we gigged had one, and I sang and sometimes played the drums. We started off as a trio and eventually went to five members, which we called a combo, but we still used the name Cremona Trio.

I had won the Lenox Theater amateur night several times

by then and had a small—*very* small—local following. Every now and then we got invited to play at a black elementary school or the high school and eventually we worked our way up to playing the noncommissioned officers club at Camp Gordon. We did stuff by Amos Milburn, Charles Brown, Wynonie Harris, and the Red Mildred Trio. I learned a lot from imitating all those different singers. For instance, Amos Milburn and Red Mildred both did "Bewildered"; Red Mildred sang high, in falsetto, and Amos Milburn sang sweet and low, but I sang like both of them. Charles Brown was the featured vocalist with Johnny Moore and the Three Blazers, and he could really sing ballads. Wynonie Harris had a real strong voice. I sang like both of them, too. But no matter who I sang like, I was always powerful. While other singers eventually gave out, I could sing at top volume all night.

When the Lenox closed, the Harlem Theater on Gwinnett Street started the Harlem Talent Review on Wednesday nights, and it wasn't long before I won their contest singing "Caldonia." I sang for my classmates, too, to raise money for the school. Like a lot of black schools in those days, Floyd didn't get nearly enough money from the Board of Education or anywhere else. Books, supplies, upkeep, everything was a struggle, and the school needed every penny it could get, so I sang and the other kids paid a dime each to see me. At first I did it in the classroom, singing and dancing without any accompaniment, but there were enough kids willing to pay that my teacher, Miss Garvin, moved the show to the library, where there was a piano. Then I really worked out, especially on that Louis Jordan tune. As often as the principal let her, Miss Garvin put me on and charged admission.

Even though I was getting into music more and more, I still didn't have a burning desire to be a professional musician. People who knew me thought I was going to play baseball because I was much better at baseball than at singing. I was a left-handed pitcher with a good fastball, a sharp curve, and a wicked floater—what they call a knuckleball today. Ty Cobb had lived in Augusta, and I knew all about him. The Detroit Tigers held their spring training there, and the city also had a Tigers farm club in the Sally League. We'd climb the trees across from the ball park and watch the games from there.

But what I really wanted to do was box. My idol was Beau

Jack, the lightweight champion of the world whose real name was Sidney Walker. He was from Augusta and had shined shoes at Ninth and Broad, same as I did. All through the forties he fought at Madison Square Garden, and we listened to his fights on the radio. In 1944, when he fought Bob Montgomery for the fourth time, you had to buy war bonds to get in; they sold more than $35 million worth that night. Later on, I met Beau and had several semi-pro fights with some of the boxers he handled, but during this time I was doing most of my fighting in the school yard, in the streets, and at the Bethlehem Community Center for Negroes.

I boxed like I pitched—left-handed. It always confused the person I was up against. I had developed a reputation for being a tough little kid, so there was always somebody wanting to test it. It didn't hurt my reputation for toughness when I broke my leg playing football and played after that with a cast on. I broke the same leg again when I jumped off a railroad trestle, and I played football with that cast on, too. I wore out both casts that way and earned the nickname "Crip."

Because of my reputation the other kids always pointed me out to the white men who came around to recruit scrappy black boys to be in the battle royals they put on at Bell Auditorium. In a battle royal they blindfold you, tie one hand behind your back, put a boxing glove on your free hand, and shove you into a ring with five other kids in the same condition. You swing at anything that moves, and whoever's left standing at the end is the winner. It sounds brutal, but a battle royal is really comedy. I'd be out there stumbling around, swinging wild, and hearing the people *laughing*. I didn't know I was being exploited; all I knew was that I was getting paid a dollar and having fun. A lot of good boxers started out in those things. I think Beau himself, when he was a kid, was in battle royals at the Augusta National Country Club. I was too classy for battle royals, though, because I could really box.

So I boxed and played baseball and football and sang from time to time or did some little gig with my group. The Cremona Trio wasn't too much happening, but it lasted, on and off, for about three years. It was also during this time that I wrote my first song, "Goin' Back to Rome." I had never been to Rome, Georgia, in my life—I just liked the way "Rome" sounded in the song. But it turned out to be prophetic.

6 GOIN' TO ROME

I DON'T REMEMBER when I first started stealing, but I remember *why* I started—to have some decent clothes to wear to school. My daddy never bought me anything, and Honey and Aunt Minnie didn't *have* anything, so it was up to me to look out for myself. I'm not making excuses for anything I did; I'm just saying what was going through my mind at the time. Every time I got sent home for insufficient clothes, it hurt me and made me mad, too.

During the war, when my father's check was coming in every month, I didn't have to worry too much. After the war, though, things got tough. Daddy was back in town, scuffling at whatever jobs he could find and losing his money gambling just as fast as he made it. Things got rough for everybody. When the services cut back, the flow of money from the soldiers slowed way down. Food prices went through the roof, and there was a lot less work around.

I kind of fell in with a bad crowd, too. There were a lot of gangs around the city: Sunset Homes and Gilbert Manor, two low-income projects, each had a gang. There was the Downtown gang, which was rough, and the Summerhill gang, which was all right. I was in a little gang around King Street led by Big Boy, Little Boy, Pete, and a boy named Harry Robinson. The gangs weren't vicious, not like a lot of 'em today. There were some rivalries but nothing deadly. We just liked to swim in the canal, keep the girls out late, shoot dice, and generally enjoy ourselves. When we were out real late the police might chase us, and when that happened I headed straight for the canal and jumped in. Sometimes I found a reed to breathe through so I could stay underwater until the police gave up.

At dice I got very good—too good. So good you can get yourself killed. The layman ain't got a chance with me. Later I won a lot of money at dice from the Moonglows, before Marvin Gaye's time, when it was Bobby Lester and the Moonglows. I beat 'em out of enough money to buy me two Cadillacs. Beat the Isley Brothers out of a lot, too.

At first we got where we might steal a pair of skates off somebody's porch, but that was about all. Later we got into everything that wasn't nailed down, and we sold it. I took hubcaps off people's cars, gas caps, whatever. Filling stations would give you a quarter for each hubcap. But the best ones were off the '46 Ford, because it had the big hub, and you could get 50 cents for one of those. A lot of times, I'd steal the battery or break into the car and take whatever was in it. Breaking in wasn't too tough because most people didn't lock their cars.

Honey must have known what I was doing because I had a little trick that almost always worked on her. See, I wore out a lot of shoes playing football, just kicked 'em right out, so I was all the time needing shoes. I'd say, "Honey, I need me some shoes; I think I might go and steal me a pair."

"Naw," she'd say, "you ain't going to steal no shoes. I'll buy you some." Then she'd give whatever little money she had, and I'd go get the shoes.

There were two things I never did when I stole. I never took from the Afro-American, and I never let Junior get mixed up in it. I didn't take from the Afro-American because I knew he didn't have anything, and I was sort of a Robin Hood. I took from the Caucasian and gave to the Afro-American—sort of redistributing the wealth. Once I stole a whole bunch of baseball gloves and passed 'em out to all the fellas. Also, there were other kids whose clothes were insufficient, too, and I didn't think twice about stealing them a jacket or a shirt or a pair of pants.

Junior was always pestering me about getting caught and going to jail. *He* didn't want to go to jail, and I didn't want to be responsible for putting him there, so when he was around and I saw an opportunity, I'd say, "Junior, I'm fixing to make a move. You go on home now." And he'd leave.

Junior was right; I did get caught. Me and another boy were digging a battery out of a car one night when the police pulled up. We were bent so far under the hood concentrating on getting the cables loose we didn't even hear the police come up behind us. They had to tap us on the shoulder. They carried us in the patrol car to the Richmond County Jail and kept us there overnight, trying to scare us. In the morning a juvenile officer talked to us real stern and then let us go. I think it scared Junior more than it did me because when I got home the next day and told him about it, he said, "I *told* you, Crip. You got to get away from Augusta."

His mother was living in New York and had written to Honey about sending him up as soon as there was enough money for a bus ticket. After I got caught he tried to persuade me to go with him.

"Why don't you come on and live with me and Mama up there?" he said.

"What would I do in New York?" I said.

"You could sing. Play the harp. Dance. New York's a *big* old town."

"I want to stay here with Honey and Aunt Minnie."

"Police catch you, they going to send you to the penitentiary," he said.

"Naw," I said, "they won't never catch *me* again."

"I'm telling you, Crip. *Please* come with me to New York."

Honey wanted me to go, too. They both knew I was going to get into trouble if I stayed down there, but I wouldn't listen. I turned right around and started breaking into cars again.

One night three or four of the fellas and I went all up and down Broad Street getting into all the cars parked along there. I must have broken into three or four myself and gotten out a whole lot of clothes. A couple of the fellas got caught that night, but I got away. The next day I went up to the shoeshine stand on Broad and heard that the police had been around looking for a boy named James Brown. Right while the fella was warning me, a patrol car pulled up and two policemen got out. I started to slip away, but somebody must have pointed me out to them because they started chasing me. They didn't have a chance. Broad Street, like its name says, was real wide, maybe two hundred feet, with a promenade down the center lined with trees and park benches. I negotiated it like a halfback—dodging cars, people, trees, benches—and man, I could *move*. After a couple of blocks of that, the cops gave out.

To me the whole thing was a game. I went back to that same shoeshine stand later that afternoon, the police got behind me again, and I got away again. The second time they chased me a lot farther, until I lost 'em behind the Dr. Pepper plant. I hid out for a couple of hours, then went back a third time. Same 'shine stand: Here I come again, there they come again. But now they're mad. When I take off running this time, instead of chasing me on foot they come after me in their car. And they can drive as good as I can run: I cut down an alley, they come screeching around the corner; I tear across a vacant lot, they charge right over the sidewalk; I duck behind a building, they barrel in the back way. I know that eventually they'll have to get out of their car, and then it'll be no contest. But they must have radioed for help because now it seems like every patrol car in Augusta is after me. I'm getting worn out, and I'm thinking, "if only I can get to the canal and jump in, I can lose them." So I cut down another alley. It turns out to be a blind one, and when I run back out I find myself surrounded by police cars and looking at a whole lot of guns.

This time they took me to jail for real—fingerprinted me, took a mug shot, and threw me in the lockup with adult offenders even though I was only fifteen years old. When the detectives asked me about breaking into the cars, I told them everything I had done. They let the other boys go because none of them had ever been in trouble before, but they charged me with four counts of breaking and entering and larceny from an automobile.

There were some pretty tough cats in that jail, some real hardened criminals, and when I was put in with them I thought I was gone. They didn't bother me too much, though, just asked for cigarettes, things like that. They did explain to me that there was no point in worrying about anything because the authorities would do whatever they felt like doing anyway. There sure wasn't any bail or legal counsel or anything like that. It's funny, but it didn't really bother me that much that I was in jail. Somehow I knew I was destined to go, and I didn't have anything to stay home for, so I passed the time lying on my bunk, thinking about things, waiting, but not really expecting anything. It reminded me of the days out in the woods when my daddy was gone because in jail, although you're surrounded by other people, you're really alone.

Sunday was visiting day. Junior would go out early in the morning and knock up some money shining shoes or whatever and bring me a pack of Camels and Juicy Fruit chewing gum.

We sat and talked in the runaround, a big room enclosed with wire mesh at one end where the visitors came in. Junior told me how Honey and Aunt Minnie were doing and what all the fellas were up to. When he left, he always gave me a few quarters. Honey never came to visit me; she said it would break her heart to see me there. My father never came to see me, either, but I'm not sure why.

After a couple of months in jail, I got hip: You could get out if you could get somebody to bribe the right person. It was like everything else in Augusta then. One boy had *stolen* a car, not just broken into one like me, and his daddy had gotten him out for $100. That was the going rate. The next Sunday I told Junior about that boy. "Tell Daddy to try and get me out," I said. After that, whenever I asked Junior about it, he said he was working on it, but he always looked like it made him uncomfortable when I brought it up.

Nearly two more months passed that way. I turned sixteen, then all of a sudden they decided to try me—as an adult. Without any advance notice, they took me and three or four other prisoners over to Richmond County Superior Court. Later I found out why it was so sudden. On that same day—June 13, 1949—they were scheduled to try a sensational bribery case against the chief of police, a civil service commissioner, and six other city officials. The prosecutor asked for a postponement, and when the judge granted it they were left with an empty calendar, so they hustled us over to the courtroom.

The prosecutor was Solicitor George Haines and he was a man who would sink you. People in Augusta loved to hear him plead a case because he put on such a show. If you were being tried for cutting somebody, he had a way of holding the knife so it looked five inches longer than it really was. Sometimes he brought a suitcase into court, and when he made his final argument he'd say: "Your Honor, here's my suitcase. If you let this man go free"—he'd pick up the suitcase and put on his hat— "I'm going to *leave* this town."

When I was brought into the courtroom there were still a lot of people left over from the postponed trial, but I could see Junior sitting way up in the balcony where black folks had to sit. The guard sat me down at the table and pointed out the state's attorney, R. Lee Chambers III, who was supposed to act as my lawyer. It was the first time I'd ever seen him.

I knew I was in trouble when they tried a little white girl right before me. She had stolen $50 from somebody, and the judge, Grover C. Anderson, gave her two to five years. When my turn came, Attorney Chambers waived the indictment, the list of witnesses, a jury trial, and formal arraignment. Then he pleaded me guilty. I was tried, convicted, and sentenced before I knew it. The sentence read that James Brown "be taken to the jail of said county to await a guard to be sent by the penitentiary of Georgia, where he shall be taken and confined at hard labor therein or elsewhere, as the State Department of Corrections shall direct for the space of not less than two years and not more than four years in each case of four cases, said term to commence from this date, and one sentence to commence at the expiration of the other." He had given me eight to sixteen years. When he asked if I had anything to say, I begged him to give me a chance.

"This *is* your chance," he said. "If you work hard in prison, you can get out when you're twenty-four years old. If you don't, you'll be thirty-two. It's up to you."

I didn't say any more. I knew they had given me all that time because I was a colored boy being tried behind a white girl who had gotten two to five. The judge had to give me the maximum sentence on each of the charges to please the whites. On top of that, he had to make the sentences run consecutively instead of concurrently. What I couldn't understand was why he was sending me away. There was a boy's home, a reformatory, right there in Augusta, but he was going to send me to a detention center in Rome.

Mine was a kangaroo court, I knew that. What I have always felt was unjust in this country is that they didn't allow us to get an education, and yet when we went to court they treated us like we were impresarios who knew what was going on. We can't be wrong on both ends. *If you don't allow a man to get an education, don't put him in jail for being dumb. That's what they did in Augusta—they sent me to prison for being dumb.*

The Sunday after the trial Junior came to see me as usual. I could see he was upset at all the time I was carrying, but I knew they were keeping me in Augusta for a few more weeks to give me one more chance to come up with a bribe from somewhere.

"Is Daddy going to get me out?" I asked.

Junior looked all over the runaround before he looked straight at me. "Mr. Joe said there wasn't nothing he could do."

I didn't say anything and neither did Junior. We both knew my daddy could have gotten me out, but he didn't do it. He just didn't have the knowledge.

"It looks like you're going away," Junior said.

Out of the blue I said a strange thing.

"Don't worry, Junior," I said, "when I get out of here the *world* is going to know about me."

I don't know why I said it, except that he looked so down-hearted. I didn't say *what* the world was going to know me for. Somewhere in the back of my mind I knew I wanted to do something with my music, to be popular, to do things for people, but I couldn't put it into words. It was something I could feel. I just knew that when I said what I said I really believed it. Junior thought I was crazy. When he went home he told Honey that being in the cell had affected my brain. He told her what I'd said. She told him, "Junior, the world *is* going to know about him." But when he was sitting there with me I could see he was worried about something else, too. Finally he told me what it was.

"Mama sent some money," he said. "We're leaving, Crip."

"Honey too?"

"Uh huh."

I don't remember if we hugged each other or not, two tough guys like us, but I remember watching him walk away through the wire-mesh door. I was splitting up from my family again. They were going to New York. I was going to Rome, like the song said.

7 PRISON

ONE DAY, without any warning, an officer took me out of my cell. He didn't tell me anything; he just led me down the hall-way and out the door. For a second, coming out into the sun-shine, I thought my daddy had come through for me, but the officer put me in handcuffs and turned me over to a man who wasn't wearing a uniform. The man looked at a document he had and asked, "Are you Brown, J.?"

"Yessir," I said.

"You're being transferred to Georgia Juvenile Training In-stitute at Rome."

He led me to a half-ton van and put me in the back of it with five or six other fellas already inside. There were two benches running along each side and no windows. This was sometime around the last of June or the first of July, and it was real hot back there, like an oven. It got hotter the longer we sat there.

After a while the van pulled away, and we rode for a long time. The whole trip must have taken about ten or twelve hours. It was already dark by the time we got to Rome, but I could see we were in a compound with a whole lot of buildings. The place had been a WAC camp before. When the federal government abandoned it, the state of Georgia bought it and converted part of it into a tuberculosis hospital, Battey State, and part into a prison for juvenile offenders, GJTI.

They took us to a holding area where they cleaned us up, deloused the ones who needed it, fingerprinted us, and issued us uniforms. The uniforms were dark gray with blue pinstripes, and the shoes were high-tops, sort of like boots. After we were done at the holding area, they took us to the old army barracks where they housed us. There were two in front of the place, where the white boys stayed, and one in the back for the black kids. The barracks were surrounded by twelve-foot-high chain-link fences with barbed wire around the top.

Nobody ever really told me what to expect. I just fell in with the routine: out of bed at 6:00 A.M. and breakfast at 6:30 in a building that they'd made into a dining hall. The whites sat on one side, the black kids on the other. At 7:00 we went to work. We maintained the hospital grounds and worked in the kitchen, the laundry, and places like that. It's a wonder we never caught TB in there—we had to have strong systems. Along with some hired labor, we helped build houses on the grounds for some of the doctors, too. Sometimes we worked on a farm about fifteen miles away. We ate lunch at noon, went back to work at 1:00, quit at 4:30, and ate supper at 5:00. After supper, if it was light, we played baseball or football. At night in the barracks we listened to the radio or played dominoes. A lot of times we used the dominoes like a deck of cards and played all kinds of poker that way. We shot dice, too, and I hadn't lost my touch.

Most of the boys were serving time for burglary, robbery, breaking and entering, and things like that. A few had killed somebody, but it was always another black person. See, if you were black and killed another black person, the state didn't punish you too seriously back then because they held black life cheap. They just put you away for a few years, same as they would if you'd stolen something from a white person. A separate system of justice existed for the black offender.

There were some rough cats in there, but some nice cats, too. Not too long after I got there a boy named Johnny Terry came in. I don't remember what he'd done, but I don't think it was much more than what I did. He later became one of the Famous Flames with me and was very free-hearted; he shared everything he had. He had a radio that he let me play whenever I wanted to, and I always wanted to because I was always trying to find a station that played the kind of music I knew. Rome didn't have but one radio station then, and it didn't play much music of any kind. One night when I found a station that played rhythm and blues, I got so excited I dropped the radio. Oh, man, it must've broken into a hundred pieces. I felt terrible because I knew what the radio meant to Johnny, and it wasn't like he could go out and buy another one anytime he wanted to. I found some tape and some wire and put it back together as best I could. It looked pitiful, but it still worked.

"I'm sorry, Johnny, I busted your radio," I said and handed it back to him.

"That's all right," he said. He just took it and laid it aside. Never even got mad. All the time I was in prison, Johnny was like that. We got to be close friends right away.

When the guards weren't around, the big, dangerous guys tried to run everything, just like in any prison, but they didn't run me because I knew how to use my fists. I was fast—couldn't nobody get to me—plus I was left-handed, which gave me an advantage because most of 'em just weren't ready for a left-hander. I was still a small kid, so I got put to the test by the bullies right away, and I identified with the other small kids and always took up for them.

For a short time, we had organized boxing, which gave me an opportunity to show the bullies without getting into trouble that they better not mess with me. Carl Noles, an old boxer who lived near Rome, came out and ran the boxing program. It didn't last too long, though, because couldn't nobody who got whipped forget about it after the matches were over. They'd be nursing a grudge against whoever beat 'em in the ring, looking for a chance to get even. One night it all broke out in the dormitory, and we wound up in a great big brawl. I mean we tore up the place. That was the end of the boxing.

GJTI was more like a school than a tough prison. The black kids were still segregated and were treated more like convicts than the white kids, but the place wasn't near as bad as being in the Richmond County Jail. The security wasn't too tight, and a lot of things were done on the honor system. The catch was that if you messed up too often they sent you to a place that was much worse.

I wanted to serve the minimum time I could and get released, but I saw pretty quick that it wasn't going to be easy. No matter how a place like that is run there's always two forces at work—one trying to help you and the other trying to hurt you. What makes it complicated is that both forces include guards and inmates. Some guards and inmates were really good influences, and some were really bad. One force tried to help me grow up and the other tried to turn me into a hardened criminal. A bad guard can do that just by mistreating you all the time. If you lose your cool, you wind up in the penitentiary. Prison is at best a balancing act.

Some guards did a lot of things to me, like they do in any prison. Mostly, they tried to play with my integrity because I was very intelligent. They gave me humiliating jobs or tried to provoke me into getting mad so I'd get in trouble. It's the kind of thing goes on in prisons right today, everywhere. One guard named Wallace, who had one eye, always watched me, following me with that one eye. It was spooky.

One time a guard who didn't like me wouldn't let me play football. He was hoping I'd get mad and try to run away so they could send me to a much rougher prison. Some of the other boys told me the best route to take if I ran away. It was like it was all set up for me to run. I wouldn't do it.

Another time a guard named Boatwright put his hands up like a boxer and talked about how nobody could get a punch through. Some of the fellas were sitting around in the barracks when he went on and on about how good his defense was. "You couldn't get in there, I don't care what you do," he said.

I sat and listened to him talk for a long time until eventually I said, "Captain Boat"—we called all the guards Captain—"I can get in there."

"Naw, you can't," he said.

"Yessir, I sure can," I said, "but if I do, you're going to put me in the hole." The hole was solitary confinement, where they put you on bread and water for several days when you did something serious. Hitting a guard was very serious.

He said, "Naw, I won't put you in the hole. Forget I'm a guard and see can you get in there."

"You promise you won't put me in the hole, Captain Boat?"

"I swear. Now come on."

He danced around a little bit and shuffled his fists. I guess he thought because he weighed about 200 pounds and I was about 135 he could whup me real bad, and that was probably what he wanted to do. I stood up, went into my left-handed stance, leading with my right and circling to the right. He wasn't ready for that. Before he knew it I hit him about twenty licks and beat him up pretty good without knocking him down. When I stopped throwing punches, he turned and walked out of there fast.

He kept his promise; he didn't put me in the hole. But after a while I started wishing I had gone to the hole. From then on he caused me a lot of problems, being real hateful because he just couldn't live with the fact that I beat him up. He always gave me the hardest jobs and tried to irritate me while I was doing them by yelling at me the whole time. I let it go; his pride was hurt, and I knew that a man whose pride is hurt is dangerous.

The assistant warden was very mean to me, too. He would probably say he was just being a strict disciplinarian, though. One day he said I was supposed to put my stool in a jar for a stool test. I did it and went back to his office carrying it at my side. I guess he couldn't see it because he said, "I thought I told you to get a stool sample."

"I got it," I said. "I brought it back in the jar like you told me."

"Where is it?"

I set it on his desk. He liked to had a fit.

"Don't you set your shit on *my* desk!" he yelled.

He grabbed me and threw me against the wall, but he didn't beat me because I wouldn't have taken it. I was different from the other people. None of the bad guards ever really beat me because they saw something in my eye that said I wasn't going to accept it—from any man.

There were a lot of good guards in there, men who tried to help me. A guard named Mr. Avery showed me how to do jobs right and taught me things. I even played basketball with his boy. For a long time after I got out I went to see him at Christmas. The warden, Walter Matthews, treated me like a son. Really, he's the person who raised me. Didn't nobody do it when I was at home, that's for sure.

Mr. Matthews got mad at me only once the whole time I was in prison. I don't even remember what for, but I think it was one of those times like when you get really mad at your child because you love him so much. We were standing in his office and he was trying to tell me something, but I wouldn't listen so he slapped me. Didn't hit me. Slapped me. And almost cried after he did it. I guess he slapped me to see if I would hit him back. I *would* have hit him back if he hadn't been a good man, but I would never have hit Mr. Matthews because he was in my corner. It would have been like hitting my father. Anyway, right after he slapped me, he hugged me. He was a good man, and after I got out I visited him many times, too, right up until his death.

In another part of the prison they had a few girl inmates. Most of them were real dangerous because almost all of them were in there for killing somebody. I didn't care. They were women, and I wanted to impress 'em. Sometimes we worked with them around the hospital, and I always tried to look sharp, which was one reason I didn't like the baggy pants they gave us in the kitchen. But a lot of it went back to not having decent clothes as a kid. Really, it was wanting better clothes that got me into prison in the first place. I'd do anything to look better. The gray pants that we wore were all right—we called 'em coyotes—but unless they were new they wouldn't hold a crease. Whenever I worked in the laundry I pulled out new pants and put my number, 33, on 'em and took the number off the pants I had on and exchanged 'em. I got all the new pants that way for a long time, then one day they caught me and gave me an old baggy pair and put me out on the farm.

Man, I couldn't stand being seen in those things, so I soaked 'em with starch and hung 'em upside the wall until they dried stiff as a board. Then I took a hot iron and steam-pressed 'em. Made 'em shine and hold a crease. Then I cut the tops off my high top shoes and made 'em look like slip-ons. When the guards saw that, they got mad and said they wouldn't give me any more shoes. So Johnny Terry, who was working on the trash truck, brought me some saddle oxfords. I cleaned 'em up and had somebody half-sole 'em and put big strings in 'em. The next day I was with the farm detail formed up at the gate. The guard said, "Brown, J. Step out." He made me stand in front of the other cats while he said "Look here. See how he refuses to be like the rest of y'all. Look how clean he is." I looked like a politician going to work. Nobody could keep me down.

There was one girl in particular I wanted to look sharp for. Her name was Eva. We looked at each other all the time, but I couldn't figure out how to get together with her. One guard who was always real good to me could tell I had my eye on her. One day he said to me, "James, you kinda like that little ole gal, don't you?"

"What gal is that, Captain?" I asked.

"Come on, now. You know who I mean—Geneva." That was her real name. I just smiled, waiting to see what he was driving at. "Well, there's a big linen closet near the laundry," he said. "It's right roomy in there. If nobody was looking, two people could get real comfortable in there."

That guard liked me and he liked her, and he was just helping us, the way some people will, just being human. He was another good man. He didn't have to say any more. The next time Eva and I worked in the laundry, as soon as that guard nodded that the coast was clear, we took off for that closet. It *was* roomy in there, and there were all those linens to make a nice bed out of. It wasn't the honeymoon suite, but I don't think anybody in a honeymoon suite ever enjoyed themselves more than Eva and I did that day.

8 MUSIC BOX

EIGHT TO SIXTEEN YEARS—it didn't seem real to me. So I tried
to make the best of things, to make some kind of life. It was like
my life outside prison had never existed. Honey and them had
moved to New York. Aunt Minnie wrote to me from Augusta a
few times, and my father came to see me once, but other than
that, nobody ever came to visit me. Come Sundays, it seemed
like I was the only boy in the place without some kind of visitor
—family, girlfriends, running buddies, somebody. Maybe that's
why some of the people like Captain Avery and Mr. Matthews
were so good to me.

I also think they were good to me because I was different. I
was good and always had a smile. No matter what happened, I
never got mad at the people who ran the place. I wasn't going
to be wrong and mad, too. You do something wrong, why you
going to be mad at somebody when you're already wrong?
That's stupid. I was good *and* I maintained my integrity. That's
what got me through—that and music.

I hadn't been there but a couple of months before I formed
a gospel quartet with Johnny Terry, a fellow called Shag, and
another called Hucklebuck. Singing gospel is a way to help
your soul and be content. Gospel gives you a *form* of contentment. I'm glad I'm in tune with God because that's the only
thing that can bail out the Afro-American or any minority that
doesn't have an education. The man has him tricked in everything else, and he cannot get out of that.

I sang a lot of gospel in prison. Gospel is contentment because it's spirit, and you feel that spirit when you sing it. It's
the same spirit I feel when I'm on stage today. I feel it when I
sing. Period. I make people happy, and *they* feel it.

Singing gospel's a good way to learn about music in general.
There's a format for gospel; you learn the different parts, and

then you start putting them together: first tenor, second tenor, baritone, bass. Instrumental music's put together the same way. That's how I knew the chords before I ever got to the piano. I had sung so much gospel with Big Junior and them in Augusta that all I had to do was to go to the piano and pick out the chords.

The other fellas in prison didn't really know too much about music, but after I taught them how to do all the parts, we got real good. We got so good that one day a guard took us to sing for the free people in the hospital. We started singing and we sang so pretty that the people started crying. I was singing "Our Father." And then the tears started running down *my* cheeks.

Meantime, the guard wandered away, and we didn't see him anymore. I was still pretty new at the prison then, and they didn't know if I'd run away or not. We kept singing, kept crying. As time went by, the guard forgot about us and went off duty. Mr. Matthews started wondering where we were. Nobody knew—none of the guards and none of the staff. Finally, one of the fellas told him we were singing at the hospital. He ran over and charged down the hall, yelling, "Where are they? Where are they?" He stumbled into a roomful of people, some of 'em singing, some of 'em listening, and *all* of 'em crying. He took a minute to get himself together, then he said, real low and gruff, "Come on." He turned and walked out of there real fast, us marching behind him. He was mad, but he was glad, too, that we hadn't run away. I wouldn't have let anybody run, and if anybody had run, I probably would have run and caught him. After that he trusted me completely.

I wasn't satisfied just singing, though. I wanted to have a band like the Cremona Trio. The only problem was we didn't have any instruments. I remembered the homemade instruments the jug and washboard bands had in the minstrel shows, and I didn't see why we couldn't make some. We started with a comb and some paper—Hucklebuck played that—then I got some empty fifty-pound lard cans from the kitchen and made a drum set from them. A washtub and a broomstick made a wash-tub bass, and I made sort of a mandolin out of a wooden box. I taught myself to play the bass, and in different keys, too. Some-how I knew where they were. You might think we would have sounded terrible with those knocked-together instruments, but when you do it right and you sing your parts correctly, it sounds real good. The jug bands on the minstrel shows sounded fine, otherwise they wouldn't have been on there.

There was a piano in the gym, and I was all the time asking to play it; after about six months they gave in. I don't know if they thought I couldn't play it or what; anyway, I walked over to it and ripped into "Caldonia." In about a second everybody was jumping up and dancing. Talk about jailhouse rock—those cats were boogying. Whenever we played basketball after that, during halftime I played the piano and sang. At night my little band entertained in the dormitory, and we still sang a lot of gospel, too.

Before too long the other fellas started calling me Music Box. Sooner or later most everybody got a nickname that stuck. You got so used to calling people by their nicknames that you forgot their real names. Hucklebuck's real name was Davis, I think, but I can't remember Shag's at all. They were good boys, though. But it's funny, as good as I knew them, I don't know their names. And they're both dead now.

Shag was killed in the state prison at Reidsville. They killed that boy for nothing. He was originally sent to Rome because of something that happened in Atlanta. He was in a place playing a record on a jukebox when a white fella came up and pulled the plug for no reason. They got into a fight, and Shag wound up getting sent to GJTI. While he was there, a guard got down on him for some reason or another. So one night the guard came into the dormitory to teach him a lesson—he beat the boy with a chain. Then he went back to the warden and lied, saying the boy had beat *him* up. So Shag got sent to the state prison. And a guard down there was beating him one day, and Shag held up his hands to protect himself and they shot him dead for holding up his hands. At Reidsville Penitentiary, Tattnall County, in the state of Georgia.

Sometime in 1951, after I had been at Rome for about two years, they moved the prison to a place near Toccoa, Georgia. Mr. Matthews and most of the guards went, too. Toccoa was a little bitty town clear on the other side of the state, right near the South Carolina border in the Appalachian foothills. An old paratrooper camp had been turned into a prison. The Flying Tigers, who jumped in China, had trained there, but now the place had twelve or thirteen dilapidated cement block buildings. Except for the fact that the buildings were so run-down

and that they had changed the name to Boys Industrial Institute, it was pretty much like Rome. We slept in the old barracks,
and there were fences with barbed wire on top to keep us in.

Toccoa was a little more exciting at first because we were
constantly finding old grenades buried on the old practice
ranges. We did everything we could to make 'em explode.
Never succeeded. We found a lot of ammunition, too, rounds
that hadn't been fired.

As soon as we found the bullets, we started making zip guns.
You made them with lead pipes. You had to find a pipe that the
bullet would fit in but that the casing wouldn't. As soon as you
found that, you had a gun. You'd make a hammer out of a spoon
or something and then make a wooden handle with a socket for
it. You put the spoon handle down in there and attach it to a
nail for it to revolve on. You wind rubber around it, put the
rubber around the nail and pull it tight. You pull the hammer
back and turn it loose, and it fires.

I made two, a singlebarrel and a doublebarrel. I fired 'em a
thousand times. Never shot anybody, though, not like some of
the cats did. I was just having fun—and making sure they
worked just in case I did need 'em. The guards never did catch
me; I guess they thought somebody had firecrackers or something.

At Toccoa I wound up being a trusty. I even helped bring
back escapees. When boys ran away, me and Johnny Terry and
one or two other boys would go out with the guards to look for
them. There were only a few routes an escapee could take—a
couple of roads and the railroad tracks—or he could hide in the
woods. Lots of nights I stayed out in the woods all night waiting
for the boy to come by. When he did I talked to him and got
him to come back with me. By that time he'd usually had
enough of wandering around in the woods, and he was ready to
go back anyway. See, something would get in a person's mind
when he'd run away. Most of them didn't have anywhere to run
to, and even when they did, it didn't take any time for them to
be picked up in their hometowns, and then they'd be in worse
trouble.

At Toccoa I still played all the sports I could and kept on
playing music. A lot of times, we'd go into town and play the
high school in whatever sport was in season. We were all muscular and strong from the work we did, and we really beat 'em

playing football. One time we beat 'em so bad that their coaches played the next time. We almost beat 'em again, except they had help from the referees.

Once, after we'd played 'em in basketball, I sat down and played the piano in their gym. When I got through, one of the town boys said, "We got a boy here who's always been the best around on keyboards, but he better look out now."

"Where is he?" I said.

"He's gone to Atlanta with the glee club."

"What's his name?" I said.

"Name's Bobby Byrd."

"Well, you tell him what you heard tonight."

Sometimes the town kids came out to the prison and hung around the fence to gawk at us jailbirds. It was just a friendly curiosity, and we went over to the fence and talked to 'em if we could. One day one of the fellas told me there were some cats out by the fence talking about music. I went over to check it out. One of 'em was a tall, thin cat, said he had a gospel group. I said I did, too. We talked about gospel, rhythm and blues, and pop. He had a lot of good things to say, and I liked him right off. When he told me he played keyboards, I said, "Say, what's your name?"

"Byrd," he said.

"I've heard about you," I said.

"You the one they call Music Box?" he asked.

"Yeah."

"Then I've heard about you, too."

It was a long time before I saw him again. We were playing the Toccoa city team in baseball at the Toccoa Recreation Center. First time up I singled. On the next pitch I took off to steal second. When I slid in, I knocked the second baseman flat. It was Byrd.

"Hey, it's you," he said. He was laughing. "They gonna keep you locked up forever?"

"It looks like it," I said. I was laughing, too. Then for some reason I got serious, maybe because I knew I was talking to another musician. "Byrd, I'm going to get out," I said, "some kind of way."

I had just turned nineteen and had been thinking that all the years I should have been in high school I had spent in prison instead, and I had a lot more years to go. It just didn't make any sense to me to be in there any longer, so one night, late, I wrote a letter to the parole board. I told them that I was like any other person, all I wanted was a chance. I explained that I was poor and didn't have anybody to help me get out and that I got in there in the first place trying to get clothes for school. I wrote: *I know I don't have any education but I can sing, and I want to get out and sing for the Lord.*

I didn't know if the letter would do any good, but I sent it off anyway. Then one day a man from the parole board came out to talk to me. "You want to get out?" he said.

"Yessir," I said.

"What do you think you're going to do on the outside?"

"Sing gospel," I said.

I tried to explain to him about the music. He was real polite, listening to everything I had to say, but I could see he didn't think singing would be enough to get me by. By the time he left, I was more discouraged than ever.

The next day one of the guards told me Mr. Matthews wanted to see me in a big way. When I went in I could see he looked happy but he looked worried too. He told me he'd seen my letter and was impressed with it, and so was the parole board. "Music Box," he said, "you can walk out of here tomorrow if you can get a job."

I couldn't believe it. In my mind I was already telling the fellas, already saying good-bye to 'em.

"I can get a job," I said. "All I did in Augusta was work. A lot of people there would hire me."

He looked downhearted. He didn't want to tell me what was coming next.

"Music Box," he said, "you can't go back to Augusta."

"Sir?"

"I've been on the phone with Solicitor Haines. He'll agree to your parole only on condition that you not be allowed to enter Richmond County."

"But that's where my father is," I said. "And my Aunt Minnie."

"I'm sorry, Music Box," he said. "It's not up to me."

"Yessir."

"You've got to get a job in Toccoa."

"Yessir."

When I left his office I was happy and sad at the same time.

At least there was a chance I'd get out, but I couldn't go back home, even to visit, and I sure didn't know where I was going to get a job in Toccoa, or how.

The next Saturday I was out in a field somewhere loading rocks on a truck, and a man who owned a Toccoa automobile dealership saw me working. I don't even know why he was out there that day. He watched me working hard for a while, then came over and said, "Boy, what would it take to get you out of prison?"

"All I need is a job, sir," I said.

"Well, I'll give you a job," he said.

Mr. Matthews let me out that day—June 14, 1952. It was exactly three years and one day since I'd been convicted. I walked to town.

9 SINGING FOR THE LORD

I GOT OUT at noon on that Saturday, and by three o'clock was pitching a crucial game for the Toccoa city team. They let me out to pitch that game. That's when I learned there's no such thing as law—coming *or* going. They gave me too much time in the first place, then they tore up the courts when they wanted me out.

At Lawson Motors, the Oldsmobile dealership where I had my job, I washed and greased cars and cleaned up around the car lot, like my daddy had done at filling stations in Augusta. I was sad about not being able to go back home and be around him. Years later, when I was living in one of the best neighborhoods in Augusta, I met Solicitor Haines's son and told him, "Your father sent me away and didn't want me to come back, but I want you to know I don't hold it against him." I *think* the boy was embarrassed.

As part of my parole I had to have a stable place to live with someone who would act as my sponsor. Finding a place wasn't easy. I saw Bobby Byrd around town—the population was only six or seven thousand—and he invited me to come home with him. I was able to stay with his family only temporarily, though, because there were already seven people in the household, but it gave me a chance to keep looking. Pretty soon I found a room at Miss Lena Wilson's, but it was available for only a couple of months. Almost as soon as I moved in I had to start looking all over again. After I had asked around a lot, some peole who had seen me pitch were talking about me in a barbershop run by a couple named Dora and Nathaniel Davis. Mrs. Davis overheard them.

"All he needs is a place to live?" she said.

"That's all," they told her.

"Well, he can stay with us," she said.

She had never met me or even seen me, and she was willing to do that. Before long I was calling her Mama and trying to give her some of the money I brought home from Lawson's. I laid the bills out side by side on the supper table. When I was finished, she pushed all the money back to me and told me to buy clothes with it.

I attended Trinity CME Church with the Davises and joined the choir there. I also started getting together with Bobby's sister, Sarah, to sing gospel. She sang in the Mount Zion Baptist Church choir. We liked each other right off, our voices blended well, and before long we were making guest appearances at churches in the area. Sarah also belonged to the Community Choir, a gospel group run by a man named Detroit Steeple and made up of the best singers from the black churches and the community at large. The choir sang all around town at churches and schools and sometimes appeared on a local radio station, WLET. Sarah talked me into auditioning for the choir. Mr. Steeple liked my singing well enough to take me on and to feature me sometimes when we were on the radio. Sometimes quartets and other small ensembles were spun off the choir to go out to various churches or to be spotlighted during a performance by the entire group. Sarah and I, along with two sisters, Yvonne and Johnnie May Wheeler, developed our own group that way, and Mama helped us and encouraged us all she could. We called ourselves the Ever Ready Gospel Singers.

In a lot of ways it was a good time in my life. I was out of prison, I had a job and a good home, and, like I'd promised, I was singing for the Lord. And I was falling for Sarah.

Meanwhile, Bobby still had his little musical group going. Besides him, it consisted of Sylvester Keels, Doyle Oglesby, Fred Pulliam, Baby Roy Scott, and Nash Knox—all friends from Whitman Street High School in Toccoa. They didn't have any instruments, just voices, and originally they started out as a gospel group. About the time I got to town they had switched to rhythm and blues, doing mellow stuff like the Moonglows and the Dells, and they had started calling themselves the Avons. They couldn't really get it going, though, because Troy Collins, a promising singer they were bringing along, had been killed in an automobile accident when the Whitman glee club made a trip to Atlanta.

I'd see Bobby when I went by his house to be with Sarah, and he started trying to talk me into joining the group. I was happy with the gospel thing I had going, and baseball, church, and my job at Lawson Motors took up the rest of my time, so I told him no. Working at Lawson's was rough, though. There was a man working there who treated me like dirt. He was nasty to many people of my color and he was always cursing me out, calling me all kinds of names and ordering me to redo work even though I'd done a perfectly good job. In Atlanta, long after I had become well known, he apologized to me publicly for the way he had treated me. I said, "You don't have to do all that, I'm not mad at you. Because you're ignorant. You should be mad at yourself."

Back in those Toccoa days, though, he wasn't doing any apologizing. One day he told me to wash a car all over again that I'd just finished washing and waxing. It was a 1950 Ford, one of the first really modern-looking cars, and I promised myself that I would take it for a drive before I did all that work over. Might as well get it dusty and make the job worthwhile. Nobody saw me take it out of the lot. Once I was clean away I really opened it up. A fine automobile, driving *good*. I drove it all the way to the prison so all the fellas could see me driving this new car. I drove real slow by the fence and honked at 'em and waved. They couldn't believe it. After I was done showing off, I had to drive fast to get back because I'd been gone a long time, but then I took this particularly sharp curve and couldn't handle it—I didn't get much driving practice in prison and wound up in a ditch. I had managed to keep from turning over, and when I got myself together and realized that me *and* the car were both in one piece, man, was I relieved. But when I backed out of the ditch and headed back toward the lot, one of the wheels started wobbling real bad. Somehow I had warped it.

Meanwhile, the fella who owned the car had come back to the lot to pick it up and discovered it was gone. Here I come driving the car real slow, sort of limping in, and I see the owner and a crowd of white fellas waiting for me. As soon as I jumped out of the car, the owner—a great big fella—came at me with a tire iron. All those other white men were going to stand around and let him do it. This grown man wouldn't jump on me with his bare hands; he was going to beat me with a piece of iron.

That told me right away that the man was a coward. He cornered me against the car and raised his arm to hit me, but I was too quick for him. I grabbed the tire iron with my left hand and held him off with my right without really hitting him. I knew that with the other white men watching I was a dead man if I actually hit the fella. Instead, I just kept a grip on that tire iron —I was still small, but boxing and football had given me a lot of upper-body strength—and I just refused to let him beat me. We wrestled that way for a long time until he started feeling silly, I guess. He let go of the tire iron and stomped away.

Naturally, I lost my job. I didn't mind leaving Lawson, but it put me in a jam with my parole officer. As soon as he found out, he threatened to have me sent back to prison. When I told Sarah how worried I was about it, she got her mother to stand up for me. The Byrd family was well known and well respected in town, and their support really helped. Mr. Matthews spoke up for me, too, and when I got a job working at a plastics factory, the parole officer decided to let it drop.

I was willing to do any kind of job, to get a foothold in *anything*. I even thought boxing might be a way to go. Some fellas in Toccoa had formed a boxing club and arranged matches. I told them I wanted to fight, so they set up some bouts. I wound up having three fights—two wins and a draw. The biggest mistake I made was fighting another left-hander, which I had never done before. We kept knocking each other down. That was the draw. I figured that was enough boxing.

After that, I sang even harder for the Lord. The Ever Ready Gospel Singers were doing well, singing in all the churches, and I thought it was time we made a record. I kept my eyes open when the Community Choir was in WLET's studio, and I thought we could make a tape there without too much trouble. We got permission from the owner of the station and taped "His Eye Is on the Sparrow," the song Ethel Waters made famous. We took the tape and had it pressed into an acetate, the kind that is cut from the inside of the record to the outside to keep you from competing with record companies.

Now that we had a record like this, we had to get somebody to play it. I vaguely knew that air play might attract the attention of a record company or at least help our little group get real gigs; beyond that, I didn't really have any sort of strategy figured out. But I did know which radio station I wanted to air it—WLAC in Nashville.

WLAC was all we ever listened to. In the daytime they played country music, which we *didn't* listen to, but late at night Gene Nobles, John "R" Richbourg, and Hoss Allen played blues, rhythm and blues, and black gospel. You could hear the station all over the eastern half of the United States. Gene Nobles hosted "Randy's Record Mart," and John R hosted "Ernie's Record Mart," both offering mail-order packages of records. The funny thing was that a lot of people, including black people, thought those disc jockeys were black, talking all this smooth jive, and then you'd go in the station and find out they were white.

Somehow word had gotten around that the WLAC disc jockeys were willing to listen to new things, including dubs and acetates, and if they liked something, they would play it. They helped a lot of artists get started that way. So I got someone to drive me to Nashville with the record. We found the WLAC studio, but instead of going in we waited at the back door until the jocks came out. We first asked Gene Nobles to play it, but he turned us down. We waited until 3 A.M. when John R came out. He listened to it but said he couldn't play it either. At least he took more interest in me than anybody else did, which is why he will always be number 1 in my book when it comes to disc jockeys. Later on, he helped me a whole lot.

I went back to Toccoa not really discouraged but sort of at a dead end. The Community Choir became less active, and the Ever Ready Gospel Singers had about saturated the local market. Like always, I listened to all the new sounds and wanted to try all kinds of music. With the gospel record and the trip to Nashville, I had made my first move toward trying to be a professional musician. The idea wasn't full blown yet, but the next time Bobby Byrd asked me to join his group I said yes.

10 THE FLAMES

WE HAD our first rehearsal one Sunday afternoon in the living room of the Byrds' house at 114 Saultee Street. This must have been late 1952 or early 1953. Besides me there was Bobby, Sylvester Keels, Doyle Oglesby, Fred Pulliam, Nash Knox, and Baby Roy Scott. We didn't have any instruments except our voices and the Byrds' upright piano, an old roller model.

We were pitiful. Our voices didn't seem to fit together. Their voices were sweet and mellow, and mine was raw and powerful. We weren't even sure what kind of music we wanted to do, gospel or rhythm and blues. I hadn't given up on gospel entirely, so I taught them some songs I knew, such as "When I Get to Heaven I'll Be Looking for My Mother." They sang their close harmony tunes for me, and then I played and sang some of the more upbeat rhythm and blues things I had been hearing. I guess a lot of groups start that way, looking for their identity.

We practiced and practiced—on Sundays, after school, whenever we could. After several weeks I brought Johnny Terry into the group. He'd been released in Toccoa, too, and we had stayed friends on the outside. After a fling at gospel, the group worked up a repertoire of about ten rhythm and blues songs, mostly things by the Dominoes, the Five Royales, the Orioles, a lot of stuff by the Five Keys, the Clovers, all those groups.

Billy Ward and the Dominoes, featuring Clyde McPhatter, had some really strong stuff, such as "Sixty Minute Man" and "Have Mercy, Baby." The Orioles, with Sonny Til singing very sweet, had hit with "Crying in the Chapel." The Five Keys, who sounded a lot like the Orioles, had "Glory of Love." The Clovers did "One Mint Julep," a favorite of ours, and "Ting-a-Ling," "Fool, Fool, Fool," and "Don't You Know I Love You." The Five Royales, who had started as a gospel group, had some powerful R & B hits in 1953 with "Baby, Don't Do It" and "Help Me Somebody."

We could sing like all of 'em. Even without instruments, we always tried to copy the sound of the records exactly, down to the last *ooh-aah*. Bobby sang bass, so he covered all the bass parts, including the instrumental ones. He could whistle real good, too, so sometimes he'd whistle the saxophone solo or whatever. We kept time by stomping our feet.

I stayed on top of all the latest dances—the slop, the funky chicken (even before it was called the funky chicken), the alligator, the camel walk. I guess the camel walk is a dance people associate with me. I first saw people dance it around 1940 and I heard Louis Jordan sing about it a little later, but I put the pizzazz into it. Really, I developed my own camel walk so that it would eventually become the James Brown. It shouldn't be confused with the moon walk that Michael Jackson does, which is really the bicycle, a move Charlie Chaplin used to do. You know how you get on a bicycle and ride it backwards? That's the moonwalk—the Charlie Chaplin bicycle done backwards.

Bobby's grandmother didn't like us rehearsing at the house. Her name was Adeline Hickman, but everybody called her Big Mama. She was very devout and she thought the kind of music we were doing was sinful. Bobby's mother was always having confrontations with her about it so that we could practice.

Big Mama didn't like me getting serious about Sarah, either. We had talked about getting married, without making anything definite. When Big Mama found out, she stepped in. "My granddaughter isn't marrying any jailbird," she said. We all laughed about it, even Sarah's mother, but it didn't do any good. Big Mama would give in on us rehearsing at the house, but she wouldn't give in on the marriage. That was the end of that. I didn't hold it against her, and later on we became good friends.

The group's first gig was at a place called Bill's Rendezvous Club in Toccoa. They had a jukebox, piano, dance floor, and booths where they served food. Bill and Delois Keith, who owned the place, lived on the same street as the Davises. I hung around the club in the daytime, and they let me practice on the piano. We started playing the Rendezvous once or twice a week and managed to come out with maybe $6 or $7 apiece each time. The Rendezvous helped us make a name for ourselves, although we didn't really *have* a name. We dropped the name Avons because we found out another group already had it. As we started playing other juke joints in the area, we became known as the Toccoa Band, and under that name, we played in Livonia, Hartwell, Cornelia, Cleveland, Kingsville, and Athens, and in Seneca and Greenville in South Carolina.

We traveled in a 1941 Ford station wagon we rented from Guy Wilson, a man in my church. The car was so dilapidated that Guy was afraid to drive it around town, but we took it everywhere. Sometimes Delois Keith went with us and acted as our bank, buying us food during intermission because the places didn't pay us until the gig was over. Then we would pay her back. By the time we paid her back, paid Guy Wilson, and bought gas, it turned out a lot of times that we just went for the trip.

These places had jukeboxes—called piccolos then—and people listened to records and danced. When we came in they cut it off and we performed, stomping our feet and singing nonstop because we didn't have any instruments outside of the piano in the place. Almost everybody in the group played a little piano, so we rotated depending on who was singing. We learned to make a whole lot of noise with very few resources, and I think that's eventually what made us so powerful and gave me the stamina to sing and dance like I do.

We didn't know anything about show business, but we came up with a few tricks to get us over. Once, in Athens, we were playing a little place where there weren't but two or three people who had drifted in. We noticed that people would come up to the windows, see the place was empty, and go on down the street. We took five and talked it over. We decided that we were going to sing louder, stomp louder and, on top of that, pull the curtains. We closed the place up tight and went back to work. Made it sound like there were a hundred people in there. Before long the place filled up. After that we always pulled the curtains first thing wherever we played. If there weren't any curtains, we covered the windows with newspapers.

We also helped attract crowds by bringing a crowd with us. A lot of our friends went along with us for the ride and the music. No matter how jammed the station wagon got, we always managed to squeeze in one more person if he was willing to make noise at the gig.

Sometimes we carried a little moonshine liquor with us, too, but not to drink. We delivered it. There were a lot of dry counties around there, and if we were heading toward one, we would drop off a load now and then. It kept a few extra dollars in our pockets and didn't hurt our popularity either.

We added Nafloyd Scott, Roy's brother, to the group because he could play guitar. But he didn't own one. So we all kicked in for an amplifier and an electric guitar, the kind with the pickup on the outside. We ordered them from Sears, and they took about four weeks to get there. This was the little bittiest amp you could imagine; it had two jacks, one for the guitar and one for a microphone. We'd be in some hot, close place, playing and singing, people up dancing, and the heat and humidity would build up in the amp. Then it gave out real loud feedback, cutting right through our voices, and we would really have to start belting. People didn't think you could sing that loud and still be soulful, but we managed it. We had to, to drown out the amp.

After our one-nighters began to increase, we got us a manager, an older man named Barry Trimier who was the town's black undertaker. The first thing he told us was that we needed something to beat on instead of stomping our feet to keep time. I used a machine out at the plastics factory to cut a big piece of metal into a cymbal. It was so big and heavy that we had to have something really sturdy to set it on when we played. It clanged when you hit it, but it didn't sound like any cymbal anybody had ever heard before. Some of the fellas who had attended Whitman Street High found, way back in a storage room at the school, a tom-tom and a big old field drum, the kind marching bands have, and we started using them. We fixed up the field drum with a pedal, just like on a regular drum kit. When someone sat behind it to play, you could hardly see him.

Barry kept a book with the names of all the places we played and the dates and how much we got paid. I don't think he made any money himself; he just enjoyed doing it for us. We really thought we were a band then. The places we played always had a piano, and we had our own guitar and amp, the great big raggedy drum, and whatever other instruments we could borrow. We even had a manager, but we still didn't have a real name.

In Toccoa we started playing some little gigs at Stephens

County High, a white high school. They had a piano and we'd use that and sing and play at intermission of their intramural basketball games in the daytime. Once, I came sliding across the basketball floor with a big dust mop and danced with it. The kids went wild. From those daytime things we moved up to doing some of the high school dances in the evening.

The daytime gigs were a problem because most of us worked, and it was hard to get off. But we had all made an agreement: When it's gig time, you go. Bobby would drive to the plastics factory where I was working, and I'd sneak away. A lot of times they never missed me. I couldn't afford to lose my job. I was still on parole, and I had been having problems with it already. The incident at Lawson's had almost put me back in prison, and then I got involved in another accident. I had a girlfriend in Cornelia a few miles from Toccoa, and one day I got stranded up there. After asking around, I caught a ride home with a fella whose name was Horace Brown. He was driving a DeSoto, flying around those curves. I said, "Horace, don't drive so fast." But he was heading for death. As were coming around a curve on one of the mountain roads near Toccoa, Horace lost control of the car and we went down an embankment. I was thrown out and shaken up real bad. Horace was killed. Dazed and disoriented, I wandered up to the highway, a two-lane blacktop with very little traffic, and ran in the direction of Toccoa. By the time I got to Toccoa, the authorities had found the wreck. When they discovered I had been with Horace, I was charged with leaving the scene of an accident.

I thought I was gone for sure. On top of the time they might give me for leaving the accident, they could make me serve the twelve years left on my original sentence. It looked like I was going to be forty before I got out this time, but after Barry Trimier and Mrs. Byrd explained what had happened, the charges were dropped and I was released.

One way or another, my troubles always seemed to involve a car. A short time later, me and another cat drove a load of stolen tires from Toccoa to Cornelia, where we sold them. A man in Toccoa had offered us part of the money if we did the driving for him. It didn't seem much different from the small loads of moonshine the band ran from time to time, but I should have known better, and I sure shouldn't have gambled with my

freedom that way. We got away with it, except that on the way
back we wrecked the car. When the police came, they thought
it was kind of funny that we were in this other man's car. They
had heard rumors about some stolen tires, too. They couldn't
prove anything, but they were suspicious enough to take me to
jail. I was sure this was it, especially when I saw Mr. Matthews
walking toward my cell.

"Hello, James," he said.

When he called me James instead of Music Box I knew he
was really mad at me. "Did you come to take me back, Mr.
Matthews?" I asked.

"They want me to," he said.

"*I* sure don't want you to," I said.

"Then you have to slow down, James. You either have to
play and sing—I know you can do that—or you have to work at
a job and stick with it. I don't care which, but you're going to
have to do one of them."

"I'm trying to do both," I said, "so I can get married."

"All right, James," he said, "I'll see what I can do, but I'm
not making any promises."

He left without even asking about the girl I wanted to
marry. I think he wanted to get away before he got any madder
at me, but when they let me out a little while later, I knew it
was because of him.

I planned to marry a very sweet girl I had met named Velma
Warren. She belonged to Mount Zion Baptist Church, and we
had been introduced when my gospel group sang there. I
started taking her with me to some of the band's gigs, which
made us even more popular because the cats in the audience
could see that I wasn't interested in their women. That may
sound peculiar, but a cat in a juke joint on a Saturday night can
get very mean if he thinks somebody is messing with his girl.
And if the guy doing the messing is up on the stage, it makes
the cat doubly jealous.

Velma and I were married in Trinity Church on June 19,
1953, a little over a year after I had gotten out of prison. The
next day I pitched a no-hitter for the Toccoa baseball team. I
think you're supposed to be drained after your wedding night,
but I was inspired. I think the *idea* of marriage appealed to me
as much as anything else. I wanted a real home and a steady

family, which I had never really had before. That was what I saw myself working for, whether as a singer or as a laborer—to be able to establish a home.

Just about the time I got married the band started having some problems, most of them brought on by jealousy. By this time I was the leader. All the songs were built around me, and on stage I stood apart from the other singers and danced differently from them. I didn't want to do all that, but Sylvester and Bobby pushed me out front. Some of the other fellas started resenting it. At first they just grumbled about it occasionally, then they called a meeting. We all sat down one night around the kitchen table at Bobby's house. The ones who had called the meeting said they didn't think it was right for me to sing most of the leads and do the solo dances, and they thought Bobby was monopolizing the spotlight, too. Consequently, they wanted to break up the group.

Sylvester, Bobby, and I couldn't believe it. Sylvester said it didn't make sense not to showcase our best singers and dancers. Bobby told them it was stupid to break up when our local popularity was about to start paying off. We were already making as much as $6 or $7 apiece per night, and we could be working five or six nights a week if we wanted. The others said they would think about what Sylvester and Bobby had said. As they got up to leave, I blew up. "How are we going to break up? We haven't *done* anything yet. We don't even know what we *can* do, and here y'all are already talking about quitting. We don't need to be talking about quitting, we need to be talking about working harder." They stopped and looked at one another kind of sheepish. One by one they sat back down.

Instead of any more talk about breaking up, we talked about how we could improve ourselves, about different ways to sing harmony, new songs we ought to learn, different arrangements we might try. Eventually we got around to the question of our name. I said we ought to come up with one right then to show that we were together again. So we sat around for a long time trying to come up with one, going over the names of other groups, throwing out ideas, and not getting anywhere. Then one of the fellas said, "How about something along the lines of the Torches?"

The Torches were a local group that sang the sweet, close harmony stuff, but what was unusual about them was that one of their singers was white. Later on, they wound up with three white and four black members, which was *very* unusual for that time and place. We all agreed that we liked their name. We played around with it for a few minutes until somebody came up with a good variation. I don't remember which one of us said it first, but I remember that we all agreed right away. It captured what we had been trying for in our music since our first rehearsal. We became the *Flames*, full of fire and romance.

11 BURNING IT UP

I HAD always absorbed ideas from whatever I was around—minstrel shows, circuses, preachers, gospel music, records—but now I started to pay attention to the way professional musicians performed on stage. A lot of big R & B shows came to Greenville, South Carolina, and I went to as many as I could to study them: Bill Doggett, Faye Adams, the Clovers, the Moonglows, Joe Turner, anybody who came through. They all had something to offer. Bill Doggett played a strong, bluesy organ. Faye Adams, who had a big hit then with "Shake a Hand," sounded like straight gospel. With "One Mint Julep," the Flames already had the Clovers' thing down. I also liked the way the Moonglows, who had "Sincerely," sang harmony. But as a showman, Big Joe Turner impressed me because he didn't waste any time on stage. "Shake, Rattle and Roll" and all of the other songs came one after the other. He really took care of business on stage, and so did the band who backed him, Paul Williams and the Hucklebucks. But I still think that the best showman of them all was Louis Jordan, even though I saw him only in movie shorts.

The best *group* we ever saw in Greenville was Hank Ballard and the Midnighters. They had "Work with Me Annie," "Annie Had a Baby," and "Sexy Ways," all hits even though most radio stations wouldn't play 'em because they thought the songs were vulgar. Really, the Annie records were just good fun, and so was the Midnighters' stage act. For instance, while the piano player was playing, his pants would drop and he'd have on longhandles, like a clown.

The Midnighters were the first professionals we'd ever seen. We traveled sixty miles to the Greenville Textile Hall and stood down front for their show. When they really got the crowd worked up, Bobby and I clasped hands real strong and I said, "Okay, one day we'll be up there, and somebody else will be down here looking up at us."

It was just one of those things that beginners say when they see someone they want to be like, but we still couldn't get it out of our minds. When we got back to Toccoa, at about two in the morning, Bobby and I went to his house and stayed up the rest of the night playing the piano and talking about our ambitions. We went through the usual stuff about getting rich and doing a lot for our parents, and for the first time we became close; we pledged that we were going to succeed as entertainers, no matter what. After that night, we were like brothers.

We had a chance to show our determination when the two of us did a tea party at a little restaurant downtown in the middle of the block. Tea parties were actually coffee breaks in the afternoon, when little cafes and places like that had some entertainment. The parties lasted only about thirty minutes, but they were a good way for a group to get exposure. This particular tea party was an audition that Bobby and I did by ourselves. We auditioned that way a lot; the two of us would give a short performance, then whoever we were doing it for decided whether to have the whole group in later on.

I had trouble sneaking away from my job the day of the gig and we were almost late, but we made it. We went in the back door of the restaurant—we weren't allowed to go in the front—and auditioned, with Bobby at the piano while I sang "Good Lovin'" without a mike. I danced and sang lead, and he did all the background vocals, jumping from voice to voice. During the bridge, when I started doing splits, slides, and the camel walk and Bobby jumped up and kicked away the piano stool, the crowd stood up, clapping and hollering and making all kinds of noise. Cars stopped on the main street outside, and people started jamming in. I danced over to Bobby and yelled to him during a spin: "We got 'em!" He beat on the piano harder and he was already pounding it pretty good.

The man paid us $5 apiece, even though it was an audition, and gave us the date for the whole group on the following Wednesday. Come Wednesday, we went in there with our mike, our guitar, and our big raggedy drum and cymbal, and we saw that the place was packed with college kids who were home for the summer. Their parents, who'd been at our audition, had told them about us. There were so many people trying to get in that the manager finally opened the doors to the sidewalk and the police blocked off the main street. A lot of 'em had never seen a raw R & B performance with singing and dancing like ours before. We did our whole show, and we killed 'em. I mean we just laid 'em out. Afterward, the man who owned the clothing store next door to the restaurant approached us.

"That was a good show," he said. "I caught your act over at the high school, too, but what really impresses me is that you at least try to look clean up there." On stage we always wore starched blue jeans and white, short-sleeved shirts. "I have some things I don't stock at the store anymore, and I want to donate them to you." He took us next door and gave us each two pairs of pants and two shirts. The pants were very shiny, like mohair. He fixed us up with some loafers, too, but we had to pay for them as we went along. I think he saw something in us that made him want to help us.

The biggest benefit from the tea party came after the kids went back to school in the fall and we started getting booked by the fraternities at all the different colleges. They'd call Barry Trimier, and we'd sneak away from our jobs and go. We played at the University of Georgia, Clemson, the University of Tennessee, Austin Peay, all those places. These were some of the biggest crowds we'd ever played for, and they treated us very well.

We were still traveling in Guy Wilson's station wagon, but now we had our instruments plus all the people—it seemed like about twenty—that we took along. We laid the guitar across our laps; someone held the tom-tom; somebody else hugged the amp, and we tied the field drum to the roof. As soon as the gig was over we piled back into the car and raced to Toccoa because we still had day jobs to get to. Sometimes I was so tired I would almost nod off standing up at work. I managed to hang on that way until we made our second round through the fraternities. They had liked us so much that almost all of them booked us again as soon as they could. Word spread to other campuses, and we began to get gigs at places that were so far away we had to sneak away from work in the middle of the day. Sometimes we were so tired after driving all night that we'd lay low the next day and miss work entirely. Before long, I got fired, but before my parole officer could get upset, I found another job, this time as a janitor at Toccoa High School.

In the middle of all this, my first son, Teddy, was born. That meant the world to me because with him I was starting the family that I had never had myself. It was hard, though, because I didn't really have any models from my own raising. I was trying to be a husband and a father, hold down a janitor job, and make it as a singer, all at the same time. That can be a lot of strain. Sometimes you struggle so hard to feed your family one way, you forget to feed them the other way, with spiritual nourishment. Everybody needs that.

The Flames and I were still staying on top of the latest records, doing material by all the other groups, when a friend of ours named Williams said something that set me thinking. "It's fine when you sing them other people's songs," he said, "but when the audience hollers, they're hollering for that song. You got to get some songs of your own." I had written a few tunes, such as "Goin' Back to Rome," and I was always hearing fresh tunes in my head, but I hadn't really thought of myself as a songwriter. It was just something that I did in odd moments. But after I thought about what Williams had said, I started to concentrate more on the music running through my head.

At that time we were doing an Orioles song called "Baby, Please Don't Go." The background vocals for it included the word "please" repeated several times. With that as a starting point, I wrote "Please Please Please," writing down the words and picking out the chords on the piano, but not writing down the chords. The next day I taught the song to the group and worked out an arrangement by humming the solos. The first time we sang it in public the crowd went wild. They asked for it over and over again. After that we always had to sing it at least three or four times a night.

We were working really regular now, at juke joints, colleges, and schools. We'd moved into South Carolina and North Carolina, getting known in a wider and wider area. In Greenville we played a place called Latham's and we were becoming well known there. When the R & B acts came to Greenville, we went to the shows ready to get up on the stage and try to cut 'em, but they wouldn't let us on. People talk about jazz musicians having cutting contests, but singing groups used to do the same thing. At a lot of little joints we jumped on the stage during intermission and did a few numbers, letting the audience decide the act they liked best, us or the one that was booked there.

We cut the other acts every time because we were hungrier than they were.

We gained so much local popularity and respect that we were able to achieve a kind of racial milestone in Toccoa: playing at the Ritz, the town's movie theater. After he lost his job at Troop's photo shop, Bobby had gone to work at the Ritz as a janitor. He kept pestering the manager to let us play during intermission. Like everything then, the Ritz was segregated, whites downstairs, blacks in the balcony. The manager worried that a black group performing would upset the whites and set off an incident. Bobby reminded him that we had played the restaurant in the middle of the block, and it had gone off fine. The manager pointed out that there hadn't been blacks and whites together at the restaurant, but Bobby kept after him until he gave in.

We were a little nervous when we set up, but once we started performing we got over it. A lot of the whites had seen us before at the restaurant and at Stephens County High, and they already dug us. The black folks had heard us all over, and most of them were our friends. The people who hadn't seen us before listened out of curiosity at first, and then they dug us, too. There wasn't anything resembling a racial incident. A few years later I remembered that when promoters tried to make me play segregated shows.

We became regulars at the Ritz. We played, the audience threw nickels and dimes on the stage, and we picked them up. But the jealousy in the group started all over again because Bobby and I were still doing most of the singing. Several times some of the fellas didn't show up for the Ritz gigs, and it looked like we were falling apart again. This time even their parents could see it was foolish, and *they* called a meeting. We all sat down at Bobby's again, but this time the parents did the talking. Nash's mother said, "If y'all are going to do anything, all this arguing has got to stop. Either stop or, starting tonight, Nash isn't going out anywhere anymore." Mrs. Keels said, "And Sylvester is going to start doing his work at home." They really laid it on the line to their own kids, and I was kind of grateful because it took care of the problem right there.

As soon as we got our personal problems worked out, we started having trouble with our churches. We were all churchgoers, me especially because it was a condition of my parole.

Our churches were opposed to the kind of music we played. They thought it was sinful, the devil's music, so each of us was hauled before the conference at our various churches and threatened with being thrown out. Maybe some of the deacons didn't want us to see them in some of the juke joints we played. The parents stopped them from throwing us out, and no matter where we were on Saturday night, we didn't let anything stop us from getting to church on Sunday morning.

When that blew over, Barry got a new car for the funeral home, a big black Ford, and we started traveling to gigs in that. There were still eight of us and all our stuff, but at least we were in a new car now.

We made a trip to Atlanta and dug the scene on Auburn Avenue where all the clubs like the Royal Peacock, the Poinciana, and the Zanzibar were located. At the Royal Peacock we heard Billy Wright, who at that time was the most popular performer in Atlanta. He had a big, luxuriant pompadour and he still sings real good today, but he's never gotten his due. We also appeared on Piano Red's radio program on WAOK. Red, whose real name was William Perryman, was an albino with red hair. He played boogie piano and later had a few R & B hits on Groove records. We were on his show along with a group that later became the Penguins and had a smash hit with "Earth Angel."

From our first pitiful rehearsal we had progressed to that— being on the radio in the big city. We had worked out our problems in the group; we'd managed to keep ourselves from being thrown out of church; we were riding in a new car, even if it didn't belong to us; and we worked five or six nights a week all around our area. We had achieved the local popularity we'd been working for.

But local popularity can hold you back. You can get so popular in a place that you won't leave. That's the position we were in. We had conquered everything in sight, and there didn't seem to be any challenges left. Then Little Richard came to town.

12 FAMOUS

LITTLE RICHARD didn't have a hit record yet, but he was still the biggest thing in Georgia and in some surrounding states, too. When we went to catch his show at Bill's Rendezvous, we couldn't believe it. He carried a big band, the Upsetters, of maybe eleven pieces, he had a group of singers called the Dominions, and he had himself—hair piled higher than Billy Wright's, who he got the style from, and all that makeup. Even so, the Rendezvous was our turf, and we were determined to cut him if we could.

Richard gave his usual wild show, beating up the piano, jumping around the stage, flirting with the audience the way he would, his band pumping out the music. But watching him, I knew I had a big advantage over him because I could really dance. The crowd loved him, but at intermission they started patting for us, yelling at us, "Go on up and sing, go on up and sing!"

That was all we needed. We jumped up on the stage; Nafloyd plugged in his guitar; somebody else took over the Upsetters' drums; Baby Roy sat at the piano; and we tore into our act. When Richard heard us, he came running out from behind the counter where he'd been talking to Delois and started screeching, "What's happening? What's happening?" He saw us and then shook his head, like we were no good, but we put so many moves on him up there on stage that he started screaming, "Get 'em off! Get 'em off!" Man, he was peepin' and hidin' til he didn't know what to do. We almost ran him out of town, we were so bad.

After the show Richard said he didn't want to have nothing to do with James Brown. "You're the onliest man I've seen who has everything," he said. He walked away, still shaking his head, and left us standing there with Fats Gonder, who ran his band. Fats told us about Clint Brantly, Richard's manager over in Macon, and told us to get in touch with him. Clint owned a nightclub called the Two Spot, booked R & B shows into the Macon Auditorium, and handled several acts besides Richard. Fats thought that Clint could help us get wider exposure but, really, Richard was behind it, even though he walked away. I have to give him the credit, because it really helped us.

I was ready to go. We had done all we could from Toccoa; we had even cut several records, although most people don't realize it. We hardly realized it ourselves. All of them were for little local labels like NRC out of Greenville; we cut "So Long" and a few other things for them. We did things on tape at radio stations and gave the tapes to these small companies, and they transferred them to plastic. Piano Red introduced us to a small label in Atlanta where we did some records we were going to use to advertise ourselves. We didn't even know whether the companies were selling the records or not. We didn't care; we just wanted to be on stage in front of all those women.

Now that I was more ambitious, the logical place to move on to was Macon, which had a very active music scene. But it was a delicate situation. Barry had done a lot for us and hadn't gotten much in return, and he couldn't leave town because of his funeral business. But Barry was a really good man; he told us he didn't want to hold us back, and he even offered to drive us to Macon if we left. There was a parole problem, too. If Clint liked us and we wound up staying in Macon, I would be violating my parole. With the parole thing, they had me in slavery—and kept me that way for ten years—but after a lot of paperwork and promises, I was given the name of a parole officer in Macon and cleared to go.

The hardest part of all was separating from my family. By this time we had another son, Terry. Since Macon wasn't but about three hours away, I figured I could get back and forth pretty easy. Plus, in the long run I thought I could provide for my family a lot better as a singer than as a janitor. So I decided to try it.

Clint sent us gas money, and Barry drove us down in the black Ford. We went straight to the Two Spot to audition. There was no piano, only a guitar that Nafloyd borrowed from the house guitar player. We had heard that Clint really liked gospel, so instead of singing anything popular we decided to do a sacred number. A song we could really tear up was the one I taught the group at our first rehearsal, "Looking for My Mother." During the group's short gospel career we had developed a little routine where we walked around like we were doing what the words said: "When I get to heaven, I'm going to look for my mother." It brought tears to Clint's eyes. After that he would always say, "I had 'em sing that song, 'Looking for My Mother,' and they looked all up under the tables, all behind the stove, and all behind the refrigerator. Never *did* find her."

Clint took us on and we moved into Dean's Hotel, where I shared a room with Johnny Terry. Clint's operation now included Little Richard, a band led by a fella from Florida named Percy, and us. Richard and Percy had been with him longer and were already established in the area, so he paid more attention to them at first. We hung around the Two Spot and saw them come in, get their bookings, pick up their gas money, and go. We didn't have day jobs, so we were anxious to start making some money. One day Clint told us he had booked us at the Club 15, a big juke joint out by the river, and he wanted to advertise the gig on the radio, but first, he said, we needed something to make us special.

"Y'all are named the Flames, right?" he said.

We said yeah.

"We've got to do something about that," he said, looking disturbed. "Just the Flames?"

We said that was all.

He thought about it for a minute, then said, "Okay, we'll put 'Famous' in front of it since y'all aren't from around here. We won't say where you *are* from, we'll just say you're the *Famous* Flames."

When we got to the Club 15 we found out we were on the bill with another group. They had all this nice equipment, new horns, a real drum kit, real amplifiers, real everything. We still had our big field drum, our little bitty amp and guitar, and Bobby was still whistling some of the instrumental parts. The other group was smooth, and when we had to follow them we were worried. We did all our songs, I did every dance I knew, and the others did the dance routines I had worked out with them. The audience wouldn't let us off the stage, and we played the rest of the night, while the other group watched.

The next weekend we were right back there, and the weekend after, too. When we told Clint we were anxious to get out on the road, he said we needed to open up Macon first. But an incident at the Club 15 almost closed the town for me for good.

Nafloyd's girl, who had come to visit him, was helping to collect money at the door with Fats. He had left Little Richard and was moving over into helping Clint manage the acts. Some fella started messing with Nafloyd's girl, so Nafloyd jumped over the railing around the stage and snatched his girl away. We thought something funny was going on with the crowd anyway, so we stopped in the middle of a song and grabbed something to use to defend ourselves. I followed Nafloyd over the rail and punched the fella. Before a big fight could get going, though, the police, who were outside already because of the crowd, swarmed over us. They grabbed me right off. When things settled down they ran a check on me and found out I was on parole. I wasn't supposed to be in a club that sold liquor, but instead of taking me to jail and then shipping me back to Toccoa and prison, they waited until Clint got there. He was one of the most well-known black people in town—even the police respected him—so he was able to squash it.

During the time we were gigging only on weekends, we drove back to Toccoa and spent weekdays there. I was able to be with Velma and my two boys and kind of keep my family life going as best I could. I don't think Velma's father liked the situation much, though, and that caused some friction. I had always felt he wanted me to be a yes-man for him, and I wouldn't be a yes-man.

Back in Macon, our gigs were improving. Little Richard was working farther and farther away, and we were taking over some of his old spots. He still didn't have a real hit—just some blues records he'd made for Peacock—and he was still washing dishes at the Greyhound bus station when he wasn't performing. He was steadily getting bigger, but we were gaining on him. One night we replaced him for a gig at Emory University in Atlanta, and Emory was ours after that.

We were working outside the state, too, and that could have caused some problems with my Macon parole officer, Donald Walters. He was a good man. I saw him once a month for the first four months I was in Macon, and after that he left me alone. He could see I wasn't any kind of a criminal that needed watching. When it came time for me to go out of state, he gave his permission right away. He wasn't supposed to do it, but he did it anyway. For the rest of my time on parole I sent him a postcard once a month from wherever I was. He never even made me meet with him again.

Not too long after I got to Macon, some people started hitting on Richard about recording for them instead of Peacock. Eventually Bumps Blackwell got him for Art Rupe's Specialty label out of Los Angeles. After "Tutti Frutti" broke, Richard left Macon for California, left everybody without saying a word —Mr. Brantly, the Dominions, the Upsetters, and a lot of bookings. Mr. Brantly asked me to fulfill Richard's dates. He put me together with the Upsetters and the Dominions and sent me out as Little Richard. Meantime, Byrd and the fellas were doing the Famous Flames bookings. I was getting paid as Richard while Bobby was getting paid as me. I guess I did about fifteen of Richard's dates. I'd come out and do "Tutti Frutti" and all those things, and then I'd do some Midnighters' stuff, some Roy Brown, and even "Please Please Please." I guess the audience thought I was really Richard. Then, near the end of the show, I'd say, "I'm not Little Richard. My name is James." After a few shows like that, Fats, who also went on the tour, started announcing me as Little James. I didn't let that stay too long, either.

Back in Macon me and the Flames would cut every group that came through. Pretty soon the word got around, and then *nobody* would let us on stage—the Drifters, the Midnighters, nobody. They had records out and were afraid to let us get on stage when we showed up at their performances. That was when I realized we had to get a record out on a good label, and it had to be our own material. First, we needed a demo. There was no question that we would do "Please Please Please"; it was our own stuff and we'd been performing and perfecting it for almost two years. We had seen the hysterical reactions of audiences when we sang it, and I had complete confidence in the song. But before we could do it, I almost wound up going back to prison to serve the rest of my time.

I was driving from Macon to Toccoa, taking some clothes to my kids, when somewhere between Madison and Athens a fella on a tractor pulled across the road in front of me, and I hit the back of the tractor. It threw the man off and hurt him, but not

real bad, I don't think. I got help for him, and with the help
came the police. When they found out I was on parole, I was
taken to jail in whatever little town we were near. After I was
in the lockup for a few days, a fella from Clayton County came
to see me.

"Brown," he said, "I represent the Georgia Board of Par-
dons and Parole, and it's my duty to inform you that a board
arrest warrant was issued for you on October 28, 1955."

"What's going to happen?"

"Your parole will be revoked, and you will be returned to
the state penal system to serve out the remainder of your original sentence."

"But, sir," I said, "that's ten more years. I have a family."

"I'm sorry," he said.

Since I'd gotten out of GJTI I'd had a couple of close calls,
but I thought this was it. And I knew I wouldn't be going back
to a juvenile institution; I would probably be going to Reidsville. All I could think about was that I wouldn't be able to see
my family, just like the time I'd been in prison before. On the
third day Mr. Brantly showed up. He had arranged to have me
released in his custody until the thing was decided. For the
next couple of weeks he did everything he could to explain to
the parole people that it was an accident, that I was only taking
clothes to my kids. He told them he would be responsible.
Finally, on November 18, they withdrew the warrant.

After that, I didn't waste any time making my demo. We
arranged to use the studio of radio station WIBB, an AM dayti-
mer in Macon. Mr. Maxwell, the owner, didn't even charge us.
Big Saul, one of the disc jockeys, was at the control board. With
Nafloyd on guitar and Bobby on piano, we all gathered around
one microphone. I was so short I had to stand on a Co'-Cola
crate. We cut loose and just tore it up. When Saul played it back
for us, it sounded very good, but I wasn't satisfied. I insisted on
recording it several times until I felt it was right. I don't think
anybody really knew what I was doing, but I always knew. I
didn't know that I knew, but I always knew.

Clint took the tape around, and everybody refused it—Specialty, Chess, Duke, and other independent labels. While they
were all turning it down, Hamp Swain, a jock on WBML, began
playing the tape on the radio. It became the most requested
song around Macon, even though you couldn't buy a record of

it. Hamp didn't care whether there was a record or not; he played the song constantly, and our bookings got better and better. Hamp knew it was a good song; the people knew it was a good song; and I knew it was a good song, no matter what the record companies said. I was sure that if I could get it to the right person, it would succeed. I took a copy and drove to Southland Record Distributing Company, sixty miles away in Atlanta. Southland was a big jukebox operation and a distributor for independent record labels, which were the only labels that recorded our kind of music in those days. Back then, music was regional instead of national like it is today. The regional distributors acted as regional talent scouts for the indies.

As soon as I walked into Southland, I met a very nice lady named Gwen Kessler. I asked her if she would listen to my tape. She accepted it and promised me she would. I thanked her and left. She had come to Atlanta in 1948 to open a branch of King Records, based in Cincinnati, and then had gone to work for Southland. She listened to the tape and liked it well enough to play it for Ralph Bass, a King talent scout, the next time he was in Atlanta. "It's a monster," he told her. "Where can I find these guys?"

We didn't know any of this was going on. We continued to play all around the area that picked up WIBB and WBML, not really letting on to people that we didn't have a record out. One night in January 1956 we were playing a club called Sawyer's Lake, not too far from Milledgeville, Georgia. There was a terrible storm outside, with rain really coming down, but the place was packed anyway. Up North the same storm was dropping snow everywhere, grounding all the planes, including the one Leonard Chess, the owner of Chess Records of Chicago, was supposed to be on. At first he had rejected "Please Please," then changed his mind and tried to get down that night to sign us. We didn't know this was going on, either.

While we were on stage we saw over in the corner a white face amid a whole bunch of black ones. We thought it had to be another club owner looking us over. At intermission he introduced himself as Ralph Bass and said he liked the show. We thanked him and waited for him to offer us a club date.

"I've heard your demo of 'Please Please,' he said. "Do you have any other tunes of your own?"

"We've got a good one called 'Good Good Lovin',' " I said.

"And a nice baseball dance routine that goes with it," Bobby said.

When we sang "Good Good Lovin'," we danced into baseball positions—pitcher and catcher and I was the batter. I took a swing and then danced real fast, like I was rounding the bases. We mentioned it because we thought he would be interested in the stage act.

"Yessir, we've got a lot of songs of our own," I said.

"Good," he said, "because I want you to record for King Records."

13 PLEASE PLEASE PLEASE

WE WERE WORKING down in Tampa when Clint called to tell us that King wanted us in Cincinnati to record right away. We hadn't heard from anyone there since Ralph Bass signed us the morning after he'd seen us at Sawyer's Lake. Since then we'd been working clubs around Tampa and Jacksonville, and we were beginning to wonder if he'd really liked us.

The club work in Florida was all right, but the club owners had a meal ticket system that could wear you out. At the beginning of, say, a week-long engagement, they gave us a meal ticket to their place. With what we were making, that meal ticket could be our margin of profit on the gig, but there was a catch: If they served breakfast at six o'clock in the morning, you better be there at six o'clock in the morning if you want to eat, even if your show the night before had lasted until 2 a.m. I missed a lot of meals that way.

We drove the four hundred miles from Tampa to Macon, stopped and picked up some money there, and continued for another six hundred miles to Cincinnati in a station wagon that had *The Upsetters* painted on the side. Clint had let Little Richard use the car before, and now we were jammed into it with all our clothes and instruments. We rode all night, stopping only for gas. It was the first time out of the South for any of us, and when we got to the outskirts of Cincinnati somebody came out from King and led us to the hotel, a place called the Manse. It was a fleabag, but it was better than anything we'd stayed in before.

Instead of sleeping we went straight over to King Records, situated in an old icehouse at the end of a dead-end street. They did everything there, recording, mastering, pressing, shipping, even printing the album covers. At one end of the building, facing the street, there was a big opening where the ice used to come down; now the rollers that shot out the ice were shooting out the records, big boxes of albums and 78s rolling down the chute. An entrance on the other side led into the studio, consisting of some microphones and a plate-glass window separating this area from the control booth, and a little mixing room behind that.

We had never seen an operation like this before and walked around the place in a daze. From the studio you could go into the stockroom, where they pressed the records. We watched them lay small balls of soft vinyl on a sort of platter, and then the press would come down and mash them into records. They were just about to move entirely from the big, old 78s to 45s.

While we were being shown around, we were introduced to Earl Bostic. He was fixing to cut that day, and he invited us to watch. Back in the control room we met Syd Nathan, who had started the company back in 1945. Syd was Little Caesar—short, fat, and smoked a big cigar. He yelled all the time in a big, hoarse voice, and everybody was afraid of him. Even though Syd didn't know one note from another, King had been successful in all kinds of music. In the country field they had Moon Mullican, Cowboy Copas, Grandpa Jones, Hawkshaw Hawkins, and a lot more. In R & B instrumentals they had, besides Earl Bostic, Lucky Millinder, Tiny Bradshaw, Bill Doggett, and Big Jay McNeely. They had singers like Bullmoose Jackson, Wynonie Harris, Cleanhead Vinson, and Little Willie John, and groups like the Midnighters, the Five Royales, and Otis Williams and the Charms. Mr. Nathan also had several companies that published most of the songs King recorded.

We were supposed to record the next day, but when we showed up we found out Hank Ballard and the Midnighters had come in unexpectedly. Everybody at the studio was tied up in a big meeting with them, so our session was postponed until the following day. When we showed up, Little Willie John had come in to record, and our session was put off again. Little Willie John was just a shade over five feet tall, and he looked really sharp. Later on he came to mean a lot to me, but when I met him that day, I was thinking more about whether my own session would ever come to pass.

When it finally did, on February 4, 1956, I almost wished it hadn't. We were set up in the studio, with Mr. Nathan and Gene Redd, the musical director, sitting in the control booth.

Through the glass we could see Ralph Bass and the engineer, too. I didn't like the idea of a muscial director because I felt I knew my music better than anyone else. Besides, our stuff wasn't put together in the conventional way. We used a lot of seventh chords. Fats played keyboards and voiced chords with the sevenths instead of the triad. And we used sevenths for passing chords, too. Playing in the key of G, for example, we might want to go from a G chord to a C chord, and to make the change we might play a G7 as the harmonic transition.

They rolled the tape, and we ripped into "Please" in our style. When we were halfway through, Mr. Nathan suddenly jumped up from the board.

"What's that? What in hell are they doing? Stop the tape," he yelled. "That doesn't sound right to my ears." He was in a rage. "What's going on here?" He turned on Gene Redd, who just shrugged because he didn't understand it, either. Then he turned to Ralph Bass. "I sent you out to bring back some talent, and this is what I hear. The demo was awful, and this is worse. I don't know why I have you working here. Nobody wants to hear that noise."

"It's a good song, Syd," Ralph said. "Give them a chance."

"A good song?" He looked at Ralph like Ralph was crazy. "It's a stupid song. It's got only one word in it. I've heard enough." He stormed out of the room and up the stairs to his office.

We were frozen in the studio. We had made it through only half a track of our first professional recording session, and the owner of the company had walked out in the middle saying we were so bad he couldn't use us. We were thinking, "Oh, Lord, we're fixing to get sent away, and we just got here." Gene came from behind the glass to talk to us.

"Can't you do it some other way?" he asked.

"That's the way we've always done it," I said.

"But Mr. Nathan doesn't like it," he said.

"Mr. Nathan doesn't understand it," I said. He looked disturbed at that. "Everybody's music can't be alike, Mr. Redd. If everybody comes up here and goes to cutting alike, then nobody's going to do anything."

I showed him the chord changes on the piano and explained to him what we were doing. Once he understood, and it made sense to to him, he said he would go and tell Mr. Nathan that they should try it, even if it sounded funny. He was gone a long time. While we were waiting, hanging out in the hall, we could hear them yelling upstairs behind closed doors. When Gene came back, all he said was , "Okay, we're going to cut it." When Mr. Nathan never showed up again, we couldn't help feeling that the session wasn't legit, but we went ahead with it anyway. We cut "Please," "Why Do You Do Me Like You Do," "I Feel That Old Feeling Coming On," and "I Don't Know"—in spite of all the turmoil that day.

Usually, King pressed and shipped a record within days after it was recorded. Before we left Cincinnati we saw a handful of 78 RPM pressings of "Please," but as soon as we got back to Macon we got worried. We heard that Ralph Bass had been fired and King wasn't going to release the record. Mr. Nathan hated the master as much as he had hated the demo. Mr. Brantly was on the phone to him every day for nearly a month. At the end of February, Mr. Nathan told him that against his better judgment he was going to put the record out on his Federal label. So on March 3, 1956, "Please Please Please" was released. Eventually, it sold a million copies.

14 UP IN FLAMES

THE RELEASE of "Please Please Please" was the beginning of a strange period in my career and the beginning of the end for the original Famous Flames. The record didn't sell a million right away; it was a sleeper that built up in different parts of the country at different times. With no support from King, we made it a hit ourselves, traveling everywhere, doing hundreds of gigs. During the course of all that, including four more recording sessions for Federal over the next year and a half, I saw a lot and learned a lot about the business on stage and off, sometimes the hard way.

Trouble within the group dated all the way back to our Toccoa days when some of the others got upset because I was doing most of the singing and dancing and Bobby and I were doing two-man performances. The record caused more problems. We were dividing up the money equally, and I decided that we ought to split the writing credit on the records, too. "Please Please Please" was credited to Brown-Terry; the flipside, "Why Do You Do Me Like You Do," was supposed to be credited to Byrd-Knox-Keels, but King printed the labels with only Byrd-Knox on them. There was some grumbling about that and more jive about quitting, but everybody realized how stupid it would be to break *up* just when we might be about to break *through*.

Now that we had a record out we began to get a lot of advice from people—girlfriends, parents, everybody—and we began to learn some things about the business. People said, "You've got to help yourself. You've got to get out there and push the record." That piece of advice made sense to me, so we started visiting disc jockeys.

We got all dressed up and went to one particular deejay and talked to him real polite: "Sir, we stopped in here today with a record of ours we hope you'll listen to and that you'll like enough to put on the air." He sat through this little speech looking kind of bored, but he let us go on. When he had each said our piece, I handed him a copy of "Please." He pulled the record out of the sleeve and laid it to one side without even looking at it. Then he turned the sleeve upside down like he expected something to fall out of it. Nothing happened. He shook it. Nothing. Without a word he picked up the record and handed it back to me.

Payola wasn't the only thing we didn't know anything about. We also didn't know we had a hit until it charted at number 60, and we didn't know how much that ignorance had cost us. See, we hadn't followed the progress of the record at first; we just went out and worked hard, playing a lot of the same places we'd played before, a lot of 'em for the same money—$25 for the whole group, even though we now had a hit tune. We didn't know enough to mind because we could all remember a gig in Atlanta once when we'd come out with a quarter apiece. I realized later that there were people who didn't want us to know how well the record was doing; they could make a lot of money from a hit group that cost them only $25.

The record company didn't do much better. When we got a statement from them, Mr. Nathan saw that they'd charged us for everything: the hotel stay in Cincinnati, studio time, tapes, *their* long-distance phone calls, even the food we ate during the session. Mr. Nathan would also under-report sales and jack up the breakage figures. That way he'd owe us even less. The biggest money we ever got for the record was the $150 apiece he gave us when we recorded it.

We went back to the studio in late March and late July. We'd usually cut four or five sides, all in one day, using our band plus some of King's house band—Ray Felder and Cleveland Lowe on sax, drummers Edison Gore and Reginald Hall, and bass players Clarence Mack and Edwyn Conley. In those sessions, we cut tunes like "Hold My Baby's Hand," "Chonnie-on-Chon," "Just Won't Do Right," "Let's Make It," and "I Won't Plead No More."

In June, King released "I Don't Know" and "I Feel That Old Feeling Coming On" before "Please" had hardly gotten started. In July they turned around and put out "No, No, No," and "Hold My Baby's Hand." You can hear a lot of where soul music came from by listening to some of those tunes. In "No, No, No" I was influenced by the Dominoes, who had started out as a gospel group, and by the Five Royales. The vocal harmony is gospel, but the chords are sevens and nines from jazz and R & B.

In October, King released "Just Won't Do Right" and "Let's Make It." "Just Won't Do Right" should have been big, but a lot of things worked against it. It should have crossed over, but my musicians held me back. They could think only in terms of R & B and didn't understand what I thought about. They were singing R & B, but their voices were too heavy; I should have had girls singing with me. Most Afro-Americans can't sing pop; they may think they can, but they can't. The Platters were the first Afro-American group to really sing pop.

I had so much faith in "Just Won't Do Right" I recut it five times in my career. In the first version the lyric goes, "Since you've been gone, I drink and gamble every night." The next time I changed it to: "I stay in the chapel every night." It still didn't do it.

"Let's Make It," on the flip side, was a sort of vocal rendition of Bill Doggett's big instrumental hit "Honky Tonk." It should have been big, too, but putting it with "Just Won't Do Right" hurt both songs. King never gave any of the records a chance to sell. All the releases coming out one on top of the other confused people, especially disc jockeys. I was competing with myself. But nothing could stop "Please." It made it to number 6 on the *Billboard* R & B chart and stayed on the chart for nineteen weeks. It even got Ralph Bass his old job back.

Once we started seeing record charts from the towns we played, the gigs got better. We even played Augusta. I had to get special permission from the district attorney's office to come to town, though. They said I could come in to do the gigs, but I couldn't stay twenty-four hours. The first thing I did there was a kid's matinee at Sunset Recreation Center on a Saturday afternoon. That night I played the Delmar Casino, a club on Ninth Street. When the job was over, the police escorted me across the bridge into South Carolina. It had been almost ten years since I had been in trouble as a teenager, and they still treated me like a dangerous criminal. But I did get to see my father and Aunt Minnie. Honey was back in Augusta, too, and Big Junior was visiting her, so I got to see everybody. They all knew about me having a record out, and except for Honey they couldn't hardly believe it.

Pretty soon we started moving north with the record. When we got as far as Richmond, we kind of stalled. We played there so much we got tired of it, but we couldn't seem to make it to Washington. Finally, the record broke there and we played the Capitol Arena, singing and dancing in a boxing ring. After that we started playing Washington as much as we did Richmond, going back and forth; then the beaches in Maryland opened up for us—Carl's Beach, Wilmer's Park—a lot of afternoon gigs for very good money. The funny one was Carl's because they called it a beach, but the water was way away. They did tell us the general direction it was in, though.

The gigs got better in the South, too. We went back to the Palms in Jacksonville and another Palms in Bradenton, but this time we had a hit record. Instead of the $25 we used to get, now we made $750. In Jacksonville we were on the bill with Guitar Slim, the blues guitarist and singer who had a big hit with "Things That I Used to Do." From Bradenton we went into the Palms of Hallandale near Miami, a premier spot on the so-called chitlin' circuit. Ordinarily you played the Palms for nine days, then you went out and played other clubs in the area for a while, coming back into the Palms for nine more days. It was a long open-air place with walls around the side, and it could hold two thousand people. The first time we performed there the bill included the Five Royales, Guitar Slim, Shirley and Lee, B. B. King, and Ray Charles. Cost 90 cents to get in.

The Five Royales was a group I had sung like in the early days. They had a real good guitarist and songwriter named Lowman Pauling who later wrote "Think" when we were all at King Records together. Shirley and Lee, out of New Orleans, had a big hit with "Let the Good Times Roll." Of course B. B. and Ray had both been out there for a long while.

It was a good gig, but Ray was always an advice type man and I was always my own man, so we were probably destined to have a little disagreement. It seems funny now, but at the time I guess we were serious. He told me I ought to change the order of the songs I did during my set. He kept after me about it, and pretty soon I started to get hot. I was pacing back and forth, arguing with him, telling him to mind his own business.

"Stand still," he said, "so I can talk to you."

I was too disturbed to stay put. I kept pacing. After a while I noticed he was turning his head back and forth, following me the whole time. It kind of spooked me for a second, and I stopped dead in my tracks. He seemed to be staring at me right through his shades.

"Listen," he said, "you may think I can't see, but I can."

That stopped me cold for a second. Then I laughed, and after that we made our peace.

When the Flames came back into the Palms for the second nine-day stand, we were on the bill with Hank Ballard and the Midnighters. They danced pretty good and they had a lot of hit records, so we really worked to outdo 'em. At that time there were no slow songs in our act, and we did almost all our own material. For the entire set we sang and danced at top speed without a break, just working hard. What we didn't realize was that the people weren't only digging our music, they were also watching to see how long we could keep up the pace. And we could keep it up a *long* time.

Back then a lot of the groups were pretty, performing with top hats and canes and singing mellow, close harmony stuff. You didn't see too many groups like us, dancing all over the place, cutting flips, slinging sweat, and singing real raw. We wore bright red suits made out of ripcord, with the jacket cut open in front to show a lot of shirt. Sometimes I was set off in a dark blue version of the same suit while the group was all in red. They were very heavy suits. You sweat, they got heavier.

Anyway, we did a good job at the Palms, and after we went back to Macon we got booked on another show in Atlanta with Hank Ballard and the Midnighters, a big bill with Solomon Burke, a group called the Turbans that later became the Tams, and several other acts. Thanks to Hank, the gig turned out to be a turning point for me, but it started off like it was going to be a disaster.

We weren't sure where we came on the show. By the time we found out we were supposed to go on second, Nash Knox and one of the other fellas, thinking they had plenty of time, had gone out for food. Time came for us to hit and they were nowhere in sight. The rest of us waited as long as we could and then went on without them; as soon as we did, they came through the stage door, out of uniform, did a double take, grabbed their uniforms, and started dressing in the wings. When they were dressed, I mashed potatoes over to the side and brought them on like it was part of the act. I always work hard, but I think they worked harder that night to make up for being late. We wound up doing such a fantastic show that after we came off, Hank went straight to the telephone—before he even went on stage for his set—and called his booking agent, Ben Bart, at Universal Attractions in New York, and told him he'd just seen an act that Universal ought to have.

Before starting Universal Attractions, Ben Bart had been with Moe and Tim Gale at GAC. He knew every aspect of the entertainment business—promoting, managing, booking, whatever—and had managed Jimmy Lunceford, Dinah Washington, the Ravens, and several others. With the Ravens he had formed Hub Records, one of the earliest independent record companies. At Universal he booked most of the major R & B acts of the day. He could do it all.

I didn't know it at the time, but that phone call was the beginning of one of the most important relationships of my life. Hank gave all the information about Universal to Fats Gonder. After we got back to Macon, Mr. Brantly called Mr. Bart. They had some lengthy conversations and decided that Mr. Bart would book us. Later, Mr. Bart became my manager and business partner. But the main thing is that he became like a father to me. I loved that man and he loved me.

We started working our way north from Macon, doing gigs, heading for New York where we were supposed to sign with Universal. In Newark we played Laurel's Garden with Little Richard and Ray Charles. By this time Richard and I had a little rivalry thing going to see who could outdo the other. His act had gotten wilder and wilder—suits made out of mirrors, hair as tall as he was, so much makeup on his face it looked like icing—and he beat up on the piano right along.

Came time for us to go on, I did my usual dancing and powerful singing, and I could tell we were getting over real good. Halfway through the act Richard was already trying to get them to make me come off the stage. But I wanted to do something to really cap it off, so when we were closing, I got the Flames to boost me up into the rafters. I worked my way across the ceiling, holding the mike, singing. When I got to the middle, I hung there by one hand above the crowd just *pleading*: "Please, please, please."

Richard liked to had a fit. He was running around yelling, "Get him down! Get him down! Get him down!" Scared him to death. Meantime, the Flames danced out to the middle of the floor and cleared out the people underneath me. For the finale, I let go, like I was overcome with emotion, and dropped down like a man going off a high bridge. The crowd gasped and jumped back. When the Flames caught me, the place went wild. Richard never had a chance.

From Newark we jumped down to Trenton before we finally got into New York and Universal. It was my first time in New York, but I never was amazed at the big city, looking up at the buildings or anything like that. I guess Atlanta helped me a lot. By going to Atlanta, I wasn't really excited by New York at all.

Mr. Bart was a nice-looking man, big, with gray and brown hair. He told us about how he had Hank Ballard, the Five Royales, and all the other big acts, and how he could do for us what he had done for them if we'd just stick together. He was going to book us, and Mr. Brantly was going to keep on managing us. We listened to him and then signed the contract without even reading it. Back then we just did what we were told. Even when we were on the road, all the money we made went to Fats, who held it for Mr. Brantly until we got back to Macon where the payoff was. We didn't mind; the system kept us from spending all our money.

While we were in New York we went to catch the show at the Apollo. It was the first time any of us had even been inside the place, but we knew what it meant. All the greatest acts in the history of black show business had played there, and it was the toughest audience in the world. What they said about New York in general was even truer of that theater: If you could make it there, you could make it anywhere. That night we saw the Dells, the Cadillacs, and several other acts, and after the show we went backstage, which was a hectic scene. All kinds of people everywhere. Naturally, the entertainers had told their girlfriends and sisters and brothers, "I'm working at the Apollo this week. Come backstage and I'll get you in free." Sign over the backstage entrance said: "If your friends and relatives won't pay to see you, who will?"

While we were back there we saw Billy Ward and the Dominoes coming in for the beginning of their week. Billy Ward wasn't really the star of the group, but it was his act. He had put it together and he kept it together. In the early days the Dominoes had been a gospel group, but they moved into R & B with "Have Mercy, Baby" and things like that, featuring Clyde McPhatter. After Clyde left, Jackie Wilson took over. They'd started out on Federal, like us, moved up to the King label and then left Mr. Nathan for another company. They'd had a lot of hits and seeing them backstage opened my eyes to a lot of things. They came through with valets pushing long garment racks, like the ones on Seventh Avenue, holding all their uniforms. For dressing rooms they took the top floor of the theater beause it had a lot of space where they could rehearse, and they put long mirrors up there so they could work on their dance routines in front of them. They also had a white baby grand piano carried all the way up the steps. Billy Ward knew what he was doing.

After we signed with Universal, our bookings improved some and "Please" started to break in the North. All this while, King kept releasing one record after another, trying to capitalize on "Please" but really working against it. In January of 1957, "Chonnie-on-Chon" and "I Won't Plead No More" came out. They wanted "Chonnie-on-Chon" out because it was supposed to sound like a Little Richard record. I think I managed to get my own style into it, though. "I Won't Plead No More" was supposed to be the answer to "Please Please Please." Mr. Nathan kept saying, "Give us another 'Please Please Please.'" That's typical of a white record company; they want you to keep cutting something just like your first hit. I gave them that, but I didn't want to. They did not want to change. They didn't change until "Papa's Got a Brand New Bag." The whole world didn't change until then. They were still playing the same thing. Some people are ahead of their time.

Tommy Sands was ahead of his time, but the industry wouldn't let *him* pull away either: "Teen-Age Crush." He was good-looking—a kind of short Tony Curtis—and super, super talented. I think Bobby Darren tried to take off on him later, but he couldn't do it. Bobby Darren was confused; he tried to be like Little Richard, then like Sinatra. He was multitalented but he didn't know what he was supposed to be doing. Like

Sammy Davis. Sammy Davis is multitalented, but he never did himself.

There are very few original people. Perry Como was original. Bing Crosby was kind of original, but he had a lot of Louis Armstrong in him. James Dean was original all the way. Fabian was a copy. He was just good looking. What killed Fabian was he started losing his hair. Same thing killed Tony Curtis. Hair is the first thing. And teeth are second. Hair and teeth. A man got those two things he's got it all.

Mr. Nathan wouldn't let us be original, and when the other records didn't do as well as "Please," he started to get down on us. I think some of the fellas in the group were getting discouraged. Sometime in early 1957 Universal called us into the office to discuss what we ought to do. Mr. Bart said he saw something in me that he wanted to see fulfilled. He decided to call the act James Brown and the Famous Flames instead of just the Famous Flames. Ever since Sylvester and Bobby had pushed me out front, that's what it had been anyway, but with all the work we'd done, the disappointments with some of the records, and the jealousy in the group, the change was too much. Everybody except me quit and went back home to Toccoa. That was the end of the group.

I was sorry. I was heartbroken. We'd been together a long time. But I think they didn't know any better. They couldn't see that we were really just getting started. There's not much more I can say about it except that they went home, and when they went home I kept going.

15 TRY ME

AFTER the breakup I spent the summer playing around Florida with Fats Gonder and pickup bands, playing every place there just like I'd played every place in Georgia. That's what you do; you just keep working. It's just like I do now.

During this time King was putting out things that I'd recorded with the original group. In April "Gonna Try" came out. You can hear gospel in it, but it's a very tired song. It was up-tempo in those days, but it's tired because it's based on an old takeoff rhythm. The sax player on the record was Little Richard's man, Wilbert Smith, who later became Lee Diamond when he started fronting the Upsetters. In July, King put out "Love or a Game" and "Messing with the Blues," one of the few blues tunes I've ever recorded. In October they released "You're Mine, You're Mine" and "I Walked Alone." "You're Mine, You're Mine" comes out of gospel, too. It might seem like a blues to some ears, but the harmony is gospel and that keeps it from being blues. Some of the records did pretty good, but none was really a hit and King wouldn't let me record any new material. Really, they had dropped me. Nobody calls you up and tells you they've dropped you. They don't call you at all. That's how you know. But I wasn't worried. It just made me work that much harder.

Then in October 1957, Little Richard, big as he was, retired from rock 'n' roll right in the middle of a tour of Australia. Just quit. He said he wanted to devote his life to the Lord. I can understand that and I don't fault him, but he left his manager, Bumps Blackwell, with a lot of bookings to honor. Mr. Blackwell called Mr. Brantly and asked him to get me to take over some of the southern bookings. I agreed to do it, but I made sure it would be as James Brown this time. I got together with the Upsetters and the Dominions again, and we did the dates.

To tell the truth, when those audiences saw what I could do with the dancing and everything, I don't think they missed Richard too much.

When my part of the tour was done, I recruited a new set of Flames out of the Dominions. I knew that to do my own stuff right I needed my own group. I got Bill Hollings, Louis Madison, and J. W. Archer, taught them the songs and the routines, and started working as James Brown and the Famous Flames again. As singers they were the best group of Flames I ever had, but a later group of Flames was better all around as a stage act.

When Mr. Nathan found out how I went over on the tour and saw that I could still put a group together, he agreed to let me record one more time. Only this time, he wanted us to use somebody else's material. We cut "Begging, Begging" and "That Dood It." Rudolph Toombs, who wrote "One Mint Julep," was one of the writers on both of them. "Begging, Begging" was a kind of slow Hank Ballard type thing, but I put my own stamp on it. "That Dood It" is rockabilly, influenced by Louis Jordan. It's a humorous story about a man who goes on a treasure hunt, tries to dig some gold, looks back, and there's a big monster standing behind him. I didn't cut many comic songs like that, and when I did they didn't come out as comedy.

Meantime, I was still doing one-nighters all over the South. Whenever I got near Toccoa, I saw Velma and the boys. Before long we had another son, Larry. As busy as I was, I couldn't get home as often as before, and when I did get home, I could tell Velma and I were drifting apart. More and more I came home a stranger. She was the best *home* woman I've ever had, and she never tried to stop me from making it. She could see what was happening, and she didn't try to fight it at all. She always had a kind word to say. And later on, she never tried to turn the children against me. After a while I started living with another woman in Macon. Her name was Dessie. We got a house and everything, but she didn't break up Velma and me. It was time. Time and distance. I still visited, but it just couldn't be put back together. Through it all, though, we tried to stay friends, and we are friends right today.

"That Dood It" came out in February 1958 and "Begging, Begging" in May. When these two records didn't do anything, Mr. Nathan really lost faith, telling people, "James Brown is through, washed up. He'll never record for me again." For almost a year I didn't, but *I* didn't think I was washed up. I thought I was getting better, but it seemed I was always having to prove myself. After eight or nine months went by without any more recording dates, I could see that Mr. Nathan wasn't going to do anything, so I decided I better do something.

I had been doing a new song on stage for a while, and I thought it could be a big hit. Back then I always stage-tested my own material; before recording something, I made sure audiences liked it. As we went around doing all our one-nighters I tried different arrangements of the same song to see how the audiences reacted, and then I decided the best way to record it. This particular song was "Try Me," really a pop tune. I had heard "Raindrops" by Dee Clark and "For Your Precious Love" by Jerry Butler and the Impressions, so I wrote my song to fit between them. Audiences loved it. Mr. Nathan hated it. When I took it to him he wouldn't even let me record it.

"I'm not spending my money on that garbage," he said.

"Okay, Mr. Nathan," I said, "I'll pay for a demo myself, and then you'll see."

I booked the studio time at King, paid Mr. Nathan in advance, and cut the demo later in the summer. At the same time I cut "Bewildered," a song I'd sung for a long time. When I heard how strong it was on the playback I decided not to let Mr. Nathan hear it. I didn't want him putting it out with "Try Me" and messing both of them up. I'd seen disc jockeys confused by all my records before, and I knew "Bewildered" could be a hit on its own. So before Mr. Nathan came down from his office to listen to what we'd done, I packed away the tape of "Bewildered" and played "Try Me" for him. He still didn't like it.

"It doesn't make sense," he said.

"But, Mr. Nathan, it's going to be a hit."

"I don't want it," he said. He waved me aside with his cigar and walked out of the control room.

Here I'd spent my own money and I was being dropped by the record company, but I didn't even try to argue with him. I still had my tape, and I knew it was good. I took it over to Nolan studios and had it made into an acetate, the kind that plays inside-out, like I'd done with "His Eye Is on the Sparrow" back in Toccoa. Only this time I had a whole bunch of copies made, took them around to the disc jockeys I knew, and got them to play it. Big Saul and Hamp Swain played it in Macon. John R, in Nashville, played it over WLAC where half the country could hear it. After a while I got it around to a whole lot of jocks, and it was getting good air play even as an acetate. When Mr. Nathan found out the stations were playing it, he still wasn't satisfied. He claimed he'd like to put it out but I'd been bumped from the Federal roster because it was full. He had officially dropped me.

"Wait a minute," I said, "the stations aren't just playing it, it's one of their most requested songs."

"Prove it," he said.

"Okay, Mr. Nathan," I said, "I'll prove it to you. And you're going to change your mind about James Brown."

I went to see all the jocks and asked them to call Mr. Nathan to tell him how the song was doing on their stations. After they'd all called him I went back to see him. He'd changed his mind, like I predicted. Wasn't because of the jocks, though, but because he discovered King had already received orders for twenty-two thousand copies, and the record hadn't even been cut yet.

"Well, James," he said, "I've decided to give the song a try."

"That's fine, Mr. Nathan," I said.

"Good," he said, "now where's the tape?"

"Oh, you don't want *that* tape, Mr. Nathan. It's just a demo, a little something I paid for myself."

"That's what they're playing on the radio," he said.

"Yessir, I know, but a record sounds a little different when you play it at home; the bad parts show up more. I think we need to recut it with some real musicians and careful production." I smiled a big crocodile grin.

He could see I had him over a barrel, so he arranged a session for the middle of September at Beltone Studios in New York. He wanted to get the song cut and get it out. Mr. Nathan was even going to send Henry Glover, his top A & R man. Over the years Henry had worked with jump bands like Buddy Johnson, Tiny Bradshaw, and Lucky Millinder. He did a lot of arranging, songwriting, and producing. But Henry wouldn't come; he didn't think we were popular enough. He sent Andy Gibson instead. That turned out to be fine with me because

Andy stayed out of my way, and that's what I wanted. They hired some experienced musicians from the New York area for the session. Hal "Cornbread" Singer played tenor sax; he got his nickname from the big instrumental hit "Cornbread" that he had in the late forties. Kenny Burrell, the jazz guitarist, was on guitar, and if you listen closely to the record you can hear that it's his style.

In a way, it was a new start for me, but in another way it was a last chance. I hadn't recorded in almost a year, the new Flames hadn't recorded with me but one time, and I knew Mr. Nathan expected something really big out of this New York session. I also knew we already had something big; I was certain enough that I wrote "Tell Me What I Did Wrong" to replace "Bewildered." If I'd been worried about it, I'd have cut "Bewildered" right then, as insurance, but I didn't. We recut "Try Me" on September 18 and released it in October. It went to number 1 on the R & B charts immediately and to number 48 on the pop charts. Everything was fixing to change for me again.

16 APOLLO ONE

THE FIRST THING that changed was my deal with King. Mr. Nathan didn't have any contract with me anymore, and when I had a number 1 record, he wanted to join up again. The deal I had had with him before was terrible; I think I received half a cent a side for writer's royalties and maybe another half a cent for performance, partly because in the original contract everything was split evenly among all the Flames and Mr. Brantly. The record companies were always under-reporting sales, exaggerating breakage, and charging for everything, so you never really knew what you were making.

My new deal was made with Hal Neely, the vice-president of King, who had come to Cincinnati in 1958 to help Mr. Nathan run things when he was sick a lot with heart trouble. Mr. Neely had been a bandleader and a trumpet player and knew something about music. On the new contract he jumped me to a 5 percent royalty, although 3 percent was standard in those days, and he made me a better publishing deal. The new contract didn't help me with "Try Me," though. They already had that. I think I made about $3,600 in royalties from "Try Me," even though it was number 1. I believe I got that $3,600 all at once and thought I was rich. I went to see Fats Domino one night in County Hall in Charleston, South Carolina, thinking how wealthy I was. That's when I realized I needed hit records because every time Fats Domino opened his mouth he had a hit record coming out of it. While watching the show, some of the people wanted me to go up and do a number, so I went on stage and ran Fats Domino off his own gig with my own record. Paid to see him, then run him off the stage. That started me thinking what I might do with a *lot* of hit records.

Universal signed me again, too. Mr. Bart flew down to

Macon to do it. See, they want you to prove yourself and *then* they want to jump back on the bandwagon.

Meantime, I recruited a new band because I knew I was going to need a permanent backup group to do my music justice on the road. I met J. C. Davis in Burlington, North Carolina, and put a band together behind him: Bernard Odum played bass, Nat Kendrick played drums, Roscoe Patrick played trumpet—you can hear him real good on "You've Got the Power," and Les Buie played guitar after Bobby Roach left. Les was a great guitarist. When we cut "I Don't Mind," he made a mistake, but it sounded so good I told him to play it again for the final recording. Albert Corley, the alto sax player, was the greatest who ever lived; he beat Cannonball and everybody. He used to roll out of his bed, pull on his clothes, and tune up his horn coming down the stairs. He'd walk in still putting on his tie and blow everybody out of their seats. Fats Gonder and I still played keyboards. It was a good band. Later, though, J. C. started to think it was his band and jumped ship and went with Etta James.

As soon as I re-signed with Universal, they set up a schedule of sixty one-nighters in a row. I think I had one day off in that time, a Sunday. During this tour I went into Masters Studio in Los Angeles and recorded "I Want You So Bad." The new set of Flames was on the record and so was Johnny Terry, who came in and out of the group for the next several years. In January 1959, King released the *Please Please Please* album and at the end of the month I recorded "Bewildered" and an instrumental called "Doodle Bug" at Beltone. I didn't tell Mr. Nathan about the tape of "Bewildered" I'd already done; we just recut it from scratch.

It's funny, the past was starting to come back on me, even in those tunes. "Bewildered" was a song I used to sing when I had the Cremona Trio as a kid, and "Doodle Bug" took me back to my days in the woods, sitting under the house, playing with the doodle bugs. I was thinking about my mother a lot, too; figuring she must have heard about me from some of my aunts. I thought she might try to get in touch with me now that I was getting well known. She didn't, and for a long time I felt bad, but that wore off. I understood that she had been going through quite a strain, and I thought it was more important to see her than to wait for her to come to me.

From Uncle Perry, the man who helped my father steal my mother away, I got an address in Brooklyn: 312 Monroe Street. It was all he knew about where she was. On a cold winter day I went out there to a kind of old, funny looking two-story building, the kind that gives you a weird feeling. I walked up the steps and rang the buzzer. Nobody answered. Somehow I couldn't leave. I stood on the stoop and waited for the longest time. I hadn't dressed warm enough, and by the time it started getting dark I was shivering. It didn't really look like anybody was living there, but I waited anyway. Finally, I gave up. The next day I was back on the road. I told Uncle Perry to keep sending the word out through the family that I wanted to find my mother.

I thrived on the one-nighters, but I was having a lot of problems with the Flames—some drinking problems and a drug problem. J. W. Archer was the really difficult one. He was difficult and I tried to keep him from drinking, and every time I tried he wanted to jump on me and fight. One night we were in Charleston, South Carolina, and I'd had enough. I said, "Let's have it out right now. We're gonna fight barefisted." He was a big fella, weighed about 195, while I weighed about 135. We started duking it out. When he saw it wasn't going to be so easy to take me, he ripped a coatrack off the wall, an iron strip with four or five coat hooks in a line on it. He gripped it in his fist so that the hooks stuck out between his fingers. Every time I hit him with my fist, he hit me with that rack. I was bobbing and weaving, but he still busted me above the eye with that iron. That was the only way he could fight me. I still beat him to the floor.

I'm not a violent man, but I know how to *be* violent. I can beat a big man like J. W. real fast. I take a big man, pick him up, and run with him. Run him into the wall and near break his back.

Sometimes you have no choice. After a show in Kansas City, during this time, some of the cats who were in the gangs around there jumped on my bass player, Bernard Odum, outside the Streets Hotel and beat him up pretty bad. When he managed to run away, they turned on me. They were mad because their girlfriends were crazy about us on stage, and they wanted to show us up in front of them.

"You better leave me alone, fellas," I said. Usually, in situations like that, when they looked at me funny I'd put the eye on 'em and they'd leave me alone, but this one fella who had jumped on Bernard wouldn't back off. He was cursing me and threatening me, so I said, "You hobo your way over here, I'm going to pay it back." "Hobo" means when somebody jumps on you they get a free ride, like a hobo jumping a train. He came at me, and I hit him thirty licks just like lightning. As a boxer I was always real fast with my hands and my feet. I finished him off with the old bolo, Kid Gavilan's punch, the one where you wind up like a whirlwind and throw it like an uppercut. Anywhere it lands, it hurts. After that, none of the other cats wanted to continue the discussion.

Lots of entertainers face problems with cats who want to fight 'em in front of their girlfriends. You just have to live with it and go on. Problems within the group are another thing; you've either got to solve the problems or break up, or solve them *by* breaking up. The problems with the Flames came to a head one night in Oakland, California. I had a big argument with 'em about discipline in the group. They didn't like it, so I left and they stayed. You can say they quit or they were fired, either way, but it was the end of the second set of Flames. It was unfortunate because they were all very good singers.

When I got back to Macon, I found out from Mr. Brantly that Universal had me booked into the Apollo for a week beginning April 24. There was no reason I shouldn't have been booked in there—I had a number 1 record—but the date couldn't have come at a worse time: no Flames and only a couple of weeks to get ready. People were advising me to put it off, to wait until I had a new group and had toured with them for a while. I said no, I was going to put on a good show no matter what. I figured the more people who could see me on stage and see what I could do, the more it would help me. A hit record gave me the opportunity to be in front of more of them, and in better places. You take your opportunities when they come.

I went on to New York with the band and started putting things together. Johnny Terry was still with me, and I had a young man named Baby Lloyd Stallworth who used to work around the Palms in Hallandale. He shined our shoes or went out for food, whatever needed doing. He must have been twelve years old at the time. When we left the Palms I asked his mother if he could go on the road with us and work for us. I promised her I'd look after him like a son, and she let him go. I sent him back to Hallandale when the first set of Flames broke up, but after I started touring he came to live in my house in Macon to help Dessie while I was gone. In New York I started showing him the routines, too. He had seen them so often on the road that he picked them up real fast. Then, while we were rehearsing one day, I noticed J. C. Davis's valet, Bobby Bennett, hanging around. I stopped the band.

"Can you dance?" I asked him.

"Not as good as you, but I can dance *some*," he said.

"Show me."

I gave the band a downbeat, and they played a little vamp while he did some mashed potatoes. He was pretty good, and he was a nice-looking cat besides.

"Okay," I said, "you open at the Apollo Theater next week. It took me five years to get there, it took you five minutes. Congratulations."

I told Johnny to take him back to the Hotel Theresa, where we were staying, and to rehearse him around the clock in the routines. I was starting to think we might actually get the thing together in time. Then Byrd showed up.

After the breakup of the original Flames, Bobby and I stayed in touch. I had told him about a job in the King stockroom, and he had been doing that. I asked him to let me know about any good new tunes that came in in case I wanted to cut them. Pretty soon Mr. Nathan had him doctoring songs. If they received a tape they thought was promising, Gene Redd and Bobby might rework the melody a little bit or change the lyrics and cut one of the King artists on it. One time they received a tape from a couple of unknown songwriters named Sam Moore and David Prater, who later became Sam and Dave. The song was called "The Sweetest Letter." At that time Bobby didn't know how people felt about having their music messed with; he worked on it, and it eventually became a hit for Little Willie John as the flip side of "Sleep."

Mr. Brantly had called Bobby and told him about the Apollo gig. When he showed up, I wasn't surprised to see him. I knew he still had performing in his blood. All I said to him was "Byrd, we open in two days." He said: "Let's get to rehearsing."

I was a seasoned performer, but under the circumstances I was a nervous wreck. The Apollo was a special place: It was *the* venue for black entertainers; it made a lot of people, but it broke a lot, too. For one thing, the schedule was grueling. You got there at ten o'clock in the morning because the first show was at eleven, and you might do as many as six or seven shows in one day. You ate there, slept there, and kept rehearsing when you were not on stage. The audience was very tough, too, and if they didn't like you, they let you know. Immediately. They made you *work*. The other performers made you work, too. Everybody was always trying to outdo everybody else. When you went on, you tried to make it impossible for anybody to follow you. I think that's why its standard of entertainment was so consistently high. We thought about all this as we rehearsed. And then we rehearsed harder.

Little Willie John was headlining the bill that week, and he was hot. He had a string of hits: "All Around the World," "Let Them Talk," "Talk to Me," and "Fever." He was on King Records, too, and they were lucky to have him because Mr. Nathan had once turned him down. He was recommended to King at the same time as Hank Ballard and the Midnighters. When Mr. Nathan signed them, he wouldn't have anything to do with Little Willie John. But Little Willie John was a determined cat. He walked into King Records one day and said: "I want to sing." Mr. Nathan said, "What can you sing?" He said, "I can sing anything." And he started singing right there in the office.

They signed him up right then and there, and he was their pet for a long time. With all his hits, he frequently headlined at the Apollo.

The Upsetters, fronted by Lee Diamond now, were on the show, too, and I *knew* they could play. The rest of the bill had the comedy team Butterbeans and Susie, Verna White, the Senators, Vi Kemp, and me. To set the record straight: the first time I played the Apollo was on that Little Willie John bill the week of April 24, 1959. When Sandman Sims, who was the Apollo's stage manager for a lot of years, says he gave me a shirt and shoes to use on amateur night, he's telling stories. I *never* competed on amateur night there.

By the time we got ready to hit the stage for the first time that week, I had whipped the group into shape, but we were way down on the bill. Little Willie John didn't want us to come on anywhere near him—he knew what we could do—so they had us opening the show.

When they got through playing the Apollo theme music and the curtain went up, I came out smoking. The audience went wild. I don't think they'd ever seen a man move that fast. I put them *on* Little Willie John's case right away. During that time I closed my set with "Please" and came out with a red suitcase that said, "Please Please Please" on one side and "Baby, Take My Hand" on the other. I fell to my knees and one of the Flames patted me on the back, threw a coat over my shoulders, and helped me off the stage. Little Willie John couldn't hardly handle it. When we came off he said I was using tricks to get over.

We kept rehearsing between shows, getting sharper and sharper. We were getting over so good that Frank Schiffman, the owner of the Apollo, promised to move us up to the co-starring spot before the week was up. We really thought we had it going then. Here I'd started out the week with almost no show and was fixing to move up to the co-star slot. But something went wrong. On the fourth or fifth day we were still opening the show, and it didn't seem right. The audience had let us know how it felt, and when the Apollo audience lets you know, it lets you know in no uncertain terms.

I decided to make a move. After one of our sets, while the audience was still stomping and cheering, I turned to the fellas.

"Pack up the stuff," I said. "Everybody grab a piece. We're leaving."

Bobby grabbed a cymbal and the snare stand, Nat Kendrick took more of the drum kit and Fats took some stuff. The Flames each took a piece of equipment, and we walked off the stage and straight up the aisles, heading for the door. Mr. Schiffman saw right away what we were doing. He stopped us at the back of the theater.

"Where do you think you're going?" he said.

"One Hundred and Twenty-fifth Street, Mr. Schiffman," I said.

"You hear what those people are doing? We can't even get the other act on the stage with all the noise they're making."

"That's why we ought to be co-starring, sir," I said.

He took a piece of drum out of one fella's hands and started back down the aisle with it. "As of now, you *are* co-starring," he said.

The next day we went on in the slot just before Willie John. He couldn't hardly stand it. He was a balladeer, and I ate him alive. He could sing, though. Later on I got where I could outsing him, too, but back then I didn't stop just to sing—I danced and sang and played keyboards and drums and did everything. He was mad because I beat him out. I can understand a fella getting mad; nobody wants to be beaten out.

By the time the week was up I felt like the Apollo was my natural home. We'd done so well that we were already booked to make the rounds of the other big theaters on the circuit—the Howard in Washington, the Royal in Baltimore, and the Uptown in Philly—and I figured that the Regal in Chicago would fall into line pretty soon. The day after we finished at the Apollo I was in my room at the Theresa, fixing to leave for Washington, when somebody knocked on the door.

"Come in," I said.

I was gathering up my belongings, not really watching the door. I heard it open, real slow, but that was all. After a minute, when I realized how quiet it was, I turned around. There was a small woman standing there, not young, not old. I hadn't seen her since I was four years old, but when I looked at her I knew right away it was my mother. I had no idea she was coming to see me that day or any day.

"I've been looking for you for a long time," I said. "I'm glad to see you."

She started to smile, and when she did I could see she'd lost all her teeth. All I could think to say was, "I'm going to get your mouth fixed for you."

She didn't say anything. She just walked toward me. We hugged, and then I kissed my mother for the first time in more than twenty years.

17 THE CIRCUIT

WE WENT into the Howard in Washington still co-starring with Little Willie John. I really thought I had something going then, and I started doing a little preaching before I sang, kind of doing the gospel thing. I talked about situations like when you went to see a lady and she had another boyfriend, blah, blah, blah, and then I started singing "Please don't go." Or you came home and she was getting ready to leave, or something like that. Cats in the audience yelled, "Don't preach, sing." Later on in the show, when I leaned out over the footlights, singing, slapping hands, sweating, really *working*, I loosened my tie and threw it out. They threw it back to me. I said to myself, "James, you got some work to do."

The same thing happened to me later on at the Apollo. The audiences on the whole theater circuit could be tough, especially on amateur nights. At the Apollo amateur night on Wednesdays, Sandman Sims sat up in a side box wearing a big sombrero with Christmas tree lights all around it. When the audience didn't like an act, they yelled up to Sandman. He blew on an old trombone, and a cat called Porto Rico came out wearing a hula skirt or something and chased the act off the stage with a cap pistol. Anyway, with an audience riled up like that, it could carry over to the featured act.

At the Apollo you opened on a Friday, and amateur night wasn't until the next Wednesday. You had all that time to win them over and let the word get out about how good you were. At the Royal Theater in Baltimore, where we went next, you opened on Monday and amateur night was on Tuesday, so you had only one day to establish yourself.

We got through the first night in Baltimore fine. Had 'em eating out of our hands, nothing to worry about, even when we saw the audience coming in Tuesday night. They came in rowdy and ready, with their baskets of eggs, lettuce, tomatoes. It was their night to howl, and if you did something they didn't like, they let you know. We had been warned: These people *come* to throw. We weren't worried, though. We knew if we kept them up in the air all the time, hollering and clapping, they wouldn't have a chance to throw. We did our stuff, singing and dancing and getting them up out of their seats, when all of a sudden there came a bottle. *Bonk.* Hit Bobby Bennett in the head and knocked him flat. I looked over and saw Byrd and them kind of dancing around him, trying to make it look like part of the act and trying to get him up at the same time. We started dancing harder. Bobby Bennett got to his feet and began *kind* of dancing. Then came the rest of the groceries. Byrd got hit with a hard-boiled egg and a head of rotten lettuce. Tomatoes went by. We were dancing and dodging, dodging and dancing. We looked like boxers up there, bobbing and weaving and looking out for the next shot.

After the show we were down in the dumps. We couldn't understand it. We'd killed 'em Monday night and hadn't nothing changed in the act, and here they had thrown at us. We sat in the dressing room trying to figure it out.

"It was all coming from one section," I said.

"And most of it was at the Flames," Byrd said.

Johnny Terry looked at Bobby Bennett. "And most of *that,*" he said, "was at *you.*"

Bobby Bennett looked uncomfortable, and not just from the bump on his head. He mentioned something about some girls he'd been messing with when we were in Washington. Finally, he admitted that it was the girls and their friends who had done the throwing. They'd come over to Baltimore from Washington. After he told us that, *we* wanted to hit him with a bottle.

The rest of the week at the Royal went fine. We closed Sunday night, took one day off, then went into the Uptown in Philadelphia. I met a local disc jockey there who talked to me about maybe getting "Try Me" to Dick Clark to play on *American Bandstand,* which at the time was still done in Philadelphia.

At the Uptown we were on a bill with the Drifters, the Vibrations, and the Isley Brothers. Harold Melvin and the Blue Notes, when they were called just the Blue Notes, were there too. They did a big opening with the chorus line and then came on later and did a few tunes. This was still the era of the nice looking top hat and cane groups like the Blue Notes; the rough looking macho thing that we had hadn't come into style yet.

We weren't headlining—the Isley Brothers were—but we weren't opening anymore, so on opening night we sat in the wings and watched the first few acts. Fine. Then here came the Vibrations—Carl Fisher, James Johnson, David Govan, Richie Owens, and Don Bradley. We had never seen them before, and we couldn't believe it. We thought we were the only ones who jumped over each other and went into splits or cut flips and wound up in a split, but the Vibrations did it, too. They worked as hard as we did, and they were nice-looking, too.

We sat there wondering how we were going to follow this. When the Vibrations came off the stage, the people were hollering so loud for them that you couldn't hardly hear our name announced. As we went on I told the Flames to really work on our closing with "Please." We went out and did our show, and when we got to the end they brought out the red suitcase. I dropped to my knees, singing "Please," and they patted me on the back and put the coat over my shoulders. I got up and then fell to my knees again. We kept doing it, and the people became aroused. The curtain closed, then it opened back up, and we went out to take our bow. The people were on their feet, stomping and cheering and yelling for us. We came off saying, "Okay, we did pretty good; we got nothing to worry about." Then we saw the Isley Brothers coming from the back of the theater, swinging on ropes, like Tarzan, onto the stage. They hardly had to sing at all. They'd *already* killed 'em. Between the Vibrations and the Isley Brothers, we had some real competition. Now we were saying, "Aw, naw, we got nine more days of this." But we perfected our closing, and by the end of the run we put a pounding on both of them.

By then the disc jockey was saying he'd take "Try Me" to Dick Clark. I was very excited about it, until he charged me $1,000 to do it, the rat. I love that particular disc jockey to this day and I'd do anything in the world for him right now, but he was a rat to do that. I paid it, though.

Back in Macon we watched "Try Me" played on *American Bandstand.* We had heard it was going to be on, so we were all sitting around the Two Spot, Mr. Brantly's club, waiting for it.

They played it on the portion of the show where the kids rated the records. One little girl said she liked it because you could dance close to it, but she was the only one who said anything good about it. The rest low-rated it pretty bad. I think we got a thirty-something, a *low* thirty-something. Man, it destroyed us. We were going crazy, saying, "Naw, naw, this can't be true." I was thinking; "I paid that jock a thousand dollars for *this*?" Mr. Brantly, God bless his soul, cut us all off. "Look," he said, "this doesn't mean the record can't be a hit. It already *is* a hit. So y'all just go on about your business and *keep* it a hit."

I knew Mr. Brantly was right. Keep working. And that's what we did, playing dates all over the South. Some weren't even our dates. We were playing a place in Birmingham with the Primes—the group that later became the Temptations—when Mr. Bart called to say Hank Ballard had stayed too long recording in Cincinnati and couldn't make a date in Jackson, Mississippi, at the Stephenson Ballroom. Mr. Bart wanted us to replace them.

"But, listen," he said, "don't tell the audience who you are. Since you've never played there and neither has Hank, they won't know the difference."

"You want us to say we're Hank and them?"

"Don't say you are and don't say you're not, don't say anything. Just go on and do the gig."

I thought I was through pretending to be other singers, but we went over there to help out Mr. Bart. The Stephenson Ballroom was a classy place where all the nice looking groups with the hats and canes went. The audience wasn't ready for what we did; as a matter of fact, they weren't ready for Hank and them, either. All they'd ever seen was the Flamingos and Billy Ward and the Dominoes. We went out and threw the three Midnighters' tunes up front—"Work with Me, Annie," "Annie Had a Baby," and "Annie's Aunt Fanny." Then we jumped into our own thing. As soon as we did our baseball routine with "Good Good Lovin'," we killed 'em. They gave us a standing ovation. We'd already recorded "Good Good Lovin'" but it hadn't been released yet, so they still thought we were the Midnighters. I stepped up to the microphone and said, "This is our tune," and we went into "Try Me." They recognized *that*. We did our own stuff the rest of the evening, and naturally we closed with "Please." From that night on the Stephenson Ballroom was ours. Every time we turned around after that, we were back there.

Ever since the Uptown we'd worked on our closing routine with "Please." I'd fall to my knees and out would come the coat to go around my shoulders. At first, we used anybody's coat that was laying around. Might belong to one of the Flames or one of the fellas in the band. It worked fine until people started hiding their coats; cleaning bills were mounting up, and didn't nobody want their coat to be the one. So they started bringing me a towel, like for a boxer. That was effective, too. Then one night in Chattanooga on a bill with B. B. King and Bobby "Blue" Bland they brought me the towel, and after a little bit I threw it into the audience. They loved it, so we did it that way for a good while.

Later on in that tour, when we were in Atlanta, we sat around the hotel one day watching wrestling on television. Gorgeous George was on, and when he got through killing whoever he was killing, he started walking around the ring taking his bows. A handler followed him and threw a robe over his shoulders. Gorgeous shook it off, went to another side of the ring, and took another bow. The fella threw the robe over him again, and George shook it off and took another bow. Watching it, I said, "We got to get a robe." So we went out and got some store-bought robes. Later on we got capes that I designed and had tailor-made, but the whole thing really started coming together while watching Gorgeous George.

Willie John or somebody might have said we were using more tricks to get over, but they didn't understand that *everything* was developing at once—the stage show, the band, the dancing, the music. There were a lot of different aspects to what we were doing. I wanted people to appreciate them, so I decided to record the band on an instrumental and kind of popularize the mashed potatoes at the same time. Most entertainers today never really understand that show business means just that, show business.

I'd been doing the mashed potatoes for years but I'd never put a name to it. The dance had been around for years, kind of of in the public domain, but nobody ever did all the things with it that I did. My mashed potatoes is really a combination of a lot of dances: the applejack, the dolo, and the scallyhop. The scallyhop takes off from the Lindy hop, the dolo is kind of like a boxing routine, a slide, almost like the skate, and if you put it all together, you have the James Brown. Plus, I have a nerve control thing that I do that makes my whole body tremble, and that adds a little bit more to it than most people can do.

I knew that an instrumental built around the dance could be a hit, but Mr. Nathan didn't believe me. He refused to let me cut it. I didn't even argue with him this time. I took it to Henry Stone who had Dade Records in Miami. I knew him from my days at the Palms there, and we had talked from time to time about doing something together. Sometime late that year, 1959, I cut the band on "(Do the) Mashed Potatoes, Parts One and Two." I did the vocal part and then got a disc jockey, King Coleman, to dub his voice over mine so I wouldn't violate my contract with King (if you listen close you can hear my voice under his). We put it out under the name Nat Kendrick and the Swans, and I used the name Rozier for my writing credit. It was released in February 1960, made the R & B top ten, and caused a lot of other people to put out mashed potatoes records. I knew it was going to be a hit, and so did Henry. Mr. Nathan should have, too.

I didn't hold it against him, though. In November 1959 I cut "I'll Go Crazy" and "This Old Heart" in Cincinnati. The *Try Me* album was released, but it was all stuff I did from 1956 to 1958. We kept touring, which helped the records everywhere we went, and we went everywhere. At the end of the year we went into the Regal Theater in Chicago in the dead of winter. I think we were on a bill with Gladys Knight and the Pips and a few others, but what I remember best is that we liked to froze walking just the one block from our hotel to the theater every day.

On December 11 we went back into the Apollo for a week with the Drifters, who had "True Love" and "Dance with Me," and Little Willie John, who had "Let Them Talk" and "No Regrets." The Apollo couldn't figure out who to headline so they headlined all of us. I had done a lot of soul-searching and fact-finding about different ways to get to an audience, and we had gotten together and vowed that we would work harder than anybody else while we were on stage, no matter what. We still didn't have all the hit records Willie John and the Drifters had, but we were getting over better than either one of them. Consequently, this time at the Apollo was the one that really got us straight in New York.

While we were there I went to Brooklyn to see my mother again. From then on that's what I did whenever I went into the Apollo, so we could get to know each other. At first she was a stranger to me because she hadn't raised me, but I knew it wasn't her fault. The whole thing was her and my father's business, and I stayed out of their business. All I cared about was that she was my mother. I saw her, we talked and talked, and eventually we got back into a mother-and-son relationship. One thing I never did, though, was tell her what I'd been through with the house on Twiggs, prison, and parole. I wouldn't do it. I didn't want to cause her a lot of pain and grief. She's my mother.

18 A THOUSAND AND ONE NIGHTERS

I WORKED all the time now, as many as 350 nights a year, most of them one-night stands. I played every place—arenas, auditoriums, clubs, ball parks, armories, ballrooms, any place that had a stage or a place you could put one. Pretty soon I became known as the King of the One Nighters. I think I took the title from Hank Ballard. But the more famous name that came out of that time was given to me by Fats Gonder. Fats used to emcee the shows, and one night—I don't even remember where we were—he introduced me and ended up with: "And now, ladies and gentlemen, here he is, the *haaaaardest* working man in show business, Jaaaaaames Brown."

A lot of the places I worked during that period don't exist anymore. After the municipal buildings opened up to black performers, most of the black clubs disappeared. By the mid-sixties integration killed them off. Performers could go into a city auditorium and do one show in front of five or ten thousand people, instead of doing a whole bunch of shows every night for a week in front of a few hundred. The Palms in Jacksonville, one of the biggest clubs, held maybe two thousand people, but the Jacksonville auditorium held seven thousand. Before the clubs went under in Texas you could work fifty days in fifty different places, and it was the same thing in Georgia, South Carolina, Mississippi, and Florida. After integration took hold, those places just evaporated.

But before they did, I played them all, and when the auditoriums and armories opened up, I played all of them, too. When I played I gave good value for the dollar, presenting a complete program and staying on stage for hours at a time. When you're on stage, the people who paid money to get in are the boss, even if it cost them only a quarter. You're working for them.

I was on stage about eighty hours in an average month. Wore out a lot of shoes that way and lost a lot of weight, too. Every night I sweated off anywhere from seven to ten pounds. In those days I built the fluid back up by drinking beer after the show; later on I took a saline and glucose solution intravenously. Today, I drink Gatorade.

I started out on the road in Guy Wilson's beat-up station wagon in Toccoa, moved up to some brand-new station wagons with Mr. Brantly, to a Cadillac and a bus, to commercial airliners, and then to three different private jets. It doesn't matter how you travel it, it's still the same road. It doesn't get easier when you get bigger; it gets harder. And it will kill you if you let it. There are lots of ways it can kill you: accidents, shootings, drugs. If you don't have the stamina, you can even work yourself to death, like Jackie Wilson did. The road has killed a lot of good people: Jackie, Sam Cooke, Otis Redding, all those great entertainers.

But even if you live, you have to see to it that you last. I wanted to last. I'd been a shoeshine boy, a jailbird, and a janitor, and I had less than a seventh-grade education: I knew there weren't a lot of opportunities for somebody like that. That's reality. Reality is what drives me. When I go around the streets of Augusta today, the same streets I grew up on, it makes me return to the stage and work that much harder.

To last you have to think about more than the performance. I started carrying an entire show, working every night, learning everything I could about the business. When you travel with a whole show it costs a lot more to run. You've got to draw and you've got to make it pay for itself. One way you draw is to have a good show in the first place; we had a good one, and it was getting better all the time. You have to be smart, too. Mr. Bart and I came up with all kinds of ways to make the whole thing work. Most acts hooked up with a regular promoter who gave them a guaranteed amount of money for the date. Acts who traveled all the time liked that system because they knew in advance how much money they were going to make and whether they'd have enough money to pay their people and get to the next town. It was comfortable, but it was limited. I thought we should promote our own shows. You take a bigger risk, but if you're good *and* smart, you can make a lot more than a guarantee.

A lot of the promoters were in trouble financially. An entertainer can always tell what shape the economy's in by how the promoters are doing. Hard times don't affect attendance that much, but they affect promoters. I could tell from all the trouble promoters were having coming up with guarantees in 1958 that the country was in a recession. You're just traveling, not thinking about things like economics, but you can always tell.

Instead of working through a promoter we sometimes rented the venue ourselves, taking all the risks—and the profit. A lot of times, we co-promoted with local disc jockeys (I think we were the first in the R & B field to do that). The jocks had the placards put up and made sure the tickets were on sale at all the outlets. There was no Ticketron or Chargit then; independent people sold the tickets—drugstores, barbershops, and things. Someone had to make sure the tickets were distributed and that we received a correct count. Counterfeit tickets were a big problem then, too, and somebody had to stay on top of that.

We worked with disc jockeys because we knew they'd make sure the people heard about the show coming in, and it created good will with the jocks so they'd play our records before and after our arrival. I knew how little jocks got paid and co-promoting was a way to help them stay honest. See, the people who ran the radio stations created the whole payola thing by underpaying the jocks, knowing the jocks could get money from the record companies. They let the whole payola situation develop, but when the time came for somebody to take the fall, it was the jocks, not the owners. By co-promoting with jocks, I helped them make the kind of money they deserved—honestly.

After I got me a Cadillac to travel in, I started doing some of the advance work myself. The show traveled in the bus while Mr. Bart, Byrd, and I, and maybe Johnny Terry, raced on ahead in the car. I went to the next town as soon as I could and visited the radio stations and did interviews. I talked to program directors, telling them how well our records were doing. If they didn't believe me, I called Roy Emory, King's promotion manager, and got him to tell them how many orders we had for a particular record. Mr. Bart checked with the ticket outlets, and Byrd went to the hall and straightened out the band when it got there. Then I went over to the hall, checked out the sound, and rehearsed the group if I thought we needed it. It might look like riding in the car made things easier for me, but really it made it harder because it allowed me to do all that extra work.

On the way to the next town, Mr. Bart and I discussed how the gig went, how we could make it better, and how we ought to promote it the next time. The funny thing was that he wasn't even managing me then. Officially, he was my booking agent, but we were becoming more like partners even then in 1959 and 1960. He had other acts at Universal, but he spent all his time out there with me, and we developed a special relationship. He called me Jimmy—just about the only person who ever did—and I called him Pop. He was like a father to me; we had mutual respect and we had love.

One time he said to me, "Jimmy, you're going to outlast them all—Jackie, Clyde McPhatter, Little Willie John—all of them."

"What you talking about, Pop?" I said.

"You're going to last in this business longer than anybody else," he said.

"Why you say that, Pop?"

"Because you're intelligent."

I couldn't understand that then. Still can't. But I *was* smart enough to know that a big group had to have discipline to succeed, like Billy Ward had with the Dominoes.

Billy had a rule that everybody had to be inside the theater forty-five minutes before they were supposed to hit. That way, if anything was wrong, you had time to take care of it. Billy lined up his group and inspected the uniforms and shoes. He carried a long tablet, and if a uniform was wrinkled or shoes weren't shined, he recorded a fine by the person's name. I watched him do this backstage once when Jackie Wilson, the lead singer then, came in about four or five minutes late. Billy chewed him out right there, saying, "This is the second time you've done this. You do it again, and the substitute will take your place." Billy always traveled with an extra person who could go on as a substitute. Jackie said, "I'm sorry. It won't happen again," and then went out and did a fantastic show.

With the original Flames I didn't worry about that stuff too much because we had all come up together and everything went smooth naturally. But when my show got bigger and I was hiring people, I saw that we had to have discipline. I put in a system of fines—so much for a dirty uniform, for unshined shoes, for being late. If somebody showed up drunk, he sat out and might get fired. Some of the cats resented the fines, but I think it gave me the tightest band in show business. I abided by the rules, too. I fined myself. When I fined somebody else, I didn't keep the money but put it in a pot to pay for parties later. I wouldn't take anybody's money.

When we had a chance and were in the right city, we recorded. When we were traveling out west, we recorded in Hollywood; up North, we recorded in New York; in the South and Midwest we went to the King studios in Cincinnati; and we recorded in Miami, too. A session might last thirty or forty minutes, or it might last twelve hours, however long it took. Usually it didn't take too long, though, because by the time I went in the studio I knew what I wanted. The material had already been worked over every kind of way on stage and in rehearsal. Most times we came out of a recording session with at least three masters; then King had a stockpile of material to draw on for releases.

Out on the road I probably had as much fun as most and more fun than the poor, but I never abused it. Besides, I still lived with Dessie back in Macon. Later on I tended to go with whoever was my lead female singer on the show at the time. So, on the road, she'd be with me.

I smoked like the rest of 'em, but I didn't get any further than that because I think cigarettes are worse than marijuana. I didn't use hard drugs; I never wanted to get so deep into something that it got me. I know some of the fellas from the old school who smoked marijuana all their lives, but they didn't get any further than that. Those are the people who are still around.

At one time I was into the whiskey drinking thing. Put seven shots of whiskey and one shot of wine in a glass—it was called a zombie. Boy, drink one of them and you start flipping over, and you can't imagine what you had or hadn't done. That's another kind of trip.

Every once in a while we had trouble traveling in the South, but not too much. I always conducted myself like a gentleman, and I think people respected that. We didn't go looking for trouble, either. But sometimes we were on a tour with white acts like the Dovells or Jay and the Americans, and at certain places where we stopped to eat we had to send them in to get the food. Once in Jackson, Mississippi, those two groups and the Hollywood Argyles, the ones who did "Alley Oop," checked into a hotel and got our rooms, too. Then here we come, all these black folks. The desk clerk gave a phony smile and said he'd made a mistake; he didn't have as many rooms as he thought, and we couldn't stay there. The other groups standing there heard this, so one of the boys in Jay and the Americans came over to the desk and told the clerk, "Well, I think I made a mistake, too. My group is checking out." One of the Dovells came right behind him. "We made the same mistake. My group's checking out." One of the Argyles came over and said, "Well, I guess that makes it unanimous. Check us out, too." The desk clerk liked to had a fit. He called the manager over, and they spoke together a long while. Then the manager sent the clerk away, came over, and checked us all in himself like we'd just walked in the door.

More often I had trouble with transportation or with promoters. Next to his instruments, the most important thing to an entertainer is his transportation. Maybe more important because he can always borrow or rent equipment for the gig, but first he has to get there. The original Flames had all kinds of trouble when we were using Guy Wilson's raggedy station wagon. We were late to a gig at a club in Birmingham because the car was acting up. When we finally got there, we pulled in front instead of going around to the back like we usually did, grabbed our stuff, and went on in. The people were already seated, waiting for us, so we went right to the stage and killed 'em—one of the best shows the original Flames ever did. When we were done we went out to the station wagon, but it wouldn't crank. We started pushing it, but now the people were coming out. We didn't want them to see us pushing our car, so we put our shoulders to the back of it and ducked our heads down by the side, hiding. We got the thing rolling, and Byrd jumped in so wouldn't nobody see him. I jumped in, too. I wasn't going to let 'em see me, either. Some of the other fellas hopped in. Now the station wagon was picking up speed. Cats were diving in through the back window. We were rolling down a hill, fixing to pop the clutch and kick the motor over. We thought we'd got away clean, but when we peeped over the back of the seat we saw Sylvester and Nash running after us in their uniforms with their bags. They were holding their arms straight down at their sides, trying to run real dignified. The people were standing there cheering 'em on. When they caught up to us and jumped in, the people applauded.

See, you're an entertainer, trying to be a star, and you think you have to keep up appearances. During the "Try Me" period, when I got a brand-new 1959 red Cadillac, we kept the windows rolled up to pretend we had air conditioning, no matter how hot it was. We had the name of the group painted on the car and on the trailer that we pulled behind it, and we wanted people to think we had that cool air. If we stopped in traffic, the windows were zipped up tight. We even did it out west, crossing the desert. If a car came up behind to pass us, up went the windows. Luckily, there wasn't much traffic on those western highways.

When we pulled in for gas or something, we had the windows shut. One time we stopped at a gas station somewhere in the desert; I don't remember where it was, but it felt like Death Valley. We sat there, and the service station attendant moved real slow so we started to sweat. This little old white lady in her car at the next pump watched us. We smiled and sweated, sweated and smiled. Now it was really getting hot. The service station man disappeared, going after our change—we just did crack the window to pay him—and we were boiling. But we weren't going to lower the windows. When she couldn't stand it anymore, the little old lady jumped out of her car, jerked open one of our doors, and yelled, "Get out quick before all you niggers die in there."

On that same trip, on a long flat stretch of highway, cruising along, we all felt kind of drowsy in the heat. The car was so crowded that sometimes Bobby Bennett rode in the equipment trailer, which had vents in it and wasn't any hotter than the car, and it gave everybody else more room. I was driving, just daydreaming, when I thought I saw something pass us. It was beginning to get dark so I couldn't really see good, but I thought it was kind of a strange-looking vehicle and it was passing us on the desert, not on the road. I said to Byrd, who was dozing, "Byrd, it's a funny looking kind of something going by out there."

He glanced out real casual, yawning. "Look kind of like our trailer, don't it?" he said.

"Sure do," I said.

"Matter of fact, it look *exactly* like our trailer."

We jerked around in the seat and looked behind us. Nothing but empty highway stretched out back there. Byrd looked back at the trailer bumping over the desert with Bobby Bennett in it. "I *thought* the car was running awful smooth all of a sudden," he said. The trailer mowed down a few cactus before it finally stopped. We had to pull Bobby Bennett out from under a pile of drums, but he was all right. He didn't want to ride in the trailer again, though.

That California trip was the first time we ever ran into Ike and Tina Turner, too. We were playing a place called the Five Four Ballroom in Los Angeles when they walked in to catch our show. Ike was already well known by then, and Tina was just getting out there good. They watched us a while, and then when I was singing "Good Good Lovin'," Tina jumped up on stage and joined in, singing it like she'd been doing it all her life. The Flames backed off and let the two of us go to work. She stayed right with me. I did a spin, she did a spin. I did a slide, she did a slide. We were bringing down the house and I wanted it to end with a bang, so I spun around, backed up, mashed potatoes over to the piano, jumped on top of it while she was at the microphone singing, and then flew off the piano and landed in a split on the stage. I thought that ought to just about do it. But she wasn't finished. She spun around, backed up, mashed potatoes over to the piano, jumped up on it, and then *she* jumped off onto the stage and landed in a split. We really upset the place that night. Ike came up and sat in on a song, and then Tina and I did "Please"; and she got down on her knees and everything. That lady knew what to do on a stage from the first.

The next day Tina brought the newspaper by our motel to show us the big write-up we'd gotten. We used to stay at a place called the Nighty Night Motel, and when we weren't making too much money the manager let us stay for free. Like a lot of people, he saw something in us and wanted to help, and he was fascinated by the fact that the maids didn't have to do any cleaning in our rooms. We emptied the trash, swept, whatever.

I think that write-up was probably the first we'd ever seen about us. It said we were "the picture of entertainment," and when it got to Tina it said, "Don't tell me what a woman can't do." We talked to Ike and Tina about doing a tour together. They were getting ready to spend a lot of time in the studio, so they couldn't do it right away, but we all agreed we'd like to someday. We never did get it together. On the road after that, it always seemed like they were right behind us or right in front of us.

Seemed like a lot of things were always happening to us in California. I was playing the El Monte Legion Hall for Alan Freed in Compton once when the bus was broken into. A lot of equipment was taken and some of the fellas' uniforms. You can replace instruments on short notice, but not uniforms. Some red suits and some blue ones were taken, so I had the cats go on in whatever suit they had. Afterwards, people told us how fantastic the mixed colors looked, so we kept it in the show.

At another gig I got to the club a little late, and the band was already on stage doing their set. They usually opened with "Do the Mashed Potatoes," and that's what they were playing when I showed up. I couldn't understand it because I knew they'd been on for a good while already, but later I found out they'd played it over and over because of a cat sitting at the front and center table. Each time they finished playing it, he requested it again and flashed a pistol at Nat Kendrick. Couldn't nobody see the gun but the fellas on the stage. After they'd played it five or six times, the cat stood up and said: "I sure do like that tune." Then he left.

Promoters can cause you problems on the road, too. Most times, you've never seen 'em in your life until you show up for the gig, so you don't have any idea whether they're honest. I was playing a club in North Carolina one time—I was up on stage, doing my show—when I saw the promoter leave the door with the cash box, so there was nobody on the door, and it looked to me like a bunch of people were coming in free. I spun around and mashed potatoes over to Byrd, and he did a slide over toward me; we talked it over while we were dancing.

"That man's done left," I said.

"Who are all these people coming in?" Byrd said.

We danced and talked about it some more—you can do a lot of talking that way—and I said, "Let's stop." So we stopped right in the middle of the song. I went to the mike and said, "Ladies and gentlemen, we want to finish our show, but I don't see the promoter on the door. I don't even see a doorman over yonder, and all these people are coming in. We have to get this straightened out before we go on."

By now the people had been drinking a long time and were having fun, and they didn't want to hear nothing about no money or stopping no music. Some of 'em started toward the stage. I gave the band a downbeat and the music started. I mashed potatoes back over to Byrd for more conversation. "They look like they're getting ugly," he said.

I looked over at the door, at the stream of people coming in. Finally I said, "Man, I'm not going for this," and I stopped the music again. The people started booing then. Some started throwing bottles, glasses, and stuff like that. Windows started busting out. Before long it was a complete riot. We fought them off the bandstand and tried to protect ourselves. During this time I had a bodyguard called Baby James. He saw what was fixing to happen and he ran out to the bus and got a .22 rifle we had fixed so it would shoot like a machine gun (nineteen rounds with one squeeze of the trigger). He came running back in and shot a burst, *brrrrrrppppp*, right across the ceiling. The people spread out then, and he was able to get to us. He gave me a pistol while the other fellas grabbed as much of our stuff as they could. We went charging out of there; me in the lead with the pistol shooting, *pow, pow, pow*, into the ceiling, and Baby James bringing up the rear with the rifle, *brrrrpppp*. Everybody ran out and jumped on the bus, and it started to pull out. But the cats carrying the amplifiers couldn't keep up, so we slowed down for them to jump on. The people came pouring out of the club and piled into trucks and cars and started after the bus. Now they had *their* guns and were shooting at us. Somebody yelled, "Get on the floor. Everybody lay down." We hit the floor and rode all the way out of town that way, window glass busting over our heads. We never did get our money. Never did go back to that town, either.

A similar incident happened in Kentucky during the same period—the promoter walked off the door with the money. But this particular club had glass all around the back and I could see him leaving, so I stopped the band like I'd done in North Carolina. This time I said to the fellas, "Everybody, put something in your hand." They all grabbed mike stands, drum stands, anything they could hit somebody with. A bunch of us walked off the bandstand and cornered the man outside while Fats explained from the stage about the previous incident in North Carolina. This time the audience cheered. They didn't do anything to us because they knew the promoter was a crook. He was always promoting shows with big names and then switching the bill to unknowns at the last minute and refusing to give refunds.

But somebody had called the police. Before they got there, Baby James had gotten me to the airport and on the plane for Cincinnati with our money. I had started flying on ahead of the rest by then so I could do advance work and be rested for the show. I hadn't wanted to do it at first, but Byrd and them insisted. He said that no matter what else happened, if I was rested then we knew we had a good show.

It turned out that one of the policemen was related to the promoter, and the others knew him well. He told them the cats were trying to rob him. That was it. They took the band, the Flames, and everybody to jail and charged 'em with armed robbery. On top of that, the police found a five-dollar bag of reefer on one of the cats in the band. Back then, a five-dollar bag wasn't some little sandwich wrapper full, it was a *bag*. Now the fellas were really in trouble.

I was up in Cincinnati trying to get them out. They finally got out by giving up all the watches, rings, and money they had on them. But they wouldn't let out the cat who had the reefer. To get him out I had to send back to the promoter the money we'd made on the gig. We found out later that the promoter also got the fellas' watches, rings, and money.

No matter what happened on the road, I was always developing the show, picking up new ideas, new sounds. There was one sound, though, I couldn't hear anywhere but in my head. I didn't have a name for it, but I knew it was different. See, musicians don't think about categories and things like that. They don't say, I think I'll invent bebop today or think up rock 'n' roll tomorrow. They just hear different sounds and follow them wherever they lead. Let somebody else give it a name. Like they'd named the stuff we'd been doing rhythm and blues. It would take the world a long time to catch up to what we were fixing to do, but when they did, they gave it a name, too: soul.

19 APOLLO THREE, FOUR, FIVE . . .

YOU CAN HEAR the thing starting to change on the records I put out during the beginning of 1960. I was changing before that, but that's when you can *hear* it. "I'll Go Crazy" came out in January; "Think" and "You've Got the Power" were released in May. "I'll Go Crazy" is a blues, but it's a different kind of blues, up-tempo, a kind of jazz blues. "Think" is a combination of gospel and jazz—a rhythm hold is what we used to call it. Soul really started right there, or at least my kind did. See when people talk about soul music they talk only about gospel and R & B coming together. That's accurate about a lot of soul, but if you're going to talk about mine, you have to remember the jazz in it. That's what made my music so different and allowed it to change and grow after soul was finished.

Recording "Think" was the strangest thing because the Five Royales were good friends of mine. Lowman Pauling, the leader of the group, wrote the song, and they had a pretty good R & B hit with it in 1957. King Records wanted me to cut it in 1960 at the same session I did "You've Got the Power," but I didn't want to. I knew that if I did, it would hurt the Five Royales. They were good, but they were still doing straight R & B while I was reaching for a different sound.

I held off until they cut "Please Please Please," then I decided it would be all right to cut "Think." The record turned out to be my third million seller and it did even better than "I'll Go Crazy." Unfortunately, "Please" didn't do anything for the Five Royales. It's a funny thing about that song. Nobody else could ever do anything with it. Tina Turner cut it and Barbara Lewis cut it, but it was like a death song for them—when they sang it, they sang their own epitaph.

"You've Got the Power" was a duet with Bea Ford, Joe Tex's ex-wife. I met her not long after they broke up, and we started dating, but I didn't know she'd been married to Joe, and she didn't tell me. That was the beginning of a lot of misunderstandings between Joe and me. He died thinking I'd messed with his woman. Bea stayed with the show for most of 1960, but that was the only time we recorded together.

Really, 1960 was the year my hard work started paying off. I played all those one-nighters around the country, and worked more and more on the stage show, and recorded all the time. In August "This Old Heart" and "Wonder When You're Coming Home" came out. In the fall, while we were playing gigs in California, we went into United Recording Studios in Hollywood and cut "I Don't Mind," "Baby, You're Right," "Come Over Here," "I Do Just What I Want," "Tell Me What You're Gonna Do," and an instrumental of "Hold It." In November "Please" and "Why Do You Do Me" were re-released, and "The Bells," and "I Do Just What I Want" came out.

"The Bells," which the Dominoes did back when Clyde McPhatter was still with them, was my first release on the King label. Everything else for Mr. Nathan had been on Federal. Being on King meant you got more support from the company. Mr. Nathan finally realized I was too strong for Federal, and he had to put me on King.

But the more the music changed, the less some of Mr. Nathan's people understood it. As soon as the band started playing for the first take when we were cutting "I Don't Mind," Gene Redd and I got into it about the arrangement. It opens with a 13, goes down to a C9, then goes to a G7 and to the A7. He couldn't understand that. He stopped us and said, "That's a wrong note."

"If you could hear it," I said, "you'd know it was right. I can hear it, and I'm telling you it's right. And that's the way we're going to record it, or we're not going to record it at all."

He backed off, and we went on and did it like we'd been doing it on the road for months, except for the mistake Les Buie made on guitar that sounded so good I made him leave it in.

By the time I went back into the Apollo in December, all the hard work had earned me the headliner's spot. It wasn't because of a particular record but because of hard work. Hard work got me there, and I knew hard work would keep me there and maybe take me beyond it.

On that particular bill we also had Maurice Williams and

the Zodiacs, who had "Stay"; the Olympics, who had "Western Movies"; Wini Brown; Larry Williams; Sam "The Man" Taylor, the sax man who did a lot of session work on those good Atlantic records; and Pigmeat Markham, the comedian who was best known for his "here come de judge" routine.

For my first time headlining at the Apollo I wanted to do a spectacular finale for each show. I'd been jumping off the piano into a split for a while, but this time I had them move the piano nearer the edge of the stage. Finale came and I got up on the piano and jumped. Everybody thought I was jumping onto the stage. But I cleared the stage and went on and plunged down to the main floor way below the stage. I hit it clean and came up out of it fine, but I didn't make it back to the stage like I'd planned. As soon as I came out of the split, the people were on me, tearing me apart. The Flames had to come down to help get me out of there.

After the first show, Pigmeat came to my dressing room and told me how much he liked the jumping off the piano. Then he came up with the idea that for the midnight show I should swing out over the crowd on a wire like Peter Pan—a thin wire so that the audience wouldn't see it. Make it look like I was flying. I said no, that really would be using tricks to get over.

Pig was one of the greatest entertainers to hit the stage. He had a lot more material than the judge routine, but that's the one everybody saw him do later on Ed Sullivan. Like a lot of comedians, Pig was a serious man offstage; it was like night and day. He did all that wild vaudeville stuff, and when he came off he was very self-possessed. I think he must have been educated, too, because he was very well-spoken. I was honored to have him on my show because as a kid I had seen him in movie shorts and always admired him.

The next week I met Louis Jordan, another idol I had seen in the movies. He was following us into the Apollo, so I stayed over for a day to see him. It was the first time I'd ever watched him live. He was a very sick man, but he still put on a great show. Afterwards, I got a chance to talk with him for a few minutes and told him what he'd meant to me as a performer. Told him that, beginning when I was a kid, I'd probably sung "Caldonia" almost as many times as he had. He was a good man, and he still hasn't gotten his due.

Less than three months later I was back at the Apollo again.

My father, with only a second-grade education, was the hardest working man I ever knew. I think I got most of my drive from him. During World War II, they took him—at age thirty-two—off the streets of Augusta and put him in the Navy, where he eventually became a second-class seaman. *(Courtesy James Brown)*

The original Flames—before we started calling ourselves "Famous"—came out of Toccoa, Georgia. *Left to right:* Sylvester Keels, Nash Knox, and Fred Pulliam are standing at the mike, I'm playing drums, Nafloyd Scott is playing guitar, Bobby Byrd is at the piano, and Roy Scott is on the other guitar. *(Michael Ochs Archives)*

en Bart started as my
ooking agent and wound up
my manager and business
artner. I called him "Pop."
ogether, we created James
rown. *(Charles Stewart)*

In the late fifties and early sixties, I
played as many as 350 one-nighters a
year—clubs, ballparks, armories,
dances—anyplace there was a stage.
That's how I earned the titled "King of
the One-Nighters" and "The Hardest
Working Man in Show Business."
(Michael Ochs Archives)

Little Willie John (*left*), a great singer, and Hal Neely (*right*), a pioneer in the record business, made up part of the family at King Records in Cincinnati. After Willie went to prison for stabbing a man, I tried to help get him paroled, but he eventually died behind bars. (*Courtesy Hal Neely*)

The first time I closed my show at the Apollo carrying a suitcase like I was headed for the next town, Little Willie John said I was using tricks to get over. (*Charles Stewart*)

The road can kill you. Luckily, nobody in the show was seriously hurt when my bus went out of control on an icy road near Hagerstown, Maryland, in the early sixties. (*Teddy Washington*)

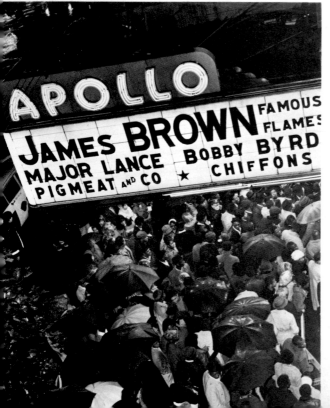

After the *Live at the Apollo* album really hit, people lined up for blocks whenever I played the theater. The first time it happened, during a week in November of 1963 when it was raining and snowing, I couldn't hardly believe it. (*Kwame Brathwaite*)

As the hit records started to come, I developed the James Brown Revue—a complete show with several musical acts, comedians, solo spots for some of the Flames, then my set. After the original Flames broke up in 1957, I had several sets of Famous Flames. Johnny Terry *(left)*, Bobby Byrd *(middle)*, and Bobby Bennett *(right)* are the three here. The band—not to be confused with the Flames—was called the James Brown Orchestra. *(Frank Driggs Collection)*

Backstage at the Apollo in 1964 with my emcee, Danny Ray. He's still with me today. *(Don Paulsen/ Michael Ochs Archives)*

Pop and I were always discussing ways to improve the show and new ways to promote it. Sometimes we argued, like all artists and managers, but he was like a father to me. One of the few times in my life I cried was when he died. *(Ebony)*

I developed my cape routine after watching the wrestler Gorgeous George on television. First, I used some store-bought robes; later, I had capes custom-made. The exhaustion I felt was no routine—I usually lost eight or nine pounds a show. *(Michael Ochs Archives)*

This 1965 show was the first integrated concert at the Memphis Municipal Auditorium. During the early sixties, I integrated a lot of venues like that. A lot of times the audiences, when they got to dancing, integrated themselves. *(Ebony)*

Roy Wilkins opened my eyes to a lot of things going on in the movement. I tried to help a little by buying a lifetime membership in the NAACP, along with Ben Bart *(left)* and his son Jack, on stage at the Apollo. *(Courtesy Jack Bart)*

I don't think the audience had ever seen a man move as fast as I did on *The T.A.M.I. Show.* Me and the Flames made it so hot out there it was hard for the Rolling Stones to follow us. *(Frank Driggs Collection)*

Vice President Hubert Humphrey was my first politician. We first met in 1966, when I started my "Don't Be a Drop-Out" campaign; in 1968, I endorsed him for president. *(Michael Ochs Archives)*

In the meantime, I recorded "Lost Someone," "Dancin' Little Thing," "You Don't Have to Go," "Night Train," and "Shout and Shimmy." All of those tunes were recorded on one day, February 9, 1961, in the King studios. With "Lost Someone" I was trying to get a pop hit; I based it on the chord changes of Conway Twitty's "It's Only Make Believe," which was popular at the time. The next day I recorded five more tunes at King. We really had a groove going, and I didn't want to stop. When we were ready to cut "Night Train," Nat Kendrick, the drummer, said he had to go to the bathroom.

I said, "Naw, I got the feel and I want to cut now."

"But, man, I got to *go*," he said.

"All right," I said, "you go on, and I'll play drums." He stepped out, and I cut it with me playing drums and singing and that's the version that became a hit.

It didn't become a hit right away because we had so many tunes in the can that some of them wouldn't be released for a year or more. "Night Train" didn't come out for thirteen months. Consequently, a lot of times I'd find myself with a big hit a year or two after I cut it and several years after I wrote it and first put it in the show. It didn't make any difference; no matter when they came out the records were still ahead of their time. Matter of fact, I also released "Bewildered" during this time, the tune I had cut on the "Try Me" session and hid from Mr. Nathan for a long time.

The engagement at the Apollo was in place of Jackie Wilson. A lady fan had shot Jackie in a hotel room in New York; he was hurt pretty bad and had to stay in Roosevelt Hospital for a while. When it looked like he wouldn't recover as fast as they thought he would, Mr. Schiffman booked us in there. By this time Jackie had left the Dominoes and was doing well as a single. He had "To Be Loved," which Berry Gordy wrote, "Lonely Teardrops," "That's Why," and "I'll Be Satisfied." He had a pretty good stage show, too, but I don't know why anybody would say he influenced me. He didn't influence me. Jackie tried to copy from me. I got nothing from him; he had nothing for me to get from him. He was singing pop stuff, and I didn't want to do that.

I used to come by and see Jackie when he was working, but it caused too much tension. See, I had caught up with Jackie real quick. And he knew that. I knew more about music than he did, I had more of a gospel background than he did, and I wrote all my own material. It intimidated him when I came around. He got shaky and couldn't perform.

What got Jackie through was his complexion. During that time, if you were light-complexioned, you had it. I was the one who made the dark-complexioned people popular. It's like Ethel Waters and Lena Horne. Ethel Waters was more popular with black people than Lena Horne, but Ethel was dark skinned and dark-skinned people couldn't make it. Eventually dark-skinned people did make it, but it took a long time for the change to come about. It started happening with Louis Armstrong, and Nat King Cole probably did more for the dark-skinned man than anybody of his era. After I came out in 1968 with "Say It Loud, I'm Black and I'm Proud," it was all over. The dark-skinned man had all of a sudden become cosmopolitan.

But I loved Jackie. He was a nice person. I liked him ever since I saw him singing with the Dominoes. The best one to come out of that group, though, was Clyde McPhatter, not Jackie, but Clyde was too dark.

Just before we went into the Apollo this time, we'd gotten five specially tailored new uniforms I designed for me and the Flames. They cost $500 apiece, which was a lot of money for stage uniforms. When a newspaper columnist found out I had insured the suits for $2,500 for the week-long engagement, he wrote that I must not trust my Harlem fans. I guess he was saying that I thought they'd steal the suits, but he didn't realize that when I jumped off the stage and got down in the audience, they'd tear at my clothes, like audiences have done to a lot of entertainers. He was trying to make the whole thing into an insult because he didn't understand the kind of love audiences can have for entertainers.

By this time Bea Ford and I had broken up, and she'd left the show. She was replaced by Sugar Pie De Santo, who had been part of a duo called Sugar Pie and Pee Wee. Etta James was on that Apollo bill, too. Etta had been big in the mid-fifties, then had quit recording for about five years because of some personal problems. But she'd come back big with tunes like "All I Could Do Was Cry," "My Dearest Darling," "At Last," and "Trust in Me." She was always a dynamic performer, and a beautiful woman, too. A lot of times, though, her personal problems got in the way of her performing. Promoters and club owners always told me how much trouble they had with her; they couldn't count on her to be in shape to go on. They couldn't handle Etta. Nobody could talk to her but me—she believed in James Brown. On the first show of the week she wasn't able to get through but one number. I took her to my dressing room and talked to her for a long time about what she was doing to the show and what she was doing to herself. For the rest of the week she didn't have any problem.

When we weren't playing the theaters, we were doing the one-nighters, traveling all the time. You see a lot of the country that way; you see it but you don't see it. You often don't know what's really going on in a particular city. In May 1961 we were doing a lot of southern gigs that it was easier for me to drive to than fly to. One day I stopped with Byrd, Bobby Bennett, and one or two others to eat at the Trailways bus station in Birmingham. Black entertainers traveling around the South frequently ate at bus stations. Their cafeterias were segregated, so you knew where you stood—you knew you could get something to eat without any hassle.

We walked into the "colored" side, sat down, and started eating. Pretty soon we heard hollering and cursing coming from the white side. We stood up and looked over the little partition separating the two sides to see what was going on. All these black people were standing around the door waiting to get a seat on the "white only" side. Most of 'em looked like they might be college kids, and there were a few whites with them. Byrd and I recognized one white boy who had been president of a fraternity the original Flames had played for. One of the white men sitting at the lunch counter got up and left in a hurry. You could see he didn't want any part of whatever was going to happen. As soon as he got up, a black kid went over and sat down. The white man next to him said, "What're you doing sitting here, nigger? You can't sit by me. What do you think you're doing?" And then *bap*, the white man knocked him off the stool. The minute he was knocked off, another came over and sat down. Then all hell broke loose. People started beating up the kids, throwing things, tearing up the place.

We took off for the car. Outside, there were all these people who had come down on the bus. Turned out they were the Freedom Riders. The college kids inside had come out to help them integrate the diner. We didn't know what a Freedom Rider was; all we knew was that there was a bunch of bleeding and beat-up people staggering around, trying to get back on the bus, and a whole bunch of white folks was coming after 'em with clubs.

We jumped in the car and pulled out onto the street. The bus pulled out right behind us, getting right on our tail, honking and trying to get around us. We moved over and let it go by, then we looked around behind and and saw *why* it wanted to get around us so bad: Chasing the bus were trucks and cars full of white folks waving axe handles and baseball bats. Now we were between them and the bus, and we knew they weren't going to care *which* side of the cafeteria we were sitting on. Now we were right on the bus's tail and trying to get around it. The trucks were on our tail trying to go *through* us. Soon as we had a chance we turned off and got away, and kept on going until we were sure none of the trucks had turned off after us. We found out later that they caught the bus, burned it, and beat up the people real bad.

It's hard to believe, but we didn't encounter much racial trouble back then, except when we were out on the road with white groups. Then we ran into discrimination at hotels and places to eat, but because we were in show business, I think people mostly just left us alone.

As soon as we finished playing all over the South, we were up North again and into the theaters. In the last week of September we were headlining at the Apollo again on a bill with Ben E. King, the Spinners, Lee Dorsey, and Pigmeat. Ben E. King left the Drifters the year before and already had hits with "Spanish Harlem" and "Stand by Me." The Spinners was a new group, put together by Harvey Fuqua, the one who had the Moonglows; Lee Dorsey had a song called "Ya-Ya" that was taking off for him; and Pigmeat did his thing. Sugar Pie De Santo was still doing her spot as part of my show, but she was about to leave. She was under contract to another record company, and I couldn't cut her on anything with me, so it was best for both of us for her to go on her own.

During this round of the theaters we were on a bill with the Chantels at the Uptown in Philadelphia. One of the young ladies singing with that group, Yvonne Fair, impressed me by how hard she worked. I could see she was conscientious, always on time, always ready to go on no matter what happened. I really dug that because the bigger the revue got, the more problems there were. A lot of people think that what's hard is when you're first starting out and playing all the little juke joints and everything, but it's not so. It's a lot harder when you have a big organization to run. Somebody who's reliable is a big asset in that situation, so I asked Yvonne to join my show. She finished up her work with the Chantels and joined the revue about two weeks later in Phoenix. I also added the Hortense Allen Dancers to the show, and they joined us in Phoenix, too; later on I renamed them the Brownies.

While we were in Philadelphia that time, the Flames and I appeared on *American Bandstand* for the first time. I was glad to make *American Bandstand;* it was going to be my first time on national television, and I was nervous. Dick Clark did everything he could to make us comfortable. He said, "Now that you've gotten used to playing big places, does it bother you to have people standing close to you while you perform?"

"Nosir," I said. "After all the small clubs I played, it makes me nervous when they're *not* crowded in on me."

We lip-synced "I Don't Mind" and "Baby, You're Right" with no band, and they had a few couples dancing close while we did it. The lip-syncing was easy, we'd done the songs so often, but I was still nervous inside, saying to myself, "Lord, let us be a hit." We were still worried when we got through because some of the fellas had gotten behind the lyrics and some had gotten ahead, and we were afraid it would look bad. Then we saw the tape. All the little hand gestures the Flames did went across their faces, so it was all right.

We talked to Dick. He was a good man, always has been. A real gentleman. He was concerned about the kids who danced on the show going straight home afterward. He said sometimes the parents called, and he felt responsible. That's the kind of man he is.

We introduced ourselves to the little girl who had given "Try Me" a high number when everybody else low-rated it. We gave her tickets to the show we were doing that night in Philadelphia, and we took her, her mother, and her little brother to dinner.

In January 1962, after the western swing, I cut Yvonne at Dukoff Studios in Miami on a song called "I Found You." It's practically the same song I had the hit on in 1965 called "I Got You (I Feel Good)." When I cut it myself, I just changed the lyric slightly. She did a good job on the song, right down to the holler.

In the spring the revue played all around California again. In Los Angeles we were at the Shriners Auditorium on a bill with Aretha Franklin, Tito Puente, Chico Hamilton, and several others. I met Aretha for the first time. She had a real strong gospel background—her father was the Reverend C. L. Franklin—and she could really sing from the first. At that time she had hit with "Rock a Bye Your Baby to a Dixie Melody." We became close after that show. What I liked about her right away was how smart she was; you could tell just talking to her once. I guess you could say that she was my girlfriend for a while, but it was hard for us to get together because we were both working all the time. We managed to see each other only about three or four times over the next year or so.

The same show, with all the other acts, went over to Long Beach, where it was picketed by the Muslims. Whenever they felt there were enough good black acts to fill out a show that had white acts, they picketed. I think they objected to the Latin acts on this particular show. I knew about the Muslims from back when I was growing up around them in Augusta, so I didn't let it bother me. I just ignored it and went on about my business. Whenever we were around the L. A. area we always counted on the Five Four Ballroom for a booking, but the Muslim thing was really getting heavy. They had a shootout with the police in front of their mosque on South Broadway near the Five Four. One Muslim was killed, and several Muslims and police were wounded. The city closed down the Five Four for a while, so we lost the gig.

We worked our way back east and wound up the tour at the Apollo the last week in May. The Olatunji Troupe, with singers, dancers, and drummers, was on the show. Yvonne did her solo spot. The Sensations, the guitarist Curley Mays, and Pigmeat with Edna May Harris, and Chuck Thompson were the rest of the bill.

The show went real good—"Night Train" was finally out and was a big hit, and the audience was better than ever—but I wasn't satisfied. Even with all the shows we gave every day for a solid week there, only a limited number of people could get in. People who couldn't get to one of my shows, especially an Apollo show, missed that special thing that always happened live. I guess some of the people who did get into the shows missed that special thing when they listened to the records. I knew there was a lot more to what I did than could be recorded in a studio anyway. By the time we wound up the week there, I knew I wanted to do a live album so that people could at least *hear* what kind of a show I had. I started hinting about the idea to a few people, to get them ready for it. Except for Byrd, everybody told me I was crazy. That's when I knew I had something.

20 LIVE

MR. NATHAN was dead set against a live album. "You mean you want to record your stage show live?" he said.

"That's right," I said.

"James, you can't keep on recording the same songs over and over again. Nobody's going to buy that."

"But Mr. Nathan, they sound different when I sing 'em live. You ought to hear the way the audience hollers."

"I'm not going to spend money on something where a lot of people are going to be screaming. Who wants a lot of noise over the songs?"

"But it'll be like you're right there at the show."

"What if somebody yells something out of the way?"

"If you can't bleep it out, then just leave it in."

"Then it couldn't even be played on the radio."

"But Mr. Nathan, it's going to be good."

"No, James, we're not doing it."

That was it. That man didn't want to hear any more about it. He'd been in business a long time, he'd made plenty of money, and he didn't see why he should do anything but the conventional thing. See, there just weren't many live albums in R & B or popular music then. It was a new thing, and he didn't understand it.

I didn't argue with him any more that day, but I didn't give up on the idea either. I'd been booked on *American Bandstand* for June 11 and thought I'd have more leverage after I appeared there again. I did "Night Train" and "Shout and Shimmy" that day, and like the other time, the bookings got better and better after that. But Mr. Nathan still didn't want to hear anything about a live album.

Some of the bookings were around Ohio, and that's when I started seeing the Supremes and the Temptations. They came over to our shows in the Cleveland hockey arena and talked about getting on my show, but they were already working with Berry Gordy, who had started the Motown and Tamla record labels. Berry had written some of Jackie Wilson's early hits—"Reet Petite" and "Lonely Teardrops"—and he'd written "You Got What It Takes," a big hit for Marv Johnson. He'd decided to send his acts around in a package tour called the Motortown Revue. His record company and most of his artists were still pretty new, and he was trying to get a better foothold in the business. He approached Mr. Bart to see if I would take them out as part of my show for a while. I agreed to do it because I thought so much of Berry. It turned out to be the only time the Motortown Revue was headlined by somebody who wasn't a Motown artist.

It was a great show: the Miracles, who had "Shop Around"; Mary Wells, who had "The One Who Really Loves You"; the Marvelettes, who had "Please Mr. Postman"; the Contours; Marv Johnson; Marvin Gaye; the Supremes; the Vandellas; and Little Stevie Wonder, who was only twelve years old at the time. I believe we started in Shreveport, Louisiana, and did forty one-nighters with maybe two Sundays off. We actually slept in hotels maybe one or two nights the whole tour; the rest of the time we were on the road on our way to the next town.

I traveled in my car and we had two buses, one for my people and one for the Motown people. Some of 'em, though, like Marvin Gaye and Marv Johnson, drove their own cars. Marvin had a brand-new red Cadillac exactly like mine. He was married to Anna Gordy, Berry's sister, and she loved me so much she made him buy a car just like mine. He'd driven it straight to Shreveport from Detroit; it still had the price sticker and the drive-out tag on it. When we went out to the parking lot after opening night, we saw that someone had taken a brick to the front and back windshields and a side window. Smashed 'em all out. Marvin had a fit. Really, though, I think whoever did it thought it was my car. Whenever you start to get well known there are people making anonymous threats against you, and I was getting some, even back then.

In Silver Spring, Maryland, someone *stole* Marv Johnson's car. They hotwired it, took it for a drive, and left it running in the parking lot. Kids had done it, and the police caught them right away. Instead of filing charges, Marv took them to dinner and talked to them about what they'd done. He kept in touch with them and later one of the boys finished school and went on to do very well for himself.

The road was a new experience for most of the Motown acts. Some, like Diana Ross, were kids, really. I don't remember too much about her from that tour; she was very shy and withdrawn, but you could already see she was very talented. She spent a lot of time with Johnny Terry, and Mary Wells was going with Baby Lloyd.

All those Motown people were talented, but the music they played was different from mine. Their stuff wasn't so strong and driving. They did lightweight, pop soul, very soft, and by being soft it crossed over into the pop market a lot easier. My music was raw, and it has never been popular to be too raw. I was always loyal to my musical roots, even when I was taking the music in a new direction. I have a lot of respect for Motown, a very strong organization and badly needed in the business, because they have that other sound. They were a good organization. When my part of the tour with them ended in Atlanta, I had a talk with Mr. Bart while we were sitting around the hotel room.

I said, "Pop, why don't you handle my business from now on?"

He said, "I *am* handling it."

"I don't mean booking, I mean managing. Why don't you manage me?"

He laughed and said, "No, Jimmy, my wife says I spend too much time on the road with you as it is."

"I want you to handle the business because I know you know how. I don't care about the money, I care about the business. If I make fifty million dollars, I'll just keep one and you take the other forty-nine as long as the tax is paid up."

He laughed again.

"I'm serious, Pop," I said. "I want you to be my partner."

He thought it over for a while and eventually agreed to do it. He worked it out with Mr. Brantly and then turned over Universal's booking to his son Jack.

As soon as Pop became my manager, I told him there were two things I wanted to do right away: Make a live album and change the deal I always got from the Apollo. "I'm booked into the Apollo starting October 19," I said. "Let's take care of both things at once."

I went back to Mr. Nathan about doing the live album, but we had another big argument. He just didn't want to spend any money on something he didn't know about. Finally, I said: "All right, Mr. Nathan, I'll pay for it myself."

"Fine," he said. "If you want to do it, James, you do it, but I'm not spending one red cent for it."

So I wound up paying for recording *Live at the Apollo* out of my own pocket. It cost me $5,700, a lot of money to me then because I really didn't make that much. It was expensive to carry around the big show I did, and there was still something funny about my records and publishing money.

Next, we had to work on Mr. Schiffman about the deal with the Apollo. Before I became really popular at the Apollo, Mr. Schiffman said we were partners, which meant I received a percentage of the door after expenses and everything had been taken out. I didn't always do a whole lot of business there, and when I did draw well, it seemed like expenses always ate up the gross. Besides that, it was hard to get an accurate count of the house because people stayed all day for all the shows on one ticket. But once I really caught on at the Apollo, I could *see* I was doing good business. I thought this arrangement was finally going to pay off for me, but when I got my money it was the same amount I had gotten before. When I went to Mr. Schiffman about it, he said, "Oh, we're not partners anymore. We're hiring you this time for a flat fee." I said, "*Whaaaaat?*" I couldn't believe it.

Later, after Pop found out about it, they came up with a few more dollars, but I wasn't going to take that again, so I said to Pop, "When we go in there this next time, we'll rent the theater."

"Jimmy, nobody has ever rented the Apollo. Schiffman is not going to go for it."

"Tell him he reneged on his agreement and that the only way I'm coming in there is if I rent it."

Mr. Schiffman didn't want to do it, but when I wouldn't back down, he gave in. Once I got the place rented, I decided to put the ushers in tuxedos and the concession people in uniforms. I wanted the audience to feel that a James Brown performance was something special, and I wanted the people who worked at the Apollo to be clean and presentable, which is something I have always been particular about. Ever since I was little and didn't have anybody to do for me, I thought a lot about cleanliness. I even tried to iron my pants when I was in prison.

Once Mr. Nathan saw I was going to go ahead with the live recording, he started cooperating. Mr. Neely took care of getting the equipment from A-1 Sound in New York, the only ones who had portable stuff—Magnacorders, I think. Matter of fact, Mr. Nathan started cooperating *too* much. He sent word that he wanted us to use cue cards to direct the audience participation. I said, "Now if y'all are going to pay for it, then I'll do it the way y'all want to, but if *I'm* going to pay for it, then please leave it alone. All I want y'all to do is tape the stuff." That was the end of it.

We had opened on the nineteenth and were building up to recording on the twenty-fourth, a Wednesday, which meant amateur night. I wanted that wild amateur-night crowd because I knew they'd do plenty of hollering. The plan was to record all four shows that day so we'd have enough tape to work with. I think Mr. Neely and Chuck Seitz, the engineers, had six or eight mikes, two crowd monitors in front, one above the crowd, and then the mikes on me, the band, and the Flames.

The other acts on the bill were Olatunji, the Sensations, Curley Mays, and Pigmeat Markham. Yvonne Fair had a solo spot, and so did Baby Lloyd. On the twenty-fourth I was going around backstage telling the Flames and the band not to get nervous, and I guess I was probably the most nervous of all. I wasn't worried about performing; I was worried about the recording coming off good. I had a lot riding on it, not just my own money but my reputation because here I was having to prove myself to Mr. Nathan and them all over again, just like when I had to demo "Try Me." I was standing in the wings thinking about all this when Fats stepped up to the microphone and did his intro:

"So now, ladies and gentlemen, it is startime. Are you ready for startime?" *Yeah!* "Thank you and thank you very kindly. It is indeed a great pleasure to present to you at this particular time, nationally and internationally known as the *Hard*est Working Man in Show Business, the man that sings, 'I'll Go

Crazy' " ... *a fanfare from the band: Taaaaa!* " 'You've Got the Power' " ... *Taaaaa!* " 'Think' " ... *Taaaaa!* " 'If You Want Me' " ... *Taaaaa!* " 'I Don't Mind' " ... *Taaaaa!* " 'Bewildered' " ... *Taaaaa!* "million-dollar seller 'Lost Someone' " ... *Taaaaa!* "the very latest release, 'Night Train' " ... *Taaaaa!* "Let's everybody 'Shout and Shimmy' " ... *Taaaaa!* "Mr. Dynamite, the amazing Mr. 'Please Please' himself, the star of the show ... James Brown and the Famous Flames."

Then the band went into the chaser—the little up-tempo vamp we used between songs—and I hit the stage. As soon as I was into "I'll Go Crazy" I knew it was one of those good times. That's a hard feeling to describe—being on stage, performing, and *knowing* that you've really got it that night. It feels like God is blessing you, and you give more and more. The audience was with me, screaming and hollering on all the songs, and I thought, "Man, this is really going to do it."

It's a funny thing, though. When I'm up on stage I'm very aware of everything that's going on around me—what the band and the backup singers are doing, how the audience is reacting, how the sound system's working, all that. When you work small clubs you watch the door, check out how rough the crowd looks, listen for little pitch changes in your one little amplifier that tell you it's about to blow out. You can't just be thinking about the song or how pretty you look up there. You learn to be aware.

As the show went along I started noticing little things and filing them away in my mind. Every now and then the band made a mistake or the Flames were a half tone off. Sometimes I hollered where I usually didn't in the song, and some of the audience down front was too enthusiastic. A little old lady down front kept yelling, "Sing it mother____r, sing it!" She looked like she must have been seventy-five years old. I could hear her the whole time and knew the overhead crowd mike was right above her. Mr. Neely had strung it on a wire between the two side balconies. Most times none of those things would've mattered, but we were recording and I was thinking, "Oh, Lord, this take's ruined."

During a quiet stretch of "Lost Someone" the woman let out a loud scream, and the audience laughed right in the middle of this serious song. I thought "Well, there goes that song, too." Then I thought I had better try to fix it some kind of way so I started preaching: "You know we all make mistakes some-times, and the only way we can correct our mistakes is we got to try one more time. So I got to sing this song to you one more time." I stretched out the song, hoping we could get *something* we could use; then I went into "Please."

Mr. Neely brought the tape into a back room between the first two shows and played it for us on a little tape recorder. As soon as we heard the little old lady, we all busted out laughing. He didn't understand. All he could hear was her high piercing voice, but he didn't really understand what she was saying, even though it was clear as a bell. Finally, somebody told him. *Then* he understood.

"Oh no," he said. "I can't have that. I have to get it out of there and make sure she's not here for the other shows, too. This is terrible."

He was getting all worked up, while all the cats were listen-ing to it over and over, laughing, having a great time, and get-ting other cats to listen to it. After a while, watching everybody carry on, Mr. Neely settled himself down and said, "Hey, maybe we've got something here."

He found the lady down front and told her he'd buy her candy and popcorn and give her $10 if she'd stay for the other three shows—he didn't tell her why. He moved the overhead mike so it wouldn't pick her up so strong. We were using two-track, which meant practically mixing as we went along. She stayed for the next three shows and hollered the same thing every time I did a spin or something she liked. It was like it was on cue. I think the shows got even better as the day went along. By the end of the last one we had four reels of tape. Mr. Neely was so excited he brought the master up to the dressing rooms and passed around the headphones for us to listen. None of us had ever heard ourselves live like that. It sounded fantas-tic. We knew we really had something.

By this time we had completely forgotten about the finale, where all the acts change clothes and come out on stage to-gether to close the show. Everybody else had changed and was waiting backstage, but we were listening to the tape over and over. Never did do that finale.

21 GETTING THE POWER— AND LOSING SOMEONE

WHEN Mr. Nathan heard how good the tape was, he wanted to get the album out real quick. I had to tell him it wasn't his tape; it belonged to me. I said I paid for it, and if King wanted it, they could buy it from me. We argued about it for a good while until I think he finally cross-collateralized it in my royalties. The funny thing was he hadn't even heard the tape and here he was already squabbling about it.

I wanted to get the record out fast, too, but first they had to do a lot of editing. Meantime, I kept on working—touring, recording, and writing—the whole conglomerate of being an entertainer. I was always working on the revue, too, changing it, adding people, keeping the music current. Baby Lloyd and Byrd started doing solo spots in the first half of the show. Bobby Bennett and Baby Lloyd also did an act called "Johnny and Bill," so called because originally I had Johnny Terry and Bill Hollings doing it. Johnny had brought me a singer named Danny Ray who later took over the announcing because of his great announcing voice. He's been with me ever since, and he and his voice are famous all over the world.

Right after doing the live recording I added a very special young lady named Tammi Montgomery to the show. Later, as Tammi Terrell, she had some big hits on Motown with Marvin Gaye, but when I met her at the Uptown in Philadelphia, where she was from, her name was Montgomery. She was the niece of Bob Montgomery, the fighter who'd had the matches with Beau Jack to sell war bonds during the war. She was just a kid really, and I helped her all I could to learn to be a performer. We became very close very quickly, and then I fell in love with her.

In December I did a session at Bell Studios in New York where I recorded four tunes with chorus and strings, arranged by Sammy Lowe. I did it because Mr. Nathan didn't think I could sing a ballad, and I wanted to prove him wrong again. "You can't sing ballads," he said, "all you can do is holler." The tunes eventually wound up on the *Prisoner of Love* album that came out in the summer of 1963.

A lot of people don't understand about the hollering I do. A man once came up to me in a hotel lobby and said, "So you're James Brown. You make a million dollars, and all you do is scream and holler."

"Yes," I said, very quiet, "but I scream and holler on key."

I was branching out in a lot of directions. At the end of 1962 I formed my own song publishing company, Jim Jam Music, and got King to give me my own label, Try Me. I had already been producing on Federal and King and Dade and wanted to bring it all together on Try Me. I wasn't content to be only a performer and be used by other people; I wanted to be a complete show business person: artist, businessman, entrepreneur. It was important to be because people of my origin hadn't been allowed to get into the *business* end of show business before, just the *show* part.

By this time Mr. Neely had finished editing the *Live at the Apollo* tape. He had a good mix of the performance and the audience, and he had fixed all the cussing so it wasn't right up front. He figured it would become an underground thing for people who knew what the lady was screaming; he was right, too. He worked on the tape a long time and did a fantastic job of mixing it.

When Mr. Nathan finally heard the tape he hated it. "This is not coming out," he said. "We have a certain standard, and we're going to stick with it." What he didn't like now was the way we went from one tune to another without stopping. He just couldn't understand that. I guess he was expecting exact copies of our earlier records, but with people politely applauding in between. He had all kinds of theories about how records should be. He wanted the hook right up front because he knew that disc jockeys auditioned hundreds of records every week by putting the needle down and playing only the first fifteen or twenty seconds. If that didn't grab them, they went on to the next record. The same thing happened in record stores, where they usually let you hear fifteen or twenty seconds on a record player on the counter. A lot of my things were more like stage

numbers, and he couldn't understand that. After more conversation, he finally agreed to put the album out. I think Mr. Neely
was the one who finally sold him on it.

After all the editing and all the arguing it was January 1963
before *Live at the Apollo* was finally released. Then discussion
began about what singles to release off it. Byrd thought
"Think" should be spun off it, especially since the live version
was so different from the version we'd put out before. Some
people thought "Try Me" was going to do it again, some people
had faith in "Lost Someone."

The idea of a smash *album* was far from anybody's mind.
Those were the days when most popular albums had only one
hit on them plus filler. Mr. Nathan was waiting to see which
tune the radio stations were going to play from the album, and
then he would shoot it out as a single. I said, "What do you
mean? We're not going to take any singles off it. Sell it the way
it is."

"James," he said, "all the money I've made in this business
I made off singles. That's how it's done. As soon as we get the
reports from the radio stations, we're going to start releasing
singles."

"Nosir, Mr. Nathan," I said. "No singles."

"You've been paid. You have no say in it anymore, James."

I didn't give him no more argument. I still had faith in the
album. While he was waiting to see what would break off the
album, King put out the "Prisoner of Love" single in April; it
crossed over into the pop market and made it to the top twenty.
It was very different from the raw stuff on the *Live* album,
which was starting to build momentum.

When Mr. Nathan checked the radio stations to see what
was being played off the album, he got a surprise. They told
him that there *wasn't* a tune the stations were playing. They
were playing the whole album. It was unheard of for a station
to play a whole album uninterrupted, but a lot of stations with
black programming were doing it. You could tune in at a certain
time each night to some of them and they would be playing it.
Mr. Nathan couldn't believe it, but it convinced him to let the
album keep going on its own.

In May my show went back into the Apollo for a week.
Olatunji, the Ward Jubilee Gospel Singers, Jimmy Pelham,
"Johnny and Bill," and Tammi were all part of it. Ever since

my first time at the Apollo the audiences had been good to me, and along about the third time I really felt the place was mine. But this time there was something different. I could feel it from the stage. I could tell that the album was really beginning to catch on because the audience seemed excited even before we started. It was like a lot of 'em had come to see what they'd heard on the live record. And it was like the ones who'd seen it before couldn't get enough of it.

Right after we left the Apollo this time, the *Live* album showed up on the charts, but by then the *Prisoner of Love* album, with the strings and things, was out, too. I was competing with myself again, and that album didn't really take off. But the *Live* was really building now. I even tried to find the woman who'd done all the screaming to thank her, but I couldn't find her.

I toured all around, putting together various shows. I think this was when we did a show in Richmond and had Otis Redding on it. I knew Otis from the talent shows at the Douglas Theater in Macon, and he now had his first hit with "These Arms of Mine." During our first rehearsal I found out Otis didn't have any charts. At that time, St. Clair Pinkney, who played sax, was my bandleader. I had known him in Augusta when we were kids. He joined me sometime in 1961 and wrote the charts for the band. Certain parts of the show were written out, and Byrd rehearsed the band until they had it memorized. I didn't believe in music stands on the stage. To play in my band you had to be able to play and dance at the same time, and you can't do that with music stands in your way. Anyway, I got St. Clair to do charts for Otis, the first ones he ever had, and I think they really helped him get over.

On October 4 I went back in the studio. Records were being released all year, but I hadn't actually recorded since the "Prisoner" sessions back in December. I recorded only one song that day—"Oh Baby, Don't You Weep"—because I had a gig to get to. I based the song on the Davis Sisters' version of the gospel tune "Oh Mary, Don't You Weep." Right away I got into a big argument with Gene Redd about it. I was playing piano, and he didn't like what I was doing. I had arguments with him like that lots of times. He didn't know what he was talking about. Neither one us would back down, and I was in a hurry to get to my gig.

"Let's call Mr. Nathan," I said, "See what he says."

We called him at home. It took him only a minute to make up his mind—I had been right so many times Mr. Nathan was on my side. He told Gene Redd that everybody better do whatever James Brown wanted or they were fired immediately. That was the last time anybody at King gave me any trouble about the way I recorded—except Mr. Nathan himself.

Somewhere during this time I cut Tammi on my Try Me label. I was crazy about her by then, but I think her family wanted her to do something else. They took her away from me because she had a lot of talent. I think they wanted me to groom her, not fall in love with her. I wanted to keep her with me, but I couldn't stop it. They took her away. But she always kept coming back whenever she got the chance and tried to talk to me. It was painful to me. I found out she even talked to the woman I was living with later on, saying to her, "You have the best man in the world, and if you ever have a problem, I'll come back and take him from you." She still loved me.

I was glad when she had all those hits with Marvin: "Ain't No Mountain High Enough," "Ain't Nothing Like the Real Thing," and "You're All I Need to Get By." But she was just a kid that people ran too fast and took advantage of. She was very talented and very warm, and they used her. She was operated on for a brain tumor, and they put her back on tour again. She collapsed in Marvin's arms on stage in 1967. While she was trying to recover I had her brought to the Apollo and made comfortable in the wings to watch the show and see her old friends. She was seriously incapacitated, and it was sad to see her like that. Three years later she died. Her death affected me very badly. It still does.

By the time I came back into the Apollo in November, she had left the revue and Anna King had replaced her. On that show I had Major Lance, who had "Monkey Time"; Betty Harris, who had "Cry to Me"; the Chiffons, who had "He's So Fine"; Jackie and the Starlites; and Pigmeat and his group. "Johnny and Bill" had their spot in the show, and Byrd had his. Sometimes Bobby Bennett did some comedy routines with Pig, too.

We were all sitting in our dressing rooms before the first show of the run when Sandman Sims, the stage manager, came around and told us we ought to take a look outside the theater. "Man, y'all got 'em lined up around the corner," he said. "You got to come see this." Byrd, Baby Lloyd, and I, and a few others, went out to the lobby, but the minute the people outside saw us they started hollering, screaming, and going crazy. We couldn't go out that way, so we went to the back door. It was the same thing on 126th Street. We ducked back inside. I said, "I want to see how long the line really is." The only time you ever saw lines was on amateur night, and this was the middle of a workday, a Friday—and it was cold out, too.

We got some big old hats, sunglasses, and overcoats and went out the back door and got in a car. We went down 126th and whipped out onto Eighth Avenue. A line went way down Eighth. We turned onto 125th to check out the front of the place. Police barricades were up and the line was doubled so that it stretched the other way, too, down to Seventh Avenue. We cut up Seventh to see the line going up to Small's Paradise. We drove back around to the stage door and ran back inside the theater. We hadn't even seen the part of the line that stretched down Eighth below 125th. We had lines like that the whole week we were there. Smashed all the attendance records.

I knew the *Live* album was doing well, but I wasn't ready for that. It stayed on the charts for sixty-six weeks and eventually made it to number 2. That means a bunch of white folks must have been buying it, too, but the funny thing was that white stations weren't playing it at all. Somehow the word had gotten around, though. As a result of that album things just got bigger and bigger, bigger than I had ever imagined. I was ready to do things I never thought I would be able to do. But just like after "Please," I had to go through a whole lot of changes first.

22

FIRST THING, I moved out of the South—for good, I thought. I wasn't bitter or anything like that, I just wanted to be closer to the center of the entertainment business. It's funny about the South. It did a lot to me, but it also made me what I am. My roots, my religion, and my music all come out of the South. Generations of my family, as far back as I can trace them, lived around one little area in South Carolina. I never even traveled outside the South until that first recording session at King.

I moved my father into the house I had on Ell Street in Macon and bought a big twelve-room Victorian place in St. Albans, Queens, in New York City. I bought it from Mr. Bart and Cootie Williams, the great trumpet player with Duke Ellington. The Ell Street house was available because Dessie and I had broken up.

She was a good woman—we were together for a lot of years —but she did a lot of wrong things. I guess I did, too. We fought a lot. She went through a lot of money, but she didn't know any better. She often played pinball, the kind that pays off—if you win; otherwise, you lose money. She lost a lot—a *lot*. She also bought presents for men with my money. Once she bought a present for a fella in the hospital and didn't even buy one for me. She was a hardworking girl, but she didn't know any better.

The house in St. Albans needed a lot of work—the basement was full of water, things like that—so I hired a bunch of people to work on it while I went on tour. The move was just one part of several big changes I was getting ready to make. First, though, I wanted to do another live album.

Even before the *Apollo* record got so big, I was talking to Pop about doing another. I wanted to do it in Washington at the Howard because I figured that was a good audience for me. Pop said, "It doesn't matter where you cut it, Jimmy, you're going

143

to have a wild audience now." So in November, after we left the Apollo with all the long lines and everything, we went into the Royal and cut *Pure Dynamite: Live at the Royal*. At just about the same time, Atlantic Records was recording all their people live at the Apollo: Otis Redding, King Curtis, Ben E. King, Doris Troy, Rufus Thomas, and the Coasters.

I think Pop was wrong, though. It did matter where we cut the album because we had some acoustic problems with the Royal. The album didn't sound bad, but it didn't sound as good as the Apollo recording. *Live at the Royal* was kind of lost in the shuffle anyway because when it was released in February 1964 the other record was still climbing the charts, hanging in there much longer than anybody thought it would.

A big hit album like that changes things. One thing it was changing was my audience. It was bigger, naturally, and the racial makeup was changing. Before that, the audience was almost exclusively black. A few hip whites came, but not many, not like they did for a rock 'n' roll singer like Richard, say. I remember one young man, a white kid, who slipped backstage at a gig in Florida in 1959 when I was still scuffling. He knew everything on the *Please* album. I couldn't believe it.

In 1963 there must've been a whole lot of white kids like him because the crowds at places like the Maryland beaches were about 35 percent white, and I know the *Apollo* album wasn't being played on white radio stations. For a performer, getting popular like that brings pressures and opportunities at the same time. Lots of times, it's hard to tell 'em apart.

There was talk about changing the show. Some people thought we should put in more stuff for the white audience. Pop was against it from the getup. "Listen," he said, "the whites are coming to see exactly what you've been doing for blacks, the gutbucket stuff. You've discussed this only with black people. You don't know how white folks think about it. You're seeing them and they're out there and they seem to be having a good time, so what do you want to change for? If they wanted Bobby Rydell, they'd go to see his show." At first we didn't listen to him. We threw in some tunes like "The Wanderer" by Dion and some pop tunes that were hot then. It didn't take us but a minute to realize they were out of place. We jumped right back into our own thing.

I was anxious, though, to break out in some kind of way.

Didn't look like I was going to do it on King. And Mr. Nathan wouldn't pay me the money I thought I had coming, and every time I asked for any kind of big advance against royalties, he wouldn't give it to me unless I let him extend the contract. But it looked to me like if anybody owed anybody, King owed me. And I was tired of fighting Mr. Nathan all the time. I loved him like a father, but I was tired of fighting him. It was a time of change at King, too. Mr. Nathan had been sick for a while, but when he got his health back he would be running the company full time again. His ideas about artist development and promotion were old-fashioned, not like Mr. Neely's. Around this time, there was a chance Mr. Neely would buy him out, but when it didn't come through I was ready to go.

Around the end of 1963, after the *Royal* album, Pop and I formed a company called Fair Deal Productions, to be run by Marty Machat, the lawyer who handled the Rolling Stones and others. I signed with Fair Deal, and Fair Deal signed me to a production deal with Mercury/Smash Records. Mr. Machat took the position that my contract with King had run out. He also got me signed to an American Federation of Musicians contract. See, my contract with King was a personal services contract for vocals, which was standard in those days to keep the company out of trouble with the union. My name never showed up on the session reports as a musician even when I did play, but King Records, like most of the other companies, was subject to the AFM union contract. Later on, when it all wound up in court, Mercury based their case on signing me as an AFM artist.

The first thing I did for Smash was cut Byrd on a tune called "I'm Just a Nobody," and it became a nice little regional hit for him. Then I cut him and Anna King on a duet—"Baby, Baby, Baby"—that came out in March 1964. The first tune by me on Smash came out in April—"Caldonia." It seemed right to start out on the new label with the song that started me out as a performer way back when I had the Cremona Trio. I was also cutting things for the *Showtime* album that came out on Smash a little later and for the *Grits and Soul* LP for them that was all instrumental.

Meantime, King released "Oh Baby, Don't You Weep" in January, reissued "Please" in February, and put out "Again" at the same time "Caldonia" came out on Smash. Then Mr. Nathan filed a lawsuit to keep me from recording for Mercury.

While the thing was tied up in the courts, I kept cutting on Smash.

I kept on touring, too, and in late May I was back in the Apollo. Anna, Bobby, and Sugar Pie were featured, and we had Patti LaBelle and the Bluebelles, too. At that time they had a big hit with "Down the Aisle." Patti's real name was Patti Holt, from Philadelphia. The rest of the group was Cindy Birdsong (who later joined the Supremes when Florence Ballard left), Sara Dash, and Nona Hendryx. Sara and Nona later became solo acts on their own. They were with the revue for quite a while. Patti was as fantastic then as she is now.

It was the same thing at the Apollo as the last time—lines in all directions as far as you could see. It was nice because I was able to sleep in my own house and drive in to work in the morning. New York was home. I guess that's why it seemed like the right time to do a homecoming concert in my other hometown, Augusta.

Now that I was off parole and was really making it, I was looking forward to going back there—until I found out the audience in Bell Auditorium would be segregated. I wasn't heavy into the human rights thing yet, but I knew I didn't want to play a segregated show in my own hometown, especially after the crowd had integrated itself when I played Jennings Stadium, the baseball park there. When I had played it a few years before, the audience had been segregated, as usual, but during the show the white kids started coming down toward the stage. Before long there were white kids and black kids crowding around the stage, dancing and hollering and having a good time. They had integrated themselves. I didn't want to turn right around and let 'em be resegregated. I had grown up with the signs that said "White Drinking Water" and "Colored Drinking Water," and it always seemed to me that water didn't have any color.

There was a long discussion with the promoter. He said it was the city. I said I wouldn't do the show—contract or no contract. That was the way we left it. The way Bell Auditorium was set up in those days there was a little section of about one thousand three-hundred seats behind the stage that was used for small affairs. The rest of the seats, several thousand of them, were on the exact opposite side of the stage. If a big black show was in there, the main seats would be for blacks and the other one thousand three hundred would be for whites. If it was a white show, it would be the other way around. You had to play to two audiences at once; when you were facing one, you had your back to the other. The stage had two curtains, one on each side, but I didn't know that. When I had been there to see a show or whatever I had never seen another side.

When the show started, we ran out and faced the audience —the major side that we thought was the only side—but we heard people yelling and screaming from both sides. I turned around, and there were all the white folks on that side. And a lot of 'em knew me, were friends of mine, yelling "James, hey James!" That got to me. They were friends of mine and the black folks were friends of mine, but they couldn't sit together. I finished the show, but I said to myself, "Never again!"

We had a few days off after the show, and I got all the fellas to hang around so I could show 'em where I was born and raised, and I took 'em all around, showing 'em the canal, the house on Twiggs, and the Richmond County Jail.

Next we went to Macon for a show at the Auditorium there. Over the years we had played in all the clubs in the area, but we hadn't played the Auditorium but one or two times back when I had "Please" and "Try Me." This was kind of a homecoming for me, too, because I had moved away. I had played the Macon Auditorium about two years before, with the audience segregated. The way it worked, if a white act was appearing, then the whites got to sit on the main floor and the blacks in the balcony; if it was a black act, then it was blacks on the main floor and whites up top.

We got into Macon a few days before the show and found out that it was going to be segregated like before. I had just been through all that in Augusta and I wasn't going to go through it again, not in my second hometown. I told Pop and Mr. Brantly, "I'm not going to do it. Not no way."

"The advertising's all out," Mr. Brantly said. "The tickets have all been sold."

"I don't care," I said. "I'm not going on. And if they say the people aren't going to be separated and I go on and see they are, I'm walking off."

Pop said, "Jimmy, just close your eyes to it. Just take the money and get out of town. Why come in here and try to change these people's policy?"

"Because it's not right, Pop."

The funny thing about it was that integrating for a black show would benefit the white people in the audience; they would have the same chance at the good seats as the black folks. I was determined to do my show that way or no way. But I didn't want to just sit there and refuse, I wanted to get it done. So I went to see a friend of mine, a very influential white fella who ran a car lot in Macon, and told him the situation.

"Let's just try it this one time," I said. "All people are going to do is walk in together and sit down. Most folks are escorted, so they're with their man or their woman. After the show, everybody goes home. Meantime, all they're doing is standing around in a place together. Nobody's going to bother nobody."

He said he'd see what he could do. I think he went around and talked to some of the city officials and got them prepared for what was going to happen. Didn't make a lot of noise about it, just explained things. The audience didn't know anything about it until they got there for the show. What we did was close the balcony until the main floor was filled. Then we opened the balcony back up. The show went off without a hitch. I think a lot of people were surprised that the building was still standing afterwards, but I wasn't.

The next time I went back to Augusta for a show—about five or six months later—I went to the leaders of the white community and the black community and talked to them about what had happened in Macon, saying that we could do it in Augusta, too. So we closed off the small rear seating section and the balcony in Bell Auditorium until the main part was filled, like we'd done in Macon. It came off fine. The next day the papers wrote it up, saying it was the first time there'd been an integrated event and complimenting everybody. After that, the audiences were integrated for all the shows. A little later, President Johnson signed the 1964 Civil Rights bill that outlawed segregation in public places, but it took a long time to take full effect in show business; it was more than a year later before a lot of venues in the South quit segregating the audiences.

In June I went into the Mercury studios and cut "Out of Sight" and "Maybe the Last Time." Like everything else for me that year, they were an ending and a beginning. "Maybe the Last Time" was a heavy gospel-based number, all about appreciating friends and everything while you can because each time you see somebody may be the last time, you don't know. Turned out that session was the last time I ever used the Famous Flames on record. They were a good stage act, but they couldn't really sing all that good. With recording becoming more sophisticated every day, this showed up more on records. Sometimes in the studio some of them had been on dummy mikes anyway; they didn't know that at the time because I didn't want to hurt anybody's feelings. After the "Last Time" session, I used only Byrd and those I told him to hire, so musically and as far as personnel went, the song was another kind of ending for me.

"Out of Sight" was another beginning, musically and professionally. My music—and most music—changed with "Papa's Got a Brand New Bag," but it really started on "Out of Sight," just like the change from R & B to soul started on "Think" and "I'll Go Crazy." You can hear the band and me start to move in a whole other direction rhythmically. The horns, the guitar, the vocals, everything was starting to be used to establish all kinds of rhythms at once. On that record you can hear my voice alternate with the horns to create various rhythmic accents. I was trying to get every aspect of the production to contribute to the rhythmic patterns. What most people don't realize is that I had been doing the multiple rhythm patterns for years on stage, but Mr. Neely and I had agreed to make the rhythms on the records a lot simpler.

"Out of Sight" went out of sight on the charts when it came out. It didn't take time to build, it didn't make it first on the R & B chart and then cross over, it just took off across the board. But even though "Out of Sight" was the biggest hit I'd ever had up to that point, I didn't put out a single *new* vocal release for almost a year afterward because of the court fight with King. It was almost like the period between "Begging Begging" and "Try Me," except this time the dry spell was after a big hit. There were still plenty of James Brown releases because with all the masters they had stockpiled King was able to put out a lot of my stuff. And they reissued a lot of my old stuff. They put out "So Long" and "Dancin' Little Thing" right before "Out of Sight" came out, and later on they released "Tell Me What You're Gonna Do" and "I Don't Care." They reissued "Think" and "Try Me" and put out a record with a medley of three songs on one side and "Fine Old Foxy Self" on the other. It went on and on like that for the next year.

In October, just about the time that I should have put out a new song, King got an injunction that prohibited me from releasing any more vocals on Mercury/Smash. Mercury even withdrew the *Out of Sight* album that had just come out. The case eventually went up through the courts; on appeal, the appellate division said I could only sing on King and play on Mercury. They divided me in half. If I wanted to sing, I was going to have to go back to Mr. Nathan. Just when I should have been reaping the rewards of ten years of hard work, I was stuck.

Nothing could stop me from performing, though. Right after the injunction I went back into the Apollo, but it was strange because Little Willie John was supposed to be there. But he had gotten arrested for killing a man at a party in Seattle. It was sad because it happened at Little Willie John's engagement party. The man he killed refused to give up a seat to a lady; Willie got on him about it, they got into an argument, and Willie wound up stabbing the man. I went back a long way with Little Willie John—my first gig at the Apollo, recording on King together, and playing a lot of shows together in the early days. We always had a friendly rivalry, and I loved him. I knew he was looking at some hard time, and I was worried because he was a little cat and I didn't think he could survive too long in prison.

That week at the Apollo the people were lined up like always, even though it was cold and snowing. The Apollo's business had been down to about a fourth of normal since August when a policeman had shot and killed a fifteen-year-old boy and a riot had broken out. Even after things settled down again, people were staying in, but they had come out for me in spite of the weather and everything. Looking out at those lines, thinking about Little Willie John and everything he was going through, and thinking about what I was going through, I suddenly realized how grateful I should be. See, back then a ticket to the Apollo was good for the whole day and night; you could stay for as many shows as you wanted. So a lot of the people out there were going to have to wait indefinitely to get in, but they were willing to do it.

I rounded up everybody on the show and told them to put on their coats and hats—we had some work to do. We had urns of coffee made and got some plastic cups, and then we went outside and went up and down the line, serving coffee to the people who were waiting to get in. I told them I appreciated their waiting in the snow and that I would try to do a good show for them. We did that for the rest of the week there, and when any act wasn't on stage, it was out there serving more people during the shows. I think they were grateful to us; I *know* I was grateful to them.

Looking back on it, I think 1964 was a strange year. A lot of tragedy came to a lot of people I went way back with in the business. Rudy Lewis, who'd been in the Drifters for five years, died of a heart attack at age twenty-seven. Not too long after Little Willie John got arrested, Ray Charles was busted at Logan Airport in Boston for heroin, and not too long after that Sam Cooke was shot to death in Los Angeles under peculiar circumstances.

I was bouncing around between two labels and wasn't sure I was going to sing on record again, but I *had* to feel blessed. It seemed like a lot of things from the past were slipping away, a lot of changes were coming around, to me and to everybody, but I was surviving. And I believed in the future. It was like standing at a crossroads. There I was playing the Apollo with the Five Royales, a group I had imitated when I first started out. Little Willie John was probably gone for good, and it seemed like a lot of cats were dying. Yesterday was gone. But I had faith in the direction of my music. And at the end of the year I knew I'd seen the future when I encountered two new acts: the Rolling Stones and the Jacksons.

23 PAPA'S NEW BAG

I SAW the Rolling Stones the first time when we were on *The T.A.M.I. Show* together. It was a TV film with a whole lot of acts that were popular then: Chuck Berry, Bo Diddley, the Supremes, Smokey Robinson and the Miracles, Marvin Gaye, Lesley Gore, Jan and Dean, Gerry and the Pacemakers. We taped it at the Santa Monica Auditorium in November 1964, and I think it came out early the next year. It was directed by Steve Binder, the cat who directed Elvis's television special in 1968.

My group and I got to the auditorium to rehearse about eight in the morning. I think we did our segment three times all the way through in rehearsal. The production crew was taping all the rehearsals and blocking the show out, and then later in the day we were going to do the actual performance in front of an audience made up of mostly white teenagers. Motown had gotten very hot by then, and there were a lot of young white kids hanging all over the Motown stars. When Byrd and some of the other fellas saw what was happening, they started worrying. "Man," they said, "it doesn't look like we're going to get such a good reception." I said, "Don't even worry about it. Once we get through, we aren't going to be able to get out of this place." I think the other acts knew it, too, even if the audience didn't. They made it plainly understood they didn't want to come anywhere after us. They knew what we could do. So the Stones, who were really big already, were scheduled to follow us.

They came in around one in the afternoon, with a bunch of guards, went straight to their dressing room, and didn't let anybody get near 'em. Meantime, we were out there doing another rehearsal. When we did, a lot of people came out of their dressing rooms to watch, Mick included. I think he'd heard about us already, but when he saw what we did, he couldn't believe it.

After he saw me, he didn't even want to rehearse. Some discussion started then about them going on sooner. I heard that Mick smoked a whole pack of cigarettes, he was so nervous. We thought that was a good sign, but we knew we still had to deal with the audience of young, young kids.

A funny thing happened when the actual show went on. Lesley Gore went out and did two songs. When she came off, a bunch of people crowded around asking for her autograph. Then this older lady—I don't know if it was her mother, her keeper, or whoever—said, "Oh, no, don't bother her, don't bother her. She's tired now. Wait until she rests." We had already been out there and nearly killed ourselves twice already, and she hadn't even done any rehearsals. When the lady said that, we all looked at each other and said, "There must be something we don't know."

We went on, a little nervous because we didn't think this audience really knew us, but when we went into "Out of Sight," they went straight up out of their seats. We did a bunch of songs, nonstop, like always. For our finale we did "Night Train." I don't think I ever danced so hard in my life, and I don't think they'd ever seen a man move that fast. When I was through, the audience kept calling me back for encores. It was one of those performances when you don't even know how you're doing it. At one point during the encores I sat down underneath a monitor and just kind of hung my head, then looked up and smiled. For a second I didn't really know where I was.

The Stones had come out in the wings by then, standing between all those guards. Every time they got ready to start out on the stage, the audience called us back. They couldn't get on —it was too hot out there. By that time I don't think Mick wanted to go on the stage at all. Mick had been watching me do that thing where I shimmy on one leg and when the Stones finally got out there, he tried it a couple of times. He danced a lot that day. Until then I think he used to stand still when he sang, but after that he really started moving around. Anyway, after they were finally able to get on the stage, they got over real good. At the end, all of the people on the show came out and danced for the finale. Later on, Mick used to come up to the Apollo and watch my shows. I used to make him come on the stage, and he became a good friend of mine. I like Mick, Keith Richards, and all the guys. I don't think of them as competition; I think of them as brothers.

I'm not sure when I first met The Jacksons, but I think it was around this time, too, late 1964 or early 1965, in their hometown of Gary, Indiana. They were called the Jackson Family then—Jackie, Tito, Jermain, Marlon, and Michael, who couldn't have been but about six years old. I think they were playing talent shows and amateur things around Gary. Their father, Joe, came to see me about getting them on the revue. Joe had played guitar with the Falcons, the group that Wilson Pickett, Eddie Floyd, and a lot of other people came out of, and he knew about the business. Joe wanted me to carry them around for a while, get them some exposure and some seasoning, but I did not want to take them out of school. I thought that if they didn't make it as entertainers, they'd regret not getting their formal education. I was hesitant also because of the record label fight I was in. If I wasn't going to be able to get any new vocal releases out, I was afraid it mighty eventually affect the popularity of the revue, so it didn't seem to be a good time to expand the payroll. I did put them on one of the shows in Gary, and they were fantastic. They could really dance, especially Michael. Their choreography was smooth, and they sang real nice. You could see Joe had really trained them to be professional.

It was about a year before I saw them again, in Chicago, when I was playing the Regal. By that time I wasn't playing the theaters anymore except for the Regal and the Apollo. I think Al Green was on the show, and Jackie Wilson, too. Jackie had gotten wild and crazy after being shot—he was drinking a lot and using drugs pretty heavy. They had to lock him in the dressing room and make him stay there until he got straight, then he came out and did a great show. But it was terrible to see Jackie in such bad shape.

The Jackson Family wasn't booked on the show, but they were backstage. Joe came to see me about letting them go on. The show was very tight, but I said they could go on at intermission. I knew the Regal would be a good shot for them—a lot better than those hometown gigs. They did another fine job. A few months later, when I went back into Chicago to

McCormick Place, which was much bigger than the Regal, they were booked on the show. I think they had a record on a little local label by then, and they were even better than before.

About a year after the McCormick Place gig, some of my people helped them get booked into the Apollo, around July 1968. Joe sent some money ahead for their hotel rooms and to see they were well looked after, since they were still just kids. Baby James, the cat who worked for me as a bodyguard, was supposed to take care of it, but something came over him and he spent the money instead. Now the kids get into New York for the first time; they're supposed to debut at the Apollo the next morning, and they don't have any place to stay, and no money to eat on. Baby James was afraid to tell me what he had done; instead he took them over to Byrd's apartment on Lenox Avenue. By this time Byrd had married Vicki Anderson, who'd joined the revue as a singer in the spring of 1965. Bobby and Vicki took in the Jacksons and fed them. After dinner they all sat around the piano and played and sang. The next morning when the kids got dressed and ready to go, they told Bobby and Vicki they wanted to sing them a song. They gathered around the piano and sang a song that had "thank you" in it. It started out 'Thank you for this, thank you for that,' and it ended with them all harmonizing on 'and we all thank you.' Byrd told me he didn't know if it was a song they knew or if they had put it together right that morning, but it was the prettiest song he had ever heard in his life.

That's the kind of kids the Jacksons were. Here they'd had all their money spent up and they were just grateful for what they did get. They were always well mannered—it was always "yessir" this and "no, ma'am" that. You could tell they'd had a good upbringing and had a lot of discipline instilled in them. They're like that right today.

On top of meeting great acts like the Stones and the Jacksons around this time, I met another great one in Vicki Anderson. She lived in Houston and had already cut a record. Her manager played her tape for me when I was in Houston. I bought the tape from him with the idea of recording her myself. When Anna King left the show a few months later, I asked Vicki to come to Miami where I could record her, and then she joined the revue. She walked into the studio while the band was put-

ting down the tracks for a song called "Baby, I Love You." Byrd
was in the corner writing the words for it. She recorded it right
then.

I've known a lot of singers, a lot of different kinds of singers,
but I will say this flatly: I've never met a person in the world
who sang better than Vicki. I used to call her Songbird. She
could outsing anybody I know. Any day. Standing flat-footed.
She can beat Aretha Franklin, and I love Aretha to death.
Aretha is Soul Sister Number One, but she cannot beat Vicki
singing. Vicki can sing "People" better than Streisand. She was
not just the best singer I ever had with the revue, she was the
best singer, period.

I also met another special person during this time—the lady
who would later become my second wife. Her name was
Deirdre, but I called her Deedee. She was from Baltimore, and
I think we first met when I was playing one of the Maryland
beaches, but I'm not sure. It wasn't one of those love-at-first-
sight things. We met several times, and things just grew from
there. We became very close, and she eventually joined me in
New York. We couldn't get married because Velma and I had
never gotten around to getting a divorce. Deedee and I weren't
ready to be married anyway; we split up a few years later and
didn't get back together for a good while after that. But we
started out good.

Around the same time I added more key people to the band:
Jimmy Nolen on guitar, Melvin Parker on drums, and Maceo
Parker on alto sax. Jimmy Nolen came from Johnny Otis's band,
and Melvin and Maceo were brothers I had heard one night in
the El Morocco Club in Greenville, North Carolina. I really
wanted Melvin but I figured I had to hire Maceo, too, if I
wanted to get his brother. Of course, Maceo turned out to be
fantastic—an aggressive, dynamic player and a real worker.
Over the years he has quit and been fired more times than
either one of us can count, but he's still with me right today.

Elsie Mae "T.V. Mama" was another regular on the revue
around this time. She was funny and talented, and very, very
large. She sang "Take All of Me" and took off her skirt; she had
tights on underneath. She was very big but very shapely. She
was a comedy act, but she also sang well, like Big Mama Thornton or somebody.

The show was tight, and I tried to keep it that way. We still had the system of fines, but now it covered fluffed notes and mistakes on the dance routines. See, a lot of the routines were worked out while we were on the road. We worked them out in rehearsal, went to eat, came back, rehearsed a little bit more, and then hit the stage. I wanted it all absolutely right. When I was dancing on the stage, I could see everything going on. If I caught a bad mistake, I'd mash potatoes over to where the person who'd messed up could see me and I'd flash my open hand once for each $5 fine—five times for a $25 fine, and so on. I did it right on the beat of the music so it looked like part of the act, but the person being fined knew what was happening. Some of the fellas might have thought it was a little rough, but it worked. I think we had the tightest band and the tightest show out there.

I was keeping busy on the road, recording a lot of the acts, doing instrumentals, and doing some television like *The Lloyd Thaxton Show* and *Where the Action Is.* The Flames and I did a cameo in a Frankie Avalon movie, *Ski Party,* dressed up in ski outfits. I was a little suprised at how much work it is to make a movie, but Frankie was a very easy person to work with. I never had any burning desire to be a movie star the way a lot of singers have —Elvis, Sinatra, or Frankie Avalon, for that matter. It wasn't something that was open to people of my origin at that time anyway. Louis made a lot of movies, but he always played himself and was never really the star of them.

Meantime, it was a standoff between King Records and Mercury. I started to think there was something funny about it; Mercury seemed more interested in putting Mr. Nathan out of business than in recording me on vocals. The doors at King were all but closed; they had beat him, he had nothing to fight with. I felt bad about it, so I went to Arthur Smith's studio in Charlotte, North Carolina, cut "Papa's Got a Brand New Bag," and sent the tape to Mr. Nathan. It was done underground—I had to sneak the tape to him.

The song started out as a vamp we did during the stage show. There was a little instrumental riff and I hollered: "Papa's got a bag of his own!" I decided to expand it into a song and cut it pretty quick to help Mr. Nathan, so when we went into the studio I was holding a lyric sheet in my hand while I recorded it. We were still going for that live-in-the-studio sound, so we cranked up and did the first take.

It's hard to describe what it was I was going for; the song has gospel feel, but it's put together out of jazz licks. And it has a different sound—a snappy, fast-hitting thing from the bass and the guitars. You can hear Jimmy Nolen, my guitar player at the time, starting to play scratch guitar, where you squeeze the strings tight and quick against the frets so the sound is hard and fast without any sustain. He was what we called a chanker; instead of playing the whole chord and using all the strings, he hit his chords on just three strings. And Maceo played a fantastic sax solo on the break. We had been doing the vamp on the show for a while, so most of it was fine, but the lyrics were so new I think I might have gotten some of them mixed up on the take. We stopped to listen to the playback to see what we needed to do on the next take. While we were listening, I looked around the studio. Everybody—the band, the studio people, *me*—was dancing. Nobody was standing still.

Pop said, "If I'm paying for this, I don't want to cut any more. This is it."

And that *was* it. That's the way it went out. I had an acetate made and took it to Frankie Crocker, a deejay in New York. He thought it was terrible, but he put it on the air and the phones lit up. Then he admitted I was right about it.

"Papa's Bag" was years ahead of its time. In 1965 soul was just really getting popular. Aretha and Otis and Wilson Pickett were out there and getting big. I was still called a soul singer —I still call myself that—but musically I had already gone off in a different direction. I had discovered that my strength was not in the horns, it was in the rhythm. I was hearing everything, even the guitars, like they were drums. I had found out how to make it happen. On playbacks, when I saw the speakers jumping, vibrating a certain way, I knew that was it: deliverance. I could tell from looking at the speakers that the rhythm was right. What I'd started on "Out of Sight" I took all the way on "Papa's Bag." Later on they said it was the beginning of funk. I just thought of it as where my music was going. The title told it all: I had a new bag.

24 SEX MACHINE

WHILE the fight between King and Mercury was still going through the courts, Mercury put out "I Got You (I Feel Good)" on Smash. The injunction was still in force, though, and they had to withdraw the record right away. Finally, the lower court ruling was upheld on appeal: I could do instrumentals on Smash, but if I was going to sing, it had to be on King. That was all right with me. I had made my point with Mr. Nathan, and I didn't want to see him driven out of business. When I came back they tore up the old contract and gave me a new one, so I came back on good terms and with a lot more power than I'd had before. You need power to get freedom. You need freedom to create.

The new contract was a ten-year personal services contract with a royalty rate of 7 percent, I think, but it wasn't too long before they raised it to 10 percent. Except for people in the classical field, I think I was the first 10-percent artist. The publishing companies were restructured, too. The key point, though, was a weekly payment: King had to give me $1,500 a week no matter what. They could charge it against my royalties, but they couldn't withhold the payment. The $1,500 figure wasn't that important; it was the principle of the thing. This way we could avoid all the squabbling over royalties and the contract extensions that caused the whole problem in the first place. Later on, in my tax case, the government came along and took all that money away from me, but at the time I was very happy about it. Mr. Nathan was happy, too; one day he said to me that if the company was ever sold I ought to get 10 percent.

So I came back to King in the summer of 1965 with "Papa's Got a Brand New Bag." The funny thing was, Mr. Nathan didn't like that song either. He was so disgusted he threw an acetate of it on the floor. I just laughed. It became my first international hit.

I had an actual new bag of my own, too. After I went back to King, every time I recorded a bunch of sides I got the masters and put them in a bag I had. I carried it with me everywhere. When I wanted to release something, I pulled the master out of the bag and gave it to the record company. I wanted to control the releases, and I didn't want to get into a situation in the future where King would have a stockpile they could draw on like they had when I was over on Smash. From then on I called all the releases.

At the end of October I went into the Apollo and had the long lines again. I think we set the Apollo record that week. A ticket at that time didn't cost but $2 and you could still stay all day on it, but we grossed about $70,000 anyway. One night while we were there we heard Ed Sullivan was in the audience. I understand he often came up to the Apollo to check out performers for his show. I think he knew how tough the Apollo audience was, and he figured if somebody could get over at the Apollo he could get over with his audience. Not too long after that I heard I got the booking on his show.

I followed up "Papa's Bag" with "I Got You (I Feel Good)." It was a much hipper, up-tempo version of "I Found You," which I had cut Yvonne on. It was another smash. Things were getting bigger and bigger, but Pop still wasn't satisfied. He was always trying to come up with some kind of promotional idea to give us that extra boost. A lot of times, we gave away cars, television sets, all kinds of things at concerts, but he was looking for something other than pushing a single concert. One day a bunch of us were sitting around his office at Universal Attractions discussing ideas. Pop was offering suggestions, and I was rejecting them as fast as he came up with them. Finally, he said, "Jimmy, I know what I can do, but you're not going to like it."

"What's that, Pop?"

"That thing we discussed before."

He wouldn't say what it was because he didn't want Byrd, who was sitting there, to know about it. *I* knew what he was talking about, though.

"Pop," I said, "just don't embarrass me. Don't make me look silly."

The next thing I knew there was an item in the gossip section of a magazine that insinuated I was going across the water to have a sex-change operation. So I could marry Bobby Byrd. Once the rumor was started, there wasn't much I could do about it. If you deny it, it just makes it bigger. Pop said to keep quiet and see what happened. Meantime, Byrd hadn't heard about it, and I didn't want to be the one to tell him. I said, "Listen, Byrd, Ben has come up with a lot of good ideas. Let's all go along with him and see what he comes up with. He's liable to make us both hotter."

When it first came out, I think we were in Raleigh, North Carolina. People were yelling from the audience about it. I was wearing a lot of makeup then, and that added fuel to the fire. After the show, Byrd and I went out the stage door together. We couldn't hardly get to the car for all the people lined up to check us out. They were hollering at Byrd: "There he is! Look at him!" Byrd said to me, "Boy, I must have killed 'em tonight."

When we got back to New York, I called him at his hotel, I think it was the Great Northern on 57th Street. I said, "Byrd, was there a bunch of people around y'all's hotel?"

"Yeah," he said, "when the tour bus pulled up, a big crowd was waiting for us, and they were all yelling at me and talking funny. Something peculiar is going on 'cause I don't have a record out now."

"I told you I was going to make you hot, Byrd."

He found out later that day what was happening. Somebody told him about the magazine story. At first he was mad about it, then he figured it didn't matter what people said about you as long as *you* know what you are. The thing did make him hot. All these people were coming to the show to see what the truth was. Once, in California, there were people jumping up on the stage to dance, and some of 'em were trying to grab me between the legs. After it all died down, we had a good laugh about it. It was all in good fun; Byrd didn't hold it against me, and I didn't hold it against Pop. But just about the time I got back with King, Pop and I got into some very heavy disagreements about other things. They were just artist and manager type problems, but they got out of hand. We had both been under a lot of pressure, and we said a lot of things we shouldn't have.

"Jimmy, I'm pulling out," he said.

"That's fine, Pop," I said. "I don't need you. You never did that much for me anyway." We both knew that wasn't true, and I think it hurt him for me to say that.

"Okay, fine," he said. "But you're going back into the clubs now because I'm going to lock up everything else."

He almost did, too. I wasn't really locked out of all the coliseums, but the prime bookings were harder to get. It was amazing how much power he had. He even stopped a show in Cincinnati one night and attached the box office. I bridged the gap by doing a lot of TV shows in the States and in England. It was never any real hardship, it was just that someone like Pop meant a lot to a black entertainer at that time. Plus, he meant a lot to me personally, and I hated to see us split up like that. It was like a family fight: Nobody knows how it starts, and nobody knows how to stop it.

Finally I went to him, we smoothed it over, and he came back. When he did, he said, "Jimmy, I'm going to take out a million-dollar life insurance policy on you." It was a humorous thing to cement our getting back together, so I said, "Okay, Pop, if I can take out a million dollars on you." I thought he was as valuable to me as he thought I was to him. We took out the policies, and after that he always joked, "You're going to die before I do, Jimmy, because you work too hard." I'd say, "Naw, Pop, you're going to die first because you don't work hard enough."

The first thing we did when we got back together was plan a concert at Madison Square Garden for March 20, 1966. It was hard to put together. People didn't think I could draw well in such a big place by myself, so to quiet 'em down I added Len Barry, Lou Christie, Slim Harpo, the Shangri-Las, and the Soul Brothers to the bill. By the time it was publicized most of the tickets had already been sold.

Right before the date, I went to England and did the *Ready Steady Go* television show. While I was there taping it several British acts came by to say hello—the Beatles, the Kinks, the Animals. I think a couple of the Stones came by, too. These groups had a real appreciation for where the music came from and knew more about R & B and blues than most Americans. I played the Palladium and the Walhamstow, and then we hopped over to Paris and played the Olympia. I wasn't really prepared for the reception we got in Europe. In London they had to put us on one floor of the hotel, clear the floor above and below us, and put guards there. During that trip the English people yelled at Byrd about the rumors they had heard, but by that time I think he was used to it.

As soon as I got back to the States I went into the Garden. It was a sellout. Things were just getting bigger and bigger real fast. "It's a Man's Man's Man's World" came out in April and took off. Then came a booking on the *Ed Sullivan Show.*

I rehearsed with Bob Beck, his son-in-law, three times to see what I was going to do so they could block it. They had to know exactly how long each act would last because it was going to go out live. They kept saying: "Once you shit, that's it." I did "Good Good Lovin' " with the baseball routine and "Please." Mr. Sullivan wouldn't let me do "Don't Be a Drop-Out." I hadn't released it yet, but I'd already written it and thought it was an important song. I wanted it to go on network television, figuring with that large an audience I should try to do something that might help people. He refused to let me do it. He was nice about it, but he never explained why he didn't want me to sing it.

The Supremes were on the show, too. We did the rehearsal, and after the dress rehearsal when it was time for the live show Mr. Sullivan couldn't get the people to stay quiet. I was *hot* for the dress rehearsal, and the Supremes were, too. The live version that went out over the air wasn't as good as that dress rehearsal.

No matter how good or how big the bookings got, I still played the Apollo, but with the size of my show now—the band was twenty pieces—I couldn't play under the old arrangement where people stayed all day for the price of one ticket. I told Mr. Schiffman, "You got to put these people out after each show."

"I've been running this place for forty years," he said. "You can't do that."

"They'll do it if you tell 'em," I said. "I'll give 'em a *complete* show, and then they'll get up and leave."

They had to make the tickets good for one show only and increase the price to $3. I hated to do it, but it was the difference between playing there and not playing there. I knew I could get people to leave feeling satisfied when a show was over. That's what I taught the people who ran the Apollo: completion.

Besides Byrd and Vicki, I had the gospel group the Swanee Quintet on the show. I did a lot of split shows with gospel acts during that time. People always said you couldn't bring to- gether church people and people who dug music like mine, but I thought you could. I used to have the Swanees, the Mighty Clouds of Joy, the Angelic Gospel Singers, Clara Ward, all of them. I had the gospel people on the first part of the show, then an intermission, and then my show. Singing is all about spirit anyway—doesn't make any difference what kind of singing.

The pace I'd been keeping was beginning to wear me down. I was tired and had some kind of virus when I started that week at the Apollo. I worked so hard on stage I was dehydrated a lot of the time and didn't even know it. I drank beer after the show to get more fluids, but I didn't know that alcohol dehydrates you even more. It all caught up with me on Saturday night's midnight show. I had already done several shows that day. I was doing "Please"—collapsing onto my knees—when I felt all the muscles in my legs freeze, then start cramping real bad. I started twitching all over, my breath got short, and I fell out right there on the stage. I thought I had done it to death for real. When the Flames helped me up, they weren't acting. I tried to continue but was too weak. I guess some of the people in the audience thought it was part of the act, but a lot of 'em could see I was in trouble and became very disturbed and started screaming. The Flames got me into the wings.

The Apollo house doctor, Dr. William Calloway—every- body called him Dr. Bill—took one look at me and knew what was wrong. They put me into a car or an ambulance—I can't remember which—and took me to his office on 135th Street. He said I had low-salt syndrome, that I had sweated out too much sodium and potassium; he gave me an intravenous solution of sodium lactate to rehydrate me. Meantime, a lot of people had followed us there from the Apollo. They were outside trying to get in, almost breaking the door down. Honi Coles or somebody went out and got them to stop before we had to call the police to protect ourselves.

After that I took an intravenous solution whenever I got really exhausted. I needed the salt and the fluids, sometimes as much as four pints, which would take two or three hours. I went to Dr. Bill's and lay there on the table until I was done and felt better right away. That's when people started saying I was a junkie because they saw the needle mark in my arm.

I thought the traveling might be taking a lot out of me, too, and things were starting to move so fast that Pop and I decided to get a jet. Right after the Apollo gig we leased full time a six-passenger Lear model 24. I think I was the first person of my origin to do that. We had it painted green and white, with "Out of Sight" written along the fuselage. With the plane I could work an eight-day week: I could get to the next gig quick, hit the disc jockeys, and still have plenty of time to rest before the show. Same reason I'd started riding in the car instead of the bus, only now everything was on a bigger scale.

We played the L.A. Sports Arena, the Cow Palace, Braves Stadium, Miami Stadium, and places like that. I played Shea Stadium for a Murray the K show that became a television special. I came down into the stadium by helicopter and climbed down a ladder onto the infield. Scared a bunch of people.

While I was doing the L.A. Sports Arena I went on *Bandstand* again—by this time it had moved to Hollywood—and sang "Man's World" and "Money Won't Change You," which had just come out in June. Jackie Wilson was playing at the Trip Club, and I dropped in on his show and did some numbers. The next night Jackie came on my show at the Arena.

I think it was on this trip to the coast that Elvis and I finally got together. We kept up with each other through mutual friends in the business, but we could never get together. He came to see my show a few times. He came in disguise, after the house lights were down, and left right before it was over. I'd get word through Mr. Neely that he'd been there. And I knew he watched *The T.A.M.I. Show* over and over.

At a big party he threw in the Hyatt Continental, I think, when it got late, we threw everybody out of the room, and Elvis and I sang gospel together. We sang "Old Jonah," "Old Blind Barnabas," all the ones I'd been singing since I was little. He knew the harmonies, too. That's how we communicated—by singing jubilee, the real upbeat kind of gospel. He told me he wanted to use my band to record. He said he wanted the horns and things behind him, but he wanted them *strong*. When he first started he was copying B. B. and them, but finally they didn't have enough fire for him. That's when he really got into his own thing. Elvis was great. People still said he was copying, but he found his own style. Elvis was rockabilly; he wasn't rock 'n' roll, he was rockabilly. He was really a hillbilly who learned to play the blues.

Cats complain all the time about white people learning music from blacks. It's true we've kind of had a monopoly on certain kinds of music, but everybody's entitled to it. They shouldn't *steal* it, but they're entitled to learn it and play it. No sense in keeping all the drive on one side, because if you're teaching people, you're teaching people. They should remember, though, that when a man teaches you, he's your best friend, but if he keeps you in the dark, you're in trouble.

Elvis and I both hit the charts at the same time, 1956; he had "Hound Dog" and I had "Please." But that night in Los Angeles we were just two country boys singing the stuff we grew up on. I could tell Elvis had a strong spiritual feeling by the way he sang that music. We sang together a long time that night.

After California we went into Kansas City and a whole bunch of mess. We got involved in a riot there when the police stopped my show for obscenity. It was funny, really. The dancers usually wore very short shorts, cut way up, with a bare midriff. In Kansas City they didn't put seats on the auditorium floor. You could crowd right up to the bandstand, which a lot of kids did. That upset the cops because the girls hadn't shaved under their arms and you could almost see some of their pubic hair when they kicked their legs up—and a lot of the routines involved kicking. The police didn't want to see no hair nowhere. So they stopped the show.

The crowd got upset, yelling, "Leave 'em alone. Let 'em dance. We want the show." This white kid jumped on the stage and pushed the cop off. When that happened, everybody with the revue left the stage. Then the fighting really started. Kids fighting the cops, cops beating up on people. The whole thing got a lot of publicity, but the obscenity charge was nothing. Kansas City had just gotten to be a very strict town, not wide open like it was in the days of Count Basie and them.

The sex-change rumor might have had something to do with the police's attitude when we were there. I think they were expecting a dirty show. I never gave a dirty show in my life. The rumor had a life of its own, though. Later on I heard that a popular version was that I was going to marry my drummer. That's funny because I used to drum on three of the tunes we did. Anyway, I never married my drummer. Never married Bobby Byrd, either. He was already married.

25 GETTING INTO IT

IN THE MIDST OF all this running around in the jet and playing in all those big places, I was starting to get involved in public issues. I guess it started when I integrated the concerts in Macon and Augusta. But it really went back to the "White Water" and "Colored Water" signs I saw when I was little. I wanted to be more than just a person who screams and hollers on stage. I wanted to use my position to help people, and I wanted to have something to say about the country I lived in.

During the week I collapsed at the Apollo, Roy Wilkins came on stage one night, and Pop, Jack Bart, and I took out lifetime memberships from him in the NAACP. The organization was trying to get new members, and I was trying to help by joining publicly. We met for the first time when Mr. Wilkins came by the dressing room beforehand. I told him I thought he was a fine man, and I was proud of the things he'd done to benefit humanity. Out on stage he talked to the people about a lot of things that were going on in the struggle for human rights, things I didn't know about. He was opening my eyes a little more.

A few days later—on June 6, 1966—James Meredith was ambushed during his "March Against Fear" in Mississippi. Meredith had integrated Ole Miss back in 1962: He tried to register four or five times, and each time the governor of the state or state troopers stopped him. It finally took several hundred U. S. marshals to get him registered. And then there was a riot, a couple of people got killed, and the army and the National Guard had to come stop it. This time around he was planning to walk from Memphis to Jackson, Mississippi, to convince black people in the state not to be afraid to register to vote. He wasn't but a few miles inside the state line when somebody shot him in the back. Like a lot of people, I was upset by it, and I wanted to do something to help. I was in Cincinnati when I heard about it. As soon as he was well enough to receive visitors, I flew to Memphis in the new plane and visited him in the hospital. We just talked and laughed. It was the first time I'd ever met him. He was a very nice fella and a very brave one, too—an Air Force veteran, I think. I told him I supported and admired what he was doing.

In Tupelo I did a show for all the people who were coming together and continuing the march. Dick Gregory was there, and Martin Luther King and his group, the Southern Christian Leadership Conference. Stokely Carmichael and his group, the Student Nonviolent Coordinating Committee, had joined in, too. There was a lot of ferment going on, and a lot of tension inside and outside the movement. Martin was trying to keep things going in a nonviolent way, and Stokely and them were starting to talk about Black Power—and upsetting a whole lot of people with it, too. Whitney Young and Roy Wilkins pulled out of the march because of it. Black Power meant different things to different people, see. To some people it meant black pride and black people owning businesses and having a voice in politics. That's what it meant to me. To other people it meant self-defense against attacks like the one on Meredith. But to others it meant a revolutionary bag.

I wanted to see people free, but I didn't see any reason for us to kill each other. Why should we kill each other, I thought, when we can talk it out? Stokely said I was the one person who was most dangerous to his movement at the time because people would listen to me. Personally, I'll take a lick on one cheek, but I won't take it if it comes to the second cheek. The Bible speaks of self-defense; you're not supposed to let another man take your life. But I was out there to preserve life, to extend it, not to take it, and I didn't want to see the country torn up, either.

I wanted to do something constructive. Not long after the Meredith thing, I wrote "Don't Be a Drop-Out." That was something I knew about firsthand because I didn't have any formal education myself and knew how it could hold you back. The record came out in October and did pretty well, too, but I wanted to do more than just put out a record. I wanted to build a whole campaign around it. As soon as the record was pressed, I took the first copy to Vice President Hubert Humphrey at the

White House and told him what I had in mind. I guess you could say he was my first politician. He was a good man, always had good things to say, meant well, and was close to the people. He said a stay-in-school campaign had come up before, but it never got off the ground. He was glad to see someone do something besides talk about it, and he said he'd help all he could.

I visited schools and talked to kids. I told them to stay in school, listen to their teachers, and stay close to their books. They were there to take care of business. I told them about my own background, and I think that made it more vivid. If I hadn't been blessed with musical ability, I said, I'd still be a janitor. I put out a newsletter to kids and started "Don't Be a Drop-Out" clubs. And I tried to get kids who had just dropped out to go back. Adults, too. I even put a routine in the show. Some of the others on the show acted like they were in school. Byrd played a drop-out, reading a book upside down. I talked to him at the mike, and then he turned the book around and acted like he was ready to go back to school. The point we were trying to make was that it didn't matter how old you were, you could always go back and get an equivalency diploma. The band played the vamp of the tune while we did this, then we sang it from the top.

During one tour, as part of the campaign, we gave away $500 scholarships to whatever black college was in the area we were working. The kids were nominated by their high schools through whatever radio station was helping to promote the show. We gave away five scholarships a show, four shows a week, for about six months. Every now and then I saw what I was up against, though. Once, in Dayton, Ohio, I was talking to one of the winners after the show, like I always did. I'd encourage them and tell them to work hard in college and all. This one kid said, "Hey, James, why don't you just give me $500 in cash, man, so I can buy some sharp clothes and be hip like you." I didn't know whether to cry or hit the kid. Some of them just didn't understand, and it broke my heart to see it.

I spent a lot of time and money on that campaign, but it's hard to know the results of something nationwide like that. We heard from a lot of places that people were going back to school and pledging to stay in school. But we still have problems right today with people dropping out of school. And there are a lot of poor schools that should have their curriculum upgraded so they can be on a competitive basis with the wealthy schools. It's not just the black kids who are suffering but poor white kids and Hispanics and everybody.

I was happy to do what I could to help, but once you start becoming a public figure and are seen with politicians, it can get tricky. People sometimes try to use you, and other people misunderstand. Later on I found out what can happen when you get involved, but it was already starting back then.

In November, the next time I was in the Apollo, Lionel Hampton dropped by and came on the stage during the show. I introduced him to the audience, and then he said some of the boys wanted to come out and say hello. I thought he meant some of the boys in his band, and I said fine. He waved to the wings, and out came Governor Nelson Rockefeller, who was running for re-election at the time. He walked over to me and shook hands right there on stage. When he did, a photographer with him snapped a picture. It was a complete surprise to me.

I said to him: 'Okay, you got what you wanted, now go." I wasn't for him or against him. I was just trying to do my show.

With all the politicians I've endorsed over the years, this will surprise a lot of people: I don't vote. I've *never* voted. In my life. I've tried to tell people which way *they* ought to vote, though. Sometimes you teach, see. A preacher says, "Don't do as I do, do as I *say*." I've always tried to guide, but I've never voted myself. I cast my vote another way. I cast my vote with ideas and concepts. I never marched in my life, either. I tried to go a step beyond being a local statesman. I'm a humanitarian, not a politician. I'm just glad God showed me the way to take that other step.

Through the "Don't Be a Drop-Out" program I became very good friends with Vice President Humphrey. We met several times after that, for official ceremonies and things, but behind the scenes we were doing a lot of serious talking. The country was going through some heavy changes, and there was a lot of unrest. Right after the Meredith march there were riots in Cleveland and Chicago and Brooklyn. Martin was leading marches for open housing in Chicago. That's when people saw for the first time that the problem wasn't just in the South, it was everywhere. In September there were riots in Dayton and San Francisco. Stokely was arrested in Atlanta for inciting to riot there.

All that turned out to be just a taste of what was coming the next year, in 1967. Mr. Humphrey and Mr. Johnson knew what might happen, and I think they sincerely wanted to avoid it. As I traveled around the country I talked to Mr. Humphrey on the phone and told him in plain language what was going on. Sometimes after a concert I talked to one of his aides about it. I told him the people were angry and that I was afraid there was going to be a bloodbath. I could feel it everywhere I went. I think I was providing the Democrats with one of the few non-white views they had of things from the street. They didn't really have anybody to give them that view. Dr. King himself wasn't a street person. I was. I came from a ghetto and was close to the people in the ghettos all over America.

I was in touch with Martin and his people a lot, too. We ran into each other in the Atlanta airport and talked, and I spoke with Andy Young and Hosea Williams, who were Martin's aides at the time. They told me what they were doing and what they had to do it with, and I told them what I was seeing around the country, just like I had told Mr. Humphrey. I told them which way I thought the politicians I spoke to were going.

Adam Clayton Powell was a friend of mine, too. He was a very intelligent man. After they barred him from Congress and he was living on Bimini, he came to see me whenever I played Miami. I remember once the two of us and Mr. Neely sat around my hotel room talking politics and the whole racial situation. We were jumping from subject to subject, the way you will, when all of a sudden Adam became very serious. He started talking about Martin and about how much he admired him and how devoted he was to Martin's philosophy of nonviolence. That was the kind of man Adam was, though a lot of people have a different picture of him.

In the midst of all this, I was working as hard as ever. I cut a bunch of Christmas songs at the end of 1966, and in January of 1967 I cut another live album, *Live at the Garden*. I did that one at the Latin Casino in Cherry Hill, New Jersey. I was cutting singles and re-releasing stuff and doing instrumentals for Smash and cutting Byrd on Smash and cutting Vicki on King. The producers for the Broadway show *Hallelujah, Baby* saw Vicki on the revue and wanted to put her in the show. I wanted her to stay with me, though, and I think Leslie Uggams wound up playing the part. In April the *Raw Soul* album came out, most of it recorded in 1966 and January 1967.

I was still playing one-nighters, but now they were almost always in stadiums and coliseums. I rented those places myself, promoted the show, and took all the risks. Like Braves stadium —I rented it and put twenty-seven thousand people in there. But I still played places like the Fox in Brooklyn and always stayed close to the Apollo. They had a birthday cake for me on stage in May; I wasn't performing there that week, they just did it as a compliment. At the end of the month I did another big show in Madison Square Garden. This time I was able to convince people I didn't need extra acts. I did put the Mighty Clouds of Joy and Joe Cuba on the bill, but the rest of it was the James Brown Revue. I think I probably put the Mighty Clouds on because the show was on a Sunday. I wanted people to have fun, but I wanted them to have religion, too.

At the end of June I was back in the Apollo, fixing to record another live album there. This time, though, we had much more sophisticated equipment and a remote truck out back. Around the same time we did that recording, I released "Cold Sweat." It was a newer, up-tempo version of a song I'd first put out on an album back in 1962 called "I Don't Care," and it was a slow, bluesy tune then. It was good that way, but I was really getting into my funk bag now and it became an almost completely different tune, except for the lyrics. It had the scratch guitar, the fast-hitting sound from the bass, and the funky, funky rhythms played by Clyde Stubblefield. "Cold Sweat" has a pattern that hasn't been duplicated yet.

Around this time I got the name Soul Brother Number One. The word "soul" by this time meant a lot of things—in music and out. It was about the roots of black music, and it was kind of a pride thing, too, being proud of yourself and your people. Soul music and the civil rights movement went hand in hand, sort of grew up together. I think Soul Brother Number One meant I was the leader of the Afro-American movement for world dignity and integrity through music.

A lot of strange things were happening in the country. Besides Adam getting barred from Congress, Muhammad Ali refused to go into the army, got arrested, and had his title taken away. The war in Vietnam was starting to tear the country apart.

Martin even came out against it and upset everybody; they said he should only talk about civil rights. In the middle of July there was a bad riot in Newark. Twenty-six people were killed. Not a week later an even worse riot broke out in Detroit. Forty-three people were killed, thousands were hurt, and many black people's homes and businesses were burned. Federal troops were called in. The whole summer of 1967 was like that—riots of some kind or another in cities all over the country. I think there were more than a hundred. It was like I had been telling Mr. Humphrey and them—the whole country was burning up.

At the end of the summer I toured Europe. By the time I got back to the States, the cities had quieted down, but there was more tension and argument in the movement than ever about the best way to go. By the first of November, when I was back at the Apollo for three days only, I ran into Rap Brown, and we had a discussion about it. Byrd and I and some of the fellas were coming out of the fish and chips place by the theater. We had just finished eating and were fixing to go back to the theater for the evening set. Rap was coming down the sidewalk behind us and hollered. I don't think I'd ever met him before, but I recognized him. He'd taken over as chairman of SNCC after Stokely, and I think he was already under indictment for inciting to riot in Maryland. I waved him inside the theater with us where we could talk.

It was very cordial, but it was very direct. He told me about some of the things he'd been doing and what they were planning. I said, "Rap, I know what you're trying to do. I'm trying to do the same thing. But y'all got to find another way to do it. You got to put down the guns, you got to put away the violence."

"You don't understand," he said. "You just travel from town to town without staying long enough in one place to find out what's really going on. I'm out in the neighborhoods, working with people. All you know is what you can see from the stage."

"Maybe," I said, "but I can see pretty good from there. I know what's happening, and I understand why. I probably come from a much poorer background than you do."

"Then you should understand how people feel. You have an enormous following in the ghettos. You ought to get them to take action."

"I'm not going to tell anybody to pick up a gun," I said.

"Besides, even if we did start a revolution, our people couldn't do nothing but lose. We're outgunned and we're outnumbered."

He talked about urban guerrillas and a lot of things like that. Finally I said, "I agree with you, Rap, we got to get justice. But people shouldn't have to die. They shouldn't have to die."

That was it. There was no more to discuss. We wished each other luck and parted company. I headed for the dressing room. He headed back out into the street.

26 DOING IT TO DEATH

A LOT OF PEOPLE at that time besides Rap and me were looking for ways to get justice. Not too long after that Apollo engagement Otis Redding called me in Cincinnati.

"Bossman"—Otis always called me that—"I've got an idea I want you to help me with."

"What's that, Otis?"

"I want us to form a union of all black entertainers. We can start by getting all the singers and musicians that we know, and then we can get actors and dancers and the rest later on."

"What do you want to do that for?"

"Well, it would give us all more leverage in the business. No more getting messed over by the white promoters and managers and people in the record business."

"Naw, Otis," I said. "I don't want to go that way. You remember when the musicians union was like two separate unions, one for white and one for black? We just wound up second-class citizens. I don't think we ought to risk going back to that."

"It wouldn't be like that, Bossman. If the big stars stuck together, they could see to it that a lot more black entertainers got work and got treated fair."

"I can't do it, Otis. I don't believe in separatism. I think that's going backwards, and I don't want to be part of that."

He dropped the subject, and we talked about the road and things we were planning to do. I told him I was fixing to get a new jet; he told me he was thinking about learning to fly the plane he was using, a twin-engine Beech 18.

"Leave that alone," I said. "Leave that to the pilot and the co-pilot. I've been flying a long time. I know. Let them do it."

That was the last time I ever talked to him. A few days later his plane crashed in a lake during a snowstorm in Madison,

Wisconsin. It killed him and his band, the Bar-Kays. He was twenty-six years old.

I used to warn him about that plane all the time. On the last morning we talked I said, "That plane is not big enough to be doing what you're doing. It can't carry all those people and all that equipment. You shouldn't be messing around with it like that."

"Aw, it's all right, Bossman," he said. "We've had a few problems, but it's doing okay."

Somebody was fooling Otis. They tried to do the same thing with his twin-engine that I did with a Lear jet, and they couldn't do it. That plane was an old plane, with a bad battery and a lot of service problems, and it had no business flying in that kind of weather.

His death was tragic to me. I knew him from way back in Macon when he was just a kid. My band did his first charts for him. I'd see him out on the road, and we always talked about how much we missed Georgia. I remember one time in Houston when I was at the Civic Center on the same night Otis was booked into a place I used to play called the Palladium Ballroom. The Civic Center held about fourteen thousand and the Palladium about twenty-five hundred. Before the concert that night Otis came by to see me and said, "Man, with you in town I'm not going to have anybody at my gig."

"Don't worry," I said, "you'll have plenty of people there. You'll have a packed house. I guarantee it."

When I finished my show I said to the audience, "Give me time to shower and change, and I'll see you at Otis Redding's show at the Palladium."

By the time I got there the place was packed. Otis invited me on stage, and we did a bunch of numbers together. There wasn't much security at the Palladium, and we both liked to got our suits torn off.

About the same time Otis was killed I heard that Tammi was very sick in Philadelphia. It was the start of the brain tumors that killed her three years later. It was as tragic as Otis. Both of them were so young and just hitting their peaks, and I loved them.

All of that was a bad end to a strange year. There had been the riots, the killings, the arguments in the movement, and it seemed like the music and the musicians were caught up in something big, too. Something no one could really control. It was like the country was coming apart, and everybody was going to suffer. I didn't think a year could be any stranger than 1967, but there was a lot worse to come.

My music was changing as fast as the country. The things I'd started doing in "Papa's Bag" and "Cold Sweat," and other tunes around that time, I was taking even further now. In the middle of 1967 Nat Jones left the band and was replaced by Alfred "Pee Wee" Ellis as musical director. He was really in sync with what I was trying to do. He played alto, tenor, and some keyboards. Maceo, after a hitch in the army, came back in April that year. I still had St. Clair Pinkney and L. D. Williams on saxes. Joe Dupars and Waymond Reed played trumpets; Jimmy Nolen and Alphonso Kellum gave me that distinctive scratch guitar sound; and John "Jabo" Starks and Clyde Stubblefield were two of the funkiest drummers you could find. They did it to *death.*

I started off 1968 by buying my first radio station. I got into the radio business because of all the things going on in the country. I believed in human rights—not civil rights, *human* rights of *all* people everywhere—and I loved my country. But I would speak out for my people, too. That was part of loving my country. I thought we needed pride and economic power and, most important of all, education. So I bought WGYW, which I changed to WJBE, in Knoxville, Tennessee.

I know people might not believe it, but I didn't go into it to make money. First, I thought black communities needed radio stations that really served them and represented them. The station I bought in Knoxville had been a black-oriented station, but it had gone off the air. When I put it back on I kept a format of soul and gospel and jazz—the whole spectrum of black music. We had talk shows, too, and editorials and programs directed at the kids to get them to stay in school. We directed a lot of it at their parents, too, encouraging them to give their kids the support they needed.

Second, I wanted my station to be a media training ground so black people could do more than just be jocks. I wanted them to learn advertising, programming, and management at all levels. Third, as owner I wanted to be a symbol of the black entrepreneur. All three of these reasons were, to me, part of education. That was real black power.

Eventually I bought two more radio stations, WEBB in Baltimore and WRDW in Augusta. At that time there were around five hundred black-oriented radio stations in the country, but only five of them were owned by black people—and three of those were mine. I did the same thing with my other two stations that I did in Knoxville. We used to joke that WEBB stood for "We Enjoy Being Black." WRDW was really special because that was in my hometown.

We did many political things on the stations, editorials that irritated a lot of people. Sometimes I would cut an editorial and just say what I was really thinking. I wasn't a radio professional, so some of 'em were a little too raw for the FCC and they got on us every now and then. With the war in Vietnam and the unrest at home, you couldn't avoid politics during that time.

In Vietnam the Tet offensive convinced a lot of people that the war was going to go on for a long time. I admired the bravery of the boys who were over there, and I knew a large proportion were black. I had been trying for a long time to get the government to let me go over there to entertain the troops. I knew the black soldiers were complaining that the USO didn't send enough acts they could identify with, and I wanted to change that. I offered to pay all my expenses and everything if they'd just let me go, but for some reason they didn't want me to go. I don't know if they thought I would be too political or what.

At home, Governor Wallace announced he was running for president and President Johnson announced that he wasn't. Senator Robert Kennedy and Senator Eugene McCarthy were already running, and Mr. Nixon looked like he'd be it for the Republicans. I knew one thing: I wanted to have some say this time in who ran the country, so I was watching it all real close.

Then another personal tragedy struck. On March 5, Mr. Nathan died. We had fought a lot, but it was like arguments between a stern father and a headstrong son. He was gruff on the outside but soft on the inside, and underneath it all he believed in me almost before anybody else did. We squabbled over money and business and all kinds of things, but Syd Nathan gave this poor country boy from Georgia the vehicle to do everything he'd ever dreamed of doing.

In the middle of all these serious events I got into a comical conflict with Joe Tex. Over the years we had this rivalry thing going. It was all in good fun. We'd say things about each other or do things, and they'd show up in *Jet* or another magazine. One time I heard he had "Soul Brother Number One" painted on the side of his bus and was going around the country that way. Next time I saw him, I stopped that real fast. Wasn't any harm in it, it was just part of the joking with each other. But this time around he stopped his show at the Uptown in Philadelphia and told the audience I was paying disc jockeys not to play his song "Skinny Legs and All." He went on Georgie Woods' radio program later and repeated it, saying I did it because I thought the song was insulting to black women. I answered him when I went into the Apollo for four days the last week in March. Before the show started I went out on stage, sat down on a stool with a mike, and told the people I didn't have a fight with Joe over "Skinny Legs and All." I said he was a good friend of mine, I thought the world of him, and I had ordered my radio stations to play *all* his songs.

A lot happened during those four nights at the Apollo. One night there was a riot outside the theater of people trying to get in. Another night a television crew taped the show for a special they were doing.

On March 27, the third day of my run, Little Willie John died in the penitentiary in Washington. Honi Coles came in the dressing room and told me. I bowed my head. I loved Willie, and I spoke about him that night on stage. Two years before he died, I started a campaign to get Willie released from prison on parole. Had a lot of papers written up. Signed things. Mr. Neely and I actually got him out for a short time, but he went down to Los Angeles, which was a violation of his parole, and they put him right back in. I knew all about how that felt. I think it broke him. When St. Clair Pinkney, Pop, and I went out to the prison to seem him later that same year, they brought him to us in a wheelchair. He had pneumonia.

"Don't worry, Willie," I told him, "we're going to get you out of here again."

"Naw," he said, "I'm going to die in here. I know that now. But thanks just the same."

It hurt me to see him so downhearted. See, the people who were all at King together were like family. Sometimes we even fought the way families will. Mr. Nathan had been like a strict father. Mr. Neely was like a favorite uncle. Willie was like a brother. When I heard he'd died, I decided while I was still at the Apollo that I wanted to record a tribute album the first chance I got. I did, too, and the album came out at the end of the year: *Thinking About Little Willie John and a Few Nice Things*.

There was a lot on my mind during those few days at the Apollo—Willie's death, Mr. Nathan's, the things that were going on in the country. During one show I brought out my accountant to present a check to CORE and another check to the H. Rap Brown Defense Fund. I disagreed with Rap about a lot of things, but I also didn't like the way the government was harassing him. And bad as things were getting, I thought we needed to stick together. I was against violence, but I was not against self-defense. At the last show of the run I closed with another speech about all the things that were going through my mind at the time. I was getting ready to go on my first trip to Africa, and I was thinking about the elections and human rights and my own origins and where I was headed.

"I will never get too big to remember I'm still a soul brother," I said. "I know I am black, always will be black, and you are my people. The way things are going in this country . . . I don't know . . . I may try to run for president. But no matter what, remember: Die on your feet; don't live on your knees."

But I never told people to burn. I told them to organize and become involved and unified. I was saying build, and Rap and them were saying it, too, but they had a shorter fuse than I did and at some point they were driven to say destroy. A short fuse is dangerous when you have a lot of people listening to you. You can be forced into creating things you can't control. I'm glad I was never pushed to that point, but I *could* have been.

A few hours after I closed at the Apollo I was on an Air France jet headed for the Ivory Coast by way of Paris. It was the first time I'd ever been to Africa. When I got there and got off the plane, I felt I was on land I should have been on much earlier. The Africans were full of pride and dignity, and they were very warm, too. It was hard to believe that they knew my music. It wasn't in their language, and most of them probably didn't have much extra money to spend on records and things. We were there for only two days, but I was overwhelmed by the spirit of the place. I think it made me understand some things about my roots as well. Later on I found out a lot of my roots were in China, a lot in Mexico, some in Germany.

It was really a whirlwind trip: We left on Friday and got back the next Tuesday, the second day of April. I intended to rest because I had a big show scheduled for the Boston Garden on Friday, April 5. Boston had always been a good town for me —I'd had ten thousand at the Garden the time before—and I was feeling kind of changed after that first trip to Africa and looking forward to the show. I spent Wednesday trying to get my sleep straightened out. Thursday, too, until I heard the news later that day: They had killed Dr. King in Memphis during a garbage strike.

27 THERE'S A RIOT GOING ON

WHEN a great man is killed for no reason and he happens to be your friend, you feel the loss twice over. In Martin's case, it was all one feeling because with him it was like the *nation* had lost its greatest friend. That's what Martin was—*America*'s best friend. And a lot of Americans didn't even realize it.

When the shock wore off I called Mr. Neely and talked to him for a long time about the assassination. Like a lot of people, I knew it was going to bring a great deal of violence, burning, and death, and I knew everybody would lose by it. I didn't want it to happen, and I knew Martin wouldn't want it to happen. I told Mr. Neely I wished there was something I could do to prevent it.

When I hung up I thought there was one thing I could do. I called my radio stations in Knoxville and Baltimore and had them put me on the air live. I urged the people to stay calm, to honor Dr. King by being peaceful. Then I made more taped messages like that and instructed the station managers to play them until the trouble passed. I believe they had some effect because those two cities had less trouble than most.

The next day, Friday, I was tied up taping some segments for a television special—the same special they had filmed my Apollo show for. I didn't want to do it that day, but it was scheduled to go on the air in early June and I didn't have any other time I could do it. I went from the studio directly to the airport and flew to Boston. I wanted to go through with my concert there because I thought it would give me an opportunity to keep some people off the streets that night—the night everybody was predicting the worst rioting for—and to talk to them about the situation.

I was met at Logan Airport by Mayor Kevin White's limousine and a city councilman named Thomas Atkins. I believe he told me he was the first black ever elected to city-wide office in Boston. As we drove to the Garden, he filled me in on the situation. The night before hadn't been too bad in Boston— everybody was still in shock—but they were worried about that night. The National Guard was on alert and standing by. He said city officials had spent the morning arguing about whether to let my concert go on. The mayor wanted to cancel it, but Atkins told him that would just make matters worse. If many people from Roxbury showed up downtown at the Garden and found a lock on the door, trouble would start. Atkins said he told the mayor he'd be lucky if his own office was left standing. Then somebody came up with the idea of televising the concert live. That way people could stay home and see the show, and the people who showed up wouldn't find a locked door. So Atkins got in touch with a disc jockey named Early Byrd on WILD, the local soul station, and Early Byrd contacted my people in New York and told them that it was either televise the concert or the mayor was going to cancel it. While they were trying to get to me, others in the mayor's office persuaded WGBH, the local public TV station, to put the concert on live. They needed some lead time to get set up, and the mayor's office needed time to get the word out about the broadcast.

My people couldn't reach me because I was taping the television program, but they gave Early Byrd a tentative okay, subject to my veto. Atkins passed the word to the mayor's office, but he told them there was no guarantee that I would agree— and then they'd really have a mess on their hands. Once the mayor got the tentative okay, Atkins told me, it was "off to the races." The mayor put out a press release announcing that the concert would be televised. Taped announcements went out over WILD urging people to stay home and watch James Brown on television. The TV people were laying cable at the Garden.

"That's where it stands now," he said.

"I really want to help," I said, "but there's a very serious problem. I just taped a television special, and the contract prohibits me from performing on television for a certain period of time before and after the show is aired and in certain geographical areas. That period of time is now, and one of the areas is Boston. If I go on TV here tonight, I'll have lawsuits and trouble every which way. I'll cooperate in any way I can, but I cannot do a show on television."

I was very disturbed. Here the people had been told they could see the show on television, and if it wasn't on, I knew they'd feel tricked and then get mad. If the mayor cancelled the show entirely, there would be more trouble. We rode along not saying anything. It was rush hour, but the streets were deserted. Sort of like the calm before the storm. After a while we both started talking about how we felt about Dr. King.

"You know," I said, "I want to do a show tonight because I want to dedicate it to him. I didn't always agree with him, but he was a great man and he did a lot for all of us."

"He was remarkable."

"Yes, he was," I said. "If I was faced with some of the same situations he was—people beating me, throwing things at me, cursing me, spitting on me—I don't know if I could stay nonviolent, not as a matter of *philosophy*."

"I know what you mean," he said. "I once spent an entire night in Mississippi in 1964 arguing that point with him. I'm nonviolent if I have to be, but I don't want anybody to ever make the mistake of thinking they could hit me and get away with it."

"Brother, that's where I'm at," I said. "But I had the deepest respect and love for him."

When we got to the Boston Garden I could see that people were coming in droves to get refunds on their tickets because they'd heard it was going to be on TV live. They didn't want to be out that night, and if they could see it free, it made sense to them to get refunds. The Garden had also stopped selling any more tickets. Now things were really a mess. For the first time I got really mad.

"Without my permission this thing has been announced, and the announcement has now had the clear effect of killing the gate. I would at least have been able to get through to the fourteen or fifteen thousand young people who would have been here. I think it would have made a difference. But now I'm going to play to an empty house; I'm going to have to pay for it myself, and the thing can't even be seen on television. The people who had tickets and the people who are excited about seeing it at home are going to be very angry. Instead of cooling things off, it's going to heat them up. The whole thing is a disaster. I want to stop riots, not start them."

I didn't blame Atkins. He was a good man and wasn't responsible for the mess. He wanted to try to fix it some way, and so did I. In a few hours people were going to turn on their TV sets expecting to see James Brown.

"Okay," I said, "I'll do everything I can to get released from my contract so I can be on television here tonight. It's not going to be easy this late on a Friday, but I'm going to try. Now tell me what you're going to do about the losses you're inflicting on me."

"I'll undertake to see that the city guarantees the gate," he said.

"Fair enough," I said. "Let's get to it."

We found an office and got on the phones. I called my people in New York, and he tried to locate the mayor. I told my people to do whatever was necessary to get the release and have the TV people call me immediately if there was any problem. Within an hour they had it worked out. I told Atkins. He told me he was having trouble getting the mayor to go along. The mayor said to him, "We're crazy to even be talking about this. If it ever gets out that we were discussing paying the city's money to some rock 'n' roll singer, we're both through in politics." The mayor hadn't been mayor that long, but people were already talking about running him for vice president.

I could see Atkins felt bad about the whole situation. I believe he was starting to feel used. He got back on the phone with the mayor and told him I had acted in good faith from the very first and that the city had caused the problem and ought to solve it. Finally, the mayor agreed—but he didn't want to. Then, I understand, they had a very interesting discusson about what it meant to guarantee the gate. Atkins told him it would be the difference between what we took in at the box office and the amount we would have taken in based on a sellout. The mayor didn't like that either, and Atkins had to explain to him that I would have sold it out. When Atkins told me that we had an agreement, I was very appreciative. I would have gone on and done the show anyway and taken the losses, but by then I thought the city ought to do *something* right, so I accepted the offer.

I went to my dressing room and changed, the band set up,

June 1968, I played for the troops in Vietnam. I could take only five members of my band—Maceo Parker on sax, Tim Drummond, bass, Clyde Stubblefield, drums, Waymond Reed, trumpet, and Jimmy Nolen on guitar, plus singer Marva Whitney (not pictured here). (*Ebony*)

We sometimes traveled around Vietnam in a bus that had wire-mesh windows to keep the Vietcong from tossing in grenades. (*Ebony*)

During the daytime shows in Vietnam, it must've been 115 degrees on the stage. But that was nothing to what our boys were going through over there. (*Ebony*)

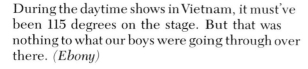

During the height of the movement, around the time of "Black and Proud," I started wearing my hair in an Afro. With a visual act like me, hair is very important. People still ask me sometimes if my hair is real: It is. *(Frank Driggs Collection)*

I played the Copa in March of 1971 and left after one week of a two-week gig. My band then included Bootsy Collins on bass; he later joined George Clinton and hit big with Bootsy's Rubber Band. *(Charles Stewart)*

When I endorsed President Nixon in 1972, a lot of people got very heavy with me. It cost me in a lot of ways, but I wouldn't back down. This particular meeting included the President's Special Assistant Robert J. Brown, the President, U.S. Marshall James Palmer, my father, me, and my manager, Charles Bobbitt. (*Official White House Photograph*)

One of my daughters "gives me five" before a concert at Bell Auditorium in Augusta. The saddest thing about my second marriage breaking up in the mid-seventies was the girls being taken away. (*Hal Neely*)

I went to Zaire in 1974 for the music festival that was supposed to coincide with the Ali–Foreman fight. When my plane arrived at the Kinshasa airport at two A.M. Ali was there to meet me. (*Kwame Brathwaite*)

I first heard Maceo Parker play in a club in
Greenville, North Carolina, around 1965. I wanted
his brother Melvin to play drums for me, so I figured
I had to hire Maceo to get Melvin. Of course, Maceo
turned out to be one of my show's biggest assets.
(*Kwame Brathwaite*)

Fred Wesley (*left*) was a trombone player who came into the band around
1968 and turned out to be a great arranger and real innovator in funk.
(*Kwame Brathwaite*)

Jimmy Nolen helped originate the distinctive scratch guitar style you hear in funk. When this shot was taken in 1983, Jimmy had just come back into the band, but he died of a heart attack not too long after. (*Mark Sarfati*)

Vicki Anderson, who married Bobby Byrd, stayed with the Revue for six years. She could outsing anybody I ever heard. (*Courtesy Jack Bart*)

The biggest and best change in my life came on February 2, 1982, when I met Adrianne, the very special lady who is my wife today. We met on the set of the television program *Solid Gold,* where she was working at the time. It was like our souls had met a long time before. *(Courtesy Mrs. James Brown)*

The thing I missed most in life was growing up without both parents. So, in the early eighties, I kind of put my family back together. My daddy was already living near me, and I got my mother to settle nearby, too. For the first time since I was four years old, we were all together again. *(Ebony)*

When I really decided to come back, I started doing a lot of television—*Saturday Night, David Letterman,* things like that—to go along with the movies. This is from a 1983 appearance on *American Bandstand. (Frank Driggs Collection)*

The scene from *Rocky IV* with Carl Weathers as Apollo Creed completed the process that started with *Blues Brothers.* Sylvester Stallone was a good man to work with, and the song "Living in America" that Dan Hartman and Charlie Midnight wrote for me went to number three on the charts. *(United Artists)*

We spent three days shooting the movie scene and the
music video for "Living in America." It helped introduce
me to a whole new generation of fans. *(Steve Schapiro)*

Even though I'm not a rock'n'roll singer, I was proud to be inducted
into the Rock and Roll Hall of Fame in January 1986, along with cats
like Jerry Lee Lewis and Fats Domino. But I'm no oldies act: I had
a record going into the top of the charts the same night. *(Hy Simon–
Photo Trends)*

and the TV people finished getting the cameras in place. Even with all the announcements about the concert being televised, about two thousand people showed up at the Garden. The mayor showed up, too, wanting to go on the air to ask for calm. That was fine with me. Atkins introduced me, and I introduced the mayor. I think I even called him a "swinging cat."

"All of us are here tonight to listen to a great talent," he said, "but we're also here to pay tribute to one of the greatest of Americans—Dr. Martin Luther King, Jr. Twenty-four hours ago Dr. King died for all of us, black and white, that we may live together in harmony, without violence, and in peace. I'm here to ask for your help—let's make Dr. King's dream a reality in Boston. No matter what any other community might do, we in Boston will honor Dr. King in peace."

I said I seconded that. "Let's not to anything to dishonor Dr. King," I said. "Stay home. You kids, especially, I want you to think about what you're doing. Think about what Dr. King stood for. Don't just react in a way that's going to destroy your community."

Throughout the show, between songs, I talked about Dr. King and urged the people to stay calm. I announced a song title and tried to work the title into a little rap about Dr. King and the whole situation. I talked about my own life and where I'd come from. At one point, when I was reminiscing about Martin, I started to cry—just a few tears rolling out, you know, nothing anybody could really see—but it was like it was all starting to really sink in what we lost. But I pulled myself together—I thought that would do the most good—and went on with the show.

"I'm still a soul brother," I said at one point, "and you people have made it possible for me to be a first-class man in all respects. I used to shine shoes in front of a radio station. Now I own radio stations. You know what that is? That's Black Power."

While the show was going on, the mayor and others backstage were monitoring the situation around the city. The police said the streets in Roxbury were almost empty. Not only was there no trouble, there were fewer people out than there would be ordinarily. Police said it was eerie. It was working so well that somebody got the idea of showing the whole thing over again as soon as we finished. I said that was fine with me. Near the end of the program I announced that the whole thing would be repeated immediately.

When we went into our finale, some of the fans at the Garden jumped up on the stage. They started dancing and shaking hands with me. That upset the police. They started to move in. I knew that all it would take to destroy everything I'd been trying to do all night long was for there to be an incident with the police and have it televised. I stopped the music and asked the police to back off. "I'm all right," I said, "I'm all right. I *want* to shake their hands." I shook some more hands and then asked the people politely to leave the stage. They did, and we finished the show without any problem. As soon as we finished, the television station started running a complete tape of the show. It wasn't over until two o'clock in the morning. By that time the danger was past. Boston got through the weekend almost without any trouble at all.

Washington, D.C., wasn't so lucky. There was looting and burning all over the city Thursday and Friday nights. They had a curfew, but nobody paid any attention to it. They had something like three hundred fires the first two nights. The burned-out buildings were collapsing and injuring people. Over two thousand people were arrested, and one person was killed Thursday and four more the next night.

Stokely was there, going around the streets trying to cool things off, I think. But it was kind of strange. I heard he was talking at Howard University on Friday and kept telling the people, "Stay off the streets if you don't have a gun because there's going to be shooting." He said it over and over, and then he whipped out his own gun and showed it to the crowd.

On Saturday they called out twelve thousand troops and put them all around the city. That morning Mayor Walter Washington and some of the other officials decided to ask me to come down there. They called Dewey Hughes, the news director of station WOL, who got in touch with my people. By that time I had received several requests like that from different cities, but I went to Washington because it was really the symbol of the whole country.

I couldn't believe the destruction: buildings smoking, smashed glass all over the streets, stores with their windows busted out. I don't think I ever saw anything like it until I got to Vietman. "Soul Brother" was written on many black-owned stores to protect them, but in a lot of cases it didn't do any good. They were looted, too. What disturbed me the most was the people dying. I didn't want to see any more people die, white or black.

I went on live television from the Municipal Center. "I know how everybody feels," I said. "I feel the same way. But you can't accomplish anything by blowing up, burning up, stealing, and looting. Don't terrorize. Organize. Don't burn. Give kids a chance to learn. Go home. Look at TV. Listen to the radio. Listen to some James Brown records. The real answer to race problems in this country is education. Not burning and killing. Be ready. Be qualified. Own something. Be somebody. That's Black Power."

I talked a lot about Martin, too, like I did in Boston. "He was our hero. We have an obligation to try to fulfill his dream of true brotherhood. You can't do that with violence."

When I got through, I met with the city officials and then went on WOL radio to make some more appeals. While I was there, Lady Bird Johnson called me to say thanks. Her daughter, Mrs. Luci Nugent, called a little later. I think that was an audience the station didn't usually get.

My next gig was in Rochester, so I went there ahead of time and went on the air to try to cool things down. I was glad to do it. I was glad to do it in all those cities. I would have gone to more if I could. Nobody gained anything from all that destruction. I knew it *then*, but a lot of people didn't like the kind of things I was saying at that time. I think they understand now.

28 VIETNAM

My PLACE CARD at the White House dinner said: "Thanks much for what you are doing for your country—LBJ." I think that upset some people because they thought it was like a pat on the head for helping cool off the riots. I don't think they understood everything I had been doing—the stay-in-school campaign, the lobbying with the vice president about job programs, and things like that. And in less than a month—the dinner was on May 8—I was going to Vietnam to entertain the troops.

I also had a song, a patriotic song, about to come out called "America Is My Home." I called it my contribution to "the long *cool* summer." I didn't know it at the time, but that record was going to disturb a lot of people. They were going to get very heavy with me over that song. Today, all anybody says about it is that it was the first rap record.

The state dinner was in honor of the prime minister of Thailand. Besides him and President Johnson, there were senators, congressmen, and other government officials: Vice President Humphrey, Sentator Birch Bayh, Senator Sam Ervin, Representative John Anderson, Secretary of State Dean Rusk, Secretary of Defense Clark Clifford, Eugene and Walter Rostow, William Bundy, General Maxwell Taylor, Cyrus Vance, and a lot more. Edward Bennett Williams, Earl Wilson, Allen Drury, and a few other private citizens were also there.

I was standing in a group with the president and others when Earl Wilson, the columnist, said, "Won't they call you Uncle Tom for doing this?"

"No," I said.

"Why not?"

"Because I'm not." And Mr. Johnson winked his eye.

I didn't talk to Mr. Johnson very much. He was eating a lot

of food. That man was *hungry*. I was honored to be there, but mostly I was just interested because I was getting ready to go to Asia and most of the people at the dinner were concerned with what was going on there. The president had just said he wouldn't run for re-election. He had stopped the bombing and was about to send some people over to start peace talks. I think he really wanted peace, but I think he wanted to reassure Thailand, too. He got up to toast the prime minister and said, "We will never abandon our commitment or compromise the future of Asia at the negotiating table."

During the meal I was seated on the other side of the room from Mr. Humphrey. Afterward, a Secret Service man came to my table and said, "The Vice President of the United States would like to see you at his table." It sounded like an order.

"Please inform the vice president," I said, "that James Brown is not his boy. I will not walk across the room to his table." The Secret Service man looked shook up now. "But you can tell him," I said, smiling a big crocodile smile, "that I'll meet him halfway."

The Secret Service man looked like he didn't believe what he was hearing. He stood there for a minute, then walked across the room, with me watching him the whole way. He leaned down and whispered to Mr. Humphrey. When he was finished, Mr. Humphrey caught my eye and started laughing. We met halfway.

It was all in good fun, but I was not his boy. I had been thinking about the election a lot since Mr. Johnson withdrew. Mr. Humphrey hadn't really jumped into it that strong yet, and I had just about decided to endorse Senator Robert Kennedy. He was a good man and was doing very well in the primaries, and I thought he was going to get the nomination eventually. He was a young man with young ideas, and at that time we needed a leader that young people could identify with. I didn't discuss my plans with Mr. Humphrey that night, but I intended to explain it to him before I went public with it.

The only other entertainer at the White House that night was Bob Hope—one of the finest men I know. I think he was partly responsible for my finally getting to Vietnam. I had volunteered a long time before and offered to pay my own way and everything, but the government kept putting me off. Mr.

Hope told some of the USO people, "If you're going to get anybody to perform for the troops, James Brown is the man." Not long after that, I received the word to go.

When I got the dates for the Vietnam trip, I cancelled $100,000 worth of bookings. We left at the beginning of June and went to Korea first. I took the whole revue over there. We stayed near Seoul and did a couple of shows a day for several days all around the country. When we went to Vietnam we could only take seven people—five musicians, me, and Marva Whitney. The musicians were Maceo Parker on sax, Waymond Reed on trumpet, Jimmy Nolen on guitar, Tim Drummond on bass, and Clyde Stubblefield on drums.

Tim was a white bass player I had used on some sessions in Cincinnati at King. I'd been asking him to join the band, and when he heard we were going to Vietnam he said yes. He told me he wanted to show the soldiers over there that *some* white and black people back home were getting along. He was a playing cat—good God a'mighty, I never could get enough of Tim.

Marva was a singer on the show, and she was also my girlfriend at the time. Deedee and I had broken up by then, and she'd left. Another woman named Florence had become my girlfriend, and she was with me in New York. We lasted about two years, until Deedee and I got back together. But Marva was my girlfriend, too. She was a fine woman. I wrote a song for her called "It's My Thing and I Do What I Want to Do and You Can't Tell Me Who to Sock It To." I think she was the strongest of all my girlfriends. Any time a woman can go to Vietnam and go through what she went through, she *must* be stronger than anybody else.

They gave us a bunch of shots, fatigues to travel around in, and steel-reinforced boots in case of booby traps, and then they put us on a plane for Saigon. The funny thing was the identification cards they gave us that said we were noncombatants. If we somehow got captured by the Viet Cong, we were supposed to show them these cards and everything would be cool. We laughed about that the whole time we were there.

We got there not too long after Tet, and the day before, the Viet Cong had launched the biggest attack on Saigon up to that time. They shot something like 135 rounds of 122-millimeter rockets into the city. Flying into Saigon you could see all the blown-up buildings and damage that had been done. Except for the gun emplacements and the sandbags everywhere, though, Saigon was a beautiful city. They put us up at the Continental Hotel, I believe, not too far from the presidential palace. The day we got there, a mortar shell hit a few doors down the street and killed seventeen people. They dropped ten rockets on Tan Son Nhut Air Base, right outside the city, that morning. We performed there that afternoon. From Saigon we traveled around the country by helicopter, did our shows, and then came back there to sleep. At night you could hear the American bombs hitting a few miles out in the countryside. You could *feel* 'em, too—the bed would shake.

We did two, sometimes three, shows a day—one in the morning, one in the afternoon, and one at night. Really, it was harder than any tour I'd ever done. For one thing, it was unbelievably hot. Being up on that stage dancing and singing in 100 degrees, the jungle sun beating down, I'd be so depleted that I'd get my intravenous after almost every show. Clyde lost a lot of fluid, too, working out on those drums. After one really hot show I said to him, "Try this." He said okay. They brought in an old field nurse who was used to seeing worse things than dehydrated musicians, and she took the needle and jabbed it into him. She didn't have any finesse at all. Clyde let out a holler, jerked the needle out of his arm, and ran out of the tent. He didn't want any more intravenous.

The reception we got was incredible, they were so glad to see us. The shows all kind of ran together, but I'll never forget the one we did for the Ninth Infantry Division. It was called Bearcat, I believe. They had the place dug out of the side of a hill—like the Hollywood Bowl—and there must have been forty thousand people there. Around the rim, at the top, tanks were pulled up like at a drive-in, with guys sitting in the hatches looking down on the show.

It must have been 115 degrees on the stage. We didn't care. Those guys went wild, all forty thousand in full field gear. About halfway through the show we heard this *ack-ack-ack-ack, boom, boom, BOOM* coming from somewhere behind the stage. It turned out Americans were firing at somebody. I didn't have any thoughts of stopping the show, but we must have looked concerned because the guys in the front yelled, "Don't worry, we won't let Charlie get you."

After a show we mingled with the troops for a little while,

then we jumped in the helicopter and headed for the next show. A soldier always sat in the open door of the helicopter with a grenade launcher watching the ground to see if anything moved. Sometimes we drew some small-arms fire. One night we were choppering back from a show and tracers came at us. It was kind of pretty if you didn't think about the fact they were meant to kill you.

When we got back to the airfield at night, they took us off the chopper and put us in a bus. The windows on the bus had screens so no one could throw a grenade in while we were riding along. One night we were standing by the chopper and overheard a guy on a walkie-talkie yell, "Get 'em out of there. A mortar attack is coming in." They hustled us onto the bus and made us lie on the floor as we drove away. I started laughing, thinking about the time in North Carolina when all those people chased us out of town, shooting at us, and we had to lie on the floor of that bus.

Another time we had to take a plane instead of a helicopter because we were going to an air base way up north. That's the only time we traveled by plane. They put us in one of those planes you always see go down in a Tarzan movie, an old prop job. They could tell we didn't like the way it looked because they said, "Don't worry, this plane's a workhorse. It'll go anywhere." We weren't in the air ten minutes when one of the engines caught fire. We came limping back, about fifty feet off the ground. We made an emergency landing—barely making the end of the runway. They ran out to the plane and got us off quick. While we were waiting in a Quonset hut for another plane, we heard this *BOOM, BOOM, KABOOM*. An officer in the hut said, "Hmmm, must be an air strike." Our planes were attacking the area we'd just brushed over. I guess we'd aroused some Viet Cong.

The whole time in Vietnam there was always a chance we'd get shot down or mortared, but nothing I did was as hard as what our soldiers had to do. Every day. For months. Some for years. A lot of 'em looked like seventeen- and eighteen-year-old kids, but they weren't kids. They were men. They had to be.

Before we left for Vietnam I had instructed Bob Patton, one of my promotion men, to make contact with Senator Kennedy. They met in the Ambassador Hotel the day of the California primary. Mr. Patton told the senator that I wanted to endorse him. He said, "That's great. Tell James I appreciate it. I'll talk to you about it a little later, but right now I have to make a speech." Mr. Patton left; I think he went to see the Righteous Brothers who were doing a show nearby. When he came back to the Ambassador later that night, he ran into a big commotion. Senator Kennedy had been shot. He died the next day. I don't remember where I was when I got the news from Mr. Patton but, for some reason, after that, Vietnam didn't seem so dangerous to me.

29 SAY IT LOUD

BY THE TIME I got back from Vietnam people were on my case about "America Is My Home," calling me an Uncle Tom, saying the song was a sellout, things like that. Some of the more militant organizations sent representatives backstage after shows to talk about it. "How can you do a song like that after what happened to Dr. King?" they'd say. I talked to them and tried to explain that when I said "America is my home," I didn't mean the government was my home, I meant the land and the people. They didn't want to hear that. I told them I was all for self-defense, but it made no sense for us to burn down our own communities. They didn't like that, either.

I was taking flak about having a white bass player, too. Over the years I have had several white cats in my bands, but Tim Drummond, was the first and it upset a lot of people. When he first joined, we were playing the Regal. There were certain people I thought would get very heavy with him if they saw him on stage, so I told him to set up offstage and watch me for cues during the show. Right before the show, though, I said, "No, let's get it over with. You go on out there."

During the band's set, before I came on, there was a big, mean looking cat in the wings motioning to Tim to get off the stage. Tim ignored him for a while. Finally, during one of Maceo's solos, he laid down his bass and came off. The fella told him, "You're not supposed to be on this stage." Tim asked him who he was. He let on that he was with the union and with the Regal, so Tim came to my dressing room while the band was still on and told me about it. I cornered the cat and said, "You don't want him to play because he's white. Well, he's going to play, and if he doesn't, I'll pull my show out of here right now. I don't care if you're with the union or the theater or who. Now get out of my sight."

Another time, in Washington, I received an unsigned tele-
gram that said, "You have a white man working for you and a
black man needs a job." A lot of people didn't like the rap I
gave in the show, either. I talked about my background—going
from shining shoes to running radio stations and owning a jet. I
talked about the importance of education. "Learn," I said,
"don't burn. Get an education, work hard, and try to get in a
position of owning things. That's Black Power." I said we had
a lot of problems in the black community that we had to solve
ourselves—wasn't anybody could do it for us.

A lot of people didn't want to hear that and didn't understand it. There were bomb threats, death threats. Once we were
ordered by the police to evacuate a hotel in Atlanta. Sometimes
there were threats about disrupting concerts with stink bombs,
things like that. Some of the threats came to Mr. Neely and
King Records. I didn't pay any attention to them. You couldn't.
Entertainers get threats like that all the time. You can never
really be sure where they're coming from anyway—it could be
political or somebody with a personal grudge or people trying
to muscle in on the business. It's hard to tell.

Pop wanted me to back off doing political things, too. From
the time I first got into integrating concerts, we got into long
discussions about it. They got a little more heated now.

"Why jump off into that?" he said. "Wait until your real hot
run is over, then if you want to dabble in politics, do it as a kind
of elder statesman, but not now. You can't do anything for anybody else if *you* don't have anything."

"If anybody's going to listen to me, it's going to be now. It
would be a shame to have this big audience, with all that's
going on, and not try to do some good."

He was afraid it would hurt my popularity. He turned out to
be right, but he didn't understand that I didn't care. I had to
say what I thought either way—whether it upset Afro-Americans or Caucasian Americans.

Meantime, my music was getting funkier and funkier. What
I'd started on "Get It Together" and "I Can't Stand Myself," I
took even further with "Licking Stick—Licking Stick." Pee
Wee Ellis, Byrd, and I put it together, and I released it at the
same time as "America Is My Home." It was another one-chord
song like "I Can't Stand Myself," but it had even more of a funk
groove. It was a rhythm section tune and exactly what the title

said, a licking stick. If the people who were on me about "America Is My Home" wanted to know who James Brown was, all they had to do was listen to "Licking Stick." My *music* said where I stood.

There were some changes in the band, too. When Tim Drummond came down with hepatitis from Vietnam, Charles Sherrell replaced him on bass. "Sweet" Charles we called him. He hasn't gotten the credit as a bass player that he should have. A lot of the stuff that Bootsy Collins and some other bass players did later—like thumping the strings—Sweets did first. Fred Wesley replaced Levi Raspbury on trombone and turned out to be a real innovator and a real creator as an arranger. Around the same time trumpeter Richard "Kush" Griffith and a third drummer, Nate Jones, also joined.

I got back from Vietnam on June 17 and five days later played Yankee Stadium. Pop and I had a discussion about that, too. He wanted me to add a whole lot of extra acts to the show so I wouldn't embarrass myself with an empty stadium. I told him I wanted to prove a soul act could fill a place like that. I believe I had forty-eight thousand people there. I dreamed a lot of dreams in my life, but I could never have imagined playing Yankee Stadium. I called the show the National Soul Festival and took it around to huge places that summer like Soldier Field to show that somebody besides the Beatles could fill venues like that. I thought it would give a sense of pride to little black kids like the one I overheard at Yankee Stadium who said, "The Yankees can't even fill Yankee Stadium."

At the end of July I campaigned for Mr. Humphrey in Watts. That wasn't too popular, either. Mr. Humphrey didn't even have the nomination yet, and a lot of people blamed him for the way the war in Vietnam was going. And a lot of Afro-Americans, including me, had really been behind Senator Kennedy, and it was hard to get over his death, coming so soon after Dr. King's. Some couldn't forgive Mr. Humphrey for being against Senator Kennedy. It's funny, though. When the election rolled around, Mr. Humphrey almost won. It took all that time for people to see he was his own man and that he was a good man.

He campaigned in Watts for several days. It was very difficult. The Saturday before I joined him, some militants booed him off the stage there. His security people didn't want him in Watts at all. When I joined him the following Monday, the

security was unbelievable. Police were on all the rooftops looking over the crowd with binoculars. There were dozens of other
policemen and Secret Service men all up and down the street
and mingling with the crowd. I'm not sure, but I think maybe
they had to know from their own informers about the threats
I'd been getting.

I didn't just get up and endorse Mr. Humphrey flatly. I tried
to get him into a discussion right there on the platform. I
wanted him to make some promises not just to me but to the
people. I said to the crowd, "I won't endorse Mr. Humphrey
unless he promises to give the black man what he wants—
ownership. He wants his own things: houses, banks, hotels. He
wants to be able to walk into a bank and see people of all
origins working there so he'll feel comfortable asking for a loan.
When he goes to a hospital emergency room, he wants to see
priority given to the people with the worst ailments, not the
lightest skin."

Mr. Humphrey stepped up to the mike and said he had been
for those things for years. "If you elect me president," he said,
"you'll get them. I promise you that."

"I got the feeling," I said. "I endorse him." The band they
had there struck up, and I even got the vice president to do a
little dance. "You can do the boogaloo, man, if you have soul."

While I was in Los Angeles I planned to cut something that
had been on my mind a long time—"Say It Loud, I'm Black
and I'm Proud." There was a vamp we'd been playing on the
show for quite a while, and during my last tour I wrote some
words for it while we were flying from Canada to Seattle. I was
ready to go into the studio with it, but I needed some kids to
be a chorus. I got all the fellas in the band and people traveling
with the show to invite their friends and relatives with kids to
come to the studio in Hollywood that night.

People were still getting very heavy with me about "America Is My Home" and the Humphrey thing, and the night we
were supposed to cut, a strange thing happened. I was in my
hotel room fixing to go to the studio when I heard a loud knock
on the door. When I went to answer it, nobody was there, but
sitting on the carpet was a grenade with "James Brown"
painted on it. I'd seen enough grenades in prison and in Vietnam to know it wasn't live, but it was the thought that counted.

We were late getting started and most of those who were

supposed to bring kids didn't show up. That was okay because I knew the thing needed a lot of work, and it was going to be way past bedtime for most kids anyway. We worked on the arrangement and I kept changing the lyrics, stopping the rehearsal and working on them. Somebody suggested we just put down the instrumental track and come back later for the vocal. I said no because I thought it ought to have a live feel to it to be inspiring, the way I intended it. We worked all night until I was satisfied. Then I was ready to cut, and when I'm ready, I'm *ready*. But we didn't have any kids. I told everybody to scatter outside the studio and just get kids off the street. Byrd got a bunch from a Denny's restaurant nearby. Other people brought them in from here and there. After a while we had about a dozen. We rehearsed them and explained about being quiet when they weren't singing. Each time I sang "Say it loud" all they had to do was answer with "I'm black and I'm proud!" The funny thing about it is that most of 'em weren't black. Most of 'em were white or Asian.

The song is obsolete now. Really, it was obsolete when I cut it, but it was needed. You shouldn't have to tell people what race you are, and you shouldn't have to teach people they should be proud. They should feel it just from living where they do. But it was necessary to teach pride then, and I think the song did a lot of good for a lot of people. That song scared people, too. Many white people didn't understand it any better than many Afro-Americans understood "America Is My Home." People called "Black and Proud" militant and angry—maybe because of the line about dying on your feet instead of living on your knees. But really, if you listen to it, it sounds like a children's song. That's why I had children in it, so children who heard it could grow up feeling pride. It's a rap song, too.

The song cost me a lot of my crossover audience. The racial makeup at my concerts was mostly black after that. I don't regret recording it, though, even if it was misunderstood. It was badly needed at the time. It helped Afro-Americans in general and the dark-skinned man in particular. I'm proud of that.

30 THERE IT IS

WHILE I was in Los Angeles I got a call one morning from my office in New York. I don't remember who it was, but the person told me Pop was dead. He was playing golf with his son Jack and had a heart attack and died right there on the golf course. I couldn't believe it because it seemed like lately his health had been better. But in another way, I could believe it: Otis, Little Willie John, Mr. Nathan, Dr. King, Senator Kennedy, and now Pop. That was probably one of the lowest points of my whole life. We were all family. Byrd and I and some of the other fellas used to lay around his house like it was ours, just like he'd come and lay around ours. For most of us, being from Georgia, Pop was the first white person we really felt comfortable with. Of all the acts he handled, I was the only one he ran with. We spent all those nights together on the plane after concerts, talking. We played tonk and talked until we got to the next city. His wife always wanted him to come off the road and be home more, but he loved me like a son and couldn't stay away.

Usually, no matter what happens, I hold my grief in. I didn't even cry much as a kid. Didn't cry when I was taken to jail or when I went away to prison. But the day I heard about Pop I cried. The only thing I was glad about was that the insurance policy I had on him had lapsed. I couldn't have taken the money. His death affected me very deeply. I never will forget Pop.

Not long after Pop died I started having problems with the Internal Revenue Service. While I was playing basketball with my son Teddy one day the mail came, and there was a letter from the IRS. I stopped playing ball for a minute and opened it. It said I owed $1,870,000 in back taxes. I just laughed and kept on playing basketball. See, earlier in 1968 I had asked them to help me with my taxes because I did not understand them. I wrote letters to Mr. Humphrey, President Johnson, and Attorney General Ramsey Clark. "I can't handle it," I wrote. "I need some help." They did not reply, not Mr. Humphrey or anybody. I wrote to Internal Revenue and to Mr. Richard Kleindienst, who later took over after Ramsey Clark. All this was after I helped stop the riots and everything, and they didn't answer.

I didn't think it would be a big problem. I thought it was a misunderstanding that eventually would be cleared up, so I went on about my life. I was about to get into the franchise restaurant business and was negotiating to buy station WRDW in Augusta. At the same time I asked the Federal Communications Commission to help other Afro-Americans get radio stations so they could reflect community views. The FCC listened to me real polite, but they didn't do anything.

Meantime, by the first of October, "Black and Proud" had gone to number 1 on the R & B chart. It stayed there for six weeks. It even got up to number 10 on the pop chart, but a lot of people still didn't understand it. They thought I was saying kill the honky, and every time I did something else around the idea of black pride another top forty station quit playing my records. Mr. Patton would come back off the road from promoting the records and tell me what was happening.

After a concert at the Washington, D.C., Armory there was a riot, which caused more misunderstanding. A fight broke out in the armory just as we finished the show, and then some people started throwing bottles and chairs and things. Several hundred people got mixed up in it. The police hustled the crowd out of the building, but outside it turned into a general disturbance, and it took them a half hour to bring it under control. That should've been the end of it, but the next day a rumor went around that a white sniper had shot and killed me. That set things off again the next night. By this time I was in Los Angeles and didn't know anything about it. The city called in all the police shifts and used tear gas and made several arrests. Station WOL broadcast over and over that the rumor about me wasn't true, but nobody believed it. So they phoned me, and I made a tape for them to play. I said I was fine and "in good health and alive in living black color." The next day they played the tape every two hours and things cooled down, but I think a lot of people associated the whole incident with "Black and Proud."

No matter what people thought, I had to say what I believed needed saying and do what I believed needed doing at the time. I was getting ready for a big concert in the new Madison Square Garden and took out a big newspaper ad with the headline "Say It Loud—I'm Black and I'm Proud." I think a lot of people only saw the headline without reading what was under it. It told the story of my life and then said: "James Brown is totally committed to black power, the kind that is achieved not through the muzzle of a rifle but through education and economic leverage." It explained what I'd done in my career and in business, and then ended with: "James Brown has won his fight, but that isn't enough. He is now fighting for his soul brothers, and the heavy odds don't discourage him." But it didn't matter what it said; people took it the way they wanted. See, just having an ad like that confused people because entertainers didn't usually advertise concerts with a lot of political commentary like that.

Count Basie and the Ramsey Lewis Trio were on the Garden bill. It was an honor to have Count Basie open up the show for me. I think I had met him somewhere before, but this was the first chance I had to really talk to him. We were all standing backstage in awe of him, but that wore off pretty quick because he was very friendly, just one of the fellas.

"It's a pleasure just to be standing here with you," I said. "When I was little I was always trying to play 'One O'Clock Jump' on the piano. Never could get it right, but I always admired your music."

"You'd make a good jazz player," he said. "I've heard your stuff."

"Can't make any money over in jazz," I said.

He laughed. "I know what you mean," he said. "But, see, the trick is to become an institution, like me. I can work until I die, even if I don't have another record. That's what *you* should do—become an institution."

He did a fantastic job on the show. And that band was *tight*. The cats in my band stood and watched them. It was like seeing where you came from.

I liked playing those big places, the Garden and Yankee

Stadium, but I still played the Apollo. I closed out 1968 with three days there in December. I had a special band shell built for the whole stage around the theme of "I'm Black and I'm Proud." I think the audience knew what I was doing. I was a symbol of pride for people who had been deprived of their civil rights and their human rights. That's what it was all about.

At the end of the year, *Cash Box* magazine named me the best pop male vocalist of the year. That was the first time in the thirty years the magazine had been doing it that they chose a black man. It was kind of funny to be chosen as the top *pop* vocalist because I didn't compromise my music and try to go pop. People just picked up on it for what it was.

In January I played Mr. Nixon's inaugural gala. I had supported Mr. Humphrey, but it was an honor to be asked to do the gala and I went—along with Duke Ellington, Lionel Hampton, Hines, Hines and Dad, Andre Watts, and Barbara McNair. There was only time to do a couple of numbers; I did "Up Tight" and "Black and Proud."

In February they held a James Brown Day in Augusta. Miss Garvin, my seventh-grade teacher, and Mr. Myers, the principal of Floyd School, arranged it. There was a parade in the afternoon, and then that night I did a benefit concert for Paine College, a black college there in the city. Their administration building had burned down in August, and they were trying to raise money to rebuild it. Unfortunately, I had to fly in from California, I believe, and after all expenses were paid there wasn't as much money left as there normally would have been. I think some of the people at the college got upset about it.

I was sorry about any misunderstanding because Augusta was my hometown, and I was planning to move back there. It was impossible for me to live in a house in New York anymore. I couldn't get any peace. Kids and fans were always jumping the fence and coming in the house and creating a disturbance. At Christmas lines of cars would come, full of people wanting to see the black Santas I put out front. I knew they meant no harm, but it was getting to be too much. Most important, Deedee and I had just gotten back together, and she wanted to get out of New York and move somewhere secluded so we could have something like a normal life. When I started talking about going back to Georgia, a lot of the cats couldn't believe it. They said, "What? You're moving back to Disgusted, Georgia." That's what they called it.

I had just about closed the deal for WRDW; it opened under my ownership officially on April 30. I was particularly proud of buying it because I used to shine shoes in front of it, and now I owned it. See, shining shoes has a lot of meanings for Afro-Americans, especially *this* Afro-American, because I actually did it. When the B'nai B'rith gave me their Humanitarian Award for 1969, I carried a shoeshine box with me to their award ceremony. "You made it possible for me not to have to carry a shoeshine box," I said in my speech, "but I carried the box just the same."

We found a house in Augusta and moved in temporarily while I looked around for something more suitable. Meantime I released "Give It Up or Turnit a Loose" at the beginning of the year and "I Don't Want Nobody to Give Me Nothing" in March. "Mother Popcorn" came out in June.

On July 3 I played the Newport Jazz Festival with Jeff Beck, Led Zeppelin, Jethro Tull, Ten Years After, and Sly and the Family Stone. I think that was the only time they had those kinds of performers for the Newport Festival—before or since. On July Fourth I was back in the Garden, and the next week I co-hosted the *Mike Douglas Show* for the whole week. I had Beau Jack on and a lot of other people who meant a lot to me.

Somewhere during this period, while sitting in my office in New York one day, a fella walked in unannounced. Didn't introduce himself or anything. He just said, "Who the hell is Velma Brown?"

"Excuse me," I said. "Who the hell are you? If you don't get out, I'm going to throw you out."

He could see I meant it and he left. He turned out to be from the IRS. After I threw him out he got a vindictive thing going against me. He was the same one who later on got the same thing against Mr. Nixon for his taxes.

Velma and I had been separated since 1964 but we were still married, and that's why he was asking who she was. Later on he came back and said he was head of the criminal investigations division of the IRS in New York. Then he presented some papers.

"You have a tax problem," he said.

"No, *you* have one," I said. "I wrote the government and asked them to help me. I asked for help, and you didn't help me."

The government is responsible for it because they didn't allow me to go to school. I have an elementary school education and didn't even graduate from there. They have no legal boundaries over me. By the Constitution of the United States. The people who represented me had shingles and sheepskins, and I didn't have any of 'em. So I owe *nothing*. My kids owe taxes because they finished high school. You pay tax when you're represented. You pay tax when you exercise all of your rights. I didn't exercise rights. I didn't have a chance to. I lived with the word *can't*, so I *can't* pay tax. They had better forget every tax case they have with people who weren't allowed to go to school because we can sue the government. They're messing around with men like me and Ali and others, people who weren't allowed to go to school and had problems. They should go to the high school graduates from now on and leave us alone.

Besides the taxes there were a lot of strange things happening during that time. I had the feeling somebody besides the IRS was watching me. Later on it came out that the FBI under Mr. Hoover had a program during this time to destroy black nationalists. They were infiltrating several groups, spying on people, taping them, like they did to Martin. Mr. Hoover wrote instructions to his agents to "prevent the rise of a 'messiah' who could unify and electrify the militant black nationalist movement." I think "Black and Proud" probably got their attention. So did my radio stations and my political raps and activities with my shows. Then *Look* put out a cover story on me headlined, "Is This the Most Important Black Man in America?"

It was silly, really. I stop trouble, not start it. They should've known that from what I did in Boston and Washington. I don't even think that way. I'm for peace; always have been. I will protect myself. I would take a life if I saw mine was going to be taken, but I don't believe you should tear up the country. I believe you should come to the table and talk out your differences. Just be fair.

The record I put out in March of 1969 explains where I've always been. It's called, "I Don't Want Nobody to Give Me Nothing." "Just open the door," it says, "and I'll get it myself." It's like "America Is My Home" and "Black and Proud" put together. Equality. If I become a bum, don't label me a nigger bum, let me be just a bum. Equal opportunity both ways. If I'm a criminal, let me be an equal criminal. Don't have a race and tell me it starts at ten o'clock when it has already started at eight o'clock and expect me to win it. The song was supposed to be the next step after "Black and Proud." I wanted to let the black people know that nobody *owed* you anything for being an Afro-American, and I wanted to let the white people know that all anybody wants is a fair chance. Don't give me a welfare check; give me a job so I can fare well.

In July I was hit with a paternity suit. A young lady in California claimed I had relations with her one time while I was out there and that her child was mine. I can't say much about it except I denied it at the trial but agreed to support him until he was twenty-one.

About the same time those charges came up I was finally getting a divorce from Velma. We'd been officially separated since 1964 and had been apart a lot longer than that. We had stayed in contact with each other, and I spent a great deal of time with the kids. The wounds had healed by then, and we were able to go through with it as friends. We're still good friends today.

A lot of *good* things were happening, too: concerts, records, WRDW, my business generally. I opened up two Gold Platter restaurants in Macon; Dick Clark wanted to produce a film of my life; I recorded half of the *Sex Machine* album live at Bell Auditorium in Augusta and wound up the year back at the Apollo.

But I was taking a lot of mess with the taxes, the paternity suit, the surveillance, and everything. That's why I announced after a concert in Memphis that I was going to retire from live performing. See, a lot of the tax problem came from the fact that the IRS didn't understand how the expenses worked on my tours. King Records paid a lot of 'em, but they were cross-collateralized in my royalties so I eventually paid those expenses myself. These were legitimate deductions. I was tired and mad and just said I was going to quit, but when I cooled off I felt it might all be worked out without a lot of mess. But, really, it was just beginning.

31 HOME FIRES

ONE DAY my real estate man in Augusta showed Deedee and me the kind of house we'd been looking for. It was on Walton Way, one of the best streets in the wealthier part of town then. It was in a white section of town, but that was all right with me —I wasn't prejudiced. It had enough room and enough yard that we could have some privacy and peace and quiet when I came off the road, which is what Deedee wanted. It didn't matter to me who the neighbors were, and it shouldn't have mattered to them. I told the agent I'd take it.

When word got out that I was going to buy there, some of the people in the area became very disturbed. They did not want a man of my origin to buy a home on Walton Way. I once had millions of dollars transferred from a New York bank to an Augusta bank in a single day, but they didn't want me living where I wanted to. They got up a campaign to keep me out, but I refused to be intimidated. They approached the real estate agent and tried to stop him from closing the deal. He told them that if he didn't sell me that house he was going to turn around and sell me some other house nearby, so they might just as well get used to it. I bought it and gave my old house to my father.

Meantime, I talked Byrd into moving to Augusta, too. I helped him find a nice place on Silverwood Drive, not too far away. Only problem he had was visitors all the time—me. Whenever I'd get an idea I wanted to discuss, I went over and talked it out with him. Kept him up all night lots of times. Liked to drove him crazy.

After I moved in on Walton Way, some of the people approached me to try and buy me out, offering me twice what the house was worth. I turned 'em down flat. After I lived there for a while it all died down and everybody forgot about it. But the results of that kind of thinking were fixing to break out real bad in Augusta. There was a lot of frustration, a lot of anger waiting to be touched off. You could feel it. I grew up on those streets and I knew.

When the spark came I was doing a gig in Flint, Michigan. I received a phone call at my hotel at about six o'clock on a Monday evening from Governor Lester Maddox. He told me there was a riot going on in Augusta. The city was in flames. There was looting, vandalism, and sniper fire. The local authorities had lost control of the situation, and he was sending in the National Guard and the Highway Patrol. He said the sheriff advised him to call me and see if I would come home and use my radio station and my personal influence to do what I could to stop it. I promised to meet him in Augusta in the morning to discuss the situation.

The whole thing had started a few days before when a sixteen-year-old black kid was beaten to death in Richmond County Jail—the same jail I turned sixteen in. A lot of people in the black community claimed he'd been beaten by the guards. The sheriff said his two cellmates did it, beating him with a shoe and belt and banging his head on the wall. Some of the black people said that even if that was so, it was the authorities' fault for not supervising the prisoners enough.

There had been a peaceful protest on Saturday in front of the jail. On Monday there was a march through downtown. Everything was fine until the march reached the Municipal Building. That's when a student from Paine College hauled down the Georgia state flag and burned it. I think some police tried to move in, some rocks got thrown, and things got out of hand from there. Windows were broken, looting started, and some gunshots went off. Fires started. The Augusta police force and the sheriff's deputies started sealing off the Terry, all 130 blocks of it.

At first the looting was mostly around Ninth and Gwinnett, but it spread to Broad Street and all over the downtown. During the night there were fires all over the area and they spread, too, because the firemen ran into sniper fire. Eventually the guard showed up with live ammunition and bayonets. They rolled in with jeeps, half-ton trucks, and armored personnel carriers with machine guns mounted on them. They set up blockades, and searched cars, and tried to contain things.

I flew in on the Lear jet early in the morning with Byrd.

From the air I could see flames and clouds of smoke; it looked like some of the scenes I had seen from the helicopter in Vietnam. I went to my father's house to get ready to meet with the sheriff to find out what was going on. I was getting into a car when the police pulled up and said they'd take me in their car. I said, "No, that'll just make people madder. I don't want any police cars near me. I know the way to the jail. Nobody'll bother me."

The street around the jail was lined with guardsmen. I went inside to talk with the city officials. They assured me the boy had been beaten to death by his cellmates. I told them I didn't want to choose sides in the thing, I just didn't want to see any more bloodshed. When we came out of the building, television cameras were waiting and I made an appeal to *all* Augustans. "Don't save face—save your city," I said. "We can't be bullheaded. We all have to deal as one, to do unto others as you would have them do unto you."

From the jail I went to my radio station offices out on Eisenhower Drive to meet with Governor Maddox. It was a cordial, businesslike meeting—no grandstanding or threats or arguments on either side. The sheriff and the Community Commission chairman briefed us on the latest developments, then the governor told me what he intended to do.

"I was advised by my intelligence people that this was going to happen," he said. "Now that it has, I'm bringing in the necessary personnel to protect lives and property. It doesn't make any difference to me whether the rioters are Republicans or Democrats, black or white. My purpose is to preserve the peace, and that's what I'm going to do."

"I understand that," I said.

"But we need your help. I can't communicate with the black community on this, but you can. If you would appeal to the people over your radio station to stop the burning and shooting, I think it could be a major contributing factor to restoring order."

"Governor," I said, "I can't back up in supporting my people and their grievances. I'm sure you recognize that."

"Yes, sir, I do."

"But I don't want to see any more lives lost, either. So I'll do better than an appeal; I'll broadcast appeals around the clock. I'll go out in the streets, I'll talk to whoever needs talking to until this thing is over."

I went on the air immediately, asking the people to think about what they were doing. I tried to make the same point I made in Boston and Washington—that it didn't make sense to burn up your own neighborhood. "This is your city, too," I said. "This country is as much yours as it is the white man's. Don't let anybody tell you it's not." I appealed especially to women and children to stay off the streets. At the same time I said that the establishment had better listen to the black citizens of Augusta. They needed to talk to the people themselves, not to so-called leaders who didn't really represent the black community. Most of the rioters were young men and teenagers, and I tried to talk about their grievances: unequal treatment in jobs, education, and just generally not having a *chance* at the finer things in life.

We broadcast around the clock. Some of the appeals were live, some taped. I made some tapes to be played on station WBBQ, too. Byrd went on the air, too, directly appealing by name to friends of ours, white and black, to come out to the station—we'd put them on the air and they'd talk about their feelings about what was going on and how they hated to see it. We put down rumors and got people to check things out in different areas and call in to tell us if things were calm and warn us if anything looked like it was about to start up. WBBQ loaned us a remote unit, and we went around the streets and broadcast back through my station with it. I spent a lot of time in the streets. I drove around in the riot area, and when I saw cats running in groups I got out and talked to them. "What are y'all doing?" I'd say. "You're burning down businesses that belong to black people. Can't you see you're making things worse for us, not better?" Most of them listened; they'd break up and get off the streets. But you couldn't talk to some of them and they were mad at me for doing what I was doing. And there were some elements who wanted me out of the way, I think. There wasn't anything I could really do about it. The police had a few plainclothes black officers out there with me, but if someone wanted to shoot me, nobody could've stopped him.

By Tuesday night things were a little calmer but still smoldering, ready to break out at any second. On Wednesday I went to Paine College and talked to the students. Some of them had been involved in the marches—that was fine—but I tried to get them to leave the rioting alone.

The police and sheriff's department were giving me all the information they had so I'd know what I was talking about. As time went by the nature of the thing was changing. At the beginning of the riot, a lot of the Chinese merchants were burned out of their stores and homes, people I had worked for when I was a kid. I felt bad about that because the Afro-Americans and the Chinese had always gotten along. Then a lot of black businesses got torched, out of ignorance. The looting changed, too. At first the Afro-Americans were doing it, but after it got started, the sheriff's department told me whites were driving across the Savannah River from South Carolina and looting stores and then trying to get back across the bridge before they got caught. The police started arresting almost as many whites as blacks. According to the sheriff's people, there were also some militant whites—Klan elements and people like that—who wanted the thing to really blow up. They hoped the Guard and maybe the police themselves would declare open season on Afro-Americans. The intelligence people were watching them to see they didn't make a move.

I started picking up hints from some of my sources in the black community about some things before they happened. There was talk about members of certain groups—the Panthers or others—heading for Augusta. I got in contact with people I knew around the country and found out it was true. There were some heavy political cats—I don't want to call their names or the names of their groups—who were coming to Augusta. I thought that was the last thing we needed—people who didn't have any stake in the community coming to tear it up. I'm not talking about that old "outside agitators" jive. The agitation had already happened—a lot of it, like I said on the radio, for good reason. What I was hearing about was people who just wanted to incite killing and burning. I felt all that would come out of that was black people in Augusta suffering and dying.

As soon as I confirmed the information, I turned it over to the sheriff's department. Under their emergency powers they closed the airport and the bus terminal; for the next week no bus or airplane could unload in Augusta, Georgia. It was strange because Warren Martin, deputy sheriff at the time, later told me they received the same information from the FBI *after* I gave it to them. I always wondered if the FBI was just slow or if they got the information in the first place by listening in on me.

The whole cooling-off process must've taken about two weeks. Things smoldered that long. There were disturbances in other places around that time that had people stirred up generally. The week before the Augusta riot, the Ohio National Guard had killed four students at Kent State, and four days into our trouble some police in Mississippi fired into a dormitory at Jackson State College and killed two black students.

Eventually, though, things went pretty much back to normal in Augusta. But they couldn't be perfectly normal, not after something like a riot. That's when the real work began—reopening lines of communication, negotiating with the city and the state about all the local issues that had everybody upset in the first place, trying to encourage good will on both sides.

Augusta is my home. I grew up there and saw a lot of changes between the time I was a kid and the time I moved back there. I *made* a lot of changes myself. But I could still see a lot of changes that needed to be made. See, you try to make things better where you are. You don't turn your back because some place or somebody has caused you pain. You work. That's why I bought the radio station; that's why I tried to make the best of a bad situation during the riots. I moved back there in the first place to be close to my roots, to be close to my memories, good and bad, to be close to my father and to people I'd known all my life. And to make a difference.

That's why, when I released the *Sex Machine* album the September after the riots, the album cover said: "Recorded live *at home* in Augusta, Georgia, with His Bad Self." Bell Auditorium, where I recorded it, kind of makes my point about me and the city. I started out there doing battle royals as a kid. Later on I played segregated shows there. Then I integrated the place. Then I recorded live there—and called the record *Sex Machine.* Any way you look at it, for better or for worse, Bell Auditorium in Augusta, Georgia, is *mine.*

On October 22 I got even closer to my roots when I finally married Deedee in Barnwell, a few miles from where I was born. The probate judge, who performed the ceremony at her house, had never even heard of me. She told *Jet* magazine later:

214 / JAMES BROWN

"I married them out there on the front porch. I got a real nice front porch. I marry most of my colored couples out there unless it's raining, then we come inside." Roots can be real tangled.

32 HOT ON THE ONE

AT THE SAME TIME I was getting back to my roots in my private life I was branching out in my career. I started 1970 by playing the showroom of the International in Las Vegas and ended the year with an extensive tour of Africa. The International had just been built to be the most luxurious hotel in Vegas; fifteen hundred rooms and thirty stories high. Barbra Streisand opened the showroom, and Elvis made his comeback as a live performer there. Matter of fact, Elvis was scheduled to be back there as soon as I closed. Colonel Parker was at my show with Mr. Neely to see what he could pick up.

Playing Vegas can create problems for a performer. The main room of the International is huge and spread out. I wasn't worried about that because I'd played stadiums and other spaces where you really had to work to connect with the audience. The biggest problem was going to be the kind of audience; it was a lot different from what I was used to, and I was a lot different from what they were used to. I knew this because I'd first played the Flamingo there back in 1967. Vegas audiences were a lot older and mostly white, and my music was funky and raw. Rock 'n' roll never had succeeded in Las Vegas, much less R & B or soul. You had to figure out a way to get over to that particular audience. I found out you can go too far.

I expanded the band, adding some strings and other things, and put in more ballads and songs like "If I Ruled the World" and some traditional show songs. There were smoke machines and other stuff that later became commonplace even in rock shows. Rehearsal went fine except for this fella who worked as a booker or something like that for the hotel. He didn't like what he saw.

"If I'd wanted Frank Sinatra," he said, "I would've *hired* Frank Sinatra. I was told that everywhere you go you have audiences standing on their seats. Well, I want to see *this* audience standing on *these* seats."

I told him not to worry. I probably told him to get out. We went on with the rehearsal and got the cues for the audio and the lights worked out, the choreography, everything.

On opening night the house was packed. I think I started with "If I Ruled the World." The strings were going, the smoke machines were pumping. I did "It's Magic," "September Song," and other tunes like that. They thought I was crazy to sing those songs. They didn't want that from me: They wanted the gutbucket thing.

Like I say, when I'm on stage I'm aware of everything from the shine on the band's shoes to how the people in the back row are reacting. That night they weren't reacting well. The applause came, but it was too polite, too restrained. After a little while I got that feeling every entertainer has had at one time or another: I felt like I was dying out there, and here it was opening night.

I decided to redo the show on the spot. I called different songs to the band, I flashed hand signals to Byrd and the others, and just rebuilt from the ground up. I started giving an Apollo show. I don't think anybody knew what I was doing, but *I* knew what I was doing. Mr. Neely caught on, though. When he saw what was happening he jumped out of his seat and ran upstairs to the control room. Nobody up there was calling the lights because now the key sheets from rehearsal didn't mean anything anymore. The union people didn't want to let him do it, but he started calling the lights and the sound anyway. He'd seen me work a hundred times so he didn't have any problem. Pretty soon all those people in their minks and suits were up on their seats, hollering and carrying on. I never worked harder in my life, and we *killed* 'em. Dead.

Between shows the booker came in again. "Great show," he said. Then he looked kind of embarrassed. "But, uh, listen . . . if they get up on the seats of their own accord, that's okay, but would you mind not *telling* them to?"

During our time there, Diana Ross and the Supremes were closing at the Frontier down the street. Between my two shows one night I caught their last show. For a long time people had been saying that Diana was leaving the group, but I didn't know this was going to be their last performance together. The show went along fine, but Diana was talking a lot. She was saying how they'd gotten together, how long they'd been at Motown. Then she said, "Whatever we do or wherever we go, we'll still be family." Then they broke off into "Someday We'll Be Together." When they got to the chorus, the crying started. I think Mary Wilson broke down first. She turned around, hung her head, and cried. Then Cindy Birdsong started crying. That was it for Diana. Tears started streaming down her face, and she walked into the wings, crying. After a minute she came back on, and they all pulled themselves together and finished the song.

Backstage there was more crying. Berry was trying to console them. "It's not like you're breaking up," he said. "We're getting bigger. We're going to have two acts—the Supremes and Diana Ross." I talked to each one of them myself, telling each one she was fixing to make a big change and had to be strong.

It's a different thing, but I lost my own band soon after that. I was doing a gig in Columbus, Georgia, when the band threatened not to go on. They wanted more money. I wouldn't give in to a threat like that—never. You cannot lose control of your group. Once you give in to that kind of thing, there's no stopping it.

I found out what was going on that afternoon while I was still at the hotel. I called Byrd in Cincinnati. He was doing some work at King and was supposed to join us in Corpus Christi in a few days.

"Byrd, you know the band we've been working with on some of the sessions? Do you think you could get hold of 'em right away?"

"Sure, James. Why?"

"Because I'm fixing to do something with them."

"Fantastic, James. I could sign 'em up right now."

"Sign 'em up right now."

"What's the rush?"

"Just do it."

They were called the Pacesetters and were all from Cincinnati. They'd hung around King for a while and then started doing session work there. I had used them myself on several things. Bootsy Collins (who later went on to become a big star with the Parliament-Funkadelic Thang and his own Rubber

Band) was the bass player; his older brother, Phelps "Catfish" Collins, played guitar; Frank "Kash" Waddy played drums; Robert McCullough played sax; a fella called Clayton "Chicken" Gunnels played trumpet.

At around six o'clock it still looked like my band wasn't going to budge. I called Byrd back.

"Bobby, you think they'd like to come down here?"

"And play on that show? I'm sure they would."

"See if you can get a flight out. I'll call you from the auditorium."

My band showed up at the auditorium and set up their stuff on the stage, but they still refused to go on unless I gave in. I called Byrd again. There were no flights that could get them there in time.

"Okay," I said, "go out to the airport. I'll send my plane from here. You come, too."

In case the Pacesetters couldn't get all their stuff on the Lear, I called a place that rented musical instruments and amplifiers. By now the auditorium was full of people. It wasn't yet time for us to hit, but I knew there was going to be a delay so I went out and asked the audience to bear with us. Then I fired my entire band.

When Byrd got there with the new band I told him to take them straight to the stage and set them up. While they got set up, Maceo, his brother Melvin, Jimmy Nolen, and the rest carried their stuff off. The audience was beginning to wonder what was going on. So was Byrd. I gave him a rundown of the show and told him to take the new men downstairs to run over it with them. They had played some of my stuff on their own gigs and knew most of it anyway, but they didn't know the vamps and things like that and how we stretched out on some of the stuff in live performance. He took them down there, wrote out some of the licks for them, and sketched out the arrangements. We were a little late starting, but the show went on.

Bootsy and the others turned out to be the nucleus of a very good band. They were studio musicians so when I hummed out solos and things they knew how to give me what I wanted. I think Bootsy learned a lot from me. When I met him he was playing a lot of bass—the ifs, the ands, and the buts. I got him to see the importance of the *one* in funk—the downbeat at the beginning of every bar. I got him to key in on the dynamic parts of the one instead of playing all around it. Then he could do all his other stuff in the right places—*after* the one.

Out on the road I'd call Bootsy into my dressing room just to talk to him. He wasn't but sixteen or seventeen years old at the time, and I kind of felt like a father to him. He reminded me a lot of my son Teddy. I was trying to keep him straight out there because he was a kid who was suddenly pushed into all this show business craziness—thousands of people screaming for you every night, money, women, drugs. All of those *possibilities.* So many different ways to go crazy. It was hard to discipline him and keep him in line; I couldn't spank him, so I lectured him. He wasn't bad or anything; he was just determined to be wrong. I saw a lot of spunk in Bootsy, a lot of life.

One night I called him in to give him a present. When I'd first seen him at King, the bass guitar he had was nothing but a regular guitar—a $29 Silvertone he had converted into a bass. It was a weird greenish blue color with a white pick guard. A very strange looking instrument. But it was all he could afford at the time. I knew his family was having a hard time paying the rent because they were moving every month. When he came out on the road with me, he was able to fix that situation, but he still had that $29 guitar. He didn't use it on the road; he had borrowed another cat's, but I knew he couldn't keep it forever. What I couldn't understand was why he didn't take the money he was making and buy himself an instrument. He'd get paid and spend his money but wouldn't buy a bass. That night I called him in and gave him a Fender bass, kind of exasperated like you'd be with a difficult child you really loved. He said a whole bunch of thank yous, but he didn't really know what to say. What's funny is that when I saw how it affected him, *I* didn't know what to say. I wasn't ready for that.

I started to build the band back up pretty quick. Maceo and some of 'em stayed out there on their own as Maceo and the Kingsmen, but I got several of the fellas to come back: Fred Wesley, guitarist Hearlon "Sharp Cheese" Martin, Clyde Stubblefield, and drummer Jabo Starks, which gave me *three* drummers. I added a couple of trumpet players called Hasaan and Jasaan. Everybody called them the dancing trumpet players because they danced and twirled their horns. When the band jelled I cut them on several records of their own. I was still cutting Byrd and Vicki and lots of other artists, and still playing lots of gigs, in addition to all the stuff going on in Augusta and getting married and taking care of my radio stations and restaurant business.

Not long after I got married I toured Africa and Europe. In Africa we toured the Ivory Coast, Zambia, Nigeria, all over. In Zambia, President Kenneth Kaunda invited us to a state dinner to welcome us to the country. We had a long talk about soul music. He knew about my music and about Aretha, Otis, and Joe Tex. He could name all the songs and everything, but he said he had to listen to it secretly now that he was president.

What surprised me the most over there was that everybody knew our music everywhere we went. One time we were riding through the countryside on a bus to a remote city, and a little kid came running out of the bush. He ran alongside the bus holding up one of my records. The funny thing was that he didn't have any way to *play* the record, but he had it anyway.

We got to Nigeria not too long after the Biafran war, where so many people starved. Things were still torn up from the fighting. We were supposed to play a big soccer field in Lagos, the capital. The day before the concert there was a group of us standing around the hotel, which was not too far from the field. We kept hearing gunshots, then bursts of cheering and clapping. We asked a Nigerian what was going on.

"Oh, nothing to worry about," he said, "just some public executions at the soccer field."

The next night there must've been eighty thousand people in the stadium for our show, a lot of 'em pressing toward the stage. For security there were soldiers everywhere, and they were very rough with the crowd. Anybody who got out of line at all got jumped on and beaten very severely with the billy clubs. We didn't know all this was going on until we got on stage, and once my show started, it was nonstop to the end.

I remember there was this one blind fella trying to get close to the stage, and I could hear him hollering, "I want to see James Brown! I want to see James Brown!"

A guard said, "You want to see James Brown? I'll show you James Brown." Then he hit him with the club—*bop, bop, bop.*

I was very disturbed by the brutality and spoke to some of the officials about it after the show. They said, "Well, we've just had a war, and many of these people are not what you think."

I believe the audience was just trying to express its appreciation. When Vicki was on, this very strange looking old woman approached the stage. None of the soldiers bothered her; they kind of stepped back to let her pass. She came straight toward Vicki and offered some kind of long silk shawl or garment of some kind. It turned out that it had some kind of spiritual significance. We didn't know it at the time, but you could tell just by the way the woman was acting. Vicki accepted it but didn't really know what to do with it, so she twirled it over her head in a circle three times. We found out later that was exactly what she was supposed to do—pass it around her body three times. The lady pressed money on Vicki's forehead, an old custom they had there when they heard a performer they really liked.

While we were in Lagos we visited Fela Ransom Kuti's club, the Afro-Spot, to hear him and his band. He'd come to hear us, and we went to hear him. I think when he started as a musician he was playing a kind of music they called Highlife, but by this time he was developing Afro-beat out of African music and funk. He was kind of like the African James Brown. His band had a strong rhythm; I think Clyde picked up on it in his drumming, and Bootsy dug it, too. Some of the ideas my band was getting from that band had come from me in the first place, but that was okay with me. It made the music that much stronger.

It's a funny thing about me and African music. I didn't even know it existed. When I got the consciousness of Africa and decided to see what my roots were, I thought I'd find out where my thing came from. My roots may be imbedded in me and I don't know it, but when I went to Africa I didn't recognize anything that I had gotten from there.

From Africa we went to Europe and played London, Paris, Brussels, Frankfurt, Berlin, and a few other places. The Europeans loved us, like always. They'd be on their feet from the minute we hit until way after we left the stage. We checked out their music scene, too, and I thought it was very strange at the time: The disco thing had already started there. These huge places, especially in Germany, were packed with people dancing to records. At some of the places we played they were doing disco before we came on. There were always clubs where you could dance to records, but this was a whole different scene and a different music. In a way it was very disturbing because it was so popular, even with people who could afford to hear live music. Working musicians don't like to see that. The music was very lightweight, just bits and pieces from everybody, including me, taken and made very simple, especially the rhythm.

It didn't worry me, though. I didn't think it would make it across the water to America. I thought it was so popular in Europe because they didn't get enough of the real thing. And the music itself was nothing. My music had passed that a long time before. Real quick. Disco just didn't make any sense.

33 SIGNED, SEALED, AND DELIVERED

WHEN I got back from Europe I went into the Copa in New York for two weeks—and left after one. I saw myself in there trying to do something the audience didn't really want to accept —the raw, gutbucket thing. The man who ran the place didn't like it, either. That was not the place for my kind of music. I saw myself playing to these people, and there weren't many of them, so I said, "Well, what am I doing here?" I gave the man back his $25,000 for the second week and said, "Here's your money, sir. I don't want to work here anymore."

At the end of the engagement Mr. Neely came into my dressing room.

"James, I think it's time to redo the band," he said. "They're a super band, but it's time for a change."

"I think you're right," I said. "We've gone about as far as we can go."

Mr. Neely and I knew I needed to change bands from time to time to get new energy and new ideas. I think Bootsy and some of the others were ready to leave anyway. They'd gone to school in James Brown and they wanted to graduate and go on their own. A lot of times, too, a band will start trying to dominate and dictate to me, and I don't like that. Or they'll think the music is all them. That's why I've had stormy times with my bands over the years. Plus my strict rules. Mr. Neely was right; it was a great group. You can hear it on the things they did with me and the things I cut them on by themselves: "The Grunt," "Across the Track," "These Are the JB's."

Bootsy and the four cats he brought with him eventually hooked up with George Clinton and the Parliament-Funkadelic. Later on they spun off from that as Bootsy's Rubber Band. I revamped my group with Fred Wesley as the leader. Clyde had left, but Jabo stayed on drums and St. Clair Pinkney on sax.

Byrd stayed, singing and playing keyboards. They were the real nucleus. Jimmy Parker played alto sax. On trumpets, Jasaan stayed, and Russell Crimes came in. "Sharp Cheese" and Robert Coleman played guitars. Fred Thomas played bass guitar. John Morgan eventually came in as second drummer. Johnny Griffin played congas. I cut that group of JB's on a lot of good stuff, too.

Bringing Fred out front changed my sound somewhat. I think it made it even funkier than when Pee Wee Ellis ran it. Pee Wee was a reed man, and Fred played trombone, which is on the same clef as the bass, piano, and guitar. So Pee Wee and Fred, as arrangers and band leaders, would come up with two different concepts of voicing the stuff. Rhythmically, Fred had more than Pee Wee did.

I think the first thing of my own I recorded with the new band was "Hot Pants (She Got to Use What She Got to Get What She Wants)," and it was one of my biggest records. It came out in July 1971 and went to number 1 on the soul charts and number 15 on the pop charts. At the same time I recorded another live album at the Apollo, *Revolution of the Mind*, a two-record set that came out in December. In August I followed up "Hot Pants" with "Make It Funky," which went to number 1 on the soul chart, and with "I'm a Greedy Man," which went to number 7. Those songs did well on the pop charts, too. Most of my music right on through the mid-seventies did, but a funny thing was happening to music on the radio then. It was starting to get segregated again, not just by black and white but by *kinds:* country, pop, hard rock, soft rock, every kind you could name. Radio formats became very rigid. Because of that and because of my political thing, about 80 percent of the popular stations in the country would not play James Brown records. But my sales were so strong to Afro-Americans and some hip whites that they couldn't keep me off the pop charts. Matter of fact, in all of the seventies I tied with Elvis for the most charted pop hits—thirty-eight. The bad thing about it is that I was making some of my strongest music during that period, and I think most whites have been deprived of it.

My son Teddy was getting into the business a little bit now. He was very talented and could do almost everything I could do. He could sing and dance. In Toccoa he formed a group called Teddy Brown and the Torches, but I didn't really want him to pursue a show business career. I didn't think he was that serious anyway because the name of his group showed he was trying to ride on my coattails. I knew how hard the business was, and if he didn't make it and had no education, he wouldn't have anything. I wanted him to go to college. The plan was for him to get that degree and then go to law school and become a music lawyer. I started carrying him with me in the summers so he could see the music business from the inside and start learning about it.

He had a chance to learn a lot right away because I was getting ready to wind up on Polydor Records. What was left of King was about to be dissolved. After Mr. Nathan died, Mr. Neely exercised his option to buy King Records and turned it into Starday-King. In late 1968 he sold it to Linn Broadcasting as a wholly owned subsidiary with headquarters in Nashville. He took me with him into Linn. I was still under a personal services contract to Mr. Neely that had six or seven years to run, but he didn't like the arrangement with Linn. A lot of their radio stations wouldn't even play my records. I don't know if they were worried about a conflict of interest or what, but it was frustrating and something was going to have to give.

Meantime, Jack Pearl, an attorney with King for a long time, said to me, "James, there's a company moving into the American market called Polydor, and I think you should be with them. I think they're going to be very big in the businesss."

"They can be what they want to be, Mr. Pearl," I said, "but I don't want to be with them." He couldn't talk me into it

Then two fellas named Julian and Roy Rifkin started talking to me about signing with them. I thought they had their own company, but it turned out they had a production deal with Polydor. They talked me into going with them before I really realized it was Polydor.

Mr. Neely thought I should go to Polydor, too. He got fed up with Linn and exercised a buy-back of all the music assets he'd sold them, including my masters. He was planning to sell my contract, my masters, and my share of the publishing companies Dynatone and Chri-Ted to Polydor. Dynatone had been owned half by King and half by me. Mr. Neely and I personally owned Chri-Ted, which was named after his son Chris and my son Teddy. Polydor had bought Mercury so they already had all my Smash stuff.

When he told me what he wanted to do, I said, "I have to decide what I want to do with my life. I don't want to go along with it."

He said they could do the deal so that Polydor didn't just pick up my contract but had to renegotiate a new contract with me. Mr. Neely was close to Polydor anyway because they distributed King records in England and Germany. See, Polydor is part of a worldwide conglomerate of record companies which at that time was owned by N. V. Philips, a Dutch electronics company, and Siemens A. G. of West Germany. After the people with the parent companies saw the response to my shows when I toured Europe the last time, they wanted to sign me up. Polydor got into the American market in 1969 and hadn't done much in their first two years even though they'd spent millions of dollars. By signing me up they could get a foothold in the American market real quick.

I had a lot of doubts about it, but if I could negotiate the new contract then I thought it might be all right. The week before I recorded the third Apollo album, Mr. Neely sold everything to Polydor. He took the money he made on the deal and bought the rest of Starday-King from Linn. He also made good on Mr. Nathan's verbal promise to me that I would get 10 percent of the sale price of the masters. After the transfer of the personal services contract and title to the masters, we negotiated a new long-term contract with Polydor that gave me a substantial advance, a production company, a separate office so I could be independent from them, and artistic control of my work. I wasn't overjoyed to go to Polydor—King Records had been my family for fifteen years—but it was a very favorable deal, and there was some talk at the time that Mr. Neely might move over with Polydor a little later. So I signed.

Right after that a rumor got started that I was going to play in South Africa along with Brook Benton, the Isleys, and Muhammad Ali. I saw a newspaper article that said I'd be playing to black audiences only. I put out a statement through Jack Bart right away, saying: "I am unwilling to undertake a tour of the Union of South Africa under any circumstances because of the policies of that country with respect to the black members of the nation."

I was still playing the coliseums and the auditoriums anywhere there was one. I was back in the Apollo in early November, instead of my usual thing of finishing up the year there. I was doing a lot of television, too; before the Apollo gig I had a special on WPIX in New York.

Because of my stuff, Polydor was really starting to hit the singles charts for the first time. My first album for them, *Hot Pants*, came out soon after I signed. *Revolution of the Mind* came out in December. At the beginning of 1972 I released "Talkin' Loud and Sayin' Nothing" and "King Heroin," which was a rap song like "Get Up, Get Into It, Get Involved" and "America Is My Home." But, really the very first rap in my career was a thing I did back in 1963 called "Choo-Choo (Locomotion)." We were in the studio at King one night recording it, and it just wasn't happening. It was about two or three in the morning, and Mr. Neely said, "Why don't you just play conductor and call off the names of the towns and talk about them?" So that's what I did.

In August 1972 I opened the Festival of Hope at Roosevelt Raceway on Long Island. It was the first rock festival held to help an *established* charity, the Crippled Children's Society. It was a big show: us, Chuck Berry, Ike and Tina Turner, Billy Preston, Sly and the Family Stone, Stephen Stills, Jefferson Airplane, Commander Cody, and so on. The festival didn't bring in as much money as everybody hoped, but it was worth it if it brought in anything. I had visited an Easter Seal summer day camp in Albertson, New York, and my heart went out to those kids.

Right before the festival I put out "Get on the Good Foot." Afrika Bambaataa says it's the song that people first started break dancing to. I feel solidarity with the breakers and rappers and the whole hip hop thing—as long as it's clean. Their stuff is an extension of things I was doing for a long time: rapping over a funky beat about pride and respect and education and drugs and all kinds of issues. I did what I said in the songs: I got up, got into it, and got involved. I was determined to have a say, and I thought anybody with a big following had a responsibility to speak out like I'd done with "America Is My Home" and with "Black and Proud." Even if it hurt, like those two songs did. I guess they prepared me for the next big storm: endorsing Nixon.

34 ENDORSEMENT

MR. HUMPHREY was my first choice for president in 1972, but as the process went along it looked more and more like he wasn't even going to get the nomination. Meantime, President Nixon's people contacted me sometime in late 1971. Robert J. Brown, who was special assistant to the president, was visiting black-owned businesses around the country, and I met him when he came by WEBB in Baltimore. He was very interested in how I got into the radio business and in the prospects for other blacks to get into it. We talked generally about the need for Afro-Americans to own things if we were ever going to have any real equality. He said the administration was pushing black capitalism even though some said it would never work. People said Nixon was trying to substitute it for domestic programs, but Mr. Brown said that wasn't what they were going to do at all.

From there we kind of struck up a relationship. He came down to visit me in Augusta one time, and when I was near Washington I stopped in at the White House and had lunch with him and some of the other people on the senior staff. We discussed several issues that concerned me. They talked about what they were trying to do in the whole area of minority enterprise. Mr. Brown explained the Philadelphia Plan they had; it was supposed to get more blacks hired in the construction industry where they'd always been discriminated against. They talked about being the first administration to ever funnel large amounts of money to private black colleges, and they revoked the tax exemption for schools and colleges that practiced segregation.

Sometimes I said hello to the president or talked with him for a few minutes. His working office was right across the hall from Mr. Brown's in the old Executive Office Building. The president knew about the discussions Mr. Brown and I were having, and he talked about what he was doing in those areas. Talking to Mr. Nixon, you could see he was very knowledgeable, very aware, even if you didn't agree with him. He knew what was going on in the government.

One time I brought up the subject of making Dr. King's birthday a national holiday. I felt very strongly about it. I told the president what Dr. King meant to me and to so many other people. "A holiday in his honor would make a lot of people feel more a part of the country," I said, "and it would stop a lot of unrest."

"I think he should be honored, too," the president said, "but I have to wait until after the election to do it. If I do it now, people will say it's calculated just to get votes."

As the election got closer I was thinking more and more about which way I ought to go, especially after Mr. Humphrey lost the nomination. When the real campaign started in the fall I could see that Mr. Nixon was going to win in a landslide. Everybody could. A situation like that puts somebody who's sort of a spokesman in a dilemma: You can either try to get inside and have some influence, or you can stay outside and be pure and powerless. Either way you're going to get criticized, especially if you're a *black* spokesman.

When I went to the White House again, on October 10, the election wasn't but a month away. I still hadn't completely made up my mind what I was going to do. I had lunch with Mr. Brown, and we continued our discussions. After lunch we met with the president. I told him that Mr. Humphrey was my first choice but that I supported what he was doing for minority enterprise and black colleges, and in minority hiring. He said that was fair enough. I talked about drugs, too. It was something that was on my mind a lot then. I had given support to drug prevention programs in Georgia—Governor Jimmy Carter had honored me for that—and I was very concerned about young people staying off drugs. Mr. Nixon talked about a White House task force that was working on it. I told him I would like to see more drug clinics in places where they were really needed. He said he would support that.

After our meeting I went to a press conference at the offices of the Committee to Re-elect the President. "I say don't quit the boat in the middle of the stream," I told them. I spoke about some of the things Mr. Nixon was doing that I supported. "And we talked about a subject very dear to me," I said, "making Martin Luther King's birthday a national holiday. He said he couldn't do it now because people would say he was just trying to get the black vote, but he said he plans to do it after the election."

I knew what people were going to say about me endorsing Mr. Nixon. People were saying he was buying endorsements with the black capitalism grants and contracts. I tried to deal with it up front. "I'm not a sellout artist," I said. "I never received a government grant. I never asked for one and don't want one. I'm not selling out, I'm selling in. Dig it?"

A lot of people *couldn't* dig it. The attacks on me and on other Afro-Americans who endorsed Mr. Nixon became vicious. Sammy Davis, Jr. almost got booed off the stage at Jesse Jackson's Black Expo show in Chicago. Jesse had to quiet down the crowd himself before Sammy could sing. People announced boycotts of Jim Brown's movies—he'd endorsed the president, too. Floyd McKissick, who had been director of CORE, was called a sellout.

Less than a week after I endorsed Mr. Nixon I did a show in Baltimore. There were pickets outside the arena discouraging people from coming to see my show. Usually I sold out all thirteen thousand seats there, but that night only about two thousand five hundred people showed up. I was disappointed. People just didn't understand. Even Mr. Neely, a Republican himself, said to me one time, "I don't think endorsing Nixon was a very smart thing to do."

"I didn't do it to be smart," I said.

After the show in Baltimore, Mr. Brown came backstage. I could see he looked kind of down about what had happened with the pickets and the small crowd.

"Look," I said, "it makes no difference to me. I'm going to do what I think is right. You're pushing people away from drugs, you're helping black colleges and black businesses. Y'all keep on doing that. That's why I'm endorsing the president. I think he can do those things better than anybody else right now. It makes no difference what happens."

A lot of the stuff was aimed at me because of a picture of Sammy Davis hugging Mr. Nixon. The picture was in newspapers and in *Jet* and it made a lot of black folks mad. But somehow the rumor got started that I was the one hugging the

president. That caused more mess, pickets and threats and boycotts, so Mr. Patton and other promotional people went around
to the program directors of black-oriented stations and explained that it wasn't me. The jocks started talking about it on
the air, cooling that down. Meantime, I went about my business, touring and performing. There was still plenty of resentment, and people got right in my face about it. There was
heckling and booing in the audience. I think they wanted to
see how strong I'd be. I always told 'em I'd do it again.

I spent most of November and December putting together
the soundtrack for the movie *Black Caesar*. In the middle of
December a very disturbing incident happened after a concert
in Knoxville. There had been some kind of incident at a black
concert a few weeks before I came in, so the city wanted to put
restrictions on other black concerts, including mine. That was
like waving a red flag in front of me. Since I had a radio station
there, I voiced some very strong opinons, and they didn't like
it.

After my concert, I was standing in the parking lot signing
autographs and rapping with the fans about community things.
There was an old fella who ran the Knoxville Coliseum and he
wanted me away from there. He called the police and told 'em
a story about inciting a riot. All of a sudden a bunch of police
cars came sweeping into the lot, and the officers came out with
shotguns. One started snatching me around and pushing me
around. It was strange because I had a .38 in my pocket that I
carried for protection. I had started carrying it during the days
when I first started speaking out about politics, wanting to protect myself against somebody trying to shoot me or do something stupid, because there is always a fool in the crowd. The
police beat two of my people, Bobby Diaz and my road manager, Freddie Holmes, but they didn't beat me. If they had, I'd
be dead today because I would have shot 'em, and then they
would've mowed me down with those shotguns. They told me
to get in the car, and I did. They took me downtown and booked
me for inciting to riot and threw me in a cell. The funny thing
was they didn't search me. They locked me up with that .38 in
my pocket. If they had come in the cell that night to beat me, I
would have shot them coming in. I never could figure out why
all that happened because they were just dead wrong from the
start. I've never been able to put my finger on it. The only thing

I could figure was that it was because I had the radio station there. The whole incident, coming when it did, really depressed me because it turned me against the system a little bit.

In January 1973 the Nixon people asked me to play the inaugural. I asked for money for the band; I thought they should be paid for their performance, at least, even if I wasn't. The Nixon people wouldn't pay, so I refused to do it. I thought they had funds for things like that.

When I went back into the Apollo in May, the Nixon thing still hadn't died down. I had SRO crowds, but there were thirty or forty pickets outside the theater with signs that said, "James Brown—Nixon's Clown" and "Get the Clown out of Town." Some of the people who bought tickets and came in were still upset about the Nixon thing, too. Some heckled and hollered things, so I stopped the show and tried to talk to them.

"You can't change a house from outside," I said. "You have to be inside the house. That's why I endorsed Mr. Nixon. I'm trying to sell us *in*. I'm trying to put pressure on the government not to forget about us. I'm trying to do some good. I think in time you'll see that."

Some people responded to that, some didn't. The protests outside the theater went on, but there was something funny about them. They were run by a black cat who called himself Rabbi Judah Anderson. He was supposed to be head of an organization called the Harlem Salute Committee and said that they wanted to raise money to do something to honor black heroes, like build a museum in Harlem or something like that. He said he was picketing me because I had "repeatedly refused to cooperate with black groups in Harlem in their previous efforts to honor our black heroes." What I'm convinced he really meant was I wouldn't do a benefit show for his group and that the whole thing was really just a shakedown.

I met with him but decided he wasn't legit, that if I simply gave him money he would back off. After a few days somebody did give him some money, and the protests stopped. I saw him every now and then after that, and when our eyes met I think he could see what I thought of him. I didn't hate the man, but had no respect for what he stood for.

There were still a lot of people who didn't like what I'd done, and they picketed a lot of shows. Many never forgave me.

I think it cost me a lot of my black audience, just like "Black and Proud" had cost me a lot of my white audience.

After the election I went to see Mr. Nixon again about making Dr. King's birthday a national holiday. My father was with me.

"People talk about a national holiday costing too much money, but I think you can get around that by making it on a Sunday," I said. "He was a minister, a spiritual man. He should be honored on Sunday, like Christ."

"I'm going to do something *better*," he said. "I'm going to see to it that a fitting monument to him is built."

"In Washington?"

"No, in Atlanta."

I didn't think that was enough. I thought there should be a holiday in Dr. King's honor. But I don't think Mr. Nixon wanted to take that step.

35 DEATH AND TAXES

I WAS at home in Augusta on the morning of June 14, 1973, when I received a call from someone at WRDW. I can't remember who it was, whether it was the station manager or who, but whoever it was told me that he thought a relative of mine, maybe a cousin, maybe one of my sons, had been hadly hurt in a car wreck somewhere in upstate New York. He knew my son Teddy had been killed, but he was trying to break it to me gently. By acting confused he gave me time to run a lot of things through my mind, to prepare myself for whatever it was. I was grateful he did it that way; I think it kept me from collapsing completely when he told me the whole truth.

I was in shock while hearing the rest of what he said, and not hearing him, too. He said I needed to go up there and identify the body. I put down the phone. I couldn't believe it. My oldest son, so talented, and I was hoping to get him to go to college. He'd been living with me and working with me on the road, and we'd become close even though I missed a lot of his early childhood. I was hard on him sometimes, but it was because I loved him so much. When I heard the news, it was like the end of the world for me.

Teddy was in New York with two friends from Toccoa visiting some cousins. At around six that morning they were on the New York State Thruway, about 120 miles north of Albany. I'm not even sure where they were going. The police thought that the boy driving might've fallen asleep. When he did, the car veered off a wet shoulder and crashed down a forty-foot embankment. It kept going for another hundred yards, hit an abutment, and turned over on its top. All three of the young men were killed.

I moved like I was in a dream. Somehow I got in touch with my pilots, and they met me at my plane. We flew to New York, but when I got there the officials, seeing how disturbed I was, wouldn't let me go in to identify my son.

Starting the night after Teddy was killed I was supposed to do three one-nighters in a row: Columbus, Dayton, and Buffalo. My people were ready to cancel them, but I told them to wait, I needed to think about it first. Those three dates weren't anything special, and under the circumstances I knew nobody would hold it against me for cancelling. But that's not what was on my mind. What *was* on my mind was preserving my sanity. I thought if I continued on with my life right away, then maybe I wouldn't have a total breakdown. And I was afraid that if I didn't go ahead with the shows, I might never be able to get on a stage again. I decided not to cancel. I tried to look past the fact that I'd lost a son by telling myself I had a show to do.

When I got to the show in Columbus, very few people showed up—maybe five hundred. Normally, I would have three thousand people there, but I think they thought I wasn't going to make it. I went ahead with the show that night and the next two nights, too. I think those shows probably weren't as good as they should have been because people were looking at me with pity. But I was glad I had that stage to turn to. Performing was the only thing that drove what had happend out of my mind. Those shows preserved me.

At the funeral in Toccoa it all came flooding back. I managed to get through the service all right—I was trying to keep my composure and not lose all my senses—but on the way to the cemetery I broke down. Later on I went to Velma's house, and we sat and talked and tried to console each other, but she was well out of it, like I was.

The thing that haunted me, that *still* haunts me, was that Teddy and I had been arguing a lot right before it happened. He'd been living in Augusta with me for a while, but then he'd gotten himself into something and had gotten a little wild. He didn't want to go to school. I had him set to go to Centre College of Kentucky, but he was determined not to go. I stayed upset with him about that. I said to him one day: "You know, you're kidding yourself. Your classmate Mike is going to school, and he's going to beat you out." Teddy and Mike had a kind of friendly rivalry thing going.

Teddy said, "He could go to school the rest of his life, and he still couldn't beat me out."

"You're crazy," I said. "There's no such thing as that, son. If you don't go to school, he's going to beat you out."

I was also trying to get him out of Augusta because he was writing some bad checks. I felt he was ducking me and didn't want me to see him because he knew how hard I'd be on him. I just didn't want him to go through what I'd been through when I was his age. He came from a broken home, like me, and a broken home is a bad thing. Doesn't matter whether it's a broken home that's poor or one that's well off. It keeps you so upset when you're young that you're never really yourself. Maybe I could have straightened him out; maybe I would have made it worse, I don't know, but he was ducking me. I never saw him again.

Not too long after Teddy died, Byrd left me. Vicki had left a year before and Lyn Collins, a fine singer, replaced her. I cut Lyn on many tunes throughout the mid-seventies. I think Bobby was despondent about several things; his mother was very sick, and he felt like he wasn't getting enough credit for his contribution to the group. I think I probably said something like, "Well, I don't need him anyway; he never did anything for me," just like I had when Pop and I fell out. But, really, I was sad about it. We'd been together for twenty years and were like brothers. We didn't have a big break or anything like that —we'd been through too much for something like that. He moved to Houston, and when I came through Texas he joined the show and stayed with it through Dallas and maybe Corpus Christi, but that was all. Every now and then I enticed him back to do one thing or another.

Pretty soon he had a nice hit with a song called "Back from the Dead," and he was playing a club in Miami. I went to see his show—he had Bootsy and them as his band—and got up on the stage with him. We did "Try Me," and then, before I could even say it, he had the band hit "Sex Machine." It was like he'd never left. Backstage we got to talking about the early days and all the things we'd been through. After we both got to feeling real sentimental, I told him I was getting ready to tour Europe. "Why don't you come along, Byrd?" I said.

"I don't know, James," he said. "I don't think I want to go back out there with you. You know how I feel."

"It'll be like old times, Byrd," I said. "Come on."

After a while he finally agreed to it. I said, "Fantastic! Johnny Terry will be here tomorrow with your uniforms."

"Johnny's coming back?"

"He'll have the shoes and everything."

I'd already bought 'em. Byrd just shook his head and laughed. We did eleven days in Europe—Brussels and then all around Germany—but when we came back he went back with his band. That Europe trip was the last time we were ever out there together.

Meantime, the government was getting very heavy about the tax case. They were saying I owed $4.5 million in back taxes for 1969 and 1970. At first I didn't really know they were doing a big investigation, but then my office started receiving calls from Treasury people all around the country. I found out somebody was trying to make it a criminal case instead of a civil one; they were going to charge me with fraud.

I had always heard fraud started with intent and intent starts with knowledge. Without knowledge, you can't commit fraud because there's no intent. See, I hired all these people with sheepskins and shingles and had them handle my business— with a seventh-grade education, I'd be crazy to do anything else —but the government held *me* responsible. By the time all the trouble started, all those people who'd worked for me were gone. I had to fight it along with two of my people, Fred Daviss and Al Garner, two of the finest people I know. They stayed with me and fought it for as long as they could.

I think it started when one of my accountants mixed some of the corporate stuff in with my personal return. He just noted on the form that some of the things on the personal return were business deductions. That was like waving a red flag in front of the IRS. They went crazy. They came into my office and confiscated a truckload of documents and records, and I just let 'em do it. There was no way they could give me a receipt for all of it. Then it was my word against theirs. They called all the time, saying, "Prove this and prove that," but they had the records. After a few years of this, they said, "Come and get your stuff." Mr. Daviss went to New York, and on a table in a conference room there they had two boxes. He said, "Where's all the material?" They said, "This is it."

Most of the argument was about the money from my shows.

The government went around to all the coliseums and auditoriums and figured how much I made on each show, and they built up a net worth picture from that. They didn't consider payroll, expenses, travel, and all of that. A lot of those things had been paid by King Records and then cross-collateralized against my royalties, but the IRS just went by the 1099 forms I received from King saying I'd earned so much money each year. Those forms just showed earnings; they didn't show all the business deductions for hotel rooms, salaries, maintaining the jet, and all the other expenses. An overhaul of the jet engine cost $50,000. The monthly payment for the plane was about $12,000. King paid those things, then charged me for them. So my people had to try to reconstruct all my expenses without most of the documents. On top of that, we got into an argument about the $1,500 a week King had paid me since I came back from Smash. King couldn't withhold it from me, but it was still charged against my royalties. The government couldn't understand that. The money was in a special account, and the government took it.

I tried not to let it get me down, but I could see we were in for a long fight. What I didn't see was how it was eventually going to affect my ability to function as an entertainer. It was going to keep me and my people tied up to the point that we couldn't take care of our other business—which was to keep all the things I did as an entertainer and artist moving forward. And it hurt my people personally. Mr. Daviss told the government they were wrong, and he took it on the chin. They ran him ragged until his family begged him to leave me, but he stayed and fought and lost his family. And I eventually lost my family, too.

But I don't blame the government. I don't hold a grudge. The government hurt my business a lot, a *whole* lot. But they didn't destroy me. Polydor did that.

36

PAPA TAKES SOME MESS

MY RELATIONSHIP with Polydor went sour almost from the beginning. I made some very good records for them—"Make It Funky," "Talkin' Loud and Sayin' Nothing," "Get on the Good Foot," "The Payback," "Get Up Offa That Thing," "It's Too Funky in Here"—but they didn't know how to promote or distribute them. It was basically a German company, and they didn't understand the American market. They weren't flexible; they couldn't respond to what was happening the way King could.

They weren't flexible about creativity, either. They expected you to go into the studio on such and such a day at such and such an hour and finish up at a certain time. Like a factory. At King we went into the studio and put together arrangements and worked at all hours until we had it *right*. Polydor back then didn't work that way. They had no respect for the artist, no personal feeling for the artist, no concern for what he had in mind. They would say this is what's going to happen: blah, blah, blah. And what the artist felt meant nothing.

I'd mix a song until I thought—until I *knew*—it was right, but they would want their machines to say whether it was right or not. It had to register certain numbers on the machines. It didn't matter whether the track was alive and moved; all that mattered was the numbers. I had a warmth in my sound I was trying to preserve, and I wanted the track to be an instrumental before it was a vocal. I wanted it to have the right feel before I put any words to it. It's like having a good bedspread but wondering if the mattress is comfortable. They wanted a pretty bedspread. I wanted to make the mattress comfortable.

In the early years with them I was hitting the singles charts in spite of the company. The songs were hits because I forced them through the company and made them hits myself. I was supposed to have creative control, but they started remixing my records. I mixed them, but when they came out they didn't sound like what I'd mixed. The company didn't want the funk in there too heavy. They'd take the feeling out of the record. They didn't want James Brown to be raw. Eventually, they destroyed my sound.

It took them a dozen different presidents of the company to do it, though. Every time a president came in that I got tight with—like Jerry Schoenbaum—he'd be replaced. They were always sending in somebody to put a bridle on James Brown.

Their artist promotion was strange, too. To me, they didn't want a man of African descent to appear sophisticated. They did not want him to come across as a man. They wanted the female Afro-American artists to look good, but not the men. That's the vibration I picked up from the company, but when you pinned 'em down one-on-one, you didn't get that. Dr. Vogelson, who was head of the whole thing, was a fine man, though, and he treated me like a gentleman. But I never got that warmth from the company. Not one time.

Whatever King Records had been about, Polydor was the opposite. Every King act was individual; Polydor tried to make all of their acts the same. King wanted to be an independent company with individual artists; Polydor wanted to be a conglomerate. King wanted to be a little company with big acts; Polydor wanted to be a big company with little acts.

The funny thing was Polydor had great facilities and Mr. Nathan didn't, but we made great records at King anyway. To me, Polydor didn't have a musical background. If you check the whole concept of the company, you see they weren't in the record business; they were in telecommunications and electronics. But they paid me; I can't get away from that. They gave me more money than anybody ever gave me. Mr. Nathan didn't pay me; he was a good man, but he didn't pay me. Polydor would pay me, but they wouldn't give me the freedom Mr. Nathan did.

Polydor might have been fed some bad information about me being difficult to work with. I *am* difficult if you want to change me from being James Brown. If I had been a new artist, it would have been different. But I had a track record—everything was a hit. Everything that Polydor did turned the other way unless I forced it. Once the door was open to them in the American market, they had no more need for me.

Besides groove tunes like "Make It Funky," I was doing a lot of message things during my first few years with Polydor. "Talkin' Loud and Sayin' Nothing" was aimed at the politicians who were running their mouths but had no knowledge of what life was like for a lot of people in this country. It was also aimed at some of the cats on their soapboxes—I won't call their names —who were telling the people one thing while manipulating their emotions for personal gain.

I was getting a lot of visions during those years. "King Heroin" was something that I foresaw. I wasn't using drugs, but it was like I had lived it anyway. During that time I had an office at Polydor, and I maintained an apartment in New York, too, but I lived in Augusta. I was seeing New York and then getting away from it and writing about it. But producers don't know the truth. They write about what they *think* is happening. I was writing about what I was living.

"The Payback" was originally supposed to be a tune for the soundtrack of *It's Hell Up in Harlem,* the answer to *Black Caesar,* but the producer said the tune wasn't funky enough.

I said, "*What* did you say?"

"It's not funky enough. We can't use it."

That was all I wanted to hear. "I'm going to put it out as a single, and you'll see," I said.

I knew the song wouldn't make sense without the movie, so I came up with a story line that you could see. It came out in February 1974 and went to number 1 on the R & B chart and 26 pop.

Somewhere during this time I picked up the name the Godfather of Soul. Fred Williamson in *Black Caesar* was supposed to be the Godfather of Harlem. I was talking to the disc jockey Rocky G about the movie one day, and he said, "You're the Godfather of Soul." I think some of the jocks started using it on the air, and it kind of stuck.

I was still playing everywhere, but I was getting ready to cut back on all the one-nighters. I did a benefit in Madison Square Garden on July 4, 1974, for the National Youth Movement. It was a self-help group for teenagers run by Reverend Al Sharpton. When I lived in St. Albans, he was just a kid, and he'd come over and we'd rap. I encouraged him and the other kids around there to stay in school and work hard and have pride. He took it to heart and started his youth movement. I think he was only about nineteen when we did the July Fourth date.

In September I went to Kinshasa, Zaire, for the music festival that was supposed to coincide with the Muhammad Ali–George Foreman fight there. The Spinners, the Crusaders, B. B. King, the Pointer Sisters, and I arrived in Kinshasa at two o'clock in the morning. When we landed thousands of fans were there to greet us. So were Foreman and Ali. The fight had to be postponed, though, because Foreman got a bad cut over his eye while sparring, but they went ahead with the music festival.

In October I was back in the Apollo for six days. By this time the Apollo was in trouble. A lot of the big acts wouldn't play it anymore because it wasn't profitable enough. I could see it wasn't going to make it, and I said that this show might mark the end of an era in black music. I think a lot of people realized it. Mick Jagger and Ahmet Ertegun showed up for the Friday show; they knew what was happening. Not too long after that, the theater closed. It reopened a few times, but it didn't stay open. I didn't play it again for almost four years.

I released another message song around this time, too: "Funky President (People It's Bad)." It was about President Ford, who had taken over from Mr. Nixon in August. Every time he made a speech, it gave people the blues. He was a nice man, but he talked a lot and didn't say anything. He was there as a caretaker after Watergate, and I think he did that. He was a good man, but I never looked at him as a *president*.

In February the next year I went back to Gabon in Africa and played for President Bongo's birthday party. We had some discussions about building a recording studio and a pressing plant there but never got any further than that. In July I was back in the Garden for Reverend Sharpton's National Youth Movement again. I had Tito Puente, Joe Bataan, Tyrone Davis, Lyn Collins, and the Swanee Quintet on the bill. Charles Sherrell had a solo spot, too. He has a sweet, high voice, and I had cut him on an album called *Sweet Charles: Music for Sweet People.*

By the middle of 1975 disco had broken big. Disco is a simplification of a lot of what I was doing, of what they *thought* I was doing. Disco is a very small part of funk. It's the end of the song, the repetitious part, like a vamp. The difference is that in funk you dig into a groove, you don't stay on the surface. Disco stayed on the surface. See, I taught 'em everything *they* know but not everything *I* know.

Disco was easy for artists to get into because they really didn't have to do anything. It was all electronic sequencers and beats-per-minute—it was done with machines. They just cheated on the music world. They thought they could dress up in a Superfly outfit, play one note, and that would make them a star. But that was not the answer. It destroyed the musical basis that so many people worked so hard to build up in the sixties. The record companies loved disco because it was a producer's music. You don't really need artists to make disco. They didn't have to worry about an artist not cooperating; machines can't talk back and, unlike artists, they don't have to be paid. What disco became was a lawyer's recording; the attorneys were making records.

Disco hurt me in a lot of ways. I was trying to make good hard funk records that Polydor was trying to soften up, while the people were buying records that had no substance. The disco people copied off me and tried to throw me away and go with young people. You can't do that. You have to come back to the source. Disco hurt live music in general. The black concert business was already hurting. Whites wouldn't come even if the black artist had big record sales. Black America was in a serious recession; there was just no money in the black community. Later on, that situation hurt records sales, too. For everybody.

By this time I was in semiretirement anyway. I still did big shows in Europe, Africa, and Japan, but I cut way back on American appearances. I was mad and I was tired and I was disgusted. The tax thing was making it hard to function, I was fighting my record company all the time, and the music business was all going one way. It was similar to the period after "Begging, Begging" or the time I was caught between Smash and King—I was stopped, but I wasn't finished. I was going to pull back and wait for it all to work itself out. After the Nixon thing, Teddy's death, the taxes, disco, and the bad blood with Polydor, I didn't see what else could happen. But a lot did. Before too much longer I thought I might be stopped *and* finished.

37 PRISONER OF LOVE

PART of the reason I pulled back from show business was my wife. Deedee wanted me to be at home more and be a good father to our children. We had two sweet little daughters, and they meant everything to me. They were a kind of consolation to me after losing Teddy. Staying home was what would make my wife happy, and that's what I did. We even moved out of Augusta to a big, secluded piece of land not too far from where I was born. If I was really going to be a family man, I wanted to do it on the same ground my family was on when I was a child. It was almost like I was trying to make good at what my own parents hadn't been able to.

I had gotten back to my roots. In 1973 Big Junior—Mr. Willie M. Glenn—started working for me in New York. We'd always stayed in touch, but he'd been working in the numbers game in Harlem for ten or twelve years until he finally got tired of being arrested. He was just trying to support his family, but one Christmas Day when he was shoveling snow on Riker's Island, he decided the risk of working policy wasn't worth it anymore. He drove a cab for a while after that and then joined me.

Honey was still living in Augusta, and I saw her all the time. I wanted to build her a nice house, but she wouldn't let me. She said she wanted to stay where she was, among the people she'd known all her life. When she died in 1974 it almost destroyed me. I think she took so many of those headache powders all her life that it just took everything out of her. Looking at her at the funeral home, I couldn't stand it anymore. I reached in and hugged her, and Junior had to pull me away.

Not long after Honey died I heard that Mr. Brantly was very sick in Macon. I went to see him and found out there was nobody to take care of him or pay his medical bills. He was more than eighty years old by then and needed constant care. I had him brought back to Augusta and put him in a convalescent home where he was comfortable up until his death a few years later.

During this time I kept my hand in the business. I started a television show, a syndicated dance program called "Future Shock" that lasted from 1974 through 1976. But it was done in Augusta and later on in Atlanta, so it didn't take me too far away. It was a strong show—I invested over a million dollars in it—but I couldn't get sponsors for it. The same thing happened to my radio stations. I had the numbers but not the ad billings.

I was still recording and producing right along, but a lot less than before. The hardest thing for me to do was to get Polydor to release a record. They were paying me to be inactive. I still did gigs occasionally in the States, but it was tough because I was really at a very low point. That's where "Get Up Offa That Thing" came from—a gig when I was really down.

I was playing Fort Lauderdale at the Bachelors III, owned by Joe Namath. The audience was sitting down, trying to do a sophisticated thing, *listening* to funk. One of the tightest bands they'd ever heard in their lives, and they were sitting. I had worked hard and dehydrated myself and was feeling depressed. I looked out at all those people sitting there, and because I was depressed they looked depressed. I yelled, "Get up offa that thing and dance til you feel better!" I probably meant until *I* felt better. My wife came down later to join me, and when she saw me, she liked to had a fit, I was in such bad shape. Nothing was going right.

There was more turnover in the band. Fred Wesley and Maceo left to join Bootsy in P-Funk. I think they wanted to work more than they were doing with me. I was sorry to see them go, but I didn't blame them.

There were lawsuits against my radio stations. Every time you play a record you're supposed to pay so much money to the performance rights societies like ASCAP and BMI. ASCAP had put in five or six lawsuits against WEBB for nonpayment of the money. That was just part of the trouble I was having in the radio business. The people I bought WEBB from in the first place were suing me for money they said I still owed them from the sale. Also, no matter how good my numbers were, I couldn't get national advertising on my stations. I was pumping the money from my record and songwriting royalties into the stations to keep them going. I didn't get into the radio business to make money in the first place, but when you have the numbers, you're supposed to get the advertising. I just couldn't understand why we didn't.

Then I got dragged into a payola trial. Frankie Crocker— who had been on all the major radio stations in New York, WLIB, WWRL, and WBLS-FM, where he was program director —was indicted in Newark for perjury. They said he didn't tell the truth about a $10,000 payment he was supposed to have received from an independent record promoter and about money he was supposed to have received from a promo man from Philadelphia International. See, a program director is very powerful because he approves every record that's put on the air. If your record was played on WBLS at that time, it meant two hundred thousand in sales in the New York area.

Charles Bobbitt, one of my managers, was subpoenaed by the prosecution, and he testified that he paid Crocker almost $7,000 to play my records. I didn't hold it against Mr. Bobbitt for testifying to that—he probably had to give Crocker some money—but I testified that the only money I ever gave to Frankie was payment for emceeing my show. To pay somebody to play a record is a little heavy, but I think to pay him to do our shows was important. I guess Mr. Bobbitt had to get my records played, and that's what independent promotion is about: You try to compete against what the other people are doing. I guess he did it with money instead of with drugs. I think they used Mr. Bobbitt for a scapegoat for what others were doing before Mr. Bobbitt even came on the scene. Later on, his testimony was thrown out on a technicality.

The whole payola thing is a hustle. A main reason for it is radio management. They underpay their people and *expect* them to make up the difference in favors from outside. With a lot of black-format stations, it was usually black jocks who suffered and white management who got off. A lot of it depends on what you consider payola in the first place. If you give some underpaid jock $50 to buy groceries, that's payola. If you're a big record company handing out $750 television sets as Christmas gifts, that's not payola. I always tried to have jocks emcee my shows and legitimately pay them. That way, everybody knew what was going on, just like the laws that make politicians tell where their campaign contributions came from.

Not too long after the Crocker trial I lost the jet. It was a Sidley-Hawker 125, the third jet I'd owned since Pop and I got the first one. There was a mechanical bill due on it, and Polydor agreed to pay it, then reneged. I wasn't going to pay that kind of money myself, so we let the plane sit while we discussed it. Then they discovered a crack in the tail. I took it to Newark, but they couldn't fix it, so I had it flown to Canada to be fixed. The authorities grounded it. When they did that, I let it sit there. It was repossessed.

All these things happening made me pull back further from the business and spend more time at home, like Deedee wanted. I have a picture from that time in my life that's the only picture in the world that doesn't look like me. You can look at it and see how far away I'd gotten from show business. I was still trying to look sharp, to look debonair, but I look at that picture and I don't know who that man was. I just did not know where I was going.

When Elvis died in August 1977, I think I got a clue. For some reason his death hit me very hard. We were a lot alike in many ways—both poor boys from the country raised on gospel and R & B. "Hound Dog" and "Please" both came out the same year. He had lived in Hollywood a long time and then, like me, had moved back home to try to preserve himself. Somehow or another he just didn't manage to do it. They kept him shut away all the time; he couldn't get out and be with the people. I knew he was a poor boy and never intended to go that way. When you're poor, you have survival in your mind.

When he died, I said, "That's my friend, I have to go." I went to Graceland that night. The crowds had already started gathering around the gate. Some agents from the Tennessee Bureau of Identification put me in one of their cars and got me in without anybody seeing. I saw Priscilla and his daughter, and I saw one of his aides who'd been a good friend of mine for sixteen years. I talked to Elvis's father, saying what I could to help console him. But when I walked over to the open casket, I needed consoling. I put my hand over his heart and said with tears in my eyes, "You rat, why'd you leave me? How could you let it go? How could you let it go?"

It was very strange; that was only the second time in my life

I'd ever touched someone who was dead. It made me think about the waste of such a great, great talent, and it made me wonder what I was doing with my own life and about everything that was going wrong. During that time I couldn't find any way out of it. Like Elvis couldn't find any way out of it except dying.

I knew things were going to get worse, too, when one day I found a book lying around the house. It was a book about women's legal rights. My wife was reading it. She'd underlined the parts about community property in divorce. I knew then she was planning to leave; I knew it in my mind, but in my heart I hoped it wouldn't happen.

I was working somewhere—I don't even remember where —and I left early to be with my family on Valentine's Day. I wanted to have a candlelight dinner and then a long talk about us to see if we could work it out. When I came up the drive she already had the station wagon packed and the two girls inside ready to leave. I talked to her, I argued with her, but it didn't do any good. She left and took the girls with her. I watched them go down the drive until they were out of sight at the bottom of the hill, heading toward the front gate. I stood there in the middle of all that land, by myself, just listening to that car fade away.

She was a very good woman and we had a lot of good years together, but she did not want a man who was in the entertainment business. She might say there was some other reason that we broke up, but I believe that my being an entertainer was the real reason. If I had been a man who came home every night, she would have been much happier. I gave up a lot to be with them, but she had no aspiration for my being in show business at all. But that's what James Brown is all about.

After she left I tried not to let it get me down. You must be intelligent about it first. When a person leaves you, the person has just expressed something to you. Understand that before you understand anything else. The person would never leave you without wanting to. That's hard to accept. She did what she wanted to do. She went where she wanted to go.

I couldn't think that way about the children, though. They weren't adults making up their minds of their own free will. I missed them, and I couldn't think it through the way I could think through a grown-up leaving me. I picked up the telephone and called Deedee to ask if she wanted to come back. I knew she didn't, but I was really asking her for the children. If it hadn't been for them, I probably never would have called her. After that, I didn't call her anymore. I accepted it and went on. But the girls—that was sad.

I was free to get back out there on the road if I wanted to, but I wasn't sure I wanted to. It had been a long time. A New York newspaper even had one of those "where are they now" stories about me, so when a group of Harlem businessmen bought the Apollo and tried to reopen it, I agreed to play it. The place had been closed for three years, and I hadn't played it in almost four. I already had a short tour of Europe planned right before that, and I could go right into the Apollo as soon as I got back. I scheduled two shows a night for a week, thinking it might rejuvenate me and the theater at the same time.

I opened on Wednesday, July 12, 1978. It was like always—lines as far as you could see. There was so much demand that I added two shows. It was like I'd never left. The crowds were fantastic. I told them, "I was here in the fifties, the sixties, and the seventies. Now I got to get ready for the eighties." I was starting to think that maybe I should come back full-time. "I'd rather play for my folks at the Apollo," I said, "than play the White House."

Everything went smooth until Sunday night. When I came offstage after the second show, there was a U.S. marshal waiting for me with a bench warrant issued by U.S. District Court Judge C. Stanley Bair in Baltimore for contempt of court. It was connected to the civil suit I was involved in with the people I'd bought WEBB from. See, the court didn't like the fact that I'd left the country. It really got me down because I'd called the judge to ask if I could leave to go overseas to do my show. He refused to talk to me. When I went, he got me for contempt.

The marshal arrested me right there and carried me to Baltimore. I went into the city jail in handcuffs and spent three days there. I couldn't understand it; the whole thing was about money in the first place, a civil suit. I thought we were way past putting people in prison for debt. What kept running through my mind was the connection between being in jail when I was a kid and being in jail as an adult. Here I was successful, well known and, most of all, *respected*—and still in jail. I'd come out of prison to do right and still wound up in jail.

I knew we still had some problems; the same problems they have in South Africa still prevail in some parts of this country.

I had to put the station into receivership. I'd already sold WJBE in Knoxville, and the beginning of the end at WRDW had come a month before when a fire damaged it real bad. I posted my bond and got out of jail.

Meantime, the show had gone on at the Apollo without me. That was it. I could get out of jail, but I could not get out of whatever had been happening to me—for years, it seemed like. I could not find another way to go. For the first time in my life I said something I never thought I'd hear myself say: "I just don't care anymore."

38 DEAD ON IT

WHEN you sit down, like I did, one of the things you think about is the danger of freezing up. It has happened to a lot of entertainers. They leave the stage, and then after they're away from it a while, they get where they can't go back even if they want to. It crossed my mind that it could happen to me. Up to that point I'd never retired completely. I had still played huge arenas and stadiums in Europe and Japan and Africa, and I still did American concerts occasionally. But now I was ready to throw in the towel entirely. It got to where I didn't care about freezing up. I wasn't going back out there anyway. Ever.

Leon Austin, the childhood friend who first showed me some chords on the piano and who I had cut on a lot of singles from the late sixties on, came by and talked to me. He's soft-spoken, but he can be very insistent and persistent. "You can't quit," he said. "You can't lay down."

"I'm tired, Leon," I answered. "I'm tired of fighting the government and the record company and the radio establishment."

"You can't let 'em beat you."

I told him what I'd been telling myself. "I don't care anymore. I just don't care."

"You *got* to care," he said.

"I wish I could, Leon. I wish I could."

He kept coming by, kept talking to me, arguing with me, encouraging me. I wouldn't budge. He could see how far down I was, so he got off the retirement thing and started talking to me about spiritual things. He told me how he'd recently let God back into his life and what a difference it made. He didn't preach to me or anything like that. He just talked real quiet about what it meant to him personally, how it gave him peace of mind.

I was always religious, even before I used to help Charlie Brown, the crippled fella, to the different churches on Sunday when I was a kid. I'd sung gospel all my life. Gospel saved me in prison and got me out. Over the years I presented a lot of gospel acts on my shows, too, but somehow, I guess, I'd just been going through the motions lately.

Really, a lot of the ways I communicate with people and *what* I communicate I owe to the church. When I'm on a stage, I'm trying to do one thing: bring people joy. Just like church does. People don't go to church to find trouble, they go there to lose it. Same thing with a James Brown show. I'd always felt that as an entertainer you shouldn't bring your personal problems to the stage. Your job is to send people home feeling better than they did when they came in. I wasn't sure I could do that anymore.

Leon got me thinking about all that and gave me the moral support I needed. We all need moral support; we don't get any bigger than that. When we don't need it, we're in trouble. And we need to trust in somebody, something bigger than ourselves. That's what I did. I rededicated myself to God. In a little country church near where I was born, I was rebaptized. I'd been baptized when I was a little boy, but I wasn't as serious then as when I went on my own as an adult. Eventually I just let go and put things in His hands.

The final turning point came one day when I walked outside the house and found my father down on his knees working around the walkway. It must have been 100 degrees in the shade.

"What you doing, Daddy?" I asked him.

"Pulling these weeds."

"It's too hot, Daddy. You don't need to do that."

"Somebody's got to, Junior."

"What you mean?"

"We can't afford to hire nobody to do it."

I got down beside him and started helping. Before long I was sweating. The more I sweated, the harder I worked, like he was doing. He had more energy than any man I've ever known. He'd never been out of work more than five days in his life, and anybody he ever worked for would hire him back in a minute. Something happened while I was down there beside my father. He knew what I was going through, and he straightened me out.

"You're lucky, Junior," he said. "The yard you pulling weeds in *belong* to you."

In his whole life he'd never stopped working. It didn't make any difference to him: turpentine, heavy machinery, filling station work, picking vegetables. That's what he was about. And his son was about working on the stage. God showed me the direction. I knew it was time for me to get up and go back to work.

That's what I did. But I had a lot to rebuild, a lot of fights still ahead. In destroying my sound, Polydor had cost me my audience, and it was around this time, 1979, that the record business in general collapsed. Except for a few blockbusters every now and then, you couldn't give records away. The whole industry was depressed. And disco had killed off live music and a lot of middle-level venues with it. I could go out of the country, where I was a superstar, but there was no place for me to work at home.

Polydor got a couple of breaks with *Saturday Night Fever* and *Grease* and had a chance to sell ten or twenty million of each album while I sold maybe two hundred thousand albums. That spoiled them. After that, all they wanted was the blockbusters. But they didn't get them and they got off their acts that were doing good but not spectacular.

They tried to take me over into disco by bringing in an outside producer, Brad Shapiro. I was against it from the first. Disco had no groove, it had no sophistication, it had nothing. It was almost over anyway. I fought against doing it but finally gave in. They called the album *The Original Disco Man*. It wasn't disco all the way, but I was very unhappy with the result. Then they had me do another one with Brad Shapiro called *People*, but I wanted to release a live album I did in Japan.

When I made the decision to *come* back, I decided to *fight* back, too. I got the lawyer William Kunstler to help me. He came down to Augusta and discussed all the aspects of the trouble I was having and decided he'd take my case. In November 1979 we called a press conference and charged Polydor with skimping on my royalties; we talked about the discrimination by national advertisers that had cost me two radio stations already; and we charged the federal government with harassing me throught the FBI and IRS. I was trying to protect some of the things that I thought were being taken from me unfairly, including my career. The idea was to fight on all fronts at once by bringing my case to the attention of the public. One thing about William Kunstler: He brings out all the injustices in a case and gets a lot of press doing it. After a while I realized that those injustices would make a lot of people angry, and when they got angry they were going to defend James Brown. I didn't want it to get out of hand. Mr. Kunstler even told me at one point, "You know, a lot of the people I defend get killed."

After that press conference I realized that the reporters would ask me questions I really didn't want to answer, because the more you answer and the more you talk, the more you hear yourself talk. Pretty soon, after all that talking, you become bitter, and I did not want to become a bitter person. So I backed off. I decided that if there was any way to work things out, I would.

After the live Japan album *Hot on the One* came out, Polydor and I separated. We'd renegotiated an album-by-album deal, and they didn't like the one I gave them, so I took it to Henry Stone—the same one who'd put out "Do the Mashed Potatoes"—and he put it on TK Records with the title *Soul Syndrome*.

I think with Polydor I was caught in the middle of some forces that you have in conglomerates that have nothing to do with the record business. I don't think everybody in Polygram and Polydor was involved, but if I had to summarize it, I'd do it this way: I think I got caught in a fight between the Jews and the Germans in the company. The Jews wanted James Brown to make it; the Germans didn't.

Meantime, I went back to work in America as a live performer. It wasn't easy. There were people who wanted to put me on oldies shows. I refused. I said, "I'm a contemporary artist." I wouldn't let 'em call my greatest hits albums golden oldies, either. Called 'em Soul Classics.

For the first time in my career I played the rock club circuit in New York, places like the Lone Star, Irving Plaza, and Studio 54. Some places that size didn't want me because I refused to cut back on my band, which was too big and expensive for the clubs. They didn't think they could make it pay. That's why I'll always be grateful to the Lone Star. They were one of the first places that would book me in New York when I came back. They showed it could be done.

Mr. Daviss and Mr. Garner thought the clubs would be a good place to expose me to people who'd never been exposed to me before, and I wanted to go into the clubs because while playing arenas and stadiums in Europe I'd started to doubt myself. From the distance of those big stages, I began to wonder if I was getting over to the people. The clubs got me back in close touch with audiences.

But I knew I'd eventually need some kind of wider exposure than that. With all the problems I was having with my record company it didn't look like the exposure was going to come from recordings. Only place it could come from was a movie. Somebody must have been reading my mind because not too long after I went into the clubs I hooked up with the two people who really turned it around for me: John Belushi and Dan Aykroyd.

39 BROTHERS

I THINK John and Danny saw me at one of the New York clubs and that hipped them to the fact that I was back working. They contacted me through a talent agent named Richard Dostal, who got the script for *Blues Brothers* to me. It was a long time before I looked at it because I was afraid of the way it might portray Afro-Americans. Once I read it, I could see it was going to bring back the blues and R & B performers that people had tried to put on the shelf.

From the time they started putting the script together they wanted me to play the role of the gospel-singing preacher. I memorized my sermon and lines on the airplane while flying out to California. On the lot at Universal they'd built a church that was a replica of a real church in Chicago. My sequence, with all the dancing and with John somersaulting down the aisle, took about three days to shoot because it was so detailed. It's funny: With all the gospel I'd sung in my life, I'd never heard of the song they picked for me to sing, but it was a genuine old gospel number. Danny found a recording of it from the thirties that was done at a tempo as fast as the one we used in the movie.

People who criticized John and Danny were confused. They didn't understand that the Blues Brothers were actors *pretending* to be R & B performers. I know Danny and John themselves weren't confused about it, and you could tell from the respect they gave the real R & B performers on the movie that they knew what they were doing. They were there for every take I did, and they treated me fantastic.

The Blues Brothers is a funny movie, and it'll never be outdated because there's a lot of information in it. It's as informative as *The Godfather* about the kinds of things people are into.

It's somewhat political too—like the part with the Nazi—and we don't want to face the things it's saying.

In my scene I was supposed to pull off the robe I had on, like the cape routine, but I wouldn't do it. I was playing a character, not James Brown, and I thought to pull off the robe would destroy the character. After some discussion John Landis, the director, agreed. I think later on they were glad they did it that way. When I did my dance I didn't get down as much as I would have if I'd been playing myself. I stayed gospel and only moved from side to side.

John wanted to do a lot of his acrobatic things, and I told him he should be careful. I'd done enough of that stuff on the stage over the years to know how dangerous it can be. He was doing a lot of those flips in my sequence, and then they used a double to do some more. John was very agile and had a lot of energy and a lot of ideas, and he seemed to be a man with so much talent that it was hard for him to define himself. I think one of the things that got to him was that he was putting on weight; he did not want to be fat. I don't think John had any kind of drug problem at that time. If he did, I wasn't aware of it. We talked about some of the pressures and problems in show business. He said to me, "I don't think you've gotten a fair shake in show business, but after this movie comes out you won't be able to walk down the street."

He was right, too. That movie exposed me to young people who'd never seen me before. I was performing all the time again. Right after the movie came out I was supposed to do a concert at Madison Square Garden with the Rolling Stones, but it went sour at the last minute. Bill Graham was promoting it. He was supposed to be the world's greatest promoter, and he wanted me to play for $5,000. I don't think he really wanted me to come at all.

Around that same time—the end of 1980—I released "Rapp Payback (Where Iz Moses)" as a 45 and as a twelve-inch. On that record I mixed rap and funk together. I was rapping about the things that "Payback" is about. It took off real strong on the English charts, but it never did what it should have here. I still wasn't on a major label, and it's hard to make a record go under those circumstances.

The next year I started doing television shows—*Saturday*

Night, Tomorrow, Mike Douglas, and others. I toured Germany and Italy. *The Blues Brothers* had triggered all this, but since I only played a character in the movie, people who saw the movie hadn't seen or heard the real James Brown. So I did television and clubs and foreign tours, just like I'd played one-nighters years before. I was determined to prove that James Brown was still relevant.

Probably the most important thing in the whole long process happened when I was on *Solid Gold* in Los Angeles on February 2, 1982. I never will forget that date because that's when I met the very special lady who's my wife today. She was the hairstylist and the makeup artist for the show. It wasn't love at first sight, it was recognition at first sight. Our souls had met a long time before.

They tape three days every other week, so they do two weeks' worth of work in those three days. They have lots of entertainers coming in and out of there. The night I was on, most of the show had already been done. I was sitting in the dressing room with the door cracked when she walked by. Our eyes met. Right there, we exchanged a long, intense look. I went out and did my spot for the show. While I was working, I wasn't really aware of her. I didn't know if she was in the booth or where. We finished the taping late that night. When it was over, all the girls, the dancers and other women, were crowded around me. I looked over their heads and saw her standing off to the side. I said, "If I'm going to talk to anyone, I'll talk to that one there." I don't know why I said that. Then I saw a fella standing behind her. He looked funny when I said that, so I said, "Well, I'm sorry, I don't think this fella likes it."

"He doesn't mean anything," she said.

He turned out to be her ex-husband who had come to talk to her about filling out their joint tax form for the last time. He was looking so mean, though, that I didn't say any more. After the wrap, I was standing over in the wing, and she was over on the other side. For some reason a spotlight split on me. I pointed over toward the other wing, and it split on her. I found out her professional name was Alfie Rodriguez and her real name was Adrianne. I didn't approach her, though, because I didn't want to come on strong or not be a gentleman. I asked one of my backup singers to see if she'd have dinner with me and with Reverend Sharpton and his wife. She said no, she

didn't socialize with entertainers. She didn't like to get involved with entertainers because they usually led such strange
lives. I found out later the only one she'd ever dated before me
was Elvis.

When I found out she was going to a cafe after the show, I
went back to my hotel and called her there. I finally managed
to talk her into coming over and having a late dinner with me
and the Sharptons in the hotel dining room. She wouldn't let
me send the limousine to get her, though. She insisted on driving her own car over. We had a very friendly dinner, and then
she went home.

A week later I called her again and invited her up to San
Francisco. I let her know that Reverend Sharpton and his wife
would be there, but by this time I think she could tell I was a
gentleman. She came, and I took her to a city that I like—
Sausalito—and we had dinner and talked some more. We
danced through the streets afterward, and then she went back
to her hotel. We dated right. I *courted* that lady.

After that I tried to fly her to meet me wherever I was performing, but she had to get right back to all the jobs she was
doing for television shows. It got harder and harder to be separated, but I could see she had a good career going. She got a
big offer from CBS, and it didn't look like we had a future
together, so I called her up one day and said that we should
stop seeing each other. She locked herself up in her house for
three weeks and just told everybody to leave her alone while
she tried to figure out what was what. She'd just been through
a divorce and then our breakup, and she had all these job offers.
Finally, she called me and asked my advice about her offer to
work on *The Young and the Restless* for CBS. She was going to
keep the job she already had, too. I advised her not to try to do
two jobs. She didn't listen. She took the job.

A month and a half later, after she'd done two shows, I
called her and she said, "I can't take doing all this anymore."

"I can't take being away from you anymore," I said.

"I can't stay away from you either."

That was what I was waiting to hear. I went to California for
a week and flew her in to meet me after each of my shows
around the state. She had to be back every morning, and we
were both so tired that we barely had time enough or strength
enough to say hello to each other. That was enough for a while,

but then I couldn't take that anymore, so I said, "I tell you what you do. If you love me, put your house up for sale and come be with me." Three days later she sold everything inside her house and then sold the house itself four days after that, and she joined me on July Fourth. I think that surprised people who knew her because they'd always known her to be very solid and rooted where she was. She said, "I finally really love somebody. If it doesn't work, so what? It's worth the gamble."

We found out we're a lot alike. She's got a lot of different bloodlines, like me. She's Italian and Afro and Jewish and Hispanic. She could penetrate the so-called white world or the black world. My wife and I are Third World people, people who are part of all the human races. When I go to a wedding or funeral in her family, I see people of all colors, and I like that.

She was from a broken home, too, growing up in Watts without her parents. That helped us really understand each other. Most of all, she had already been in show business for a long time, even though she was very young. She was able to understand the kind of life I live, and she started working with me. And because she knew so much about makeup and hair, she was able to give me a more contemporary look. A lot of people don't realize how important that is to somebody who's a visual act, like me.

During the time I was courting my wife, John Belushi died of a drug overdose in a hotel room in Beverly Hills. It was a tragedy to me. John and Danny both had been very good to me, and I knew I was going to miss him. The last time I'd seen him was at Studio 54 when I was playing there. Keith Richards and John came backstage and sat around the dressing room talking with me. But John was well out of it that night, and I remember thinking I wish I could be with him more and talk to him and help him straighten out.

When I heard that Danny's brother Peter and John's wife Judy were planning a memorial at the Lone Star, I knew I had to go. Flying up on the plane, I thought for a long time about exactly what I was going to say, but when I got there I was so overwhelmed I couldn't say any of it, so I let my performing speak for me. I thought John would have appreciated that.

I don't think I saw Danny again until he came to see me at a club in Los Angeles. He was working on a movie project called *Dr. Detroit* that he wanted me to be in. I agreed right away. The next time I saw him was on the set. He was distraught about John's death, very, very low. We talked about it, and I did my best to support Danny any way I could. I explained to him that I'd lost someone very dear to me when my son was killed but that you had to go on.

The more we talked about it, I think the better it was for him. He told me what he thought was bothering John in his last days—that show business was stressful anyway, that John had a lot of heavy pressures on him at the end and just tried to escape them through drugs. We talked for a long time about the viciousness of coke and drugs like that. I'd known a lot of people in the music business over the years that it had gotten to, and it was always sad, especially because it always seemed to get people so young.

Without his partner, Danny sounded like he was doubting his own future in the business, too. I said, "You're very talented —you can write and act and do it all—and now you're going to have to prove it all over again. People are going to wonder if you can do it without John. If you're as strong as I think you are, you will." I threw my arms around him and hugged him. I missed John, and I felt terrible for Danny. They really were like brothers. And they really did wind up with the blues.

40 LIVING IN AMERICA

Dr. Detroit was great, but the song I sang in it was an old one, "Get Up Offa That Thing." It took *Rocky IV* and a new song, "Living in America" to complete the process that started with the earlier two movies. At first I didn't want to do it, because I thought four Rockys was too many. I didn't think it would be able to sustain its popularity. But Sylvester Stallone is a strong force in the business; he knows what he's doing. He turned out to be an easy man to work with and a concerned man, too. He told me he thought *Rambo* sent a positive message to the Vietnam War veterans and made people aware of the whole MIA issue, but he was worried about its effect on kids. It was making them go out and buy bows and big knives, and he was against that. He said he didn't want them to dress up in that kind of outfit and pretend they were bloodthirsty, savage killers.

We shot my scene for the movie in three and a half days at the MGM Grand in Las Vegas. Part of that time was spent shooting the music video. It was the biggest production number they'd ever done for a Rocky picture. The song was written by Dan Hartman and Charlie Midnight, and, really, it could be about my life with all the stuff about all-night diners and all the cities in it. Richard Dostal put me together with Dan, and thank God he did. Dan is my man. He helped produce the recording session at Unique Recording in New York, and he did a fantastic job.

During the filming, Sly said to me, "You think *Blues Brothers* was something. I'm going to really show you something." He was right. The movie and the record took off together. A whole new audience saw me for the first time. The soundtrack went platinum, the single went into the top five on the charts, and I signed a new record deal with Scotti Brothers and CBS. They understood that I'm a contemporary artist.

That movie gave me the final boost I was looking for, but there were other things that helped, too, during the time I was playing the clubs. Maceo came back into the band in November of 1983. He's a Pied Piper: He plays so much horn that you could do with him what Motown did with Junior Walker. Jimmy Nolen had been back with the band, too, but he died of a heart attack at the end of that year.

In 1984 I recorded a six-part twelve-inch with Afrika Bambaataa called "Unity." It was a message directed to world leaders to get the nuclear thing under control before people all over the world *make* 'em do it.

I admire the rap and the break dancing and all the stuff coming out of hip hop. A lot of the records are messages that express community problems. Used right, those records could help prevent the riots of the sixties from happening again. If you know how a community feels about things, then you can do something about it. I'd advise all elected officials, policemen, and judges to buy those records and listen to what they're saying before we have the confusion again. Nobody wants another 1968. All they have to do to find out what's wrong is get those records. That could be their platform. If the president got up and said, "Hey, I got some new rap for you," imagine what that would do. Or if the Pope said, "You know what—I got a rap for you."

That's what my song "Brother Rapp" is all about. A fella is calling on his lady and protesting at the same time: "Don't put me in jail before I get a chance to rap. Hear what I'm saying. When you see me on a soapbox out there complaining, don't lock me up. Sit down and join me." And that's what I'm saying about these records. Let 'em testify. Let the brothers rap.

Another thing that helped me was that writers were interested in me again and helped bring attention to what I was doing and what I'd accomplished throughout my career. Also, Polydor started putting out a series of albums that told the story of my career from the beginning. That was one thing they did right.

A lot of the younger performers came to see me, too. During a show I did at the Beverly Theater in Los Angeles with B. B. King, Michael Jackson and Prince both came by. Michael sang "Man's World" and sounded fantastic. When we broke into "There Was a Time," it blew his mind. He sang and danced, and the place went wild. Prince played some guitar, but I think he was a little nervous because Michael fit into my thing a little better since Michael had been studying me for years. But later on Prince studied, and he got into it real good. When I was in California later, he came to a show and lay on the floor backstage and watched my feet. Afterward, he asked me if I had roller skates on my shoes.

But a lot of disturbing things were going down, too. I was supposed to do an album for Island Records—I went to Nassau and put down some tracks with Sly Dunbar and Robbie Shakespeare—but there were problems, and the record never came out. Island wanted me, but I don't think they could deal with me. They paid me, though, and so I think maybe Chris Blackwell, who started Island, wanted to help sustain me through that period.

I needed sustaining, too, because I was using whatever money we made to keep the show—the big band and all—going. My wife couldn't understand how I could work so much and when I got finished have no money. She'd say, "Baby, when are we going to take some money home with *us?*" I'd laugh. It never bothered me. Keeping the show alive was more important to me.

I could have gotten a lot of money by playing South Africa, but I wouldn't do it. In 1980 they started making these unbelievable offers to me through Universal Attractions. They offered me almost unlimited amounts of money; at one time the figure was $3 million. One of the fellas in the Universal office would relay the offers to me. I kept telling him not to even mention it to me, but I guess he felt it was his duty to do it. Finally, I almost had to insult him to show I was serious. He was Jewish, so I said to him, "When you've had dinner with Arafat, I'll go to South Africa." I didn't hear any more about it.

I don't want to go there because I don't even want to *see* why I'm not supposed to play it. I might be able to go in and play and cleanse people's nerves, but the sin would continue. I wish they could bring it to a harmonious end, but I'm afraid they're going to have to go through the bitter part first.

Another thing that disturbed me was the way my own government treated me. The IRS never let up. They still haven't. A man named Mr. Roof came and took all the cars out of my yard for no reason. I let him take 'em. They got seizure papers on my house. Mr. Roof—that was a man who *came* to cause a problem. One day he went through everything in my house. I said, "Mr. Roof, you're walking through my house, pulling things out and disrupting things. Why're you doing this?"

They lied to me over and over, and I spent money over and over, and kept paying. They don't want to do anything right. They just want to do what they want to do. At one point I felt so bitter about it that I was thinking of going to Canada. I even talked to a friend of mine about arranging it. And once, when I was in Italy, I started to just not come back. I had had enough. But when I cooled off, I changed my mind.

America *is* my home. Why should Afro-Americans leave it? We helped build it. The Afro-Americans and the Chinese-Americans did more of the hard labor in this country than anyone else. Someday we're going to have an Afro or Chinese or Indian president. I can understand a president going back to his heritage like President Reagan did when he visited Ireland, but a true president won't have to go anywhere to look for his roots. They'll be here.

For me, that American dream has been fulfilled. But my trouble with the government tells the story of our shortcomings, too. For the IRS to be on my neck shows some of the things we still need to accomplish. The South is the same story. The South made me what I am. When I was coming up, there were still a lot of diehard people in the South. That made me try harder. The South made me an individual. There were no avenues; they made me find an avenue that wasn't there. Later on, those diehard people grew up. Now the South is more advanced in human relations than the North is. That's why I live where I do. I want to be able to walk out of show business and come to a relaxed atmosphere and breathe the good clean country air and then go back to work and grab it again. I couldn't stay behind the plow, and that's behind the plow up there. Six o'clock is sundown, and I don't want to plow at night.

A few years ago I put my family back together. My father was already in Augusta, and my mother had been there off and on over the years. I finally got her to move back permanently and be near me. For the first time since I was four years old I had my mother and father around me. I had a chance to be with them for a little while before it was too late. More than anything else in my life, I would like to have been raised by both parents.

When Adrianne and I got married, that completed things. To make it in life you and your wife need to be in the same business. That has been my problem all along. My wives didn't know what I was doing. I would come back home from the road to a stranger. That's no good. She has to know what I'm doing, what I'm about. She goes on the road with me. We come and go together, and it's about that. My wife is me and I am my wife. Anything else doesn't mean anything. But any time you have two souls like ours coming together it takes a long time for them to become one. She has a strong self, and I have a strong self. I'm making her stronger and solid, and she's making me sharp and taking the rough edges off me. I'm giving her energy, and she's giving me the finished product.

Meantime, everything that had been started by the movies I was in and by "Living in America," and, really, by "Please Please Please" way back in 1955 in the studio of WIBB in Macon culminated when I was inducted into the Rock and Roll Hall of Fame at the beginning of 1986. Ahmet Ertegun and the people putting it together made me one of the first ten people chosen. I went in with Elvis, Chuck Berry, Ray Charles, Fats Domino, the Everly Brothers, Bill Haley, Buddy Holly, Jerry Lee Lewis, and Little Richard. I've never been a rock 'n' roll singer, but I was glad to be honored with all those other great people. That night, while I was being inducted, I think I felt for the first time that the struggle was over. I was being enshrined for posterity, and I had a record going into the top of the chart on the same night.

But honors and gold records and all that aren't what I'm proudest of. I'm proudest of what I have become, as opposed to what I *could* have become, and I'd like to be remembered as someone who brought people together.

Not long after I was put in the Hall of Fame I was in a restaurant with a white friend of mine. Another white fella came up and said, "Elvis was the greatest, and you're next." That was from his side. Then a black girl came up and said to my white friend, "The black people love him—y'all *like* him— but he's still ours." Between those two people, I bridged the gap.

Elvis was American as apple pie. Years ago I couldn't be American as apple pie. It took me four generations to be apple pie. On the other hand, if you look on the soul chart today, sometimes six of the top ten records are by white artists. Nobody has a monopoly on soul, just like nobody has a monopoly on apple pie.

People realize now they got to go the whole trip—all cultures—to enjoy life. When I play a show now and there are ten thousand people, seven thousand of 'em are white. The reason is education. Unless they were well educated, Afro-Americans never knew what they really had right in their own community. Now I think they're going to know.

I don't consider myself better than anyone. I consider myself luckier than most. People say I have a big ego, but I had to have an ego to make anything of myself in the first place. I had to have an ego to stay out there and continue to work no matter what, and I have to have one now to say, "Yes, I'm James Brown, and it's still happening for me." Because it doesn't just happen. You have to *make* it happen.

Where I grew up there was no way out, no avenue of escape, so you had to make a way. Mine was to create JAMES BROWN. God made me but with the guidance of a Ben Bart, I created the myth. I've tried to fulfill it. But I've always tried to remember that there's JAMES BROWN the myth and James Brown the man. The people own JAMES BROWN. That belongs to them. The minute I say "I'm JAMES BROWN" and believe it, then it will be the end of James Brown.

I'm James Brown.

EPILOGUE:
Prisoner of Race

It's obviously impossible to write a finished biography of a living subject, but the unwritten chapters of *James Brown: The Godfather of Soul* are more significant than most. When this book was first published in hardcover four years ago, Brown's career was at its greatest pinnacle of public adulation in nearly twenty years. In one of modern popular music's most remarkable comeback stories, the blaring, implausibly patriotic "Living in America" gave Brown his first top ten pop single since the late sixties. In January 1986, he'd been inducted into the Rock and Roll Hall of Fame. While he received that honor mainly for his best-known early hits, the minimally melodic, maximally funky albums he'd made in the early seventies, at the beginning of his commercial eclipse, were beginning to be seen (quite accurately) as groundbreaking excursions into the future of dance music, which eventually dominated pop. The rap, hip hop, and Europeanized funk records that monopolized black pop radio—and a good deal of what was left of the pop top forty—were so dependent on Brown's earlier rhythmic inventions that many of them dispensed with imitation and, using a new generation of digital equipment developed for the purpose, simply presented "samples"—that is, what amounted to tape loops—from his hallowed repertoire of riffs and beats. Although Brown wasn't paid cash for this use of his music, dozens of those musicians honored him with specific lyric citations and acknowledged his influence in interviews. He had converted "Godfather of Soul" from a promotional boast to a statement of fact. James Brown, somewhere close to sixty years old, was truly one of the revered father figures of the music revolution engendered by rock and soul.

On a September weekend in 1988, however, the mighty world of James Brown came crashing down. On Saturday, September 24, Brown was in his office in Augusta, Georgia. He discovered that somebody had used his private bathroom without permission and became enraged, angry enough to pick up a handy shotgun and enter the building next door to find out who, among the attendees at an insurance seminar, had trespassed. He was reportedly unsteady on his feet, but he did not fire his weapon nor (according to all the accounts I've read) even so much as point it at anyone.

No matter. To those in the room, he must have seemed nothing less than the bogeyman incarnate. What have Americans been trained to fear more than an enraged, possibly intoxicated black man carrying a weapon?

Somebody called the cops. Brown heard the sirens, jumped in his pickup truck, and drove away. The cops pursued him and, when he didn't stop, shot out his front tires. A total of twenty-three bullet holes were found in his vehicle when it was all over, after Brown finally surrendered because he'd run his truck into a ditch.

Brown took a voluntary drug screen. It showed that his bloodstream contained "angel dust," or PCP, an animal tranquilizer soaked into marijuana and smoked, with personality-deforming consequences. Brown nevertheless was charged with nothing more serious than a so-called blue light violation, that is, failure to stop for a police car with its flashers running. He was charged in both Georgia and South Carolina, because the roads he'd been chased on ran along that border. By the end of the evening, he was released on bail, only to be arrested again the next day—Sunday the 25th—this time for driving under the influence of PCP and marijuana. He was again bailed out.

For a time, his wife, Adrianne, threatened to file assault charges; she'd been so badly beaten on Sunday that she had to be hospitalized. According to press reports, the police had been called to the Brown home to investigate beating complaints on several occasions over the previous three years. But Adrianne had never filed charges, and this time, she dropped the complaint.

In October, James Brown came to trial in South Carolina. The charges included fleeing the police—the so-called blue light violation—driving under the influence, and aggravated assault (necessary to justify the shooting the cops had done, but not backed up by much evidence). Brown pleaded guilty and was sentenced to six years in a South Carolina prison. The bulk of the time was for the traffic charge; the assault conviction—or as he told Reverend Jesse Jackson, "I aggravated them and they assaulted me"—carried only six months. He was never convicted for driving under the influence.

Several weeks later, Brown was again tried, this time in a one-day Georgia hearing. He again copped a plea and was given a concurrent six-year term, which had the effect of ensuring that he would not be released from prison as soon as if he'd been convicted in South Carolina alone. In February 1990, a Georgia judge amended Brown's sentence to make him eligible two months earlier for work release—not to be confused with freedom.

Rolling Stone called the Georgia sentence, without bothering to note its implications, a "slap on the wrist," which is fairly amazing since it represents perhaps the longest sentence ever given in the United States for a traffic charge. Of course, *Rolling Stone* and the many other journals that have written about Brown's sentence are careful to lay against Brown many other allegations, including drug use and wife beating. The court, they want us to believe, took all this into consideration when sentencing James Brown.

It's worth recounting, then, what Reverend Jesse Jackson learned when he visited James Brown in prison. "There is some contrast between media suggestion and what the facts are on paper, and I saw the papers," Jackson said. "Number 1, James Brown is not in jail on any drug-related matter—neither consumption, possession, nor distribution. There is nothing in the record about drugs, which has been projected as the suggestion.

"Second, there is no evidence that James shot at or engaged in any violent act toward the police. . . . He is in jail for what they call the blue light high-speed chase, running from the police between South Carolina and Georgia. For that, he got six years. James' truck was shot up twenty-three times. So his motivation for running could have been well founded. If he had been shooting at them, he would be dead."

Jackson called on Governor Carroll A. Campbell, Jr., of South Carolina to commute Brown's sentence. He also asked Senator Strom Thurmond to intervene. They ignored him.

No drug charges—nor any of wife beating—have ever been raised against James Brown in a courtroom, let alone settled there. The way the justice system works, we are told, is that you go to jail only for the crime of which you're convicted, not for any felony, misdemeanor, or smear with which you may have been accused but not indicted. That is the basis on which the courts justify putting Lieutenant Colonel Oliver North, certainly more intimately familiar with drug traffickers than James Brown ever was, back on the street with no punishment but "community service" or for sentencing retired Major General Richard Secord, a gunrunner and proud subverter of national sovereignty, to a mere sixty days. Unless all of the evidence against you is presented in open court, you can't be convicted of anything at all. When "national security" prevented CIA agent Felix Rodriguez from fully documenting his involvement with Colonel North and then Vice President George Bush, he was immediately set free. Against that standard, James Brown's six-year sentence is not only suspicious; it's a blatant example of rank injustice.

James Brown is doing six years, and while an early exit from his squalid cell is a moot question as I write, Georgia law made sure he served at least eighteen months before work release, and he won't be entirely free until he's served at least half his sentence. This would be nearly equivalent to the time served by Lieutenant William Calley, who oversaw the murder of between four hundred and five hundred innocent Vietnamese civilians at My Lai. (Except that Calley actually had it easier, because he did his time under house arrest.)

There is one explanation for the sentence given James Brown and only one: He was a black man on trial in an American courtroom (not incidentally, in the state that prides itself on having been the first to secede in the Civil War). He is not an especially radical black man. In fact, he has been associated with the Republican party since 1969, at such personal expense that it has to be the result of strongly held beliefs. (Thus, my favorite dialogue in this book: "I don't think endorsing Nixon was a very smart thing to do," says record executive Hal Neely. "I didn't do it to be smart," Brown replies.) "Living in America," the hit that restored him to the top ten, served as the theme song for *Rocky IV*, in which Sylvester Stallone sought, with frightening success, to meld *Rambo*'s crazed anti-Communism with his usual chauvinism and jingoism. Brown sang it with pride and conviction.

"The American Negro has the great advantage of having never believed that collection of myths to which white Americans cling," wrote James Baldwin three decades ago in *The Fire Next Time*. Baldwin died, so far as I know, without ever having had that dearly held principle shattered by an encounter with James Brown, a black man who clings—in word and deed—to a belief in those myths.

Clings to them even in jail. Some weeks before this epilogue was written, I arranged to speak with Brown in prison, to interview him for a story I was writing for *Playboy* on racism in the American music industry. Brown was reached through a series of petitions from *Playboy* editors and stringers and myself to officials in the Atlanta offices that still represent his interests. He called collect from some semipublic area in the prison. Although we'd never spoken before, I'd seen enough James Brown interviews over the years to know that I was getting undiluted vintage JB: rapid-fire, rambling dialogue, as befits someone who long ago absorbed the music industry principle that you should never give up the floor, because it won't be easily taken back. Much of what he had to say was boiler plate about his belief in the system, how honored he felt to have been visited even in prison by so many important figures, his confidence that he'd be out soon, his pride in having transformed American music.

Although he strenuously insisted on the unfairness of being put away for so long on nothing more than a "blue light" charge,

Brown grew agitated only when I suggested that the reason he was still in prison was racism, that he was jailed in the first place because America is a racist country. "Oh no, Mr. Marsh, please don't say that," he pleaded, so ardently that I half expected to hear Danny Ray creep up behind him, bearing a cape. "America's not racist. This is all a misunderstanding, but it doesn't have anything to *do* with racism."

Had Brown and I been face to face, I'm quite sure I would have pressed him harder. However, as Baldwin also wrote, "To defend oneself against a fear is simply to insure that one will, one day, be conquered by it; fears must be faced." James Brown, God knows with great excuse and in the best of company, has yet to face the greatest fear his nation has produced. This truth is best expressed by another great black author, Richard Wright, who wrote, "The secret, black hidden core of race relations in the United States . . . is this: nobody is ever expected to speak honestly about this problem."

Trying to do so most often leads to charges of exaggeration, and perhaps for that reason, it is unwise to compare James Brown's sentence to those meted out to political criminals, as I've just done. It would probably be even more antagonistic to point out that Bernhard Goetz, the white New York City vigilante who shot four unarmed black youths in a subway car and left one of them permanently quadriplegic, served less than one year. So let us compare the charges against James Brown to those laid against other contemporary musicians. As Reverend Jackson says, "We, the people, need to *know* that John Lennon and Elvis Presley and Jerry Lee Lewis would *not* be in jail for six years for running from the police."

I'm unaware of any other pop star who's ever been accused of fleeing red-neck cops on a southern border road. However, in 1984, Vince Neil, of the all-white heavy-metal band Mötley Crüe, killed two people and seriously injured another in a drunken driving incident. He served no jail time, merely paying large fines, agreeing to "community service," and submitting to drug and alcohol counseling. The South Carolina prisons in which Brown has served time do not offer drug counseling, though he has promised *Jet* magazine to seek it on his own.

The hypocrisy about drugs in the rock world that this case reveals is unconscionable. Band members of the Grateful Dead, one of rock's most revered institutions, have advocated substance abuse since the day they became famous; few dare criticize them for it. When lead guitarist Jerry Garcia was found sitting in his car in Golden Gate park, drugged so badly on heroin and cocaine that he nearly died, he was regarded not as a criminal but as a victim. Similarly, when Paul McCartney was thrown into a Japanese jail for possession of marijuana, his case was considered a travesty of justice. Not one of these people or their apologists has stepped forward on behalf of James Brown.

In 1988, Doc McGhee, who manages Mötley Crüe and Bon Jovi, among others, got caught underwriting a drug-smuggling ring, which imported several hundred million dollars' worth of marijuana. McGhee served no time and a major part of his "community service" consisted of shepherding his clients to an "antidrug" pop festival in Moscow. On that basis, Brown did his bit in advance, with 1972's "King Heroin," a top forty rant against the most ruinous illegal chemical of that day, or with the time he served on President Ronald Reagan's antidrug commission.

As to wife beating—to my mind the most serious of the unfiled charges against Brown—when Jerry Lee Lewis' spouse was found dead under highly suspicious circumstances at his Mississippi home, he was barely interrogated, let alone charged. The fact that James Brown faced southern justice as a black man is not to be underestimated; chances are, if Richard Pryor lived in South Carolina rather than southern California, he might be doing time, too.

It is also alleged, in *Rolling Stone* and elsewhere, that James Brown engaged in unfair business practices with his various backing bands and with artists who recorded for his production company. I can relate to the concept of sentencing people for such transgressions, but if we do that, it's hard to imagine what major record executive of the past four decades will be left on the street—certainly, John Hammond having passed on, none of those I've met in the past twenty years will escape.

It's extremely difficult—for me, at least—not to hear as an undercurrent in all the charges against James Brown the idea that he was, beyond anything else, guilty of a certain hubris, that he was one more pop star grown too big for his britches. As we have seen when similar indictments have been made against Elvis Presley (another poor Southerner, and one of JB's few contemporaries who might be judged a peer), there is a class and regional bias in such allegations. Because James Brown's pursuit of wealth and fame—and his flaunting of whatever amount of them he laid hold of—doesn't meet northern middle-class standards of acceptability, some of his putative fans feel free to stand by while he is dealt with unjustly.

So let us remind ourselves, at least briefly, who James Brown really is. The best way to do that is, in fact, to read *James Brown: The Godfather of Soul*. Almost despite itself, this book is very revealing of its subject.

The Godfather of Soul belongs to two significant groups of popular literature: the superstar show-biz autobiography and the black cultural hero autobiography. As a generic black cultural hero autobiography, *The Godfather of Soul* is more-or-less typical—I'm thinking here of books such as Richard Wright's *Black Boy*, the personal passages of James Baldwin's *The Fire Next Time* and *Notes of a Native Son*, *The Autobiography of Malcolm X*, and *The Quality of Hurt* by Chester Himes. These works involve not only the typical autobiographical search for identity, but cast that search in a peculiar way, as the struggle to find one's name amidst a powerful, white-run society that uses all its authority and strength to keep that name (and the power derived from knowing it) hidden. This is perhaps clearest in Malcolm X's tale, where his true name is finally granted to him through divine revelation, but the same search and struggle takes place in the others.

Consider the opening passage of *The Godfather of Soul*: "I was marked from the getup. You might say that I've got a mark on my back that I never knew was there. That's because they fixed it where I couldn't see it myself. . . . I was marked a lot of different ways. With names, for example. I was marked with a lot of different names. And each one has a story behind it." This leads, some three hundred pages and many stories later, to the concluding passage: "Where I grew up there was no way out, no avenue of escape, so you had to make a way. Mine was to create JAMES BROWN. God made me but with the guidance of a Ben Bart, I created the myth. I've tried to fulfill it. But I've always tried to remember that there's JAMES BROWN the myth and James Brown the man. The people own JAMES BROWN. That belongs to them. The minute I say "I'm JAMES BROWN" and believe it, then it will be the end of James Brown.

"I'm James Brown."

And who James Brown thinks JAMES BROWN might be is the real story. Unlike any other superstar autobiography I've ever come across, this book concentrates on its subject's actual work. The center of *The Godfather of Soul* is not just James Brown, but JAMES BROWN's music and performances.

If James Brown's music and stage persona is the subject, the theme is encapsulated in the title of the record that any Brown biography must recognize as the watershed of his career: "Say It Loud, I'm Black and I'm Proud." Brown lives up to both degrees of this title; he's proud of his blackness, and especially of his stature among black Americans, to the point of boastfulness—"I was the one who made the dark-complexioned people popular." He reiterates this pride at the top of his lungs, and not at all inappropriately.

As a singer, James Brown found his métier in the shout, not so much the gospel kind as the field holler. His cracked and rasping yell in "Papa's Got a Brand New Bag," "I Got You (I Feel Good)," "Night Train," "Cold Sweat," "I Can't Stand Myself (When You Touch Me)," "Please Please Please," "Out Of Sight," and "Get Up, I Feel Like Being Like a Sex Machine" doesn't just declare a man exulting in his search for and discovery of a new identity, but proclaims a new order of American popular music, one based on the triumph of polyrhythm over the restrictions of conventional Western harmonics and melodies. (And though I prefer the balladry of Jackie Wilson and Little Willie John, it's also true that when

Brown reworked old Billy Eckstine tunes such as "Prisoner of Love," he cut a new and previously unimaginable groove with them, too.)

I once joked that one day in 1967, James Brown grew weary altogether of the tyranny of chord changes and so he banished them and thus begot "Cold Sweat." Looking back over his career now, I fail to see the humor. It's no joke, just the truth, the bare facts of what the man did—and if you don't think it amounted to much, try turning on the radio. You will hear a myriad of recordings in which everything is subordinated to beats—beats generally far less complex and subtly interwoven than those in the great James Brown hits (of which there are far more than those listed in the previous paragraph, perhaps three or four times as many). Beats heard today are often fragments taken directly from James Brown records a decade or more old.

Which is to say that even if James Brown boasts incessantly in these pages, he never brags. By critical acclimation, he is now quite clearly seen as the most influential American popular musician of the second half of the twentieth century. (My only qualm is whether "American" is too restrictive.) I would argue that as a radical innovator within popular music, only Louis Armstrong indisputably stands before him in the century's first half. What Brown has in common with Armstrong is a willingness to reinvent the ground of his work on the spot. Arranger Pee Wee Ellis claims that "Cold Sweat"—the most minimally melodic record ever to reach the *Billboard* top ten when it appeared there in 1967 and the record that, more than any other, set the pattern for funk, disco, and hip hop—was literally mumbled into his ear in the dressing room after a show, then recorded live, with only a few moments for rehearsal, after the tour bus rolled into Cincinnati the next day. "Then [we] got back on the bus and went back to work." *That's* improvisatory composition.

Intellectuals may greet with outrage the suggestion that Brown belongs in the same rank as other American musical geniuses of our time, let alone that someone would seriously elevate him above Duke Ellington and Charlie Parker, no matter how carefully defined the context. "James Brown, to my ears, has merely learned

the same lesson as the creators of *The Great Train Robbery*,"
Ishmael Reed wrote, in a 1972 essay titled without apparent irony,
Music: Black, White and Blue. "That is, you can play the same
scene over and over merely changing the titles and still get a
gullible public to go for it." The bias at work here isn't so hard
to understand; Reed himself has scorned other intellectuals for
their snobbery and condescension in dismissing Louis Armstrong
as a mere entertainer. Armstrong, like Brown (and unlike, say,
Charlie Parker) was an entertainer, but there was nothing "mere"
about it. Pops did not idly invoke the shark's pearly teeth in "Mack
the Knife." Underneath the simplest of his declarations of romantic
fervor, Armstrong hid fangs of ironic convolution, ready to rip at
anyone with the insight to pierce the veil. Nothing ever quite meant
what he said, or even (maybe especially) what he said it said.

James Brown has a different approach; he portrays his insights
as simplicity personified. Much of what he has to say is not only
simple, but reflects a simplistic faith, particularly in the political
and economic system of which he is a creature, the system that
has for these past months all but entombed him. (Another aspect
of the harm done him deserves to be carefully considered; prison
is hard on young men, and James Brown is pushing sixty.) These
are the convoluted simplicities of the skilled evangelical preacher,
in which the Bible means literally what it says and literally says
what you never imagined it contained when you were reading it
yourself. Listen to James Brown sing of his fervor for "Living in
America" right now. You will not hear mere Reagan-period jingoism, but rather the expression through sheer blind willpower of
one man's version of the American Dream, a dream Brown
believed he had no right to expect, having been raised in a
whorehouse and without a name.

Brown's only gripe with the government, in fact, is with its
taxation policies. The passage in which he expresses his doubts is
worth repeating here, because it's the only hint we have of political
self-doubt in James Brown, because it grounds those doubts solidly
in exactly the racism he would otherwise deny, and because it
expresses so well the fundamental eccentricity of his thought.
"The government is responsible for [my tax problems]," he writes

in chapter 30, "because they didn't allow me to go to school. I have an elementary school education and didn't even graduate from there. They have no legal boundaries over me. By the Constitution of the United States. The people who represented me had shingles and sheepskins, and I didn't have any of 'em. So I owe *nothing*. . . . You pay tax when you're represented. You pay tax when you exercise all of your rights."

Such is the totality of James Brown's faith in the system that raised him to riches and certain kinds of glory (though it barred him, because of his race, from others equally his due), that he'd probably be willing to try that argument in court. Nevertheless, you can't measure the fullness of his faith in the system until you know the story of what he did in Boston, Massachusetts, on April 5, 1968. Brown was scheduled to play the Boston Garden that night, to a crowd that would have totaled more than ten thousand. But the night before, Dr. Martin Luther King, Jr., was assassinated in Memphis. City officials were terrified, as well they should have been. King's death symbolized the end of an era in the movement for black civil rights; the dream of a nonviolent solution had been demolished. Presiding over probably the most racist city in the country and certainly the most strictly segregated urban area in the North, Mayor Kevin White verged on panic, especially since a powerhouse black entertainer was set to bring together such a large crowd the next evening.

To cool the tension caused by Boston's benign neglect of and overt hostility toward its black citizens, James Brown agreed to play his show before a much smaller audience at the Garden and to send it out live on television. Brown and Bruce Tucker tell this story better than I ever could (in chapter 27 of this book). I have seen a videotape of the event (actually, it seems a fuzzy old kinescope), and it is one of the most riveting performances of any kind I've ever witnessed. Brown's act has been better captured, notably on *The T.A.M.I. Show*, but almost always out of context.

The Boston Garden tape presents Brown so far out of context that he snaps back in. Mayor White and other city fathers crowd the stage at the beginning and they are all but trembling, so deep is their fear of what may occur. Throughout the tape, you can see them in the shadows just offstage, lurking, pacing, fretting. The Apollo Theater might as well exist on another planet, Brown and the JB's might be toying with time bombs rather than chopping up backbeats. At the end, the crowd storms the stage, as it might have been predicted would happen, and the cops surge in, but Brown cools out both sides and saves the day for what passes for democracy in America's supposedly most liberal city.

"For Brown, never lacking in self-esteem, this confirmed his power in black America," writes Nelson George. And indeed, Brown had been honored by Vice President Hubert Humphrey for similar, though less dramatic aid in quelling urban insurrections in 1967. His next gig was for U.S. troops in Vietnam. Like America's other veterans of urban and Southeast Asian battles, Brown gets no credit for what he risked. In January 1969, having switched allegiance, he appeared at Richard Nixon's inaugural ball (joining a truly impressive lineup of black talent, including the orchestras of Duke Ellington and Lionel Hampton; the dance team of Hines, Hines and Dad; singer Barbara McNair; and pianist Andre Watts).

The previous August, James had released his recording of "Say It Loud, I'm Black and I'm Proud." It squeezed into the pop top ten, but it was the last top ten visit he'd make until "Living in America," seventeen years later. In chapter 29, Brown argues that this record damaged him with white audiences because they (and the radio programmers who influenced them) found it antiwhite. I'm not so sure; the real reason might just as well have been the music, the most intense and skeletal funk he'd made up to that time. I am certain that having such records in your catalogue does you no good when it comes time for the white county prosecutors and state judges of South Carolina and Georgia to pass sentence upon you. (Even when, as with "Black and Proud," the song is the follow-up to "America is My Home," which was a statement of pride of a whole different order.)

That's one reason, beyond their lack of sympathy for his seemingly undeveloped music, why such intellectuals as Reed feel justified in dismissing James Brown. True child of the American system that he is, he can absorb any blow, no matter how potentially deflating, and convert it into ammunition for his argument of faith. "People came around after awhile and bought 'Living in America,' didn't they?" I can hear JB arguing. "See, the system works. You just have to give it another chance."

Well, you can see that a man is blind to certain things without denying his talent in others—Mark Twain said that every man is a genius if we can only place him. Placing James Brown is not difficult: his achievements are musically immense, as a funk-steeped generation of black intellectuals younger than Reed would agree. And though, as the most musically astute critic of that generation, Nelson George, wrote in *The Death of Rhythm & Blues*, "it is simply impossible to resolve all the contradictions in James Brown," it is equally impossible to abandon him to the unkind mercies of America's separate, viciously inequitable justice system, merely because he's often behaved inexplicably and sometimes destructively.

I don't mean that James Brown does not deserve to serve six years in prison because he is a great artist. Artists aren't, and ought not to be, socially exempt. I mean that the failure to recognize James Brown as a great artist is also a crime of some magnitude, and that it is unlikely that the former inequity would exist without the latter. Ask yourself, as James Brown tells you his story, if America would permit such a prison sentence to be visited upon Elvis Presley, JB's close friend and fellow substance abuser. Ask yourself, as you read these words, if any of us are free as long as any man—let alone one as well-known, important, and beloved as James Brown—can receive and serve a sentence such as this one. Ask yourself why, more than half a century after Richard Wright declared it so, we still cannot tell one another the truth about race relations in America and acknowledge that what has happened to James Brown happens to other black men and women in America every day. Ask yourself why we have not—especially why those in the music world so heavily indebted to him have not—begun to do something about it, to demand his freedom at the top of their lungs. Ask yourself what happens if we continue to treat people this way and, as long as we do so, why it is that America has any right to consider itself privileged among nations.

And the answers will come back, if not at great volume, at least in a still, small voice. When they do, I think you will know why I say, without knowing whether James Brown will have been released from jail by the time you read this: Free James Brown!

DAVE MARSH
1990

DISCOGRAPHY

Compiled by Cliff White

JAMES BROWN SINGLES

The following section is a chronological listing of all James Brown single releases credited principally to James Brown as the performer, whether with or without the Famous Flames, "featuring his band," or some other variation. Recording dates, where known, follow titles. Numbers following titles indicate chart position: *Left* is Rhythm & Blues ranking; circle ○ indicates that it was in the top ten. *Right* is Pop ranking; circle indicates that it was in the top forty.

1956

March	Please Please Please (2/4/56)	⑥	Federal	F12258
	Why Do You Do Me? (2/4/56)			
June	I Don't Know (2/4/56)		Federal	F12264
	I Feel That Old Feeling Coming On (2/4/56)			
July	No, No, No (3/27/56)		Federal	F12277
	Hold My Baby's Hand (3/27/56)			
October	Just Won't Do Right (7/24/56)		Federal	F12289
	Let's Make It (7/24/56)			

1957

January	Chonnie-on-Chon (3/27/56)		Federal	F12290
	I Won't Plead No More (3/27/56)			

April	Can't Be the Same (7/24/56)	Federal	F12292
	Gonna Try (7/24/56)		
July	Love or a Game (4/10/57)	Federal	F12295
	Messing With the Blues (4/10/57)		
October (?)	You're Mine, You're Mine (3/27/56)	Federal	F12300
	I Walked Alone (3/27/56)		
November	That Dood It (10/21/57)	Federal	F12311
	Baby Cries Over the Ocean (10/21/57)		

1958

May (?)	Begging, Begging (10/21/57)			Federal	F12316
	That's When I Lost My Heart (10/21/57)				
October	Try Me (9/18/58)	①	48	Federal	F12337
	Tell Me What I Did Wrong (9/18/58)				

1959

February	I Want You So Bad (12/18/58)	20	Federal	F12348
	There Must Be a Reason (9/18/58)			
April	I've Got to Change (0/18/58)		Federal	F12352
	It Hurts to Tell You (1/30/59)			
July	Good Good Lovin' (6/27/59)		Federal	F12361
	Don't Let It Happen to Me (1/30/59)			
October	Got to Cry (12/18/58)		Federal	F12364
	It Was You (12/18/58)			

1960

January	I'll Go Crazy (11/11/59)	15	Federal	F12369
	I Know It's True (I Found Someone) (11/11/59)			

May	Think (2/20/60)	⑦	㉝	Federal	F12370
	You've Got the Power (2/20/60)	14	86		
August	This Old Heart (11/11/59)	20	79	Federal	F12378
	Wonder When You're Coming Home (11/11/59)				
November	The Bells (10/4/60)		68	King	K5423
	And I Do Just What I Want (9/29/60)				

1961

January	Hold It (Instrumental) (10/4/60)			King	K5438
	The Scratch (Instrumental) (10/4/60)				
February	Bewildered (1/30/59)	⑧	㊵	King	K5442
	If You Want Me (2/20/60)				
April	I Don't Mind (9/27/60)	④	47	King	K5466
	Love Don't Love Nobody (9/27/60)				
May	Suds (Instrumental) (2/9/61)			King	K5485
	Sticky (Instrumental) (2/9/61)				
June (?)	Cross Firing (Instrumental) (6/9/61)			King	K5519
	Night Flying (Instrumental; maybe reissue) (6/9/61)				
July	Baby, You're Right (9/27/60)	②	49	King	K5524
	I'll Never, Never Let You Go (2/20/60)				
September	I Love You, Yes I Do (2/10/61)			King	K5547
	Just You and Me, Darling (9/29/60)	17			
November	Lost Someone (2/9/61)	②	48	King	K5573
	Cross Firing (Instrumental) (6/9/61)				

1962

March	Night Train (2/9/61)	⑤	㉟	King	K5614
	Why Does Everything Happen to Me? (4/10/57)				
June	Shout and Shimmy (2/9/61)	16	61	King	K5657
	Come Over Here (9/29/60)				
August	Mashed Potatoes U.S.A. (5/20/62)	21	82	King	K5672
	You Don't Have to Go (2/9/61)				
November	I've Got Money (5/21/62)		93	King	K5701
	Three Hearts in a Tangle (7/31/62)	18			

1963

January	Every Beat of My Heart (Instrumental) (1/8/62)		99	King	K5710
	Like a Baby (5/21/62)	24			
April	Prisoner of Love (12/17/62)	⑥	⑱	King	K5739
	Choo Choo (Locomotion) (Instrumental) (7/30/62)				
July	These Foolish Things (12/17/62)	25	55	King	K5767
	(Can You) Feel It, Part 1 (Instrumental) (9/4/62)				
September	Signed, Sealed, and Delivered (7/31/62)		77	King	K5803
	Waiting in Vain (7/31/62)				
November	I've Got to Change (9/18/58)			King	K5829
	The Bells (10/4/60)				

1964

January	Oh Baby, Don't You Weep, Part 1 (10/4/63) Oh Baby, Don't You Weep, Part 2 (With overdubbed crowd) (10/4/63)	㉓ King	K5842
February	Please Please Please (With overdubbed crowd) (2/4/56) In the Wee Wee Hours (Of the Nite) (5/21/62)	95 King	K5853
April	Caldonia (3/64) Evil (Instrumental) (3/64)	95 Smash	S1898
April	Again (12/17/62) How Long, Darling? (7/31/62)	King	K5876
June	So Long (12/17/62) Dancin' Little Thing (9/9/61)	King	K5899
June	The Things I Used to Do (3/64) Out of the Blue (3/64)	99 Smash	S1908
July	Out of Sight (3/64) Maybe the Last Time (6/64)	㉔ Smash	S1919
August	Tell Me What You're Gonna Do (10/4/60) I Don't Care (5/21/62)	King	K5922
September	Think (2/20/60) Try Me (9/18/58)	King	K5952
October	Fine Old Foxy Self (4/10/57) *Medley:* Found Someone, Why Do You Do Me?, I Want You So Bad (Live) (10/24/62)	King	K5956
December	Have Mercy, Baby (6/9/61) Just Won't Do Right (6/9/61)	92 King	K5968

1965

Month	Title	R&B	Pop	Label	Number
March	Devil's Hideaway (Instrumental) (5/64)			Smash	S1975
	Who's Afraid of Virginia Woolf? (Instrumental) (6/64)				
Unissued	I Got You (7/64)			Smash	S1989
	Only You (3/64)				
May	This Old Heart (11/11/59)			King	K5995
	It Was You (12/18/58)				
July	Papa's Got a Brand New Bag, Part 1 (2/65)	①	⑧	King	K5999
	Papa's Got a Brand New Bag, Part 2 (2/65)				
September	Try Me (Instrumental) (8/65)	34	63	Smash	S2008
	Papa's Got a Brand New Bag (Instrumental) (8/65)				
November	I Got You (I Feel Good) (5/65)	①	③	King	K6015
	I Can't Help It (I Just Do-Do-Do) (5/65)				

1966

Month	Title	R&B	Pop	Label	Number
February	Lost Someone (Live) (10/24/62)		94	King	K6020
	I'll Go Crazy (Live) (10/24/62)	38	73		
February	Ain't That a Groove, Part 1 (12/13/65)	⑥	42	King	K6025
	Ain't That a Groove, Part 2 (12/13/65)				
March	Prisoner of Love (12/17/62)			King	K6029
	I've Got to Change (9/18/58)				
March	New Breed, Part 1 (Instrumental) (2/7/66)			Smash	S2028
	New Breed, Part 2 (Instrumental) (2/7/66)				

April	Come Over Here (9/29/60) Tell Me What You're Gonna Do (10/4/60)			King	K6032
April	It's a Man's Man's Man's World (3/66) Is It Yes or Is It No? (3/66)	①	⑧	King	K6035
May	Just Won't Do Right (6/9/61) I've Got Money (5/21/62)			King	K6037
June	James Brown's Boo-Ga-Loo (Instrumental) (2/7/66) Lost in a Mood of Changes (Instrumental) (2/8/66)			Smash	S2042
June	It Was You (12/18/58) I Don't Care (5/21/62)			King	K6040
June	This Old Heart (11/11/59) How Long, Darling? (7/31/62)			King	K6044
July	Money Won't Change You, Part 1 (6/9/66) Money Won't Change You, Part 2 (6/9/66)	11	53	King	K6048
October	Don't Be a Drop-Out (8/16/66) Tell Me That You Love Me (4/24/66)	④	50	King	K6056
November	The Christmas Song (Version 1) (10/17/66) The Christmas Song (Version 2) (10/17/66)			King	K6064
November	Sweet Little Baby Boy, Part 1 (10/18/66) Sweet Little Baby Boy, Part 2 (10/18/66)			King	K6065

December	Let's Make Christmas Mean Something This Year, Part 1 (10/19/66) Let's Make Christmas Mean Something This Year, Part 2 (10/19/66)			King	K6072

1967

January	Bring It Up (10/4/66) Nobody Knows (4/17/66)	(7)	(29)	King	K6071
January	Let's Go Get Stoned (Instrumental) (4/20/66) Our Day Will Come (Instrumental) (4/20/66)			Smash	S2064
Withdrawn	Let Yourself Go (1/14/67) Stone Fox (Instrumental) (1/67)			King	K6086
February	Kansas City (1/25/67) Stone Fox (Instrumental) (1/67)	21	55	King	K6086
March	Think, with Vicki Anderson (1/25/67) Vicki Anderson only		100	King	K6091
April	Let Yourself Go (1/14/67) Good Rockin' Tonight (3/64)	(5)	46	King	K6100
June	Jimmy Mack (Instrumental) (6/66) What Do You Like? (Instrumental) (6/66)			Smash	S2093
June	I Loves You, Porgy (7/64) Yours and Mine (Instrumental) (?/67)			Bethlehem	B3089
July	Cold Sweat, Part 1 (5/67) Cold Sweat, Part 2 (5/67)	(1)	(7)	King	K6110
Withdrawn	It Won't Be Me (4/5/67) Mona Lisa (7/64)			King	K6111

October	Get It Together, Part 1 (9/5/67)	11	40	King	K6122
	Get It Together, Part 2 (9/5/67)				
November	Funky Soul—No. 1 (Instrumental) (8/67)			King	K6133
	The Soul of JB (Instrumental) (8/67)				
December	I Can't Stand Myself (When You Touch Me) (10/30/67)	④	㉘	King	K6144
	There Was a Time (Live) (6/25/67)	③	㊱		

1968

February	You've Got to Change Your Mind, with Bobby Byrd (4/5/67)	47		King	K6151
	Bobby Byrd only				
March	You've Got the Power, with Vicki Anderson (1/25/67)			King	K6152
	Vicki Anderson only				
March	I Got the Feelin' (2/15/68)	①	⑥	King	K6155
	If I Ruled the World (2/15/68)				
April	Maybe Good, Maybe Bad, Part 1 (Instrumental) (11/12/67)			King	K6159
	Maybe Good, Maybe Bad, Part 2 (Instrumental) (11/12/67)				
May	Shhhhhhhh (For a Little While) (Instrumental) (5/5/68)			King	K6164
	Here I Go (Instrumental) (5/5/68)				
May	Licking Stick— Licking Stick, Part 1 (4/16/68)	②	⑭	King	K6166
	Licking Stick— Licking Stick, Part 2 (4/16/68)				

Month	Title			Label	Number
May	America Is My Home, Part 1 (5/31/67)	13	52	King	K6112
	America Is My Home, Part 2 (5/31/67)				
July	I Guess I'll Have to Cry, Cry, Cry (10/4/67)	15	55	King	K6141
	Just Plain Funk (Instrumental) (8/67)				
August	Say It Loud, I'm Black and I'm Proud, Part 1 (8/7/68)	①	⑩	King	K6187
	Say It Loud, I'm Black and I'm Proud, Part 2 (8/7/68)				
Not on General Release	I Love You (8/7/68)			Colgate promo on King	Cold Power Axion
	Maybe I'll Understand (11/12/67)				
November	Goodbye, My Love (9/5/67)	⑨	㉛	King	K6198
	Shades of Brown (Instrumental) (8/68)				
November	Santa Claus Goes Straight to the Ghetto (10/7/68)			King	K6203
	You Know It (Instrumental) (10/8/68)				
November	Tit for Tat (Ain't No Taking Back) (10/8/68)		86	King	K6204
	Believers Shall Enjoy (Instrumental) (10/8/68)				
November	Let's Unite the Whole World at Christmas (10/7/68)			King	K6205
	In the Middle, Part 1 (Instrumental) (4/29/68)				

1969

Month	Title			Label	Number
January	Give It Up or Turnit a Loose (10/29/68)	①	⑮	King	K6213
	I'll Lose My Mind (Instrumental) (8/67)				

February	"Steve Soul" A Talk with the News Shades of Brown, Part 2 (Instrumental) (8/68)		King	K6216
March	You've Got to Have a Job, with Marva Whitney (1/13/69) Marva Whitney only		King	K6218
March	Soul Pride, Part 1 (Instrumental) (8/7/68) Soul Pride, Part 2 (Instrumental) (8/7/68)	33	King	K6222
Unissued	You Got to Have a Mother for Me, Part 1 (1/13/69) You Got to Have a Mother for Me, Part 2 (1/13/69)		King	K6223
March	I Don't Want Nobody to Give Me Nothing, Part 1 (2/23/69) I Don't Want Nobody to Give Me Nothing, Part 2 (2/23/69)	③ ⑳	King	K6224
Unissued	The Little Groove Maker, Me, Part 1 (Live) (6/25/67) The Little Groove Maker, Me, Part 2 (Live) (6/25/67)		King	K6235
Unissued	The Little Groove Maker, Me (Live) (6/25/67) Any Day Now (4/21/69)		King	K6235
Withdrawn	The Little Groove Maker, Me (Live) (6/25/67) I'm Shook (12/2/68)		King	K6235
May	The Popcorn (Instrumental) (8/26/68) The Chicken (Instrumental) (8/26/68)	11 30	King	K6240

June	Mother Popcorn, Part 1 (5/13/69)	①	⑪	King	K6245
	Mother Popcorn, Part 2 (5/13/69)				
August	Lowdown Popcorn (Instrumental) (6/13/69)	16	41	King	K6250
	Top of the Stack (Instrumental) (6/13/69)				
August	World, Part 1 (7/17/69)	⑧	㊲	King	K6258
	World, Part 2 (7/17/69)				
October	Let a Man Come In and Do the Popcorn, Part 1 (5/13/69)	②	㉑	King	K6255
	Sometime (12/2/68)				
Unissued	I'm Not Demanding, Part 1 (8/13/69)			King	K6273
	I'm Not Demanding, Part 2 (8/13/69)				
November	Ain't It Funky Now, Part 1 (Instrumental) (10/14/69)	③	㉔	King	K6280
	Ain't It Funky Now, Part 2 (Instrumental) (10/14/69)				
November	Let a Man Come In and Do the Popcorn, Part 2 (5/13/69)	⑥	㊵	King	K6275
	Gittin' a Little Hipper, Part 2 (Instrumental) (11/67)				
December	It's Christmas Time, Part 1 (8/13/69)			King	K6277
	It's Christmas Time, Part 2 (8/13/69)				

1970

January	"Steve Soul" Soul President (5/13/69)			Federal	F12551
	Popcorn with a Feeling (Instrumental) (5/13/69)				

November	Ain't It Funky Now, Part 1 (Instrumental) (10/14/69)	③	㉔	King	K6280
	Ain't It Funky Now, Part 2 (Instrumental) (10/14/69)				
Unissued	Brother Rapp, Part 1 (10/14/69)			King	K6285
	Brother Rapp, Part 2 (10/14/69)				
March	Funky Drummer, Part 1 (Instrumental) (11/20/69)	20	51	King	K6290
	Funky Drummer, Part 2 (Instrumental) (11/20/69)				
February	It's a New Day, Parts 1 and 2 (9/3/69)	③	㉜	King	K6292
	Georgia On My Mind (1/4/70)				
April	Let It Be Me, with Vicki Anderson (2/14/70)			King	K6293
	Vicki Anderson only				
Unissued	Talkin' Loud and Sayin' Nothing, Part 1 (2/24/70)			King	K6300
	Talkin' Loud and Sayin' Nothing, Part 2 (2/24/70)				
May	Brother Rapp, Parts 1 and 2 (10/14/69)	②	㉜	King	K6310
	Bewildered (4/12/69)				
July	Get Up, I Feel Like Being Like a Sex Machine, Part 1 (4/25/70)	②	⑮	King	K6318
	Get Up, I Feel Like Being Like a Sex Machine, Part 2 (4/25/70)				
July	A Man Has to Go Back to the Crossroads (5/11/70)			Bethlehem	B3098
	The Drunk (Instrumental) (5/70)				

Unissued	I'm Not Demanding, Part 1 (8/13/69)		King	K6322
	I'm Not Demanding, Part 2 (8/13/69)			
October	Super Bad, Parts 1 and 2 (6/30/70)	① ⑬	King	K6329
	Super Bad, Part 3 (6/30/70)			
November	Hey, America (10/7/70)		King	K6339
	Hey, America (Instrumental) (10/7/70)			
November	Santa Claus Is Definitely Here to Stay (10/7/70)		King	K6340
	Santa Claus Is Definitely Here to Stay (Instrumental) (10/7/70)			
December	Get Up, Get Into It, and Get Involved, Part 1 (11/3/70)	④ ㉞	King	K6347
	Get Up, Get Into It, and Get Involved, Part 2 (11/3/70)			
Withdrawn	Talkin' Loud and Sayin' Nothing, Part 1 (2/24/70)		King	KP6350
	Talkin' Loud and Sayin' Nothing, Part 2 (2/24/70)			
Unissued	Talkin' Loud and Sayin' Nothing, Part 1 (10/1/70)		King	KS6359
	Talkin' Loud and Sayin' Nothing, Part 2 (10/1/70)			

1971

February	Spinning Wheel, Part 1 (Instrumental) (10/1/69)	90	King	K6366
	Spinning Wheel, Part 2 (Instrumental) (10/1/69)			

Month	Title			Label	Catalog
March	Soul Power, Part 1 (1/26/71)	③	㉙	King	K6368
	Soul Power, Part 2 (1/26/71)				
April	I Cried (2/14/70)	15	50	King	K6363
	World, Part 2 (7/17/69)				
May	Escape-ism, Part 1 (4/8/71)	⑥	㉟	People	P2500
	Escape-ism, Part 2 (4/8/71)				
July	Hot Pants, Part 1 (5/13/71)	①	⑮	People	P2501
	Hot Pants, Parts 2 and 3 (5/13/71)				
August	Make It Funky, Part 1 (7/13/71)	①	㉒	Polydor	PD14088
	Make It Funky, Part 2 (7/13/71)				
October	My Part/Make It Funky, Part 3 (7/13/71)		68	Polydor	PD14098
	Make It Funky, Part 4 (7/13/71)				
November	I'm a Greedy Man, Part 1 (5/13/71)	⑦	㉟	Polydor	PD14100
	I'm a Greedy Man, Part 2 (5/13/71)				

1972

Month	Title			Label	Catalog
February	Talkin' Loud and Sayin' Nothing, Part 1 (10/1/70)	①	㉗	Polydor	PD14109
	Talkin' Loud and Sayin' Nothing, Part 2 (10/1/70)				
February	King Heroin (1/18/72)	⑥	㊵	Polydor	PD14116
	Theme from King Heroin (Instrumental) (1/17/72)				
March	It's a Man's Man's Man's World (Reissue)			Polydor Soul Classics	SC501
	Mother Popcorn (Reissue)				

	Cold Sweat (Reissue) Night Train (Reissue)			Polydor Soul Classics	SC502
	Sex Machine (Reissue) The Popcorn (Reissue)			Polydor Soul Classics	SC503
March	Think (Reissue) Licking Stick (Reissue)			Polydor Soul Classics	SC504
March	Papa's Got a Brand New Bag (Reissue)			Polydor Soul Classics	SC505
	I Got the Feelin' (Reissue)				
March	I Got You (I Feel Good) (Reissue)			Polydor Soul Classics	SC506
	I Can't Stand Myself (Reissue)				
March	Try Me (Reissue) Money Won't Change You (Reissue)			Polydor Soul Classics	SC507
March	Super Bad (Reissue) Ain't It Funky Now (Reissue)			Polydor Soul Classics	SC508
March	Give It Up or Turnit a Loose (Reissue)			Polydor Soul Classics	SC509
	Soul Power (Reissue)				
March	Hot Pants (Reissue) Out of Sight (Reissue)			Polydor Soul Classics	SC510
May	There It Is, Part 1 (2/7/72)	④	43	Polydor	PD14125
	There It Is, Part 2 (2/7/72)				
June	Honky Tonk, Part 1 (4/72)	⑦	44	Polydor	PD14129
	Honky Tonk, Part 2 (4/72)				
July	Get on the Good Foot, Part 1 (5/9/72)	①	⑱	Polydor	PD14139
	Get on the Good Foot, Part 2 (5/9/72)				
October	Interview and There It Is (Flipside by Elton John [Rocket Man]) (10/72)			What's It All About Records	
November	I Got a Bag of My Own (9/19/72)	③	44	Polydor	PD14153
	Public Enemy No. 1, Part 1 (2/22/72)				

December	What My Baby Needs Now, with Lyn Collins (9/19/72)	17	56	Polydor	PD14157
	This Guy's (Girl's) in Love With You (9/19/72)				
	Santa Claus Goes Straight to the Ghetto (10/7/68)			Polydor	PD14161
	Sweet Little Baby Boy (10/18/66)				

1973

January	I Got Ants in My Pants, Part 1 (10/10/71)	④	㉗	Polydor	PD14162
	I Got Ants in My Pants, Parts 15 and 16 (10/10/71)				
March	Down and Out in New York City (11/22/72)	13	50	Polydor	PD14168
	Mama's Dead (12/7/72)				
Unissued	The Boss (12/5/72)			Polydor	PD14169
	Like It Is, Like It Was (12/5/72)				
April	Think (1/22/73) (Release overdubbed 2/73)	15	77	Polydor	PD14177
	Something (1/17/73)				
June	Think (Alternative version) (1/22/73) (Release overdubbed 4/73)	37	80	Polydor	PD14185
	Something (1/17/73)				
Unissued	Woman, Part 1 (5/3/72)			Polydor	PD14193
	Woman, Part 2 (5/3/72)				
August	Sexy, Sexy, Sexy (2/15/71)	⑥	50	Polydor	PD14194
	Slaughter Theme (4/23/73)				
Unissued	Let It Be Me, with Lyn Collins (1/17/73)			Polydor	PD14199
	It's All Right (1/17/73)				
November	Stone to the Bone, Part 1 (10/73)	④	58	Polydor	PD14210
	Stone to the Bone, Part 2 (10/73)				

1974

February	The Payback, Part 1 (4/8/73) (Overdubs, 9/73)	①	㉖	Polydor	PD14223
	The Payback, Part 2 (4/8/73) (Overdubs, 9/73)				
April	My Thang (11/29/73)	①	㉙	Polydor	PD14244
	Public Enemy No. 1, Part 1 (2/22/72)				
August	Papa Don't Take No Mess, Part 1 (8/23/73)	①	㉛	Polydor	PD14255
	Papa Don't Take No Mess, Part 2 (8/23/73)				
October	Funky President (People It's Bad) (3/24/74)	④	44	Polydor	PD14258
	Cold Blooded (3/24/74)		99		

1975

January	Reality (10/8/74)	19	80	Polydor	PD14268
	I Need Your Love So Bad (11/22/71)				
March	Sex Machine, Part 1 (1/31/75)	16	61	Polydor	PD14270
	Sex Machine, Part 2 (1/31/75)				
Withdrawn	Dead On It, Part 1 (1/31/75)			Polydor	PD14279
	Dead On It, Part 2 (1/31/75)				
June	Hustle!!! (Dead On It) (5/75)	11		Polydor	PD14281
	Dead On It, Part 2 (1/31/75)				
September	Superbad, Superslick, Part 1	28		Polydor	PD14295
	Superbad, Superslick, Part 2				
December	Hot (I Need to Be Loved, Loved, Loved)	31		Polydor	PD14301
	Superbad, Superslick,				

1976

February	Dooley's Junkyard Dogs (Long version) Dooley's Junkyard Dogs (Short version)			Polydor	PD14303
March	(I Love You) For Sentimental Reasons Goodnight My Love	70		Polydor	PD14304
May	Get Up Offa That Thing Release the Pressure	4	45	Polydor	PD14326
October	I Refuse to Lose Home Again	47		Polydor	PD14354
December	Bodyheat, Part 1 Bodyheat, Part 2	13	91	Polydor	PD14360

1977

March	Kiss In 77 Woman	35	Polydor	PD14388
July	Give Me Some Skin People Wake Up and Live	20	Polydor	PD14409
September	Take Me Higher and Groove Me Summertime, with Martha High		Polydor	PD14433
December	People Who Criticize If You Don't Give a Doggone About It	45	Polydor	PD14438

1978

February	Love Me Tender Have a Happy Day		Polydor	PD14460
April	Eyesight I Never, Never, Never Will Forget	38	Polydor	PD14465
June	The Spank Love Me Tender	26	Polydor	PD14487
September	Nature, Part 1 Nature, Part 2		Polydor	PD14512
December	For Goodness Sakes, Look at Those Cakes, Part 1 For Goodness Sakes, Look at Those Cakes, Part 2	52	Polydor	PD14522

1979

February	Someone to Talk To, Part 1		Polydor	PD14540
	Someone to Talk To, Part 2			
May	It's Too Funky in Here	15	Polydor	PD14557
	Are We Really Dancing?			
August	Star Generation	63	Polydor	PD2005
	Women Are Something Else			
October	Let the Boogie Do the Rest		Polydor	PD2034
	The Original Disco Man			

1980

January	Regrets	63	Polydor	PD2054
	Stone Cold Drag			
March	Let the Funk Flow		Polydor	PD2078
	Sometimes That's All There Is			

1980

	Rapp Payback (Where Iz Moses), Parts 1 and 2	46	TK	TK1039 (7")/ TKD452 (12")
	Get Up Offa That Thing (Live)		Polydor	PD2129
	It's Too Funky in Here (Live)			

1981

	Stay with Me (Flipside unknown)	80	TK	TK1042
	God Has Smiled on Me, with Reverend Al Sharpton and the Gospel Energies, Parts 1 and 2		Royal King	RK7-900

1983

	Bring It On . . . Bring It On		Augusta Sound	CAS94023 (7")/ CAS94500 (12")
	The Night Time is the Right Time			

Unissued	As Long as I Love You (I'm Searchin')	Augusta Sound	
	For Your Precious Love		
	King of Soul (from *Dr. Detroit*) (Flipside by Devo)	Backstreet	
	Unity, with Afrika Bambaataa, Parts 1 and 2	Tommy Boy	TB847 (7")/ TB847 (12")
	Unity, Parts 1 to 6		

1985

	Living in America (R & B dance version)	Scotti Brothers	4Z9.05310 (12")
	Living in America (Instrumental)/ Living in America (LP version)	④	

JAMES BROWN ALBUMS

1959

January	*Please Please Please* (16 tracks, recorded 2/56 to 9/58)	King	K610
Late	*Try Me* (16 tracks)	King	K635

1960

Late	*Think* (12 tracks, recorded 1/59 to 9/60)	King	K683

1961

Midyear	*The Amazing James Brown* (12 tracks, recorded 9/60 to 2/61)	King	K743
Late	*James Brown Presents His Band/Night Train* (12 instrumentals, 6 by JB band, recorded 10/60 to 6/61; later reissued in U.S. as *Twist Around*, then *Jump Around*)	King	K771

1962

February	*Shout and Shimmy* (12 tracks, some reissues from above, recorded 10/57 to 6/61; later reissued in U.S. as *Good Good Twistin'*, then *Excitement*)	King	K780
Late	*JB and His Famous Flames Tour The U.S.A.* (12 tracks, includes 6 instrumentals, recorded 2/61 to 7/62)	King	K804

1963

January	*Live at the Apollo* (Genuine live recording, Apollo Theater, New York City, 10/24/62)	King	K826
Midyear	*Prisoner of Love* (11 tracks, 8 recorded 7/62 to 12/62, plus 3 reissues)	King	K851

1964

February	*Pure Dynamite: Live at the Royal* (Mostly genuine live recording, Royal Theater, Baltimore, 11/63, but includes 2 studio tracks with overdubbed audience)	King	K883
Midyear	*Showtime* (11 studio tracks with overdubbed audience, recorded early 1964)	Smash	S67054
Midyear	*Please Please Please* (Reissue of K610)	King	K909
Midyear	*Grits and Soul* (10 instrumentals, recorded early 1964)	Smash	S67057
Late	*Out of Sight* (12 tracks, recorded 1964; LP withdrawn within days of issue)	Smash	S67058
Late	*The Unbeatable James Brown/ 16 Hits* (Reissue of K635)	King	K919

1965

Late	*Papa's Got a Brand New Bag* (12 tracks: both parts of hit single plus 10 reissues)	King	K938

1966

January	*I Got You (I Feel Good)* (12 tracks: both sides of hit single plus 10 reissues)	King	K946
February	*JB Plays JB Today and Yesterday* (11 instrumental tracks, recorded 1965)	Smash	S67072
Midyear	*Mighty Instrumentals* (12 instrumentals, recorded 1960 to 1965)	King	K961
Midyear	*JB Plays New Breed (The Boo-Ga-Loo)* (9 instrumentals, recorded 1965)	Smash	S67080
July	*It's a Man's Man's Man's World* (12 tracks: both sides of 2 hits plus 8 reissues)	King	K985
November	*Christmas Songs* (12 tracks, recorded 10/66)	King	K1010
Late	*Handful of Soul* (10 instrumentals, recorded 1966)	Smash	S67084

1967

February	*The James Brown Show* (Genuine live recording, 1966, of various artists on the JB Revue)	Smash	S67087
April	*Raw Soul* (12 tracks: 2 from 1964, others recorded 4/66 to 1/67)	King	K1016
May	*JB Plays the Real Thing* (8 instrumentals, recorded 1966)	Smash	S67093
June	*Live at the Garden* (Genuine live recording, Latin Casino, Cherry Hill, NJ, 1/13 to 14/67)	King	K1018
July	*Cold Sweat* (12 tracks: 6 from 1964, 6 recorded 1/67 to 5/67)	King	K1020

1968

February	*JB Presents His Show of Tomorrow* (12 tracks: 2 by JB, others by various artists on the JB Revue)	King	K1024

March	*I Can't Stand Myself (When You Touch Me)* (12 tracks, recorded 1/67 to 10/67)	King	K1030
June	*I Got the Feelin'* (12 tracks, recorded 3/67 to 3/68)	King	K1031
August	*JB Plays Nothing But Soul* (6 instrumentals, recorded 1967 to 1968)	King	K1034
August	*Live at the Apollo* (Double LP; genuine live recording, Apollo Theater, New York City, 6/25/67)	King	K1022
September	*JB Sings Out of Sight* (Reissue of S67058, with one track missing)	Smash	S67109
December	*Thinking About Little Willie John and a Few Nice Things* (12 tracks, includes 6 instrumentals, recorded 1968)	King	K1038
December	*A Soulful Christmas* (12 tracks, recorded 8/68 to 10/68)	King	K1040

1969

April	*Say It Loud, I'm Black and I'm Proud* (12 tracks, recorded 9/67 to 9/68)	King	K1047
May	*Gettin' Down to It* (12 tracks with the Dee Felice Trio, recorded 12/68 to 2/69)	King	K1051
August	*The Popcorn* (10 instrumentals, recorded 1968)	King	K1055
August	*It's a Mother* (12 tracks, recorded 6/67 to 7/69)	King	K1063

1970

January	*Ain't It Funky* (7 instrumentals, recorded 1966 to 1969)	King	K1092
April	*Soul on Top* (11 tracks with the Louie Bellson Orchestra, recorded 11/69)	King	K1100
June	*It's a New Day—Let a Man Come In* (9 tracks, recorded 10/68 to 1/70)	King	K1095

September	*Sex Machine* (Double LP) (Record B: genuine live recording, Bell Auditorium, Augusta, Ga., 10/1/69, record A: studio tracks with overdubbed audience, recorded 10/69 and 7/70)	King	K1115
December	*Hey, America* (8 tracks, recorded 10/70)	King	K1124

1971

January	*Super Bad* (6 studio tracks with overdubbed audience, recorded 12/68 to 6/70)	King	K1127
April	*Sho Is Funky Down Here* (6 instrumentals with the David Matthews Trio, recorded 2/70)	King	K1110
August	*Hot Pants* (4 tracks, recorded 4/71 to 7/71)	Polydor	PD4054
December	*Revolution of the Mind (Live at the Apollo), Volume 3* (Double LP; genuine live recording, Apollo Theater, New York City, 7/21 to 22/71)	Polydor	PD3003

1972

June	*Soul Classics* (10 track hit compilation)	Polydor	PD5401
June	*There It Is* (11 tracks, recorded 10/70 to 2/72)	Polydor	PD5028
November	*Get on the Good Foot* (Double LP; 13 tracks, recorded 10/70 to 9/72)	Polydor	PD3004

1973

March	*Black Caesar* (Soundtrack; 11 tracks, recorded 11/72 to 12/72)	Polydor	PD6014
July	*Slaughter's Big Rip-off* (Soundtrack; 13 tracks: 10 recorded 5/73, 3 earlier)	Polydor	PD6015
November	*Soul Classics, Volume 2* (10-track hit compilation)	Polydor	PD5402

1974

January	*The Payback* (Double LP; 8 tracks, recorded 2/73 to 10/73)	Polydor	PD3007
August	*Hell* (Double LP; 14 tracks, recorded 1973 to 1974)	Polydor	PD9001

1975

January	*Reality* (9 tracks)	Polydor	PD6039
Midyear	*Sex Machine Today* (6 tracks)	Polydor	PD6042
Late	*Everybody's Doin' the Hustle and Dead on the Double Bump* (7 tracks)	Polydor	PD6054

1976

January	*Hot* (9 tracks)	Polydor	PD6059
Midyear	*Sex Machine Live* (Double LP; reissue of K1115)	Polydor	PD9004
Midyear	*Get Up Offa That Thing* (6 tracks)	Polydor	PD6071
Late	*Bodyheat* (7 tracks)	Polydor	PD6093

1977

Midyear	*Mutha's Nature* (8 tracks)	Polydor	PD6111

1978

May	*Jam 1980's* (5 tracks)	Polydor	PD6140
	The Fabulous James Brown (Double LP; 20-track hit compilation)	HRB Records	HRB1004

1979

Early	*Take a Look at Those Cakes* (5 tracks)	Polydor	PD6181
Midyear	*The Original Disco Man* (6 tracks)	Polydor	PD6212

1980

Early	*People* (7 tracks)	Polydor	PD6258
Midyear	*Hot on the One* (Double LP; genuine live recording, Tokyo, Japan, 1/80)	Polydor	PD6290
Midyear	*Live and Lowdown at the Apollo, Volume 1* (Reissue of K826)	Solid Smoke	SS8006
December	*Soul Syndrome* (6 tracks, recorded mid-to-late 1980)	TK	TK615

1981

Nonstop! (7 tracks)	Polydor	PD6318
Live in New York (Double LP; genuine live recording, Studio 54, New York City, 1980, except for two instrumentals by the "Bay Ridge Band")	Audio Fidelity	
Can Your Heart Stand It? (10-track compilation, 2/56 to 5/69)	Solid Smoke	SS8013
The Best of James Brown (11-track hit compilation, 2/56 to 1971)	Polydor	PD6340

1983

Bring It On (6 tracks)	Churchill/ Augusta Sound	CAS22001

1984

The Federal Years, Part 1 (15-track compilation, 3/56 to 7/59)	Solid Smoke	SS8023
The Federal Years, Part 2 (15-track compilation, 6/56 to 8/60)	Solid Smoke	SS8024
Ain't That a Groove—The JB Story 1966–69 (10-track compilation, 1/66 to 2/69)	Polydor	422-821231-1
Doing It to Death—The JB Story 1970–73 (9-track compilation, 10/69 to 1/73)	Polydor	422-821232-1

1985

Dead on the Heavy Funk 74–76 (9-track compilation, 9/73 to 1976)	Polydor	422-827439-1
The CD of JB: Sex Machine and Other Soul Classics (Compact disc; 18-track, digitally remastered compilation, 2/56 to 9/73, including one previously unissued track)	Polydor	422-825714-2

1986

Live at the Apollo, Volume 2, Part 1 (Reissue of record one, K1022)	Rhino	RNLP-217
Live at the Apollo, Volume 2, Part 2 (Reissue of record two, K1022)	Rhino	RNLP-218

1986

Live In Concert	Sugar Hill	
Gravity	Scotti Brothers	SB75212
In The Jungle Groove	Polydor	PLG829624
James Brown's Funky People	Polydor	PLG829417

1988

Motherlode	Polydor	
Santa's Got A Brand New Bag	Rhino	
I'm Real	Scotti Brothers	SB75213
James Brown's Funky People, Pt.2	Polydor	PLG835857

1989

Soul Session Live [James Brown & Friends]	Scotti Brothers	SB75214
Tribute	Scotti Brothers	

1991

Love-Over-Due	Scotti Brothers	SB75225
Soul's Alive	Koch International	
20 All-Time Greatest Hits!	Polydor	PLG511326
Messing With The Blues	Polydor	PLG847258
Star Time	Polydor	PLG849108

1992

Is Dua.k	Hollywood	HLY458
Love Power Peace	Polydor	PLG513389
Universal James	RCA	SB75274
Greatest Hits of the Fourth Decade	Scotti Brothers	SB75259

1993

Can't Get Any Harder	RCA	
Soul Pride: The Instrumentals (1960)	PolyGram	PLG517845

1994

Turn It Loose	Drive Archive	DRV41011

1995

Living In America	Scotti Brothers	SB75480
James Brown's Funky Christmas	Polydor	PLG527988

1996

Try Me	Polydor	PLG531017
Funk Power—1970:	Polydor	PLG531684
A Brand New Thang		
Foundations of Funk:	Polydor	PLG531165
A Brand New Bag		
Move On	Scotti Brothers	
James Brown	Audio Fidelity	
Spank	PolyGram	SPM837726
Live At Chastain Park	Charly	
Soul Jubilee	Magnum	MAGM43
Original Showman Live	Onyx Classix	
Please, Please, Please/James Brown	Blues Journey	PLG531016

1997

James Brown's Golden Classics	Intercontinental
Golden Hits	Galaxy
James Brown Live:	Columbia River
Roots of Rock n' Roll	

1998

Funky Goodtime	Prism
The Masters [Live]	EDM
Greatest Hits	PSM
Dead on Heavy Funk, 1975–1983	Polydor
The Very Best of James Brown	Polygram
Say it Live and Loud:	
Live in Dallas 1968	Polygram
Gold Collection	Fine Tune
Godfather of Soul Live	Mastertone
Goldfather of Soul	Spectrum

1999

James Brown: The Masters	Cleopatra
Prisoner of Love	Madacy
The Godfather Live in New York	Dressed To
City	
On Stage	Charly
20th Century Masters	Polygram
Cold Sweat	Hallmark

2000

Magic Collection	Magic
Great James Brown	Platinum Disc
Forever Gold	St. Clair
The Great James Brown	Goldies
Ballads	Polydor

2001

Best of James Brown	St. Clair
Get Up Offa That Thing	Bianco
Gold Collection	Retro Music
Papa's Got a Brand New Bag	Goldies
Live at the Apollo: Volume II	Polydor
James Brown Live	Delta
The Legends Collection	Legends
The James Brown Collection Vol. 1	Dressed To
The James Brown Collection Vol. 2	Dressed To

2002

Best of James Brown	Universal
20th Century Masters	Polydor
Out of Sight	Universal
It's A Man's Man's World	Universal
James Brown and Friends	Legend
Original Funk Soul Brother	Recall
The Next Step	Red Ink

JAMES BROWN EPs

1959

Early	Please Please Please
	Please Please Please/That's
	    When I Lost My Heart
	Try Me/Tell Me What I Did
	    Wrong
		King EPs	KEP-430

1963

Early	The Fabulous James Brown
	    Live at the Apollo
	Intro/I'll Go Crazy
	Lost Someone/*Medley:* Please
	    Please Please, You've Got
	    the Power, I Found
	    Someone, Why Do You Do
	    Me?, I Want You So Bad
		King EPs	KEP-826

SINGLES BY JAMES BROWN BANDS
and/or BAND MEMBERS

1959

Midyear	James Davis Doodle Bee/Bucket Head	Federal	F12360

Late	Nat Kendrick and the Swans
	Mashed Potatoes, Parts 1 and 2
	   (reissued on Dade D5004)
	   5/25/63)
		Dade	D1804

1960

May	Nat Kendrick and the Swans Dish Rag, Parts 1 and 2	Dade	D1808

1960/1961

	Nat Kendrick and the Swans Slowdown/Hot Chile	Dade	D1812

1963

	The Poets (JB and band) Devil's Den, Parts 1 and 2	Try Me	TM28006

1964

June	Al Brisco Clark Soul Food, Parts 1 and 2	Fontana	S1909

1965

June	Bobby Bennett and the Dynamics Soul Jerk, Parts 1 and 2	Loma	L2016
Unissued	The James Brown Dancers (The Dapps) It's a Gas, Parts 1 and 2	King	K6087

1968

January	The Dapps, featuring Alfred
	   Ellis
	Bringing Up the Guitar/Gittin'
	   a Little Hipper
		King	K6147

June	The Dapps, featuring Alfred
	   Ellis
	There Was a Time/The Rabbit
	   Got the Gun
		King	K6169

November	Alfred "Pee Wee" Ellis Little Green Apples/Come On In This House	King	K6199

1969

February	The Dapps I'll Be Sweeter Tomorrow/A Woman, A Lover, A Friend	King	K6201
February	Alfred "Pee Wee" Ellis In the Middle, Parts 1 and 2	King	K6214
Unissued	The New Dapps (The JB's) More Mess on My Thing, Parts 1 and 2	King	K6271

1970

June	The JB's The Grunt, Parts 1 and 2	King	K6317
October	The JB's These Are the JB's, Parts 1 and 2	King	K6333

1971

June	The JB's My Brother, Parts 1 and 2	People	P2502
August	The Believers (The JB's) Across the Track, Parts 1 and 2	Brownstone	B4201
Late	The Sons of Funk (The JB's) From the Back Side, Parts 1 and 2	King	K6398
December	The JB's Gimme Some More/The Rabbit Got the Gun	People	PE602

1972

April	The JB's Hot Pants Road/Pass the Peas	People	PE607
July	The JB's Givin' Up Food for Funk, Parts 1 and 2	People	PE610
October	Fred Wesley and the JB's Back Stabbers/JB Shout	People	PE614
Unissued	Fred Wesley and the JB's Everybody Plays the Fool/Use Me	People	PE616

1973

January	Fred Wesley and the JB's Watermelon Man/Alone Again, Naturally	People	PE617
March	Fred Wesley and the JB's Sportin' Life/Dirty Harri	People	PE619
April	Fred Wesley and the JB's Doing It to Death/Everybody Got Soul	People	PE621
August	Maceo and the Macks Parrty, Parts 1 and 2	People	PE624
September	Fred Wesley and the JB's If You Don't Get It the First Time/You Can Have Watergate	People	PE627
October	Maceo and the Macks Soul Power '74, Parts 1 and 2	People	PE631
December	Fred Wesley and the JB's Same Beat, Parts 1 and 2	People	PE632

1974

January	Maceo and the Macks I Can Play For (Just You and Me)/Doing It to Death	People	PE634
February	The Last Word Keep on Bumping Before You Give Out of Gas/Funky and Some	Polydor	PD14226
March	The Devils The X-Sorcist/Hip Hug-Her	People	PE637
April	Fred Wesley and the JB's Damn Right I Am Somebody, Parts 1 and 2	People	PE638
May	Maceo Drowning in the Sea of Love/ Show and Tell	People	PE640
June	Fred Wesley and the JB's Rockin' Funky Watergate, Parts 1 and 2	People	PE643
July	The First Family Control (People Go Where We Send You), Parts 1 and 2	Polydor	PD14250

Unissued	Fred Wesley and the JB's Little Boy Black/Rockin' Funky Watergate, Part 2	People	PE646
October	Maceo and the Macks Cross the Track (We Better Go Back)/The Soul of a Black Man	People	PE647
October	Fred and the New JB's Breakin' Bread/Funky Music Is My Style	People	PE648

1975

January	Fred and the New JB's Makin' Love/Rice 'n' Ribs	People	PE651
March	A.A.B.B. (Above Average Black Band) Pick Up the Pieces One by One/ C.O.L.D.	Identify	ID8003
Unissued	Fred and the New JB's Thank You for Lettin' Me Be Myself and Be Yours, Parts 1 and 2	People	PE654
May	Fred and the New JB's (It's Not the Express) It's the JB's Monaurail, Parts 1 and 2	People	PE655
Midyear	The Hustlers Hustling/Soft Hustle	People	PE658
Late	The JB's Thank You For Lettin' Me Be Myself, Parts 1 and 2	People	PE660
Late	Maceo Future Shock, Parts 1 and 2	People	PE661

1976

January	The JB's All Aboard the Soul Funky Train/ Thank You for Lettin' Me Be Myself, Part 1	People	PE663
Midyear	The JB's with James Brown Everybody Wanna Get Funky One More Time, Parts 1 and 2	People	PE664
December	JB's Wedge Bessie, Parts 1 and 2	Brownstone	7072

1977

Midyear	JB's International Music for the People/Crossover	Polydor	PD14396
November	JB's International Nature, Parts 1 and 2	Brownstone	7073

1978

	JB's International Disco Fever (Flipside unknown, probably Part 2)	Polydor	PD(?)

1979

	The JB's Rock Groove Machine, Parts 1 and 2	Drive	Dr6277

JAMES BROWN PRODUCTIONS, ALBUMS BY VARIOUS ARTISTS

1964

Midyear	Anna King, *Back to Soul*	Smash	S67059

1969

Midyear	Hank Ballard, *You Can't Keep a* *Good Man Down*	King	K1052
Midyear	Marva Whitney, *I Sing Soul*	King	K1053
Midyear	The Dee Felice Trio, *In the Heat*	Bethlehem	B1000
Late	Marva Whitney, *It's My Thing*	King	K1062

1970

February	Marva Whitney, *Live and* *Lowdown at the Apollo*	King	K1079
December	Bobby Byrd, *I Need Help*	King	K1118

1972

June	The JB's, *Food for Thought*	People	PE5601
September	Lyn Collins, *Think (About It)*	People	PE5602

1973

	Fred Wesley and the JB's, *Doing It to Death*	People	PE5603
	Maceo, *Us*	People	PE6601

1974

Fred Wesley and the JB's, *Damn Right I Am Somebody*	People	PE6602
Sweet Charles: For Sweet People	People	PE6603
Fred and the New JB's, *Breakin' Bread*	People	PE6604

1975

Lyn Collins, *Check Me Out If You Don't Know Me by Now*	People	PE6605
The JB's, *Hustle with Speed*	People	PE6606

1978

JB's International, *Disco Fever*	Polydor	PD6153

1979

The JB's, *Groove Machine*	Drive	Dr111
Martha High, *He's My Ding Dong Man*		Salsoul(?)

JAMES BROWN PRODUCTIONS, SINGLES BY VARIOUS ARTISTS

The following section is a listing of single releases by various artists associated with James Brown. It is organized alphabetically by artist, then chronologically under each.

VICKI ANDERSON

1964

August	My Man I Won't Be Back	Fontana	S1922

1965

June	I Love You Nobody Cares	Smash	S1985
October	Never, Never, Never Let You Go, Part 1 Never, Never, Never Let You Go, Part 2	Fontana	F1527

1966

June	I Can't Let You Go, Part 1 I Can't Let You Go, Part 2	New Breed	NB1102

Fall	Wide Awake in a Dream Nobody Cares (Also scheduled for Federal 12543 [unissued])	DeLuxe	DL6201
November	You Send Me Within My Heart	King	K6066

1967

March	Think, with James Brown Nobody Cares	King	K6091
July	If You Don't Give Me What I Want Tears of Joy	King	K6109
November	Baby, Don't You Know? The Feeling Is Real	King	K6138

1968

March	You've Got the Power, with James Brown What the World Need Now Is Love	King	K6152
September	Here Is My Everything, with Bobby Byrd Loving You, with Bobby Byrd	ABC	ABC11134
March	I'll Work It Out What the World Needs Now Is Love	King	K6221

1969

September	Answer to Mother Popcorn (I Got a Mother for You) I'll Work It Out	King	K6251
December	I Want To Be in the Land of Milk and Honey Wide Awake in a Dream	King	K6274

1970

April	Let It Be Me, with James Brown Baby, Don't You Know?	King	K6293
June	No More Heartaches, No More Pain Never Find a Love Like Mine	King	K6314

October	as Myra Barnes: The Message
	  from the Soul Sisters, Part 1
	as Myra Barnes: The Message
	  from the Soul Sisters, Part 2
		King	K6334

December	as Myra Barnes: Super Good, Part 1 as Myra Barnes: Super Good, Part 2	King	K6344

1971

May	Yesterday (Live) Message from the Soul Sisters	King	K6377
Unissued	I'm Too Tough for Mr. Big Stuff In the Land of Milk and Honey	People	P2505
August	I'm Too Tough for Mr. Big Stuff (Hot Pants) Sound Funky (Instrumental)	Brownstone	B4202
November	I'll Work It Out In the Land of Milk and Honey	Brownstone	B4204

1972

| September | Don't Throw Your Love in the
Garbage Can
In the Land of Milk and Honey | Brownstone | B4207 |

1975

| March | *as Momie-o.:* You're Welcome, Stop
on By, Once You Get Started | Identify | ID8004 |

LEE (LEON) AUSTIN

1967

| April | Two-Sided Love
I'm Mad | King | K6093 |

1968

| May | Two-Sided Love (Reissue)
I'm Mad (Reissue) | King | K6161 |

1969

| July | Turn Me Loose
Respect | King | K6247 |

1970

| January | Steal Away
Yesterday | King | K6201 |

1971

| Late | Put Something on Your Mind
Screwdriver (Instrumental) | International
Brothers | I801 |

1972

| May | Gimme Your Hand
Moonlight | People | PE609 |

September	Real Woman Gimme Your Hand	People	PE612

1973

March	The Truth Moonlight	People	PE620
August	Tutti Frutti Moonlight	Polydor	PD14195

1974

March	I'm in Love Moonlight	People	PE635
August	I'm a Man Gimme Your Hand	Polydor	PD14251

1975

	Missin' You Gimme Your Hand	Identify	ID8005

1975

	Georgia Peach, Part 1 Georgia Peach, Part 2	Polydor	PD14500

HANK BALLARD

1963

August	It's Love, Baby (24 Hours a Day) Those Lonely Lonely Feelings	King	K5798

1967

September	You're in Real Good Hands Unwind Yourself	King	K6119
April	Which Way Should I Turn? Funky Soul Train	King	K6131

1968

July	Come On Wit' It I'm Back to Stay	King	K6177
November	How You Gonna Get Respect (The Dapps) Teardrops on Your Letter (The Dapps)	King	K6196

1969

January	You're So Sexy (The Dapps) Thrill on the Hill (The Dapps)	King	K6215
April	With Your Sweet Lovin' Self Are You Lonely for Me, Baby?	King	K6228
September	Butter Your Popcorn Funky Soul Train	King	K6244
September	Blackenized Come On Wit' It	King	K6246

1971

October	Annie Had a Baby Teardrops on Your Letter	People	PE604

1972

February	Finger Poppin' Time With Your Sweet Lovin' Self	People	PE606
May	From the Love Side Finger Poppin' Time	Polydor	PD14128
Unissued	Gonna Get a Thrill, Part 1 Gonna Get a Thrill, Part 2	Polydor	PD14166
Unissued	GonnaGet a Thrill, Part 1 Gonna Get a Thrill, Part 2	Identify	ID8002

BOBBY BYRD

1963

Midyear	I Found Out They Are Sayin'	Federal	F12486
Late	I'm Just a Nobody, Part 1 I'm Just a Nobody, Part 2	Smash	S1868

1964

Early	Baby Baby Baby, with Anna King Baby Baby Baby (Instrumental)	Smash	S1884
May	I Love You So Write Me a Letter	Smash	S1903
September	I've Got a Girl I'm Lonely	Smash	S1928

1965

February	We Are in Love No One Like My Baby	Smash	S1964
April	The Way I Feel Time WIll Make a Change	Smash	S1984
September	Let Me Know You're Gonna Need My Lovin'	Smash	S2003

1966

Early	Oh, What a Night Lost in the Mood of Changes	Smash	S2018
Late	Let Me Know Ain't No Use	Smash	S2052

1967

Early	I Found Out I'll Keep Pressing On	King	K6069
September	Funky Soul, Part 1 Funky Soul, Part 2	King	K6126

1968

February	You've Got to Change Your Mind, with James Brown I'll Lose My Mind	King	K6151
Withdrawn	My Concerto You Gave My Heart a Brand New Song to Sing	King	K6165

1970

March	Hang Ups We Don't Need
	    (The Hungry We Got to Feed)
	You Gave My Heart a Brand
	    New Song to Sing
		King	K6289

May	It's I Who Loves You (Not Him Anymore) I'm Not to Blame	King	K6308

August	I Need Help (I Can't Do It Alone),
	    Part 1
	I Need Help (I Can't Do It Alone),
	    Part 2
		King	K6323

November	You've Got to Have a Job You've Got to Change Your Mind, with James Brown	King	K6342

1971

May	I Know You Got Soul It's I Who Loves You (Not Him Anymore)	King	K6378
August	Hot Pants, I'm Coming, Coming, I'm Coming Hang It Up	Brownstone	B4203
December	Keep on Doin' What You're Doin' Let Me Know	Brownstone	B4205

1972

April	If You Got a Love You Better
	  (Hold on to It)
	You've Got to Change Your Mind,
	  with James Brown
		Brownstone	B4206

July	Never Get Enough My Concerto	Brownstone	B4208
October	Sayin' It and Doin' It Is Two Different Things Never Get Enough	Brownstone	B4209

1973

May	I Need Help (I Can't Do It Alone) Signed, Sealed, and Delivered (Live)	Brownstone	B4210

LYN COLLINS

1971

December	Just Won't Do Right Wheels of Life	Polydor	PD14107

1972

March	Oh, Uncle Sammy Ain't No Sunshine	Polydor	PD14119
May	Think (About It) Ain't No Sunshine	People	PE608

October	Me and My Baby Got Our Own Thing Going I'll Never Let you Break My Heart Again	People	PE615
November	What My Baby Needs Now, with James Brown This Guy's (Girl's) in Love with You	Polydor	PD14157

1973

February	Mama Feelgood Fly Me to the Moon	People	PE618
May	How Long Can I Keep It Up?, Part 1 How Long Can I Keep It Up?, Part 2	People	PE623
	Take Me Just as I Am People Make the World a Better Place	People	PE626
October	We Want to Party, Party, Party You Can't Beat Two People in Love	People	PE630

1974

January	Don't Make Me Over Take Me Just as I Am	People	PE633
March	Give It Up or Turnit a Loose What the World Needs Now Is Love	People	PE636
June	Rock Me Again and Again and Again and Again and Again and Again Wide Awake in a Dream	People	PE641

1975

February	You Can't Love Me, If You Don't Respect Me Rock Me Again and Again and Again and Again and Again and Again	People	PE650
June	How Long Can I Keep It Up? Baby, Don't Do It	People	PE657
September	If You Don't Know Me By Now Baby, Don't Do It	People	PE659

1976

| February | Mr. Big Stuff
Rock Me Again and Again and Again
and Again and Again and Again | People | PE662 |

JAMES CRAWFORD

1964

| May | Farther On Up the Road
When Loneliness Knocks at Your Door | Mercury | 72282 |
| November | Much Too Much
Strung Out | Mercury | 72347 |

1965

February	I Don't Care, I Don't Care, I Don't Care Help Poor Me	Mercury	72393
Midyear	If You Don't Work You Can't Eat Stop and Think It Over	Mercury	72441
November	Got No Excuse Hooray for the Child Who Has Its Own	Blue Rock	B4033

1966

| | Honest I Do, Part 1
Honest I Do, Part 2 | Omen | O12 |

1967

| April | Stone Fox
Hold It (Instrumental) | King | K6103 |
| October | I'll Work It Out
Fat Eddie (Instrumental) | King | K6130 |

1968

| January | Bringing Up the Guitar, featuring
Alfred Ellis (Instrumental)
Gittin' a Little Hipper, featuring
Alfred Ellis (Instrumental) | King | K6147 |
| June | There Was a Time, featuring
Alfred Ellis (Instrumental)
The Rabbit Got the Gun, featuring
Alfred Ellis (Instrumental) | King | K6169 |

1969

February	I'll Be Sweeter Tomorrow A Woman, a Lover, a Friend	King	K6201
May	I'm Ready, I'm Ready (I Got Me Some Soul), Beau Dollar At the Dark End of the Street, Beau Dollar	King	K6241

1970

January	Where the Soul Trees Grow, Beau Dollar Who Knows, Beau Dollar (Instrumental)	King	K6286

YVONNE FAIR

1962

Early	I Found You If I Knew	King	K5594
June	Tell Me Why Say So Long	King	K5654
September	It Hurts To Be in Love You Can Make It If You Try	King	K5687

1963

Early	Straighten Up Say Yeah Yeah	Dade	D1851
November	Straighten Up (Reissue) Say Yeah Yeah (Reissue)	Dade	D5006

1965

End	Tell Me Why You Can Make It If You Try	King	K6017

1966

Autumn	Baby Baby Baby Just as Sure (As You Play, You Must Pay)	Smash	S2030

THE JEWELS

1967

Early   This Is My Story   Federal   F12541
         My Song

1965

Late   This Is My Story   Dynamite   D2000
         Papa Left Mama Holding the
             Bag

1966

November Lookie Lookie Lookie   King   K6068
          Smokey Joe's

1968

March   Never Find a Love Like Mine,   King   K6153
              as the Brownettes
          Baby, Don't You Know?,
              as the Brownettes

NAT KENDRICK AND THE SWANS

1959

Late   Mashed Potatoes, Part 1   Dade   D1804
         Mashed Potatoes, Part 2

1960

May   Dish Rag, Part 1   Dade   D1808
         Dish Rag, Part 2
         Slowdown   Dade   D1812
         Hot Chile
         Wobble, Wobble, Part 1   Dade   D5003
         Wobble, Wobble, Part 2
         Mashed Potatoes, Part 1 (Reissue) Dade   D5004
         Mashed Potatoes, Part 2 (Reissue)

ANNA KING

1963

End   If Somebody Told You   Smash   S1858
         Come and Get These Memories

1964

Early	Baby Baby Baby, with Bobby Byrd Baby Baby Baby (Instrumental)	Smash	S1884
May	If You Don't Think Make Up Your Mind	Smash	S1904
August	Come On Home Sittin' in the Dark	Smash	S1942
End	That's When I Cry Tennessee Waltz	Smash	S1970

KAY ROBINSON

(?)	In the Bosom of the Lord This Old World	Federal	F12550
(?)	Lord, I'm Yours This Old World	Federal	F12553

1968

July	Try Me, Father What a Feeling	King	K6182

1970

June	Lord Will Make a Way Somehow, Part 1 Lord Will Make a Way Somehow, Part 2	King	K6316

1971

April	Amazing Grace, with the Charles Fold Singers This Old World	King	K6362

MARVA WHITNEY

1967

June	Your Love Was Good for Me Saving My Time for My Baby	Federal	F12545
September	If You Love Me Your Love Was Good for Me	King	K6124

1968

January	Unwind Yourself If You Love Me	King	K6146
April	Your Love Was Good for Me What Kind of Man	King	K6158
May	Things Got to Get Better (Get Together) What Kind of Man	King	K6168
August	I'll Work It Out All My Love Belongs to You	King	K6181
September	I'm Tired, I'm Tired, I'm Tired If You Love Me	King	K6193
November	What Do I Have to Do to Prove My Love to You Your Love Was Good for Me	King	K6202
November	Tit for Tat In the Middle (Instrumental)	King	K6206

1969

March	You've Got to Have a Job, with James Brown I'm Tired, I'm Tired, I'm Tired	King	K6218
June	It's My Thing Ball of Fire	King	K6229
August	Things Got to Get Better (Get Together) Get Out of My Life	King	K6249

September	I Made a Mistake Because It's
	    Only You, Part 1
	I Made a Mistake Because It's
	    Only You, Part 2
		King	K6268

1970

January	He's the One This Girl's in Love with You	King	K6283

INDEX

WESLEY CHAPEL-WILLIAM C. BROWN

10/03